LEADER'S GUIDE

Correlates with David C. Cook Bible-in-Life® and other curriculum lines!

NexGen® is an imprint of
Cook Communications Ministries, Colorado Springs, CO
Cook Communications, Paris Ontario
Kingsway Communications, Eastbourne, England

NOAH'S PARK® CHILDREN'S CHURCH LEADER'S GUIDE (Red Edition)
© 2007 by Cook Communications Ministries.

First printing 2007   Printed in the United States

                             1 2 3 4 5 6 7 8 9 10 Printing/Year 12 11 10 09 08 07

Editor: Carol Pitts
Contributing Writers: Mary Brite, Judy Gillispie, Karen James, Gail Rohlfing, Scott Stewart, Nancy Sutton
Interior Design: Mike Riester
Cover Design: Todd Mock
Illustrations: Aline Heiser, Chris Sharp
Photography: © 2001 Cook Communications Ministries by Gaylon Wampler

Music: "In the Beginning," "Hallelujah! Jesus Is Risen"
                             Words and Music by John H. Morton

                             "When God Makes a Promise," "I Wanna Live God's Way," "God Wants You"
                             Words and Music by Phil Reynolds

                             "God's Already There," "It Pays to Obey"
                             Words by John J. DiModica

                             "Glory to You," "Take a Stand," "Good News"
                             Words and Music by Sarah Moore

                             "Trust Him and Obey"
                             Words and Music by Darren Roos

                             "Living for You"
                             Words and Music by Shelly McFalls

Vocals: Kara DePriest, Carter Garrison, Kelsi Kinney, Aria Morton,
                             Jonah Upton, Noah Upton
Producer: John H. Morton
Arrangements: John H. Morton, John J. DiModica, Tom Rau
Bass: Marty Wilhite, John J. DiModica
Drums: Pete Generous
Synth/Loops/Sequencing: John H. Morton, John J. DiModica, Tom Rau, Blair Masters
Electric Guitar: Jeff Smith, Mike McAdoo, Tommy Calton, Paul Brannon
Acoustic guitar: Phil Reynolds, Mike McAdoo, Tommy Calton, Paul Brannon
Mandolin/Dobro/Banjo: Paul Brannon
Clarinet: Ed Maina
Recorded and mixed at: Music Precedent, Ltd.
Engineer: John H. Morton

ISBN 978-0-7814-4494-1   105097

TABLE OF CONTENTS

INTRODUCTION

Welcome to what we are certain will be an exciting year of learning and worship for both you and the children who attend Children's Church.

The focus of this material is to provide for an extended Sunday school learning experience as well as a worship experience for children in preschool through upper elementary. By using this material, the concepts and lessons learned in the Sunday school hour can be reinforced and extended through the use of activities, games, and crafts that are different from those used in the Sunday school lesson.

This curriculum provides Bible study, Bible memory activities, Music activities, Puppet skits, Prayer time, Snacks, Crafts, Games, and more. It gives you, the leader, the flexibility of choosing the activities that fit the time you have for your program. If you have a 30-minute, 60-minute, or 90-minute program (or another variation), you can effectively use the time to lead the children in meaningful worship.

Included in this kit you will find the following:

- **Leader's Guide** (with music CD in front cover pocket)
- **Craft Book**
- **Snacks and Games Book**
- **Puppet Skits Book**
- **Park Patrol Training Book**
- **Two Puppets**

The pages of these books are reproducible for use with the Noah's Park® Children's Church program. You may need to reproduce additional pages of the Leader's Guide to give to several leaders. The craft pages need to be reproduced (usually one page for each child—either preschool or elementary). Because of this feature, you don't have to worry about running low on material. Just reproduce extras as your program grows.

This curriculum emphasizes the involvement of the children. There are two Bible Stories provided for each lesson—one for preschool children and one for kindergarten through third grade. You may choose to keep all the children together for the Bible Story. In that case, we suggest that you use the Elementary Bible Story. If you so desire, you can use the Preschool Bible Story with preschool through kindergarten or first grade.

PARK PATROL

Children in fourth, fifth, or sixth grade can participate in the program as the "Park Patrol." Through this participation, these older elementary children will be learning about service as they assist the leader. By using the *Park Patrol Training Book* as the basis for preparing the students to be effective helpers, they can feel confident as they assist with the program. By using the Park Patrol, you will find that you do not need as many adult leaders to teach and guide the children.

This program will work equally well for small or large churches. Because you can combine these age groups for worship, you can have an effective, meaningful worship time for any number of children.

A CLOSER LOOK

To help you understand the curriculum, let's take a look at each section.

Introduction

As you look at the Table of Contents, you will notice that the material is divided into twelve units. Most units take four weeks to complete; some take five. The units correspond basically to the months of the year. However, some units might take one full calendar month and one more week. So don't think in terms of months, but rather units.

This is especially important if you rotate your Children's Church leadership. Ask for volunteers to consider teaching for one unit. That way they will be able to help the children focus on the unit theme and can emphasize it consistently through the teaching of it.

Turn now to the first lesson of the first unit. You will notice the unit theme at the top of the page. This is the emphasis of all the lessons in the unit. In the special box on the left side of the page, you will see an outline of what is included in the lesson with suggested times. This can help you as you plan for the time schedule you have in your program. Do not feel that you are required to do every activity. We suggest that you select activities from each of the areas, however, in order to reach the different types of learners in your group. By having a Bible Story, puppet skit, time of singing, games or crafts, you are appealing to children who need to learn by listening, moving, doing, etc.

Discovery Trails

The first section is Discovery Trails. We include a Teacher Feature that you can use to begin your session. This is designed to help the children begin thinking about the unit theme and help prepare them for the Bible Story to follow. The Teacher Feature may be a story, an activity, or an object lesson. Sometimes the children just listen, but often they participate more actively.

Following the Teacher Feature, we suggest that you divide up your group of children into preschool and elementary ages. If you have sufficient space, it would be best to have a separate area for the two groups as you teach the Bible Stories. Use the Preschool Bible Story for your preschoolers. If you have a small group of children, or if you just choose to keep the children in one larger group, use the Elementary Bible Story to teach the lesson.

Bring all the children back together following the Bible Stories. At this point, we suggest that you use the Noah's Park Puppets. The puppet skits are written to reinforce the unit theme and the Bible story. It's a fun way for the children to begin moving toward the next part of the worship session.

We offer a Bible Memory section. You will notice that we do not give you a specific Bible verse to use. You may choose to use a Bible memory verse that the children studied in Sunday school or you may choose to select a verse that emphasizes or reinforces the Bible Story. We provide an activity to help the children quickly and easily learn the Bible memory verse.

Worship Trails

Now we move into Worship Trails. At this point, you can have the children involved in a time of Singing Praises to Jesus. We suggest that you use the songs on the CD included with the program. The songs are all original music written specifically for the program. Each song on the

INTRODUCTION

CD correlates with one unit. You can use other favorite songs that help to emphasize the theme as you have the time in your program.

We also offer a Share and Prayer time. Here's an activity specifically designed to help your children worship God through prayer. Many times the children will be making something that they will take home. This will help them to remember the importance of prayer in their daily lives as well as assist them in this time of worship.

WILDLIFE TRAILS

Wildlife Trails offers the children a chance to move and create. This section of the lesson includes Snack Shack, Campsite Capers, and Cozy Cave Crafts.

We offer a snack suggestion (Snack Shack) to correlate with each week's lesson. You can use these snack suggestions or others of your own choosing. All the children can have their snack time together or you can separate them into preschool and elementary groups at this time.

As you begin the Campsite Capers (Games) and Cozy Cave Crafts (Crafts) notice that there are options for preschool and elementary. These activities are designed with age-appropriate activities for each of these groups.

HAPPY TRAILS

Happy Trails gives you a chance to gather all the children back together into one large group and wrap up your session. Everyone can help with cleanup and then have a time of review just prior to leaving. We give suggestions for Closing Activities as well as Overtime Activities. During the time at the close of your session while you wait for parents to pick up the children, we give suggestions to help you extend the session.

The Park Patrollers are your assistants. Take time before beginning your year of Children's Church to train the children. Using the *Park Patrol Training Book* will help these kids become confident helpers as they assist with the movement of the younger kids, help with the snack time, games, crafts, puppets, etc. Be sure to make assignments for the kids so that they know what is expected of them and when it's their turn to help if you use them on a rotating basis. You will find that they are learning a great deal from the Bible Stories, puppet skits, prayer time, etc. as they listen and help.

Refer to the *Craft Book, Puppet Skits Book*, and *Snacks and Games Book* for more information about supplies and preparation.

As the children leave your session, they will be taking home a craft that they have made. Included with many of the crafts is a "HomeLink" to help parents extend the learning even further. Be sure to send it home with the children if it is not already attached to the craft project in some way.

Now that you have made it through this introduction, you're ready to begin!

R1 Lesson: We Can Trust God's Plan in Creation

Choose from the options listed below to follow Adventure Trails that lead to Jesus:

DISCOVERY TRAILS
TEACHER FEATURE (5 min.)
Planning a Batch of Cookies
BIBLE STORY (10 min.)
Trusting God's Plan for Creation (Elem.)
God Made Day and Night (Preschool)
NOAH'S PARK PUPPETS (5 min.)
Shooting Stars
BIBLE MEMORY (5 min.)
Created Shapes

WORSHIP TRAILS
SINGING PRAISES TO JESUS (10 min.)
SHARE AND PRAYER (5 min.)
Prayer Stars

WILDLIFE TRAILS
SNACK SHACK (5 min.)
Star Cookies
CAMPSITE CAPERS (15 min.)
The Creator Said (Elementary)
Daytime and Nighttime Toss (Preschool)
COZY CAVE CRAFTS (15 min.)
Heavenly Mobile (Elementary)
Creation Quilt—Square 1 (Preschool)

HAPPY TRAILS
CLOSING ACTIVITIES (5 min.)
OVERTIME ACTIVITIES (as needed)

DISCOVERY TRAILS

TEACHER FEATURE
Planning a Batch of Cookies

Supplies: Empty cookie jar and cookbook with recipes for cookies

Show the children an empty cookie jar. **What should be inside this?** (Cookies!) **How could we make some cookies for the cookie jar?** Let the children tell their ideas. **How would a cookbook help us?** (It would have a recipe.) **Well, I have a cookbook! Let's see if it has a recipe for some good cookies.**

Let the children search the cookbook for a cookie recipe (or picture). Read aloud some ingredients, such as sugar, chocolate, raisins, etc., for several recipes. Guide the children to understand that the recipe will help you make some yummy cookies.

What do you think we would need to do to actually make the cookies? Let the children suggest ideas. Work with children to make a reasonable plan. These might include reading the recipe, making a grocery list, shopping, and following the recipe. Help the children understand that making a plan is important.

Do you think we have a good plan to make some delicious cookies to fill the cookie jar? We do have a good plan. In fact, it's a plan we should trust to work for us.

When God created everything, do you think He had a plan? Yes, He did! We can trust God's plan in creation even more than we trust our plan for making cookies! Let's learn more about God's plan in creation.

At this time, ask the Park Patrol to lead the preschool children to the area for their Bible story. The preschoolers will rejoin the elementary-age kids after the Bible story for more large-group activities.

ELEMENTARY BIBLE STORY
Trusting God's Plan for Creation
(Genesis 1:1–31; Psalm 111:2, 7)

Supplies: Bible, poster board, marker, scissors, string or yarn

Preparation: Cut large circles from poster board. Label them *sun, moon, earth, planet* (make several), and *stars* (make several). Attach string or yarn to each so it easily hangs around a child's neck.

In the Bible God tells us about the beginning of everything—in Genesis and other Bible books, like Psalms. Show the children Genesis 1 and Psalm 111. Hold your Bible open to Genesis 1 as you tell the story so the children know the story comes from God's Word.

God made the heavens and the earth. He had a plan, and He put our earth and everything in the universe in its place. One thing God made with a plan was our solar system. Ask for volunteers to wear the sun, earth, and planet signs. Have the sun stand in the center of the room, with earth and the other planets "rotating" in a circle around him or her. Have the other children give them room to move. If your room is not large enough for this demonstration, so much the better; it will reinforce God's careful planning.

Are our planets bumping into each other? Are they making perfect orbits? We didn't plan a very careful a solar system. But God made the planets good and planned them to not bump into each other. Aren't you glad that earth isn't bumping into Saturn or rotating too near the hot sun? We can trust God's plan in creation. Have the solar system children remove their signs and let all be seated.

When God made the earth, darkness was everywhere. It was *completely* **dark, like when you close your eyes in a dark room at night.** Ask the children to close their eyes and "see" the darkness for a moment. **But God didn't plan for all of creation to be dark. He said, "Let there be light," and there was light! God called the light "day" and He called the dark "night." This is God's plan for daytime and nighttime. God made both good. That shows we can trust God's plan in creation.**

Ask more volunteers to wear the sun, moon, and star signs. **God made the sun and put it exactly where He planned in the sky so it would light the day.** Place the "sun" on one side of you. **He made the moon and stars and put them in their place to light the night.** Place the "moon" and "stars" on the other side of you. **It's because of God's plan in creation that the sun, moon, and stars work perfectly to give us light. It's a plan we can trust.**

Day and night are good for us. And God planned the right amount of each. Have the children wearing signs crouch down. As you take answers for the next question, have either the sun or the moon and stars spring up if it's an activity that happens during their time of day or night.

What are some things you like to do? Take answers from children. If it's usually a nighttime activity, like sleep, stargaze, or have a sleepover, the moon and stars should stand up. If it's normally a daytime activity, such as go to school, eat, or play, the sun should stand up. If it's an activity that could happen in either day or night, such as watching TV or praying, all the sign-wearers should stand up. Encourage the children to watch carefully and make sure the proper signs are standing up.

Take the signs and have all the children be seated. **God had a great plan when He created our universe. The Psalms praise God for making creation so wonderful. One says this: "Great are the works of the Lord!" Let's say that together. "Great are the works of the Lord!" We can trust God's plan in creation.**

Discuss these questions to make sure the children understood the main points of the Bible story: **Who had a plan for creation?** (God.) **What things were part of God's plan?** (The solar system, light and darkness, sun, moon, stars, etc.) **Why can we trust God's plan in creation?** (Because everything God made is so good.)

PRESCHOOL BIBLE STORY
God Made Day and Night
(Genesis 1:1–31; Psalm 111:2, 7)

Supplies: Bible, completed preschool craft (*Craft Book*, p. RC-8), flannel board

Preparation: Make a large-sized preschool craft from page RC-8 of the Noah's Park *Craft Book*.

Show the children where Genesis 1 is in your Bible. **Our story today comes from the very beginning of the Bible, from the Book of Genesis.** Keep your Bible open as you tell the story.

Cover your eyes with your hands. What do you see? (Nothing.) **The Bible tells us this is how the world looked at the very beginning. But God had a plan.** Put the black square from the prepared craft on your flannel board.

God said, "Let there be light!" And there was light. Tell the children to open their eyes. **God**

called the light "day." Put the white rectangle over half of the black square.

But God's plan was for there to be more than day. God knew the world also needed a little darkness. Have the children cover their eyes, then uncover them. **God called the darkness "night."** Point to the dark fabric on the square.

God put lights in the sky. The lights help people know when it is day and when it is night. So God made two special lights. God put the big light in the sky for the day. Make a big circle above your head with your arms. Have the children copy your actions. **God called the big light the "sun." The sun shines in the day.** Put the sun figure on the white rectangle. **What do you do in the day?** Let the children give suggestions.

God put the little light in the sky for the night. Make a small circle with your hands. Hold your hands above your head. Have the children do the same. **God called the little light the "moon." The moon shines at night.** Put the moon figure on the black rectangle. **God also made some lights called stars. He put the stars with the moon in the night sky.** Add the star figures. **What do you do in the night?** Let the children offer some ideas.

God looked at the day and night. He looked at the sun, the moon, and the stars. God saw that they were all good. They were all a part of God's plan when He made the world.

Use the quilt square to review the Bible story. Beginning with the dark square, put each piece on the square asking, **What did God make?**

NOAH'S PARK PUPPETS
Shooting Stars

Signal the Park Patrol members who will perform today's puppet skit to get ready. You will find the puppet script and instructions in the Noah's Park *Puppet Skits Book* on page RP-7. Gather the children in front of your puppet stage, and begin when everyone is seated and ready.

BIBLE MEMORY
Created Shapes

Supplies: Poster board, marker, scissors, paper clips, Bible

Preparation: Select a Bible verse that connects with today's Bible story, or use the verse from today's Sunday school lesson. Cut poster board into large stars, crescent moons, and round earths so you have a shape for every three or four children. Make the shapes at least six inches across. (For sample shapes, see page RC-7 in the craft book. Print the Bible memory verse on one side of each shape. Cut all but one shape into five to eight puzzle pieces each. For older children, you may cut the shapes into more pieces. Clip puzzle pieces together.

Hold up the whole shape so the children can see it as you point to the words. Children should listen while you read the verse, pointing to each word as you say it. Ask the children to join you in saying the verse and reference. Repeat this several times.

Divide the children into small groups. Give each group a prepared verse puzzle and have them put it together. Park Patrol may help as needed.

When finished, ask each group to say the verse together and tell what shape its puzzle made. **Remembering this verse is a great way to honor God. Let's praise Him because we can trust His plan in creation.**

SINGING PRAISES TO JESUS

Supplies: Noah's Park CD and CD player

Begin teaching the Unit 1 song, "In the Beginning," from the Noah's Park *Children's Church CD*. First, play the song while children listen, or project the words onto a wall with an overhead projector so children can read them. Invite the class to tell what the song is about. Then, replay the song and let children sing along. (See page R-247 for reproducible lyrics.) Discuss how the song's message relates to today's Bible lesson. As time permits, lead the children in other songs praising God.

SHARE AND PRAYER
Prayer Stars

Supplies: Paper, pencil, scissors

Preparation: Draw a large, six-pointed star on paper. Print the Bible memory verse or today's lesson title in the center. Print one day of the week inside each star point. Photocopy this Prayer Star for each child in your class.

We can trust God's plan in creation and thank Him for it. Ask for volunteers who would like to pray aloud to thank God for something in His creation. Have volunteers come to the front and face the class in the order each will pray. Ask the first child to begin and then each of the others in turn. Encourage the others who are listening to pray along in their hearts with the one who is praying aloud.

We can pray each day this week to thank God for His plan in creation. Park Patrol members should give each child a star and scissors. Have the kids cut out their stars on the outline.

Take your Prayer Star home and use it to help you pray. On each point, you can write one thing in creation that you are thankful to God for. Then thank God for making that thing. Color the star-point for each day that you pray. Have the children put their names on the back of their stars. Put them in a safe spot until the end of class.

The preschoolers and elementary children have separate activities for this part of the lesson. Use the Park Patrol or the Noah's Park puppets—or both—to help the children move to their separate areas.

SNACK SHACK
Star Cookies

See page RS-7 in the *Snacks and Games Book* for a lesson-related snack suggestion: Star Cookies. Use the Park Patrol to help give out snack supplies and clean up afterward. You might also want them to sit among the children to chat and help them make friends with one another.

CAMPSITE CAPERS
The Creator Said (Elementary)
Daytime and Nighttime Toss (Preschool)

Have your Park Patrol lead the children to an open area for today's game. The elementary game, "The Creator Said," is on page RS-7 in the *Snacks and Games Book.* The preschool game, "Daytime and Nighttime Toss," is on page RS-8 in the same book.

COZY CAVE CRAFTS
Heavenly Mobile (Elementary)
Creation Quilt—Square 1 (Preschool)

The elementary craft that supports today's lesson is a "Heavenly Mobile." Complete instructions are on page RC-7 in the *Craft Book.* The preschool craft project, "Creation Quilt—Square 1," is on RC-8 of the *Craft Book.*

CLOSING ACTIVITIES

A few minutes before class is over, have the children help straighten the room. Then gather them around to review the Bible memory verse and close in prayer. As children leave, be sure they take their crafts and remind them we can trust God's plan in creation.

OVERTIME ACTIVITIES

If you have extra time while waiting for parents to pick up their children, ask the Park Patrol to lead children in another round of "The Creator Said" game.

R2 Lesson: God's Useful and Beautiful World

Choose from the options listed below to follow Adventure Trails that lead to Jesus:

DISCOVERY TRAILS
TEACHER FEATURE (5 min.)
"What Do You Need?" Game Show
BIBLE STORY (10 min.)
A Useful and Beautiful World (Elem.)
God Made the Sky, Water, Land, and Plants (Preschool)
NOAH'S PARK PUPPETS (5 min.)
Beautiful and Useful
BIBLE MEMORY (5 min.)
Verse Flower

WORSHIP TRAILS
SINGING PRAISES TO JESUS (5–10 min.)
SHARE AND PRAYER (5–10 min.)
Prayer Flowers

WILDLIFE TRAILS
SNACK SHACK (5 min.)
Useful Plant Snacks
CAMPSITE CAPERS (10 min.)
Water Relays (Elementary)
Plant Hide-and-Seek (Preschool)
COZY CAVE CRAFTS (15 min.)
Beautiful Plant Pot (Elementary)
Creation Quilt—Square 2 (Preschool)

HAPPY TRAILS
CLOSING ACTIVITIES (5 min.)
OVERTIME ACTIVITIES (as needed)

DISCOVERY TRAILS

TEACHER FEATURE
"What Do You Need?" Game Show

Supplies: Whiteboard or newsprint and marker

Divide the children into small groups for a game show. Ask teams the same questions. Teammates may confer to select one answer, then stand up to answer. It's okay if teams repeat answers.

Have a Park Patrol keep score where everyone can see. Don't tell kids what answers are best, but ask them to see which answers score highest.

Begin the game show with some hype. **Let's welcome the contestants of the "What Do You Need?" Game Show! Here's the first question!**

What do you need to surf? Let teams decide answers, stand, and respond. Award five points for ocean, wind, waves, and other things that God made. Award two points for surfboard, swimsuit, and other things not created.

What do you need to play soccer? (A grassy field and other created items get five points; a man-made ball and goal and similar items get two points.)

Have the children think about what the high-point answers have in common, but don't tell them the answer yet.

What do you need to make a fruit salad? (Award five points for any fruit; award two points for anything related that people made.)

What do you need to make a bouquet? (Award five points for any flower or plant, award two points for ribbon, vase, etc.)

What do you need to snow ski? (Snow, hill, mountain, cold weather, etc. for five points; two points for skis, boots, poles, etc.)

Congratulate all teams for doing a great job. See who figured out that the high-scoring answers were things God created. **Today's Bible story will teach us more about God's beautiful and useful creation.**

ELEMENTARY BIBLE STORY

A Useful and Beautiful World
(Genesis 1:6-13, 28-29)

Supplies: Bible, large basin, sand, water, plastic plants

Preparation: Place a thick layer of sand in the bottom of the basin. Cover it with an inch of water.

Show the children Genesis 1 and hold your Bible open to that spot while you tell this Bible story.

The Bible teaches us that God created a useful and beautiful world. **What does it mean when something is beautiful? What does "useful" mean?** (It's good to use; it does a job.)

When God first made the earth, the land, water, and sky were not neatly separated, as they are now. So God separated the sky from the earth. The sky is the air we breathe. That's pretty useful, isn't it? How are clouds beautiful? (They have interesting shapes and color.) **How do they help us?** (They make rain and snow for water.) **God created a useful and beautiful world.**

Gather the class around the basin. **The earth was completely covered with water—like this sand. Then God said, "Let dry ground appear on the earth," and land pushed up from under the water.** Let volunteers gently push the sand into a pile that sticks up above the water.

Most of earth's land is still covered with water. God called the water "seas." We also call them oceans. Gently rock the basin to make waves. **Oceans are beautiful. How are the oceans useful?** (For swimming or boating; home for fish.)

God made the dry ground take different forms. What are they? (Mountains, valleys, plains, deserts.) **They are beautiful, but they are also useful. What do these landforms provide us?** Let children share their ideas.

Then **God said, "Let plants grow on the land." And it happened!** Place the plastic plants in the wet sand so they stand up—in and out of the water like bushes and seaweed. **God made plants grow on all the different landforms. He even made plants that grow in the land under the sea! All plants are pretty in their own way. How are plants are useful, too?** (We eat fruits and vegetables, bake with grains and spices. We get wood and paper from plants, and cotton for clothes.) **God created a useful and beautiful world.**

Use review questions like these to check for understanding: **Who made the water, clouds, land, and plants?** (God made them all.) **Why do we have a beautiful and useful world?** (Because God made it that way.)

PRESCHOOL BIBLE STORY
God Made the Sky, Water, Land, and Plants (Genesis 1:6-13, 28-29)

Supplies: Bible, completed preschool craft (*Craft Book*, p. RC-10), Creation Quilt—Square 1 (from last week), flannel board

Preparation: Make a preschool craft from page RC-10 of the Noah's Park *Craft Book*.

Show the children Genesis 1 in your Bible and keep it open as you tell the story. **Our story today comes from the very beginning of the Bible, from the Book of Genesis.**

Put the quilt square from Lesson 1 on the flannel board. **God made the day and night.** Point to each item as you name it. **He made the sun, the moon, and the stars. God saw that they were all good. But there was more to God's plan for creating the world.**

God said, "Let there be sky with the water below." Move your hands from left to right, rippling your fingers. Have the children copy your actions. **And there was water on the earth and the sky above it.** Take down the square from Lesson 1. Put the light blue square on the board. Put the dark blue water figure on the bottom left corner. Put the cloud figure in the sky.

God told all the water to come together in one place. Clap your hands once. Have the children copy your actions. **When all the water came together, ground appeared. God called the ground "land."** Put the land figure on the bottom right of your square.

Then God said, "Let the land have plants on it." And so there were plants—many plants! There were tall plants like trees. Stand up tall with your arms stretched up. Have the children do these actions with you. **There were little plants like grass.** Crouch down low. **There were plants with flowers that looked and smelled pretty.** Pretend to smell a flower. **There were plants with fruit like bananas.** Pretend to eat a banana. Put the tree and flower on the land.

God looked at the water and land. He looked at the clouds and the plants. God saw

that they were all good. They were all a part of God's plan when He made the world.

Use the quilt square to review the Bible story. Have the children choose a figure to put on the square that answers each question. **What did God make?** (Water and land.) **What kinds of plants did God make?** (Trees and flowers.)

NOAH'S PARK PUPPETS
Beautiful and Useful

Lead the children to your Noah's Park puppet theater while the Park Patrol members who will present today's puppet play get ready. You will find this lesson's puppet script in the Noah's Park *Puppet Skits Book* on page RP-9.

BIBLE MEMORY
Verse Flower

Supplies: Green and yellow paper, scissors, marker, tape

Preparation: Select a Bible verse about creation or use the memory verse from Sunday school.
Cut a large green circle and yellow flower petals. Print the verse, one word per petal. Put the verse reference on the last petal. Lightly tape the petals in order around the green circle.

Hold up the verse flower where all can see it. Say the verse and reference aloud as you point to each word. Have the children say the verse as you point to the words. Repeat a few times.

Choose children to each "pick" a petal. Ask them to make a line holding their petals in order. Have everyone read the verse together. Put the verse flower back together. As time permits, repeat this activity with different children until every child has had a turn to hold a flower petal.

God is pleased when we learn Bible verses. He's also pleased when we sing praises to Him for the useful and beautiful world He created.

WORSHIP TRAILS

SINGING PRAISES TO JESUS

Supplies: Noah's Park CD and CD player

Ask the children to join you to sing with the Unit 1 song, "In the Beginning," from the Noah's Park CD. Work with the children to plan hand motions to go with the lyrics. Then sing the song again using the motions. Repeat so all can learn the motions. As time permits, sing other songs praising God for who He is and the beauty of His creation.

SHARE AND PRAYER
Prayer Flowers

Supplies: Craft foam in two colors, scissors, hole punch, resealable plastic bags, light string, whiteboard or newsprint and marker, colored markers

Preparation: From craft foam, cut two-inch circles. From a second color of foam, cut two-inch-long oval petals. Punch a hole near the edge of the circle and also the end of each petal. Cut nine-inch lengths of string. Put one circle, six petals, and a string in a bag for each child.

We used a flower to help us learn our Bible verse. Now we'll make Prayer Flowers to help us thank God for beautiful things He created. Give each child a bag and have them set their pieces on the table in the shape of a flower.

Show the children how to tie one end of the string to the center and then put the loose end through the hole in each petal. Tie the remaining end of string to the last petal.

Distribute colored markers, and have the children write, "Thank You, God," on the circle. On each petal, the children should write a word for something beautiful or useful God created.

Set your Prayer Flower on the table with the circle in the middle. Place the petals around the edge to make a flower. Pray the words in the center and then what you wrote on each petal. You can pick it up and put it back together whenever you want to pray with it.

Ask your Park Patrol members to gather small groups of children with their Prayer Flowers and thank God for things they wrote.

The following age-appropriate activities work best when elementary and preschool kids are separated. Children could be in the same room at different tables and in different areas. Or you can use separate rooms for each group.

SNACK SHACK

Useful Plant Snacks

This lesson's snack is on page RS-9 of your Noah's Park *Snacks and Games Book.* Snack Shack is a fun time to let Park Patrol bring out the Noah's Park puppets to interact with the children. Be sure to have children clean up after they finish eating their snack.

CAMPSITE CAPERS

Water Relays *(Elementary)*
Plant Hide-and-Seek *(Preschool)*

Have the elementary-age children gather in a large area for "Water Relays." Directions are on page RS-9 of the Noah's Park *Snacks and Games Book.* Directions for the preschool game, "Plant Hide-and-Seek," are on page RS-10 of the same book. Each group needs a separate game area.

COZY CAVE CRAFTS

Beautiful Plant Pot *(Elementary)*
Creation Quilt–Square 2 *(Preschool)*

The preschool children will work again on their Creation Quilts, found on page RC-10 of the *Craft Book.* Elementary children will do the "Beautiful Plant Pot," on page RC-9. Both crafts will give the children opportunity to appreciate the beauty and usefulness of God's creation.

CLOSING ACTIVITIES

Ask the children to help straighten the room. Then gather them together. Ask the children to name useful and beautiful things God created. **We can praise God for these during the week. What do you have to help you remember?** (Prayer Flower, Beautiful Plant Seed Pot, songs, and Creation Quilt.) Lead your class to thank God for His useful and beautiful world.

OVERTIME ACTIVITIES

While waiting for parents to pick up their children, the Park Patrol can act out clues about water, clouds, land, or plants. Let kids guess what is being pantomimed. For example, arch your arms overhead and puff out your cheeks like a cloud, tapping fingers on the floor like raindrops. Or, crouch down like a seed, unfolding to sprout leaves. Act out peeling and eating a banana.

R3 Lesson: God Created All Kinds of Animals

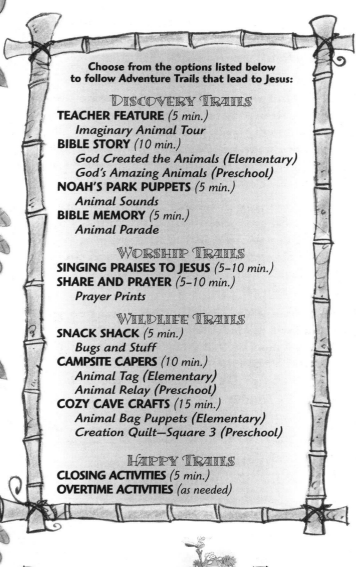

Choose from the options listed below
to follow Adventure Trails that lead to Jesus:

DISCOVERY TRAILS
TEACHER FEATURE (5 min.)
Imaginary Animal Tour
BIBLE STORY (10 min.)
God Created the Animals (Elementary)
God's Amazing Animals (Preschool)
NOAH'S PARK PUPPETS (5 min.)
Animal Sounds
BIBLE MEMORY (5 min.)
Animal Parade

WORSHIP TRAILS
SINGING PRAISES TO JESUS (5–10 min.)
SHARE AND PRAYER (5–10 min.)
Prayer Prints

WILDLIFE TRAILS
SNACK SHACK (5 min.)
Bugs and Stuff
CAMPSITE CAPERS (10 min.)
Animal Tag (Elementary)
Animal Relay (Preschool)
COZY CAVE CRAFTS (15 min.)
Animal Bag Puppets (Elementary)
Creation Quilt—Square 3 (Preschool)

HAPPY TRAILS
CLOSING ACTIVITIES (5 min.)
OVERTIME ACTIVITIES (as needed)

DISCOVERY TRAILS

TEACHER FEATURE
Imaginary Animal Tour

Supplies: None

Let's go on an imaginary tour. I'll describe things and you can guess what they are. Here's a hint—God made them all. When you know what we're pretending to look at, raise your hand. Read the "tour" dramatically. You might lead the children around the room as you pretend to look at different animals.

Here we are in a field watching a little, furry fellow who just came out of his hole in the ground. He's sitting tall and every once in a while barks like a dog. Oh! Lots of his friends just came up out of their holes and they're all sitting up too! It's a colony of these guys. (Children should guess prairie dog or groundhog.)

You guessed very well what we saw at that first stop on our tour. (Look down.) **Now we're looking at a, um, is it a stick? No, it's alive and slithering off into the grass! My, it's already hiding. What was that?** (A snake.)

That last site was a little surprising. Hmmm. What's that up there? (Point and look up to a corner.) **Sitting on a branch is a . . . whoa, he just turned his head way around and looked straight behind himself! Wow, such big round eyes. Listen, what's that he said? "Whoo, whoo." I wonder whooo he is?** (An owl.)

Well, let's move on now that you know WHO was at that last stop. There's something! Funny feet with toes all connected together. She waddles along with all her little ones in line behind her. Yep, there she goes, right into the pond with her family right behind. (Duck, goose, swan, etc.)

That was a fun! What things did we pretend to see? (Animals.) **Yes, God created all those animals. Let's learn more in our Bible story.**

At this time, let the Noah's Park puppets lead the children to their separate Bible story areas. If you keep the groups together, use the Elementary Bible story.

ELEMENTARY BIBLE STORY
God Created the Animals

(Genesis 1:20–25)

Supplies: Bible; a wide variety of plastic, rubber, or stuffed animals, including mammals, birds, fish, reptiles, and insects (it's okay if they are not proportionate in size to one another)

Keep your Bible open to Genesis as you tell the story. Explain that Genesis tells us how God created the animals. Gather the children in a circle on the floor or at a table and spread out all the animals in the center. Let the children handle them and use them as prompts during the Bible story.

God made the heavens, earth, day, night, sun, moon, stars, clouds, oceans, land, and plants. Then when He was finished, He said, "Let the waters be filled with living creatures, and let birds fly in the sky." And it happened! By simply speaking the words, God made all the animals that live in water and those that fly. Let the children look for these kinds of animals in the pile.

Some animals that God made to live in water are fish with gills so they can breathe underwater. What do we call some of them? Let the children name fish they know of. Let children hold up any fish from the pile. **Other animals that live in water come up to the surface to breathe because God made them so. What are some of their names?** (Whale, dolphin, etc.) Let children hold up any of these.

God made many animals in the water move in different ways. What do you know about these? The children might talk about fish, mammals, and reptiles that move in the water with fins, flippers, water jets, or even drift until they grab onto or attach to something. **God really is creative, isn't He? God saw that all the animals He made to live in water were good.**

God made all kinds of birds with the power of His words. What do birds have in common? (They have wings and beaks.) **What are some of the differences between the kinds of birds?** (Colors, size, songs, etc.) Let the children hold up any birds and describe them.

We can see God's creativity in all the different kinds of animals He made to live in the water and sky. Then God said, "Let there be living creatures all over the land." Just by speaking the words, God made all the animals that walk, hop, or crawl on the land. Each kind of animal is different.

Many land animals are mammals. They're different in that they give birth to live young and breathe with lungs. **Can you name any mammals?** The children might suggest animals such as bears, rabbits, deer, dogs, and bats. Younger children may not yet know about mammals; gently correct those who name a non-mammal. Others may be able to tell more characteristics of mammals. Children may find mammals in the pile.

God's land animals also include reptiles and insects. Reptiles are different because many can swim very well, but they aren't fish. What are some names of reptiles? (Turtles, crocodiles, lizards, snakes, etc.) Let volunteers name some and hold up any they find.

Insects are very different. Some fly but aren't birds. God made some insects with many legs and others without legs. Those without legs slither along the ground. What insects do not have legs? (Worms.) Encourage the children to find and name insects.

How many different kinds of animals do you think God made? Reinforce the huge but unknown numbers that show God's creativity. **Who created all the different kinds of animals?** (God.) **Let's praise God today because He created all kinds of animals!**

PRESCHOOL BIBLE STORY
God's Amazing Animals
(Genesis 1:20-25)

Supplies: Bible, completed preschool craft (*Craft Book*, p. RC-12), flannel board, quilt squares from Lessons 1 and 2

Preparation: Make a large-sized preschool craft from page RC-12 of the Noah's Park *Craft Book*.

Our story today comes from the Bible. It is found in the beginning in the Book of Genesis. Keep your Bible open to Genesis 1 as you tell the story.

Put the first quilt square on the flannel board. **God made the day and night.** Point to each item as you name it. **He made the sun, the moon, and the stars. God saw that they were all good.**

Put the Lesson 2 quilt square next to the one for Lesson 1. **God made water, clouds, land, and every plant. God saw that they were all good** too. But God wasn't done making things yet!

God said, "Let there be animals in the water and birds in the sky." And there were fish that swam in the water—big fish, little fish, and even yummy fish. Put your hands together and wiggle them like a fish. And there were birds that flew in the sky—robins, sparrows, and even eagles. Have the children pretend to fly by flapping their arms like wings.

God had plans for even more animals. He said, "Let there be all kinds of animals that live on the land." There were animals everywhere! God made some animals to live on farms. A cow lives on a farm. Have the children say "moo!" Who else lives on a farm? Let children name other animals.

God made animals and bugs that move on the ground. An ant moves on the ground. Have the children crawl their fingers up an arm. Who else moves on the ground? (Insects and reptiles.)

And God made wild animals that live in the forests, the deserts, and the jungles. An elephant is a wild animal. Ask the children to put their arms together and raise them like a trunk. What else is a wild animal? Encourage children to respond.

The animals could drink water from the oceans and lakes. They could eat from the plants. God looked at all the animals He had made—and He saw that they were all good.

God looked at the day and night. He looked at the sun, the moon, and the stars. God saw that they were all good. They were all a part of God's plan when He made the world.

Use the quilt square to review the Bible story. Put the quilt square on the flannel board. Put all the animals on the floor in front of the square. God made animals. What did He make? Have children name animals and put them on the square.

NOAH'S PARK PUPPETS
Animal Sounds

Have the children walk like elephants (bent forward with arms down and swinging like a trunk) to your Noah's Park puppet theater. Ask them to sit with

their legs folded like a clam and be quiet as a mouse for today's puppet program presented by the Park Patrol. See page RP-11 of the *Puppet Skits Book*.

BIBLE MEMORY
Animal Parade

Supplies: None

Preparation: Choose a verse for the children to memorize that reinforces this lesson. Say the first few words of the verse. Have the children repeat after you. Continue increasing the amount of the verse until the children are saying the entire verse and reference.

Lead the children around the room walking slowly like elephants while saying the verse, one word on each step. Repeat the verse hopping like kangaroos, and then crawling like a spider, and so on.

Wouldn't it be fun to be able to swim like a fish and say our verse underwater! God didn't make us that way, but He did make us to sing praises to Him. Let's do that now.

SINGING PRAISES TO JESUS

Supplies: Noah's Park CD and CD player

Have the children join you and the Park Patrol in singing the Unit 1 song, "In the Beginning," from the Noah's Park music CD. You might do the motions the class created for the song last week. Sing other worship songs the children know to praise to God.

SHARE AND PRAYER
Prayer Prints

Supplies: Blank paper, colored pencils

Across the top of the board or paper print "Dear Jesus, please . . ." Ask the children to share prayer concerns they would like the class to pray about today and through the coming week. Write each in two- or three-word phrases on the board.

Hand out paper and colored pencils. Have the children copy, "Dear Jesus, please . . ." at the top of their papers.

Explain how to draw circles to make a paw print as you draw one on the board. It should be one larger circle (about the size of their fists) with four smaller circles around the top half. Make it large enough to write a two- or three-word prayer concern inside the largest circle. Have the children copy it.

Pick one of the prayer concerns on our board to copy into the large circle of your paw print. That way you will turn it into a "prayer print." Write one of the prayer items in your paw print on the board. Tell the children they may choose any one they want to pray about. Then ask them to draw more paw prints and write other items from the prayer list on the board for each paw print.

Take time to pray as a class, letting kids talk to God about the requests they wrote in their prayer prints.

Be sure the children all write their names on the back of their Prayer Print paper to take home with them. Encourage the children to continue to pray about these concerns during the week.

In this part of the lesson, age-appropriate activities are provided for crafts and games. You may want to let the preschoolers and elementary-age kids have their snack separately as well. You might use the Noah's Park puppets to lead the children between activities.

SNACK SHACK
Bugs and Stuff

See page RS-11 in the Noah's Park *Snacks and Games Book* for a suggestion for today's Snack Shack. Children will have fun creating their own snacks!

CAMPSITE CAPERS

Animal Tag (Elementary)
Animal Relay (Preschool)

You will find directions for "Animal Tag" for the elementary-age children on page RS-11 of the *Snacks and Games Book*. If conditions are good outside,

you might take the children outside for this game. The preschoolers will play an "Animal Relay," described on page RS-12 in the *Snacks and Games Book*.

COZY CAVE CRAFTS
Animal Bag Puppets (Elementary)
Creation Quilt—Square 3 (Preschool)

The crafts for this lesson provide opportunities for the children to use their creativity in celebration of God's creativity when making all the different kinds of animals. The preschool children will continue work on their "Creation Quilts," found on page RC-12 of Noah's Park *Craft Book*. For the elementary-age children, see the "Animal Puppets," on page RC-11 of the *Craft Book*. If time allows, invite the elementary-age kids to use their animal puppets to create and perform their own Animal Puppet Play.

CLOSING ACTIVITIES

A few minutes before class ends, ask the children to help clean up craft projects. You could play the unit song as they work. As children finish, Park Patrol can lead them to collect their craft projects and Prayer Prints and join you for the following Closing Activity.

Huddle with a few children to quietly plan an animal charade. As they act it out, let the other children guess the animal. **God created all kinds of animals and you did a good job acting out one of them!** Repeat with another group of children, then close by thanking God for creating the animals.

OVERTIME ACTIVITIES

Let Park Patrol members occupy the children while they wait for parents to arrive so you are available to greet parents. You might have some Park Patrol members continue with the charades from Closing Activities. Or you might play the unit song again and let the children sing along and do motions.

R4 Lesson: God Created People to Be Like Him

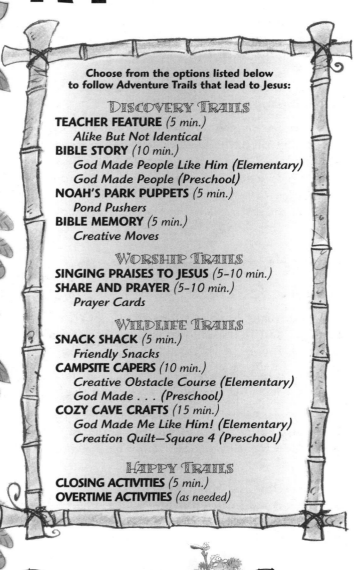

Choose from the options listed below to follow Adventure Trails that lead to Jesus:

DISCOVERY TRAILS
TEACHER FEATURE *(5 min.)*
  Alike But Not Identical
BIBLE STORY *(10 min.)*
  God Made People Like Him (Elementary)
  God Made People (Preschool)
NOAH'S PARK PUPPETS *(5 min.)*
  Pond Pushers
BIBLE MEMORY *(5 min.)*
  Creative Moves

WORSHIP TRAILS
SINGING PRAISES TO JESUS *(5-10 min.)*
SHARE AND PRAYER *(5-10 min.)*
  Prayer Cards

WILDLIFE TRAILS
SNACK SHACK *(5 min.)*
  Friendly Snacks
CAMPSITE CAPERS *(10 min.)*
  Creative Obstacle Course (Elementary)
  God Made . . . (Preschool)
COZY CAVE CRAFTS *(15 min.)*
  God Made Me Like Him! (Elementary)
  Creation Quilt—Square 4 (Preschool)

HAPPY TRAILS
CLOSING ACTIVITIES *(5 min.)*
OVERTIME ACTIVITIES *(as needed)*

DISCOVERY TRAILS

TEACHER FEATURE
Alike but Not Identical

Supplies: Paper, pencils, golf balls, pictures of ice cream

Divide the children into multi-age teams. Give each team a paper and pencil, and have them choose a writer. A Park Patrol member may help each team, but let children do the thinking.

Some things are alike, but not exactly the same. For example, what is a lot like a pencil, but is not exactly a pencil? (A pen, marker, or chalk because they also write; a stick or other object that is straight and made of wood.)

I will say a word. Work with your team to list things that are similar to what I name. When time is up, we'll count the number of items you list on your papers and compare ideas.

Here's the first item—a golf ball. Hold up the golf ball. If you have extra, let each group pass one around. **Brainstorm with your team a list of all the things that have a lot in common with a golf ball. Have your team writer write down your ideas.** Let team members talk and write.

After one minute, call time. Ask teams to count the number of items on their list. Have a group name one item from its list. Other groups should raise hands if they listed the same item. Ask how the item is like a golf ball. Repeat this process with other items on their lists. Children might name things which are round, things you hit with a stick, or things which are small, round, and white.

Let's do another one: ice cream. Make a list of things that have something in common with ice cream. Pass out pictures of ice cream. Let the teams brainstorm. After a minute, let teams count the items and share ideas. Children can tell how things are similar to ice cream. (Whipped cream or milk because of taste, snow because it's cold, etc.)

Things can be *like* something else, but not exactly the same. This is true for people, too. Today we will learn that people are like Someone else. God made people like Him. Let's go to our Bible story areas now. Have the Park Patrol, using puppets, lead the way.

ELEMENTARY BIBLE STORY
God Made People Like Him *(Genesis 1:26-28; 2:7-8, 18-22, 25; 3:8; Psalm 8)*

Supplies: Bible

Open a Bible to Psalm 8. Explain that God teaches about creation throughout the Bible. Ask the children to listen for ways God made people like Him.

God made Adam from the dust of the earth, but God made Adam like Him in some ways. Adam was alone until God made Eve. Adam and Eve were made for each other. Both were happy with each other and they cared for each another because God made people to need and love other people. Who do you need and love? (Family and friends.) Let the children all give high fives or hugs to their friends in the room.

Adam and Eve got along with each another, just as we do. What do you do with people? (Talk, play, work, eat together, etc.) **That's called being in a relationship with someone. We are like God because we have relationships with others.**

God had planted a garden and called it Eden. He put Adam and Eve there for a place to stay and to take care of it. Adam and Eve enjoyed their home in the Garden of Eden and the work God gave them. God also enjoys His home in heaven and His work.

One of Adam's jobs was to think of names for the animals. Let each child name an animal. **Adam could do this job well because God made people with creative minds like Himself. What are some things that you've created or made up?** Let kids share. (Pictures, music, jokes, games, gifts, etc.)

God told Adam to rule over the earth, with its plants and animals. This is another way we are like God. He rules over all creation. We rule over the earth. Let a few volunteers act out some ways we rule over the earth and take care of it. You may whisper suggestions in their ear, such as gardening and building. **God made us like Him so we can care for creation.**

We rule over animals, too. What are some ways we take care of them? Let a couple more volunteers act out ways we rule over animals. They might pantomime giving food to a pet or teaching a dog to do tricks. Let the other children join in. **We rule over animals and that means we must take good care of them. We can do this because God made people like Him.**

God created people so He could enjoy them and be friends with them. He visited Adam and Eve in the Garden so they could spend time together. We also want to be friends with God and enjoy Him forever. How can we be friends with God? Let kids act out things like praying, singing, reading the Bible, coming to children's church, etc. **It's great that God created people to be like Him.**

Use a few review questions to check children's comprehension of the Bible story. **What are some of the ways God created people to be like Him?** (People enjoy relationships and care for one another; we enjoy our homes; we are creative; we rule over the earth, plants, and animals; we enjoy friendship with God.)

PRESCHOOL BIBLE STORY
God Made People (Genesis 1:27; 2:25; 3:8)

Supplies: Bible, completed preschool craft (Craft Book, p. RC-14), flannel board, quilt squares from Lessons 1, 2, and 3

Preparation: Make a large-sized preschool craft from page RC-14 of the Noah's Park Craft Book.

Show the children where Genesis 1 is in your Bible. **Our story today comes from the Book of Genesis in the Bible.** Keep your Bible open to Genesis 1 as you tell the story.

Put the quilt square from Lesson 1 on the flannel board. **God made the day and night.** Point to each item as you name it. **He made the sun, the moon, and the stars. God saw that they were all good.**

Put the Lesson 2 quilt square next to the one for Lesson 1. **God made water, clouds, land, and every plant. God saw that they were all good too.**

Put the Lesson 3 quilt square below the Lesson 1 square. **And God made all the different animals: fish, birds, animals that live on farms, animals that move on the ground, and wild animals. But God wasn't done making things yet! He still had something very special to make.**

God's special creation didn't live in the sea.

Shake your head no. **It wasn't a fish. His creation didn't fly in the sky.** Shake your head no. **It wasn't a bird. The creation didn't say "moo," so it couldn't be a cow.** Shake your head no.

What did God's creation have? It had two legs. Have children point to each body part as it is named. **It had two arms. God's special creation had two eyes to see with, a nose to smell with, two ears to hear, and a mouth to eat. God's most special creation had a brain to think and a heart to feel. What do you think is God's special creation?** Let children respond. **Yes, you're right! It's people!**

First God made a man. God took dirt from the ground and formed it into a man. God named him Adam. God put Adam in a garden called Eden. Adam would take care of God's creation. Put the quilt square on the flannel board below the second square. Ask a child to put the figure of Adam on the square.

Then God made a woman. One day while Adam was sleeping, God took out one of Adam's rib bones. Help children find their ribs. **God used the rib bone to make a woman called Eve. God put Eve with Adam in the garden. She would be Adam's helper and friend.** Ask another child to put the figure of Eve on the square.

God looked at all of His creation. He saw that it was good.

Review questions: **What did God make?** Let children answer by pointing to different parts of the quilt. **What is God's special creation?** (People.)

NOAH'S PARK PUPPETS
Pond Pushers

The puppet skit for today is found on page RP-13 of the Noah's Park *Puppet Skits Book.* Lead the children to the puppet stage and have them be seated. When ready, have the Park Patrol perform.

BIBLE MEMORY
Creative Moves

Supplies: Bible

Preparation: Select a Bible verse for the children to

memorize that reinforces today's focus on God's creating us to be like Him.

Read the verse aloud from your Bible and show them where it is located so they understand a reference is like an address to help us find the verse again.

Remind the children that God formed Adam from dust and made Eve from Adam's rib. We are like God because we create things using our brains and hands.

Ask the children to use their brains to create hand signs and body motions that go with the verse. Then lead the children in saying the verse with the signs or actions. Repeat a few times, letting different children help lead.

God is creative. He made us like Him so we can create things too. Remember the actions we've created for our Bible memory verse? Teach them to your family and friends so they know that God created them to be like Him too.

Now let's praise God for making us like Him.

SINGING PRAISES TO JESUS

Supplies: Noah's Park CD and CD player, rhythm instruments

Lead the children in singing the Unit 1 song, "In the Beginning," with the Noah's Park CD or the music in the back of this *Leader's Guide.* Ask the children to use their memories—another likeness we have with God—to help them remember the motions your class created together in Lesson 2 for this song. Sing the song and do your motions.

SHARE AND PRAYER
Prayer Cards

Supplies: Note cards, pencils

As we get to know people, we learn about them and what they need. We also can get to know God and talk with Him about our needs and the needs of our friends. Praying for our friends is something we can do only because God make us like Him.

Ask the children to share needs and requests for prayer for their families and friends. Make a list of the prayer concerns. Ask for volunteers who will pray for each request mentioned. Ask volunteers to pray aloud in turn; then conclude the group prayer time.

We can pray for the people we know all week. Let's make prayer cards to let people know we care about them and will pray for them. Hand out small note cards (or paper to fold as cards). Have children write on each card, "I'm praying for you because I care for you." Let them sign their names.

Explain that during the week they can give a card to someone they will pray for because they care for him or her. Talk about the possible family members and friends the children might pray for.

Age-appropriate activities are suggested below to help engage children meaningfully in the lesson. You might consider alternative uses of your space to accommodate the groups. Utilize the Park Patrol to help the children at each activity as needed.

SNACK SHACK
Friendly Snacks

We enjoy friends because God created people to be like Him. An activity many enjoy with friends is to make and eat food together. Today's snack suggestion can be found on page RS-13 in the **Snacks and Games Book.** Ask the children to form groups of two or three to prepare their snacks.

CAMPSITE CAPERS
Creative Obstacle Course (Elementary)
God Made . . . (Preschool)

Lead the children to an open area for today's games. The elementary "Creative Obstacle Course" can be found on page RS-13 in the Noah's Park **Snacks and Games Book.** The preschool game, "God Made . . .," is on page RS-14 in the same book.

COZY CAVE CRAFTS
God Made Me Like Him! (Elementary)
Creation Quilt—Square 4 (Preschool)

Copy page RC-13 in the **Craft Book** for each child. Review the ways God made people like Him from the Bible story. Let the children draw pictures showing the ways in which they are like God. Instructions for the last quilt square of the preschool craft, "Creation Quilt—Square 4," are on page RC-14.

CLOSING ACTIVITIES

When the children have completed the snack, games, and craft, play the unit song from the CD as a signal for cleanup time. Encourage all the children to help straighten the room. Use Noah's Park puppets to suggest what could be straightened and to give encouragement for a job well done. When finished, gather the children for a wrap-up time.

Talk with the children about places they will be and things they will do this week that might remind them of how God made them to be like Him. For example, in art class at school they will be creative like God. Each day they will relate with friends in many ways—just like God.

Allow time to pray and thank God for making each child participating in Noah's Park Children's Church. As the children leave with their parents, be sure they are taking their Prayer Cards and crafts with them.

OVERTIME ACTIVITIES

Assign Park Patrol members to select books about creation to read aloud to groups of children as they wait for their parents to arrive. Alternately, you might play another round of the games found in Campsite Capers.

R5 Lesson: Sin Is Wrong and Has Consequences

Choose from the options listed below
to follow Adventure Trails that lead to Jesus:

DISCOVERY TRAILS
TEACHER FEATURE (5 min.)
Decisions and Consequences
BIBLE STORY (10 min.)
Adam and Eve's Wrong Choice (Elem.)
A Very Bad Day (Preschool)
NOAH'S PARK PUPPETS (5 min.)
Following Signs
BIBLE MEMORY (5 min.)
Word Fruits

WORSHIP TRAILS
SINGING PRAISES TO JESUS (5–10 min.)
SHARE AND PRAYER (5–10 min.)
Rotating Prayers

WILDLIFE TRAILS
SNACK SHACK (5 min.)
Fruit Garden
CAMPSITE CAPERS (10 min.)
Listen Up (Elementary)
May I, Please? (Preschool)
COZY CAVE CRAFTS (15 min.)
Road Signs (Elementary)
Apple Printing (Preschool)

HAPPY TRAILS
CLOSING ACTIVITIES (5 min.)
OVERTIME ACTIVITIES (as needed)

hand up flat (as if motioning "stop") for a consequence.

The teacher said to make shoe box dioramas for a story. Jason moaned out loud, "Ugh, I hate reading." Children show thumbs-down. **Jason got in trouble for that.** Flat hand up.

Sarah walked by Jason and said, "Ha, ha. You have to stay in for recess!" Thumbs-down. **Jason wanted to trip Sarah, but didn't.** Thumbs-down for his thought or thumbs-up since he didn't act on it.

But Sarah went to Jason later and said, "Could we work together on our projects? I'd like that." Thumbs-up. **Jason knew he needed help, but said, "No, I don't want any help with that stupid story."** Thumbs-down. **So Sarah left Jason alone.** Flat hand up.

Later Jason apologized to Sarah. Thumbs-up. **Sarah said, "I forgive you. Let's work together now."** Flat hand or thumbs-up. **They read the story and worked hard on their dioramas.** Thumbs-up. **Jason and Sarah received the most applause for their dioramas.** Flat hand.

Jason and Sarah's decisions had consequences. Ours do too. When we make good decisions there are good consequences. But when we sin—do something wrong—there are unhappy consequences. Our Bible story today helps us learn more about decisions and consequences.

Have the Park Patrol lead children to their separate areas to hear their Bible stories.

DISCOVERY TRAILS

TEACHER FEATURE
Decisions and Consequences

Supplies: None

What are decisions? (Choices we make.) **What are consequences?** (Things that naturally result from our decisions, good or bad.)

Have children listen for decisions and consequences in the story. Ask them to show a thumbs-up for good decisions, a thumbs-down for bad ones, and the whole

ELEMENTARY BIBLE STORY
Adam and Eve's Wrong Choice
(Genesis 2:15-17; 3:1-24)

Supplies: Bible, table or desk, a pretend gavel

Preparation: Ask two Park Patrol members to play Adam and Eve. Copy the script for them to refer to as they act. Set up the classroom like a courtroom, with the judge's desk at the front.

Show the children that today's story comes from Genesis 3 in the Bible. Then take your seat as the judge behind the desk. Have Adam and Eve stand next to the desk where all can see and hear them.

Judge: (Pounds the gavel.) **This court will come to order! We are here for the trial of** (glances at notes) **Adam and Eve. We will decide if what they did was sin and if the consequences are fair. Adam and Eve, do you swear to tell the truth, and nothing but the truth?**

Adam and Eve: **We do!**

Judge: **Be seated. First, state your address.**

Adam: **We live in the Garden of Eden. Well . . . we DID.**

Eve: **It was beautiful! It had room to play and lots of yummy fruit trees!**

Judge: **And yet, my records show,** (shuffles papers) **there was one tree God said do not eat—the Tree of the Knowledge of Good and Evil. Is that true?**

Eve: **Yes . . . but we NEVER ate from it—well, except that one time.**

Adam: **That's right, we were very good and obeyed God. Except once.**

Judge: **What did God say would be the consequence if you broke the rule?**

Eve: **Um, He said we would die . . . But you know, that's not what the snake said! And why shouldn't I trust that beautiful, friendly snake?**

Judge: **That snake was only being friendly so he could trick you. What did he say?**

Eve: **The snake told me I could eat from the tree and NOT die! He said—it sounded so wonderful—that we would become like God. It looked sooooo yummy. So I ate fruit off that tree. But it wasn't my fault!**

Adam: (Bursting out to Eve.) **It IS all your fault, Eve! You shouldn't have listened to the snake. You got us kicked out of the Garden of Eden!**

Eve: **You ate the fruit too, Adam!**

Adam: **Not until after you told me to!**

Eve: **But you knew it was wrong!**

Adam: **Did not!**

Eve: **Did too!**

Judge: **Silence!** (Pounds the gavel.) **This is what**

got you in trouble in the garden! You each blamed someone else. Eve, you blamed the snake. Adam, you blamed Eve. But you each chose to do wrong. You both sinned.**

Adam: (Looking sorry.) **Afterward, we tried to hide from God because we knew we did wrong. But we wanted God to forgive us.**

Eve: **We knew we deserved being sent from the garden. And I would have pain when I had children. And Adam would have to work hard in the field to grow food. But worst of all, we were separated from God.**

Judge: **That's a very sad consequence. But there's good news too. Adam and Eve, God loved you. He loved you enough to let you live many more years. He loved you enough—all of us—to make a plan for us to be forgiven when we sin. He sent Jesus.**

Adam: **So we all can be forgiven when we believe in Jesus and tell God we're sorry?**

Judge: **Yes. Sin is wrong and has consequences. But God forgives us through Jesus. Now it's time for my decision.** (Pretends to write notes and shuffle papers. Clears throat loudly.) **I find that Adam and Eve did sin.** (Strike the gavel once.) **I further find that the consequence God gave them was fair.** (Strike the gavel once.) **And I also find that because they were sorry and because God sent His Son, Jesus, to pay the price, that God will forgive them.** (Strike the gavel once.) **This case is closed!** (Strike the gavel a few times and exit.)

Discuss these review questions with the children. **How did Adam and Eve sin?** (They ate from the tree, they blamed others.) **What were the consequences for their sin?** (Pain, hard work, separation from God.) **What way did God make for us to be forgiven?** (Forgiveness through Jesus.)

PRESCHOOL BIBLE STORY
A Very Bad Day (Genesis 2:15–17; 3:1–24)

Supplies: Bible, flannel board, Adam and Eve figures (Craft Book, p. RC-14), stuffed snake

Preparation: Copy, cut out, and color the figures

of Adam and Eve from page RC-14 in the *Craft Book*. Glue a small piece of felt to the back of each piece. If you don't have a stuffed snake, make one by lightly stuffing a necktie and closing the ends.

Our story today comes from Genesis in the first part of the Bible. Show children Genesis.

Parts of our story today will be happy. When it is happy, put your thumbs up. Make a thumbs-up action. **But parts of our story will be sad. Then, we'll put our thumbs down.** Show children how to do thumbs-down.

God made a wonderful world. Is that happy or sad? (Thumbs up.) **Then God made Adam and Eve to take care of God's creation.** Put the figures of Adam and Eve on the flannel board. **Is that happy or sad?** (Thumbs up.)

Adam and Eve lived in a garden and took care of God's wonderful world. God told them they could eat from any tree in the garden except the Tree of the Knowledge of Good and Evil. If they disobeyed, they would die.

Now in the garden lived a snake. Drape the stuffed snake over the board so it hangs by the figure of Eve. **This snake was very, very sneaky.** (Thumbs down.)

One day the snake asked Eve, "Did God really say you couldn't eat any tree in the garden?" He was trying to trick Eve. And she told him, "We can eat from any tree except one. If we do, we'll die."

"No you won't!" said the snake. But he was lying. Is that happy or sad? (Thumbs down.)**The snake said, "If you eat the fruit from that tree, you'll be like God."**

The snake's trick worked! Eve disobeyed God and ate fruit from the tree. Eve gave some to Adam and he ate it too. Is that happy or sad? (Thumbs down.)

When Adam and Eve heard God walking in the garden they tried to hide because they did something wrong. But God called Adam. Adam answered, "I hid because I was scared."

"Why were you scared?" God asked, though He knew the answer. "Did you eat from the tree?"

Adam said, "It wasn't my fault! Eve gave it to me." So Adam blamed Eve instead of saying he was sorry. Is that happy or sad? (Thumbs down.)

Eve said, "It wasn't my fault! The snake tricked me and I ate it." Eve blamed the snake instead of saying she was sorry. Is that happy or sad? (Thumbs down.)

Adam and Eve didn't obey God. That is called sin. Is that happy or sad? (Thumbs down.) **God loved them, but had to punish them. He put them out of the Garden of Eden. Sin kept Adam and Eve away from God. God punished the snake too. Then God promised He would send Jesus, His Son, to save the world from sin.**

Each of us does sin. We get into trouble because of sin and sin keeps us away from God. But God still loves us. He loves every one of you. Is that happy or sad? (Thumbs up.)

To review the Bible story, put the Adam figure on the board. **Tell me what happened to Adam in the story.** Put the Eve figure on the board. **Tell me what happened to Eve in the story.** Finally, lay the snake over the flannel board. **What did the snake do in the story?** (He tricked Eve into disobeying.)

NOAH'S PARK PUPPETS
Following Signs

Bring all children together at your puppet theater for the skit performed by the Park Patrol. The puppet skit is on page RP-15 in the *Puppet Skits Book.*

BIBLE MEMORY
Word Fruits

Supplies: Bible, construction paper, scissors, marker, (optional: paper clips, masking tape)

Preparation: Choose a verse that supports the Bible lesson, or use today's verse from Sunday school. Cut fruit shapes from construction paper. On each fruit, print one word of the memory verse. Print the reference on another fruit. Spread the fruit words all around the room, and hang some at eye level too.

Open your Bible to the verse and teach it to the children, one phrase at a time. Once it is familiar, let the children search for the fruit words around the room. Encourage them to pick up only one word. If group is larger than the number of words in the verse, some children will not pick a fruit this round.

Let children arrange the words in order and read them aloud. Then, mix up the words and let a different group of children find them.

SINGING PRAISES TO JESUS

Supplies: Noah's Park CD and CD player

Have the children listen to the Unit 2 song, "When God Makes a Promise," from the Noah's Park Children's Church CD. Lyrics are on page R-247. Play the song again and sing it together. If time allows, sing more praise songs.

SHARE AND PRAYER
Rotating Prayers

Supplies: Paper, marker, masking tape

Preparation: Make three signs labeled: "Choice at home," "Choice at school," and "Forgiven." Hang them at children's eye level in the room.

Ask children to name situations at school where they have to make a choice about right or wrong. (Cheating on a test, etc.) Next, ask the children to name some choices they make at home (helping mom rather than watching TV, etc.). Finally, ask children why it feels good to be forgiven by God.

Divide the children into three groups and assign a Park Patrol member to each. Have each group gather by a different sign. Ask Park Patrol members to lead a brief prayer time for their group. Have children ask for God's help with a choice at home or school or to thank God for forgiving them. After a minute or so, signal the groups to move to another sign and repeat.

Age-specific activities have been provided for this part of the lesson. You may want to keep the preschoolers with the elementary kids for snack.

SNACK SHACK
Fruit Garden

Today's suggestion on page RS-15 of the *Snacks and Games Book* builds on today's lesson. Let the Park Patrol help out the younger children!

CAMPSITE CAPERS
Listen Up (Elementary)
May I, Please? (Preschool)

The elementary game, "Listen Up," is found on page RS-15 in the *Snacks and Games Book.* For the preschool game, "May I, Please?" see page RS-16.

COZY CAVE CRAFTS
Road Signs (Elementary)
Apple Printing (Preschool)

The elementary "Road Signs" craft is on page RC-15 of the *Craft Book.* The preschool craft, "Apple Printing," is on page RC-16 in the same book. Assign Park Patrol members to help both groups.

CLOSING ACTIVITIES

A few minutes before the end of class, ask the children to help clean up. Play the Unit 2 song from the Noah's Park CD as they work.

Gather the children briefly to review today's Bible verse. Randomly lay out the fruit words from the memory activity and ask for volunteers to put words in order. Say it in unison and repeat as time allows.

OVERTIME ACTIVITIES

With extra time, organize another "Listen Up" game from Campsite Capers. Preschool children will catch on very quickly by watching the older kids.

R6 Lesson: God Is Able to Save Us

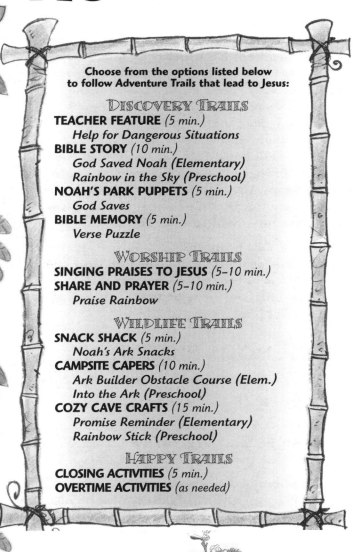

Choose from the options listed below
to follow Adventure Trails that lead to Jesus:

DISCOVERY TRAILS
TEACHER FEATURE *(5 min.)*
Help for Dangerous Situations
BIBLE STORY *(10 min.)*
God Saved Noah (Elementary)
Rainbow in the Sky (Preschool)
NOAH'S PARK PUPPETS *(5 min.)*
God Saves
BIBLE MEMORY *(5 min.)*
Verse Puzzle

WORSHIP TRAILS
SINGING PRAISES TO JESUS *(5–10 min.)*
SHARE AND PRAYER *(5–10 min.)*
Praise Rainbow

WILDLIFE TRAILS
SNACK SHACK *(5 min.)*
Noah's Ark Snacks
CAMPSITE CAPERS *(10 min.)*
Ark Builder Obstacle Course (Elem.)
Into the Ark (Preschool)
COZY CAVE CRAFTS *(15 min.)*
Promise Reminder (Elementary)
Rainbow Stick (Preschool)

HAPPY TRAILS
CLOSING ACTIVITIES *(5 min.)*
OVERTIME ACTIVITIES *(as needed)*

DISCOVERY TRAILS

TEACHER FEATURE
Help for Dangerous Situations

Supplies: Objects and pictures of things that help protect us (smoke alarm, fire extinguisher, sunglasses, swimming float tube, parachute, life raft, fire truck, ambulance, telephone, whistle, jacket, helmet, knee pads, shoes, gloves, sunscreen, sun hat, goggles, etc.)

Spread your pictures and items from the supply list on a table or floor where children can see them and touch them. **These are all things that can**

protect us or help save us. Think about how these things might help us. You will each get to pick one and tell the rest of us about how it might protect us. Let the children take turns picking a picture or item and telling how it helps save us from potential harm. If necessary, ask children to find partners and work in pairs or threes. It's okay if children repeat an item or picture. Ask leading questions as needed to keep the emphasis on how the object helps save or protect us.

We have a lot of things that help protect us, and you know a lot about them. These are good things to have and know how to use for our safety and health.

There are some risks or dangers that we are not able to protect ourselves from. Today we will learn about a man and his family who faced a very dangerous situation. It was so dangerous that if he didn't have a way out, he would have died. Let's learn more in our Bible story.

Divide the children into two groups—preschool and elementary—and have the Park Patrol lead them to their Bible story areas. If you keep the groups together, use the Elementary Bible Story for the lesson.

ELEMENTARY BIBLE STORY
God Saved Noah *(Genesis 6:9, 12–14; 7:24; 8:1, 18, 21–22; 9:1, 12–17)*

Supplies: Bible, large brown paper grocery bags, scrap wood without splinters, hammer, real or fake animal fur (or a realistic-feeling stuffed animal), bowl of water, dry sand, a leafy branch (real or fake), paper streamers or ribbons in the colors of the rainbow

Preparation: Place each item in its own brown paper grocery bag: scrap wood, hammer, fur or a furry animal, a wide bowl half filled with water, sand, a branch with leaves, streamers or ribbons. Set out the bags on a table in order (you might number them). Be sure the children can reach into them, but can't see inside. If you have a large class, you may have duplicates of the bags so more can participate.

Show the children Genesis 8 in your Bible. Explain

that as you tell the Bible story you'll ask volunteers to reach into each bag and feel what is in there without looking. They'll describe it for the others and then try to guess what it is. Choose a volunteer for each bag and have them line up.

God made people to fill the earth. But there was a time when hardly anyone loved God. They all did evil. Only a man named Noah loved and obeyed God. So God decided to destroy every living thing on earth—except for Noah and his family and some animals.

So this was God's plan. Have your first volunteer go up to the bag with the wood in it, reach in without looking, and try to guess what it is. Have him or her describe aloud what it feels like. After guessing, bring out the wood and show the class. Do the same with the second bag with the hammer. **God's plan was for Noah to build a giant boat, called an ark. God told Noah how much wood to use and how to build it. Noah's followed God's plan.**

Then God was ready for the next step of His plan. Repeat with the next volunteer and the bag with the fur. When a close guess is made, have the child remove the fur and show it. **Next, God called animals to come to the ark. A male and a female of every living creature came. The animals went into the ark and so did Noah's family. God shut the door.**

Encourage the next child to gently dip a hand in but not try to pick anything up. Let kids guess water, then take out the bowl and show them. **Then it began to rain . . . and rain . . . and rain. It wasn't a lovely spring rain or even an exciting summer thunderstorm. It was a huge rain that went on for 40 days and 40 nights. It flooded the entire earth. But Noah was safe on the ark. God was keeping His promise.**

When the rain finally stopped all Noah could see was water, like the ocean. After a long time, the water started to go down. Noah sent out birds to see if they could find a place to land. But they came back. Have the next two volunteers reach into the bags with the sand and the branch. Let them describe what they feel and guess. Then let them show the class. **God made the water go away until the ground was dry and plants grew again.**

Noah brought his family and the animals off the ark. The animals went on to fill the earth again. Noah's family went on to fill the earth with people again. But first, Noah stopped to build a special altar and thank God for saving them. God kept His promise to save Noah, and now He made another promise. Your last volunteer won't guess a rainbow by feeling the streamers, but once the volunteer gives a good description, bring out the ribbons and let the children guess what the colors might be if put together. **God put a colorful rainbow in the sky. He promised never to flood the whole earth again. Every time we see a rainbow we can remember that God keeps His promises and that He is able to save us.**

What did God promise? (To save Noah, to never flood the whole earth again.) **How did God save Noah?** (Told him to build an ark.) **What do we need to be saved from?** (Our sins.) **Who is able to save us?** (Only God.)

PRESCHOOL BIBLE STORY
Rainbow in the Sky (Genesis 6:9, 12–14; 7:24; 8:1, 18, 21–22; 9:1, 12–17)

Supplies: Bible, box, variety of stuffed animals in pairs (it's okay if the pairs are not identical), completed Rainbow Stick craft (*Craft Book*, p. RC-18)

Preparation: Make a Rainbow Stick from the directions on page RC-18 of the *Craft Book*. Collect a pair of animals for each child, or at least one per child.

Show the children Genesis 6 in your Bible and keep it open during the story. **Our story today comes from the part of the Bible called Genesis.**

The Bible tells us about a man named Noah. Noah obeyed God, but the other people did not. So God decided to send water to cover the earth. Noah loved God, so God had a plan to save Noah.

God told Noah to build a very big boat, called an ark. The boat would keep Noah and his family safe. Animals, too! Let's build the boat. Pretend to hammer with your fists. **After many years, Noah and his family finished the boat.** Put the box in front of you. **Let's pretend this is Noah's big boat.**

Then God told Noah and his family to get on the boat. God sent two of every animal to Noah. Let's put our animals on the boat. Hand out the animals to the children. As each child puts a pair of animals in the box, name the animals as a class. If you don't have enough animals, let children work in pairs.

When all the animals were in the boat, God closed the door. Then it started to rain. It rained for 40 days and 40 nights. Wiggle your fingers to show rain falling. Have the children join you. It rained until water covered all the earth.

Finally, God made all the water go away. Noah sent out a bird. The bird flew and flew. Hook your thumbs together and pretend to fly your hands. Have the children make this motion. But the bird didn't find any place to land. Everything was still covered with water. So it came back to the boat.

A few days later Noah sent out another bird. Again hook your thumbs together and pretend to fly your hands. This time the bird came back with a branch in its mouth. The water was going away and plants were growing again!

Finally it was time for Noah, his family, and all the animals to leave the boat. Have the children help take the animals out of the boat. Noah took time to thank God for keeping them safe.

Then God put a rainbow in the sky. Wave the Rainbow Stick in an arc. It was a promise that God would never again send water to cover all the earth. When we see a rainbow in the sky we can remember that God is able to save us.

Let the children use the toys to review the story. What did God tell Noah to build? A boat. What did Noah put on the boat? All the animals. What did God put in the sky to remind us that He is able to save us? A rainbow.

NOAH'S PARK PUPPETS
God Saves

Lead children from their Bible story areas to your Noah's Park puppet theater while the Park Patrol readies the skit. The puppet skit for today will help reinforce how God is able to save us. You will find the script on page RP-17 in the *Puppet Skits Book*.

BIBLE MEMORY
Verse Puzzle

Supplies: Bible, poster board, marker, scissors

Preparation: Choose a Bible verse to memorize with the children that teaches about God's ability to save us. Print the verse in large letters on a rainbow-shaped poster board. Cut the poster into several puzzle pieces.

Read today's memory verse from your Bible. Talk about any words that might be new to the children. Say the verse for the children, phrase by phrase, and have them repeat after you.

Give out the verse puzzle pieces to children and ask them to come put the puzzle together. Say the verse with the class from the puzzle. Repeat with a different group of children and let them rebuild the puzzle.

Remove one puzzle piece and have the class say the whole verse. Repeat this piece by piece until the class is saying the verse by memory with no clues.

We know God is able to save us because He promised this in the Bible. Let's praise God now with worship, just like Noah did after the flood.

SINGING PRAISES TO JESUS

Supplies: Noah's Park CD and CD player

Play the Unit 2 song, "When God Makes a Promise," from the Noah's Park CD, and sing along with the children. Encourage the children to clap along or think of a few clapping patterns in appropriate spots. Continue worship with other songs that praise God for being our Savior.

God was pleased by Noah's praise and worship and He's pleased by ours too. Prayer is another way to worship God. Let's do an activity that will help us praise Him for saving us.

SHARE AND PRAYER
Praise Rainbow

Supplies: butcher paper, masking tape, crayons or colored markers

Preparation: Hang a length of butcher paper on a wall at the children's level to serve as a mural. Draw a very large rainbow on it.

Our Bible story taught us that God is able to save us. How does God save us? (He sent His Son, Jesus, to die on the cross to take the punishment for our sins and to come back to life to be our friend and helper forever.)

Let's write and draw our thanks and praise to God. On the rainbow let's write words that thank God for things He's done for you, like *love, saving me,* **or** *help.* **You could also draw a picture that reminds you of what Jesus did for you. For example, you might draw a cross or a picture of Jesus. You may write or draw anything that helps you think about the great things God has done for you.**

Give out crayons or colored markers and let the children draw their worship pictures. Don't worry about spelling or pictures that are hard to make out. Just encourage the children to be praising God in their hearts as they work.

After five minutes, ask the children to set down their crayons and gather in a semicircle around the mural. Open a prayer time for the children to thank God for what they just wrote or drew. If children need help getting started, you might suggest sentence starters, such as, "I praise You, God, for . . ." or "Thank You, God, for . . ."

Allow time for the children to pray. If some children choose not to pray aloud, that's okay. Encourage them to pray silently. Encourage the children to pray every day for the person they drew. When finished, be sure the children have their names on their Healing Hope Pictures, and collect them until it is time to go.

Ask the Park Patrol to lead the preschoolers and elementary-age children to their separate activities. Be

sure the Park Patrol helpers have their assignments before class so they know how to help.

SNACK SHACK
Noah's Ark Snacks

The lesson-related snack suggestion can be found on page RS-17 of Noah's Park *Snack and Games Book.*

CAMPSITE CAPERS
Ark Builder Obstacle Course (Elem.)
Into the Ark (Preschool)

The elementary "Ark Builders" game on RS-17 in the Noah's Park *Snack and Game Book* and the preschool "Into the Ark" game on RS-18 reinforce today's Bible lesson in age-appropriate ways.

COZY CAVE CRAFTS
Promise Reminder (Elementary)
Rainbow Stick (Preschool)

See page RC-19 of the Noah's Park *Craft Book* for the elementary "Promise Reminder" and page RC-20 to find directions for the preschool "Rainbow Stick."

CLOSING ACTIVITIES

Ask the children to help with cleanup activities and then gather with you. You might sing the Unit 2 song as the children finish up.

Briefly review the Bible memory verse. Ask for volunteers to pray aloud about any concerns or thanks. Close your class time thanking God for each child by name.

OVERTIME ACTIVITIES

While waiting for parents to arrive, you could let the children play with the Noah's Park puppets or play another round of the Campsite Capers games.

R7 Lesson: God Keeps All His Promises

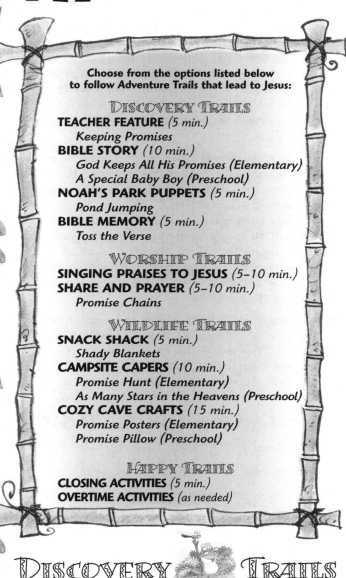

Choose from the options listed below
to follow Adventure Trails that lead to Jesus:

DISCOVERY TRAILS
TEACHER FEATURE *(5 min.)*
Keeping Promises
BIBLE STORY *(10 min.)*
God Keeps All His Promises (Elementary)
A Special Baby Boy (Preschool)
NOAH'S PARK PUPPETS *(5 min.)*
Pond Jumping
BIBLE MEMORY *(5 min.)*
Toss the Verse

WORSHIP TRAILS
SINGING PRAISES TO JESUS *(5–10 min.)*
SHARE AND PRAYER *(5–10 min.)*
Promise Chains

WILDLIFE TRAILS
SNACK SHACK *(5 min.)*
Shady Blankets
CAMPSITE CAPERS *(10 min.)*
Promise Hunt (Elementary)
As Many Stars in the Heavens (Preschool)
COZY CAVE CRAFTS *(15 min.)*
Promise Posters (Elementary)
Promise Pillow (Preschool)

HAPPY TRAILS
CLOSING ACTIVITIES *(5 min.)*
OVERTIME ACTIVITIES *(as needed)*

DISCOVERY TRAILS

TEACHER FEATURE
Keeping Promises

Supplies: Noah's Park puppet, empty candy bag

Preparation: Have a Park Patrol member familiar with the Noah's Park puppet read the following script and be prepared to present it with you. Have the puppet hold an empty, bite-size candy-bar bag.

Teacher: **Hello, (puppet's name). How are you?**

Puppet: **Hey, I'm fine, um, but mostly very full.**

Teacher: **Full of . . .? (Points to the empty bag.)**

Puppet: *(Nods head.)*

Teacher: **Oh my. Did you eat them all?**

Puppet: *(Nods yes.)* **I thought I'd promise them to the kids if they listened and learned today.**

Teacher: **I see. You can't do that very well now, can you?**

Puppet: **No. I don't have another bag. But, hey, let's try it anyway! Hey kids, listen. If you all listen and learn well, I promise to give you each a candy bar before we all go home.** *(Holds up the empty bag and nods.)*

Teacher: **Kids, do you think** *(puppet name)* **will keep his** *(her)* **promise? I don't think** *(puppet name)* **can keep this promise. Why not?** *(Let children answer that there isn't any more candy.)* **(Puppet name) can't keep this promise because there isn't any more candy. We should only make promises we can keep.**

Puppet: *(Hangs head.)* **I'm really sorry!**

Teacher: **Today, we get to learn about someone who keeps ALL His promises. Let's follow the Park Patrol to our Bible story areas.**

Divide the children into preschool and elementary groups and have the Park Patrol lead them to their separate Bible story areas. They will come back together for the puppet skit.

ELEMENTARY BIBLE STORY
God Keeps All His Promises (Genesis 18:1–16; 21:1–6)

Supplies: Bible, paper, marker

Preparation: Use paper to make large cue cards labeled, "Laugh," "Bow," and "I'm so old!"

Show the children Genesis 18 in a Bible, where today's story begins. Hold the Bible open while you tell the story.

Give the cue cards to three Park Patrol members, and have them stand at the front. Help the children read the signs and practice what they mean: When the "Laugh" sign is held up, the children should laugh loudly. When the "Bow" sign is held up, the children should stand and bow deeply once. When the "I'm so old!" sign is held up, the children should bend over with one hand on their back and say, "I'm so old!" After each sign, the children should sit.

Begin the story and cue the helpers to hold up the appropriate sign where indicated. **Abraham was a man who loved God. He and his wife, Sarah, were very old.** Cue for the "Old" sign. **They were as old as great-grandparents.** "Old" sign. **But they had never been able to have children together.**

One hot afternoon, Abraham sat in the shade at the entrance to his tent. He saw three men standing nearby. Abraham ran to greet them. "Bow" sign. **He invited them to eat, drink, and rest in the shade of a nearby tree. Since the men had come to see Abraham, they accepted his invitation.** "Bow" sign. **They sat on a blanket in the shade. Everyone was happy to have this visit.** "Laugh" sign.

Abraham had a servant bring water for the men to drink and a large basin of water to wash their feet. "Bow" sign. **These were ways to let the men know they were important guests.** "Bow" sign.

One of the guests was even more important than Abraham imagined. It was the Lord! But Abraham didn't know that. The Lord came to give Abraham a promise.

Abraham hurried to tell his wife, Sarah, to prepare a meal for the men. She was happy to have company. "Laugh" sign. **Sarah started right away. Soon, Abraham served the meal under the shady tree. Serving a meal was another way to honor guests.** "Bow" sign.

While the men ate they asked Abraham, "Where is your wife?" Abraham replied, "She is inside our tent over there." Then the Lord said, "I will come back in one year. By then, you and Sarah will have a son. I promise."

Sarah heard what the man said. "Laugh" sign. **She did not believe him. She thought he was just joking around and laughed to herself, "Ha, ha.** "Laugh" sign. **How could Abraham and I have children since we're so old?** "Old" sign.

That's ridiculous." "Laugh" sign.

The Lord knew what Sarah was thinking. He said to Abraham, "Why does Sarah not believe what I say? Does she think I'm just trying to joke around? "Laugh" sign. **Nothing is too hard for God. You will have a baby even though you're old.** "Old" sign. **God keeps all His promises." Sarah knew the man was right and felt bad that she laughed. The men thanked Abraham for the meal and got up to leave.** "Bow" sign.

That year, Abraham learned that God keeps all His promises. He kept His promise to Abraham and Sarah. Even though they were too old to have children, "Old" sign, **by the next year they had a son and named him Isaac, which means** laughter. "Laugh" sign. **Sarah was so happy that God kept His promise that she laughed out loud when Isaac was born.** "Laugh" sign. **We also can be happy that God keeps all His promises.**

Check your children's understanding of this story by discussing with them questions such as these. Who keeps all His promises? (God.) Who was happy that God keeps all His promises? (Sarah, Abraham, and we all can be too.)

PRESCHOOL BIBLE STORY
A Special Baby Boy (Gen. 18:1-16; 21:1-6)

Supplies: Bible

Our story today comes from the part of the Bible called Genesis. Show the children Genesis 18 and keep your Bible open as you tell the story.

The Bible tells us about a man named Abraham. Hold up one finger. Have the children copy your actions throughout the story. **God had promised Abraham that he would have a son. Abraham was very old, as old as a great-grandpa, but he knew God would keep His promise.**

One day, three men came to visit Abraham. Hold up three fingers from your other hand. **Abraham asked the men to stay a little while.** Put your four fingers together. **He washed the dust from their feet.** Pretend to scrub your feet. **He had them rest under a shady tree.** Lay your head on your hands. **Abraham and his wife, Sarah, made a meal for the three men.**

Pretend to eat.

While Abraham was serving his guests, one of them asked, "Where is your wife, Sarah?"

"She is in the tent," said Abraham. Point over your shoulder.

"In the next year she will have a baby boy," the visitor said. And you know who the visitor was? It was the Lord. Point up.

Sarah heard what the Lord said. Cup your hand around your ear. **She laughed at having a baby. She was as old as a great-grandma. She was too old to have a baby!**

But the Lord told Abraham, "I know that Sarah laughed. But I keep my promises. She will have a baby in the next year."

God did keep His promise. Point up. **Abraham was very old—100 years old! Sarah was very old. But Sarah did have a baby boy at the very time God had promised.** Pretend to rock a baby. **Abraham and Sarah named their baby boy Isaac. God kept His promise to Abraham and Sarah.** Point up. **God keeps all His promises.**

Use the following questions and actions to review the story. **Who was very old? (**Abraham.) Hold up one finger. **Who was his wife?** (Sarah.) Hold up another finger. **What did God promise them?** (They would have a son even though they were very old.) Pretend to rock a baby.

NOAH'S PARK PUPPETS
Pond Jumping

Today's puppet skit is found on page RP-19 of the *Puppet Skits Book.* While the Park Patrol is getting the puppets ready, lead the children to the puppet stage by playing "Follow the Leader." Follow a circuitous route using a variety of actions. When the Park Patrol is ready, ask children to be seated.

BIBLE MEMORY
Toss the Verse

Supplies: Soft foam ball or beanbag, Noah's Park puppet

Preparation: Choose a Bible verse about God's

keeping His promises. You may want to use the same verse the children started learning in Sunday school.

Say the verse for the children. Say it again, pausing after each phrase to have them repeat it. Do this a few times. Then, line up the children in two lines facing each other. Give the ball or beanbag to a child at one end of the line. He or she should say the first word of the verse and toss the ball to the child across from him or her. That child says the next word of the verse and tosses the ball across the line to the next child, and so on.

Continue to zigzag the ball or beanbag back and forth all the way down the line, saying a word of the verse on each toss. When the ball reaches the end on the line, reverse the direction and continue until the whole verse has been said. Keep playing until the children are fairly confident with the verse. Have a Noah's Park puppet whisper words to children who can't remember the next word of the verse.

If time permits and if the children know the memory verse fairly well, you may start a ball or beanbag at each end of the line so that the verse is being said twice and the balls are moving in opposite directions.

We learn about God's promises from His Word, the Bible. Now you can remember this verse all week long and remember that God keeps all His promises.

SINGING PRAISES TO JESUS

Supplies: Noah's Park CD and CD player

Let the children sing the Unit 2 song, "When God Makes a Promise," along with the CD. Use a couple of Noah's Park puppets (worked by the Park Patrol) to sit among the children and sing along. As time permits, sing more songs about God's love and forgiveness.

SHARE AND PRAYER
Promise Chains

Supplies: Construction paper, scissors, pencils, tape

Preparation: Cut several 1" x 9" paper strips for each child.

God promised Abraham and Sarah that they would have a son. God kept His promise, even though they were too old to have children! What has God promised us? Print a shortened version of the children's appropriate answers on the board or newsprint. They might include food, love, forgiveness, joy, peace, eternal life, etc. **God will keep all these promises for us.**

Give each child several paper strips, and let them copy a promise onto each one. Then show the children how to tape one strip in a loop and continue adding links to make their own chains of God's promises. Let Park Patrol members help by handing short pieces of tape to the children.

Gather the children with their prayer chains in small groups including at least one Park Patrol. Have the Park Patrol lead the children to thank God for keeping His promises, especially those named on the children's Promise Chains.

Conclude the prayer time by leading the whole class in praise to God for the joy we have because He keeps all His promises.

The following snack, games, and crafts reinforce this lesson on God's keeping His promises. Assign duties ahead of time to the Park Patrol so they can help you provide separate, age-appropriate experiences for the preschool and elementary-age groups during the following lesson portions.

SNACK SHACK
Shady Blankets

The snack suggestion on page RS-19 in the *Snacks and Games Book* will reinforce the Bible story for this lesson. Encourage the children to have fun pretending and acting the meal portion of the Bible story.

CAMPSITE CAPERS
Promise Hunt (Elementary)
As Many Stars in the Heavens (Pre.)

You will find directions to the "Promise Hunt" game for the elementary-age children on page RS-19 of the *Snacks and Games Book*. If weather conditions

are good outside, you might take them out for this game. The preschoolers will play "As Many Stars in the Heavens," found on page RS-20 in the same book. Both activities will help reinforce today's lesson for the children.

COZY CAVE CRAFTS
Promise Posters (Elementary)
Promise Pillow (Preschool)

Directions for the "Promise Posters" craft for the elementary students are on page RC-19 of the **Craft Book**. Preschool craft instructions for the "Promise Pillow" are on page RC-20. Crafts will help the children recall today's lesson throughout the week.

CLOSING ACTIVITIES

Have children stop their activities and begin to clean up the room. You could play the unit song and let children sing along as they work.

Help kids review the Bible memory verse. See who can say the verse by heart. Then wrap up today's lesson by asking volunteers to pray aloud to thank God for His promises, naming specific ones they like. Close by thanking God for your class time and for keeping all His promises. Have the children gather their crafts and Promise Chains and be ready to leave as their parents arrive.

OVERTIME ACTIVITIES

Park Patrol members can lead a variation of "Mother, May I?" using the elementary Promise Hunt clues. Children line up against a far wall and face the Park Patrol members leading the game. The first child in the line says, "Park Patrol, may we take one giant step forward?" The leader replies, "Yes, if God promises to love us." The children take a step because it's true that God promises to love us. Kids take turns asking as above. Leaders respond with God's promises or slight variations that test children's listening and memory. For example, if a leader says, "Yes, if God promises to love us only when we are good," then children stepping forward return to the wall because it's false. God loves us *always*!

R8 Lesson: God Helps Us When We Ask

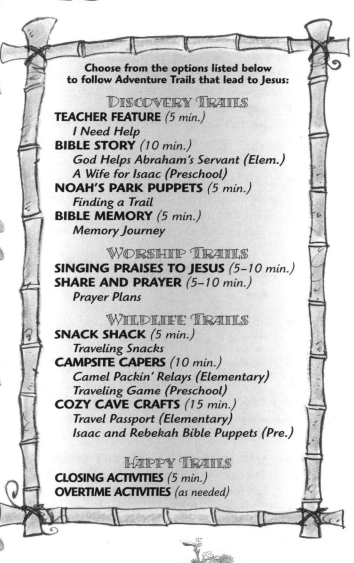

Choose from the options listed below
to follow Adventure Trails that lead to Jesus:

DISCOVERY TRAILS
TEACHER FEATURE *(5 min.)*
I Need Help
BIBLE STORY *(10 min.)*
God Helps Abraham's Servant (Elem.)
A Wife for Isaac (Preschool)
NOAH'S PARK PUPPETS *(5 min.)*
Finding a Trail
BIBLE MEMORY *(5 min.)*
Memory Journey

WORSHIP TRAILS
SINGING PRAISES TO JESUS *(5–10 min.)*
SHARE AND PRAYER *(5–10 min.)*
Prayer Plans

WILDLIFE TRAILS
SNACK SHACK *(5 min.)*
Traveling Snacks
CAMPSITE CAPERS *(10 min.)*
Camel Packin' Relays (Elementary)
Traveling Game (Preschool)
COZY CAVE CRAFTS *(15 min.)*
Travel Passport (Elementary)
Isaac and Rebekah Bible Puppets (Pre.)

HAPPY TRAILS
CLOSING ACTIVITIES *(5 min.)*
OVERTIME ACTIVITIES *(as needed)*

DISCOVERY TRAILS

TEACHER FEATURE
I Need Help

Supplies: (Optional: Noah's Park puppet)

Gather the children where everyone can see you, and have them watch as you act out various activities. After each action, ask the children to guess where you are, what you are doing, and what you might need. For example, you might act out doing a difficult task at school, looking for a lost item, taking a test, pulling a sticky zipper, hitting your finger with a hammer, nervously playing piano at a recital, etc. Feel free to use sounds to give the children clues.

After you have acted out several situations where you needed help and the children have guessed them, discuss the kinds of help they sometimes need.

We all need help at one time or another and in different ways. It's okay to need help and ask for help. Even grown-ups need help with things. The Bible tells us about a man who needed help. He knew that God helps us when we ask. Our Bible story will help us understand this better.

Divide the children into two groups—preschool and elementary—and have the Park Patrol lead them to their Bible story areas. You might have the Park Patrol use the Noah's Park puppets to lead the children.

ELEMENTARY BIBLE STORY
God Helps Abraham's Servant

(Genesis 24)

Supplies: Bible

As you tell the story today, let your expressions and actions reinforce important points. Invite the children to do all the actions with you.

Abraham was an old man who had a grown-up son named Isaac. Abraham and Isaac lived far away from where Abraham had grown up. They were living among people who didn't trust in the one true God. So when it came time for Isaac to be married, Abraham wanted to be sure his son would marry a girl who loved God too. Put your hands over your heart and then point up.

Abraham decided to look for a wife for Isaac in his old country, a faraway town called Nahor. Abraham was too old to travel back there himself. So he asked his best servant to travel there to find a wife for Isaac who loved God. Put your hands over your heart and then point up.
The servant was to look among Abraham's relatives who lived in Nahor.

This wasn't easy. Would a young woman leave

her family and travel far to marry a man she didn't know? **The servant loaded camels for the trip.** Pretend to lift bundles up onto camels. **The servant got on a camel and left for Nahor.** Have everyone rock as if riding a camel.

After several days of riding, he arrived in the town where Abraham's relatives lived. He stopped at a well where young women came to fill water jugs. The servant knew that God helps us when we ask, so he prayed, (fold your hands in prayer) **"Lord, please show me which woman Isaac should marry." The servant asked God to have the right woman give him a drink and give water to his camels, too.**

Before the servant had even finished praying, a beautiful, young woman came carrying an empty water jar on her shoulder. Lift hands to shoulders as if holding a water jar. **The servant asked her for a drink. She said, "Yes, I'll give you a drink. And let me give your camels water too."** Pretend to pour water out of a jug. **This was the one!**

It turned out exactly as the servant had prayed. Fold your hands in prayer. **This girl was God's choice for Isaac's wife! Right away, the servant thanked God for helping him.** Fold hands in prayer. **Then he gave the girl expensive jewelry that Abraham had sent.** Pretend to put on jewelry. **He asked her name, and she told him, "Rebekah." He also asked about her father and learned she was Abraham's grandniece, the granddaughter of Abraham's brother. Rebekah took the servant home to meet her family.** Have the children shake hands with someone sitting next to them.

Rebekah's family took the servant in, prepared a meal for him, and invited him to spend the night. Pretend to eat. **They were all so glad to get news about each other's family. The servant told them about Abraham, his wife, and Isaac and how God helped him find Rebekah when he prayed.** Fold hands in prayer. **Then he invited Rebekah to travel back to the promised land with him to become Isaac's wife.** Motion the word "come."

Rebekah's family knew that God had helped the servant when he asked. Fold hands in prayer. **They thought that Abraham's family**

would be good for Rebekah, and they trusted God. So they said, "Yes, Rebekah may go and become Isaac's wife." And Rebekah agreed. The servant gave more gifts to Rebekah and her family.**

In the morning Rebekah said good-bye to her family. Wave good-bye. **She went with the servant to marry Isaac.** Have the children pretend to ride camels. **When Isaac met Rebekah, he fell in love with her and married her.** Place hands over heart.

Who asked God for help? (Abraham's servant.) **How did God help?** (God brought Rebekah to the well and helped the servant know she was the one for Isaac.) **Who can ask God for help?** (We can.) **When can we ask God for help?** (Anytime.)

PRESCHOOL BIBLE STORY
A Wife for Isaac (Genesis 24)

Supplies: Bible, completed set of Isaac and Rebekah Bible puppets (*Craft Book*, p. RC-22)

Preparation: Make the Bible puppets from page RC-22 of the *Craft Book*.

Our story today comes from the part of the Bible called Genesis. Keep your Bible open to Genesis 24 as you tell the story.

The Bible tells us about an old man named Abraham. It was time for his son Isaac to find a wife. Show the puppet of Isaac and put it down again. **Abraham knew the people who lived near him didn't love God. Abraham wanted Isaac's wife to come from the land where his family lived.**

So Abraham called his best servant. Hold up the servant puppet. **"Isaac needs to get married," Abraham told his servant. "Go to the land of my family and find a wife for her." So the servant packed up many gifts and started off on his long trip.** Hold the camel puppet in front of the servant. Move the puppets in front of you as if they were traveling.

The servant came to the land where Abraham's family lived. He stopped near a well where there would be water for his thirsty camels. Hold up the well. Put the camel down; hold the servant and the well in the same hand. **It was the time of day when the women came to get water from the well.**

The servant prayed, "Dear God, please help me. When the women come to the well, I will ask one for a drink of water. Let her answer that she will give me a drink and my camels, too. Then I will know that she is the one that You have chosen to be Isaac's wife."

A pretty girl named Rebekah came to the well, carrying a jar for water. Hold up the Rebekah puppet in your other hand. Move her next to the well. **The servant asked Rebekah, "May I please have a drink of water from your jar?"**

"Take a drink," said Rebekah. After she had given the servant a drink, she said, "I will give some water to your camels, too."

It happened exactly as the servant had prayed! Rebekah told the servant her father's name. He was from Abraham's family! Then Rebekah invited the servant to come visit her family. The servant thanked God for helping him when he asked.

The servant went to the house of Rebekah's family. Put down the well. Move the servant, Rebekah, and camel a little bit away from the well area. Put down the camel.

Rebekah's family welcomed the servant and invited him to spend the night. They were all so glad to get news about each other's family. The servant told them how God helped him find Rebekah. Then he invited Rebekah to go with him to become Isaac's wife.

Rebekah's family said, "God is helping you. Rebekah can go back to marry Isaac." The servant gave gifts to Rebekah and her family. In the morning, Rebekah went with the servant to marry Isaac. Have the servant, Rebekah, and camel move away together.

Pick up Isaac in your empty hand. Hold it close to the other puppets. **When Isaac met Rebekah, he was very happy.** Put down the servant and camel. Hold Rebekah and Isaac side by side. **Isaac and Rebekah loved each other. They got married. God helped the servant when he asked. God helps us when we ask too.**

Lay the puppets where all the children can see them.

Have the children point to the puppet that answers the question. **Who needed to get married?** (Isaac.) **Who traveled to find a wife for Isaac?** (The servant.) **Who gave the servant and his camels water?** (Rebekah.) **What did God do for the servant?** (He helped him.)

NOAH'S PARK PUPPETS
Finding a Trail

Let a Noah's Park puppet lead the children to the puppet stage. When the children are seated and quiet, begin the puppet show found on page RP-21 of the Noah's Park *Puppet Skits Book.*

BIBLE MEMORY
Memory Journey

Supplies: Bible

Preparation: Choose a verse that reinforces the truth that God helps us when we ask. You might use the memory verse for today's Sunday school lesson.

Read the verse from your Bible. Then have the children form a line behind you, pretending to be the servant. Lead the children in taking one giant step for each word of the verse. Be sure to include the reference. Repeat the verse several times, increasing speed of travel as you go.

God helps us when we ask, so let's praise Him!

SINGING PRAISES TO JESUS

Supplies: Noah's Park CD and CD player

Begin a time of worship by singing the Unit 2 song, "When God Makes a Promise," from the Noah's Park CD. The sheet music is also found in the back of this *Leader's Guide.*

SHARE AND PRAYER
Prayer Plans

Supplies: Paper, crayons or colored markers

Our Bible story from Genesis told how

Abraham's servant asked God to help him with a hard job. We learned how God helped. God will also help us when we ask. **What are some places we can ask God for help?** (School, home, church, the playground, friends' homes, etc.)

What are some situations or times when you could ask God to help? Children need help at school, learning to ride a bike, skate, dribble a ball, etc. They might mention problems they know friends or family are having. Affirm that God also helps others when we ask for them.

God helps us with any problem in any place. We're never too far away for God to help.

Give out paper and crayons or markers. Have the children draw pictures of places they will be today or next week where they will ask God to help them. Ask the children to write a caption under each picture about the help they might ask for at that place. Kids should write their names on their papers.

Gather the children into small groups for prayer time. If possible, have a Park Patrol member lead each group to share one or two pictures and then pray aloud to ask God for help in that situation.

The following age-appropriate activities work best by separating the older and younger children. Let the Park Patrol lead the groups to their activities.

SNACK SHACK
Traveling Snacks

Abraham's servant took food with him on his long trip. Today's snack suggestion on page RS-21 of the Noah's Park *Snacks and Games Book* will help you take the children on a short trip for their snacks.

CAMPSITE CAPERS
Camel Packin' Relays (Elementary)
Traveling Game (Preschool)

The elementary "Camel Packin' Relays" game is on page RS-21 of the *Snack and Games Book,* and the preschool "Traveling Game" game on page RS-22.

COZY CAVE CRAFTS
Travel Passport (Elementary)
Isaac and Rebekah Puppets (Preschool)

These crafts reinforce that God helps us when we ask. You will find the elementary "Travel Passport" on page RC-21 of the *Craft Book.* You might explain and show a real passport. Look on page RC-22 for the "Isaac and Rebekah Puppets" craft for preschool.

CLOSING ACTIVITIES

A few minutes before class is over, have the children clean up their activities and straighten the classroom. Encourage kids to "travel" around the classroom, as the servant traveled, to look for items to clean up.

Then lead children on a Bible memory trip around the room, taking a big camel step for each word of the verse. Let children lead several times, then bring them to sit in a circle with you.

If time permits, lead the children in a brief review of the Bible story. Tell the children to show a thumbs-up if the following statements are true and a thumbs-down if false. You may add your own statements to remind children of key points of the Bible story.

Abraham told his servant to find his son's wife next door. (False.)

God helped the servant because he prayed and asked for help. (True.)

Abraham found Rebekah for Isaac. (False.)

Abraham's servant carried Rebekah back to Isaac. (False. She rode a camel.)

God helps us when we ask. (True.)

As children leave, pass out their crafts and Prayer Plans and remind them to pray and ask God for help this week.

OVERTIME ACTIVITIES

With any extra time, let the children reenact the Bible story. They might even use the Noah's Park puppets to play the parts of the servant and Rebekah.

R9 Lesson: Doing More with God's Help

Choose from the options listed below to follow Adventure Trails that lead to Jesus:

DISCOVERY TRAILS
TEACHER FEATURE *(5 min.)*
I Think I Can, I Think I Can't
BIBLE STORY *(10 min.)*
God Proved He Would Help Moses (Elem.)
The Bush That Didn't Burn (Preschool)
NOAH'S PARK PUPPETS *(5 min.)*
Hiding Out
BIBLE MEMORY *(5 min.)*
Memory Cards

WORSHIP TRAILS
SINGING PRAISES TO JESUS *(5–10 min.)*
SHARE AND PRAYER *(5–10 min.)*
Prayer Journal

WILDLIFE TRAILS
SNACK SHACK *(5 min.)*
Burning Bushes
CAMPSITE CAPERS *(10 min.)*
Here I Am (Elementary)
Helping Chairs (Preschool)
COZY CAVE CRAFTS *(15 min.)*
Burning Bushes (Elementary)
Exodus Stand-up Figures—Part 1 (Pre.)

HAPPY TRAILS
CLOSING ACTIVITIES *(5 min.)*
OVERTIME ACTIVITIES *(as needed)*

DISCOVERY TRAILS

TEACHER FEATURE
I Think I Can, I Think I Can't

Supplies: Newsprint paper, marker, masking tape

Preparation: Make two large signs labeled *Yes, I Think I Can* and *No, I Think I Can't*. Hang them at opposite spots in the room.

Point out the signs to the children and read them together. **Let's find out what you think you can do and what you think you can't. I will name** an activity or skill. If you think you can do it, go stand by the sign that says, "Yes, I Think I Can." If you think you can't do it, go stand by the sign that says, "No, I Think I Can't."

Have everyone stand and be ready to listen. Below is a list of skills for you to read. Have fun learning what the children think about their abilities. Accept their responses, even when you might think otherwise.

Fly like a bird.

Ride a bicycle.

Get up for school tomorrow morning.

Drive a car.

Jump over a house.

Learn the alphabet.

Become president of our country.

Brush your teeth three times every day.

Never eat candy again.

Be kind to people who are mean to me.

Keep from taking something that isn't mine but I really want.

Read the Bible every day.

Do what is right even when others are doing wrong.

Memorize some Bible verses.

Do everything God might ask of me.

Gather everyone together. **There are lots of things we think we can do and some we think we can't. The good news is that there is always help for us. Let's go to our Bible story areas to learn about that.**

Let the Park Patrol lead the children to the separate preschool and elementary areas where they will hear their Bible stories. The groups will rejoin after the Bible story for puppets and the Bible memory verse.

ELEMENTARY BIBLE STORY
God Proved He Would Help Moses

(Exodus 3:1—4:20)

Supplies: Bible, Bible-time clothes, something to resemble a microphone

Preparation: Have a Park Patrol member play the role of the reporter while you play the part of Moses. Copy the skit so it is easy to follow. Dress in Bible-time clothes. The reporter may wear contemporary or Bible-time clothes and hold a pretend microphone.

Show the children where today's Bible story is found in Exodus 3. Explain that the word *Exodus* means "to leave." This book of the Bible tells the story of God's people leaving slavery in Egypt.

Reporter: *(To audience.)* **We interrupt this lesson for an important news story! A man named Moses just saw something amazing.** *(Turns to Moses.)* **Moses, what just happened to you?**

Moses: **Let me say that I've seen many amazing things because I used to be a prince in Egypt. Then I became a shepherd in this rocky desert.**

Reporter: **Wow! Really? You're kidding!**

Moses: **It's true. Just a little while ago I was out in the hills with my flock of sheep. Over there I saw a bush that was on fire all by itself.**

Reporter: **Wow! Really? You're kidding!**

Moses: **Really! The bush kept on burning, but it didn't burn up! It was strange, so I went closer to take a look. As I got close to the bush, God's voice spoke from out of it!**

Reporter: **Wow! Really? You're kidding!**

Moses: **It really happened! God saw that His people, the Israelites, had been slaves in Egypt for hundreds of years. Now was the time for their freedom! I was pretty happy about that. Then God said, "Moses, YOU will bring them out of Egypt."**

Reporter: **Wow! Really? You're kidding!**

Moses: **That's what *I* said! I told God that I couldn't face Pharaoh, the king. I told God that the king wouldn't listen to me. I told God that the people wouldn't follow me. I told God that I didn't talk very well. In fact, I told God He should find someone else to do it!**

Reporter: **Wow! Really? You're kidding!**

Moses: **I knew I couldn't do it. So God did two miracles to prove He would be with me.**

Reporter: **Wow! Really? You're kidding!**

Moses: **Yes, really! God made my staff turn into a snake. And He made my hand get an instant skin disease—and then He healed it. I wasn't convinced.**

Reporter: **Wow! Really? You're kidding!**

Moses: **Yup, I thought this job was more than I could handle. So God told me he'd send my brother Aaron to help me. And best of all, God would be with me. Now I'm off to Egypt!**

Reporter: **Wow! Really? You're kidding!**

Moses: **No kidding! And God will be with me. With God's help I can do more than I think.** *(Exit.)*

Reporter: *(To audience.)* **And that's our wow-filled, really real, no-kidding, Bible news story. Tune in next week to find out what happened when Moses faced the king in Egypt!** *(Exit.)*

Use these questions to check comprehension: **Why didn't Moses want to do what God asked?** (He was afraid he couldn't.) **How did God help Moses?** (He did miracles and sent his brother with him.) **How can we do more than we think?** (By trusting God.)

PRESCHOOL BIBLE STORY
The Bush That Didn't Burn

(Exodus 3:1—4:20)

Supplies: Bible, real or artificial plant, orange tissue paper, robe, long stick, Exodus Stand-up Figures *(Craft Book,* p. RC-24)

Preparation: Cut out flames from the orange tissue paper and attach them to the plant to create a burning bush. Put the burning bush in a corner of your area. Make a set of Exodus Stand-up Figures from the preschool craft *(Craft Book,* p. RC-24).

Keep your Bible open to Exodus 3 as you tell the story. **Our story today comes from the part of the Bible called Exodus. The Bible tells us about a man named Moses. Moses was a shepherd. He took care of sheep.** Put on the robe and pick up the stick. **He probably wore a robe and carried a stick called a staff. Moses used the staff to take care of the sheep. Let's pretend to follow Moses.**

Have the children follow you to where you have put the burning bush. **One day, Moses saw a bush that was burning but didn't burn up. He didn't know why the bush was like that so he went over to look at it. Moses heard God's voice call him from the bush, "Moses! Moses!"**

Moses said, "Here I am."

"Don't come any closer," God said. "Take off your shoes. You are standing on holy ground. I am God."

Moses took off his shoes and hid his face from the bush. He was afraid to look at God. Take off your shoes and look away from the bush. Then sit down for the rest of the story.

"Moses," said God. "I have seen how hard my people have to work in Egypt. I have heard them crying. So I will rescue them from the mean Egyptians and their king, Pharaoh. *You are going to be My helper. Go to Pharaoh now and tell him to let the people leave Egypt."*

Moses wasn't sure he had heard God right. "You want *me* to go? He won't listen to me!"

"I will be with you," God told Moses. "With My help, you can do more than you think. Bring the people back to this place so they can worship Me."

Moses didn't think God understood. "But God, what if the people don't believe You sent me?"

God told Moses, "Tell that people 'I AM' has sent you. Then the people will listen to you. I will help you." 'I AM' was God's special name.

But Moses still wasn't sure. "What if they don't listen to me?" he asked God.

"Throw your staff on the ground," God told him. Drop your stick in front of you. **Moses' staff turned into a snake! God told Moses to pick up the snake by its tail. It turned back into the staff!** Pick up the stick. **God told Moses other things to do to get Pharaoh's attention.**

But Moses had one more problem. "God, I can't speak very well. What will I say?"

God told Moses, "Take your brother Aaron to talk for you. Now go, lead My people out of Egypt."

So Moses put on his shoes, took his staff, and went home. Stand up and walk back to the Bible.

God helped Moses do more than he thought he could do. God helps us do more than we think we can do.

Have the children use the Exodus Stand-up Figures to review the Bible stories. **Show me Moses. What did Moses see? Who was in the burning bush?** (God.) **Where is Moses' staff? Put it on the ground. What did it become?** (A snake.) **What did God tell Moses to do?** (To lead the people out of Egypt.) **Who helped Moses?** (God.)

NOAH'S PARK PUPPETS
Hiding Out

Have Park Patrol lead the children from their Bible story areas to the puppet theater. As they walk, Patrol members can talk about how they will depend upon God's help to perform the puppet play. The script is on page RP-23 of the *Puppet Skits Book.*

BIBLE MEMORY
Memory Cards

Supplies: Index cards or paper, markers, Bible

Preparation: Select a Bible memory verse that reinforces this lesson or use the verse from Sunday school today. Write the verse with reference on index cards or slips of paper, one word per card. Make a set of verse cards for every three or four children.

Divide the children into groups of three or four. Read the verse from your Bible. Give each group a set of verse cards to lay out in order. Read the verse aloud as kids point to each word. Now have the groups turn over one card. Say the verse together again. Repeat this until all cards are turned over.

We can trust God to help us with things we think we can't do. Let's praise God now for His power to help us.

WORSHIP TRAILS

SINGING PRAISES TO JESUS

Supplies: Noah's Park CD and CD player

Introduce the unit song, "God's Already There," from the CD. You will find the lyrics in this *Leader's Guide.* You might want to copy the lyrics to a transparency to project with an overhead projector. Play the song on the CD and ask the children to listen closely. Play it again as the children sing along.

SHARE AND PRAYER
Prayer Journal

Supplies: Paper, stapler, colored pencils

With God's help we can do more than we think. What are some of the things God asks us to do? (Love others, pray daily, be kind even when it's hard, etc.) **We can ask for God's help.**

Let's make Prayer Journals. In them we can write some of the things we've mentioned.

Show the children how to stack three or four half sheets of paper, fold them in half, and staple to make booklets. On the cover, children write "With God's help I can do more than I think." Inside, they write or draw pictures of things they need God's help for. For example, write names of people it's hard to be kind to, difficult tasks, etc. Leave some pages blank so they can add more this week.

Divide the children into small groups for prayer with a helper in each to lead the prayer time. Children may refer to their Prayer Journals as they pray.

We can ask God for help with things we think we can't do. Use your Prayer Journals throughout the week to remind you to pray. You can add more to your journals this week.

Use the Park Patrol to lead each group to their separate areas for age-appropriate activities. You may want to have the snack before dividing.

SNACK SHACK
Burning Bushes

Today's snack will be a reminder of the Bible story. It is found on page RS-23 in the Noah's Park *Snacks and Games Book.* Let your Noah's Park puppets visit with the children as they eat to talk about new things the children are learning.

CAMPSITE CAPERS
Here I Am (Elementary)
Helping Chairs (Preschool)

The games will give the children opportunity to actively reinforce today's Bible story. You will find the elementary game, "Here I Am," on page RS-23 in the Noah's Park *Snacks and Games Book.* The preschool game, "Helping Chairs," is on page RS-24 of the same book. Both games will be good opportunities for your Park Patrol members to help.

COZY CAVE CRAFTS
Burning Bushes (Elementary)
Exodus Stand-up Figures—Part 1 (Preschool)

The crafts for today's lesson will allow the children opportunity to make reminders of this lesson and enjoy crafting. See page RC-23 in the Noah's Park *Craft Book* for the elementary "Burning Bushes" craft and page RC-24 for the preschool "Exodus Stand-up Figures—Part 1."

CLOSING ACTIVITIES

A few minutes before class is over, have the Noah's Park puppets each child give a suggestion of something they could clean up or straighten. The children could collect supplies, pick up trash, and push in chairs. Then gather everyone again for closing.

Let the children practice the Bible memory verse using the Memory Cards. You might also play the unit song on the CD and sing it again while Park Patrol distributes the Prayer Journals and crafts.

OVERTIME ACTIVITIES

If you have extra time while waiting for parents to pick up their children play one of the Campsite Capers again.

R10 Lesson: Trust God, but Keep Trying

Choose from the options listed below to follow Adventure Trails that lead to Jesus:

DISCOVERY TRAILS
TEACHER FEATURE (5 min.)
Challenging Situations
BIBLE STORY (10 min.)
Moses Trusts God and Keeps Trying (Elem.)
Let the People Go! (Preschool)
NOAH'S PARK PUPPETS (5 min.)
Whistling Wannabe
BIBLE MEMORY (5 min.)
Circle Verse

WORSHIP TRAILS
SINGING PRAISES TO JESUS (5–10 min.)
SHARE AND PRAYER (5–10 min.)
Group-created Prayer

WILDLIFE TRAILS
SNACK SHACK (5 min.)
Celery Frogs
CAMPSITE CAPERS (10 min.)
"Keep Trying" Charades (Elementary)
Ball Test (Preschool)
COZY CAVE CRAFTS (15 min.)
One-Way Airplanes (Elementary)
T-Rings (Preschool)

HAPPY TRAILS
CLOSING ACTIVITIES (5 min.)
OVERTIME ACTIVITIES (as needed)

DISCOVERY TRAILS

TEACHER FEATURE
Challenging Situations

Supplies: None

Preparation: Ask a Park Patrol helper to read the following scripted dialog and be prepared to present it with you.

Teacher: **Hi, (Park Patrol member's name). How are you doing?**

Park Patrol helper: **I'm okay, except I'm not looking forward to tomorrow.**

Teacher: **Oh, sorry to hear that. Why not?**

Park Patrol helper: **We have to run a mile for gym class.** (May substitute some other realistic, challenging activity.)

Teacher: **You can't run a mile?**

Park Patrol helper: **No, not yet. Well, I've tried. We've been practicing for weeks. The first day I probably ran a block and walked the rest of the mile. That took a long time.**

Teacher: **Well, did you ever get any better so you could run farther?**

Park Patrol helper: **Yes, I did. Almost every day I kept trying to run farther and I actually did. I ran maybe a couple of blocks farther each time. But I'm still not fast enough and I can't run the full mile.**

Teacher: **And tomorrow you are supposed to be able to run the full mile, right?**

Park Patrol helper: **I don't know what to do.**

Teacher: **You've got a big challenge.**

Park Patrol helper: **So what should I do? Do you have an idea for me?**

Teacher: **Well, I might. Our Bible story today is about someone who was facing a big challenge. Let's find out what he did.**

Have the Park Patrol lead the preschoolers and elementary children to their separate Bible story areas.

ELEMENTARY BIBLE STORY
Moses Trusts God and Keeps Trying
(Exodus 5:1—10:29)

Supplies: Bible, toy snake, clear container of red liquid (red food coloring in water or watered-down ketchup), rubber frog, picture of gnats, plastic farm animals, picture of boils or blisters, clear bowl of ice cubes, baseball, picture of locusts

Open your Bible to Exodus chapters 5—10. Then

teach the children this response: Whenever you say, "The Lord God says," the children respond loudly in unison, "Let My people go!"

The king (Pharaoh) of Egypt, was using the people of Israel as slaves. Their job was to make bricks for the king. He didn't pay them and he treated them badly. God knew the time was right to free His people and lead them to a country all their own. God told Moses and his brother, Aaron, to lead the people of Israel out of Egypt.

Moses and Aaron went to Pharaoh. Moses said, "The Lord God says, (let children respond) **'Let My people go!'" But Pharaoh said, "No!" Then Pharaoh ordered the people of Israel to work even harder making bricks. Then he sent Moses and Aaron away.**

But God sent them back to Pharaoh. Moses said, "The Lord God says, (let children respond) **'Let My people go!'" Pharaoh said, "No!" So God started doing miracles through Moses to make Pharaoh change his mind.** Show the snake. **First, Moses threw down his staff in front of Pharaoh, and it turned into a snake! But Pharaoh wasn't impressed.**

Moses was discouraged. He wanted to give up. But he had to trust God and keep trying. God sent Moses to Pharaoh again. Moses said, "The Lord God says, (let children respond)**'Let My people go!'" But Pharaoh wouldn't let them go.** Hold up the red liquid. **So Moses touched his staff to the water, and the Lord turned all the rivers into blood! But Pharaoh wouldn't change his mind.**

Moses decided to trust God and keep trying. Moses told Pharaoh again, "The Lord God says, (let children say) **'Let My people go!'"** Hold up the frog. **When Pharaoh said no this time, God sent a plague of frogs. It was awful!**

Moses trusted God and kept trying. "The Lord God says, (let children join) **'Let My people go!'" But Pharaoh said, "No!"** Hold up the drawing of gnats. **Billions of tiny gnats invaded the land. There were so many they looked like a cloud of dust filling the sky.**

Moses tried again. He told Pharaoh, "The Lord God says, (let children join) **'Let My people go!'"** Hold up toy farm animals. **This time the plague came on the farm animals—donkeys, camels, sheep, and goats all started dying! Still Pharaoh would not let them go.**

Moses trusted God and kept trying. "The Lord God says, (let children join) **'Let My people go!'"** Hold up the pictures of blisters or boils. **The Egyptians became covered with painful sores. Again Moses told Pharaoh, "The Lord God says,** (let children join) **'Let My people go!'"** Hold up the ice cubes and baseball. **Then hail came—huge, hard hailstones that destroyed the crops in the fields. Moses kept trying: "The Lord God says,** (let children join) **'Let My people go!'"** Hold up the picture of locusts. **Huge swarms of locusts came to eat anything left. But still Pharaoh said no.**

Still Moses trusted God and kept trying. Have the children cover their eyes. **God caused darkness to cover the land. It was like nighttime—but even darker. It lasted for three days. But still Pharaoh said no.**

Who would give up first, Pharaoh or Moses? Our Bible story for today stops here, and we will learn the outcome next week. But what's important to know is that Moses didn't give up. He kept trusting God and going back to the stubborn king over and over.

Ask some review questions: **What did God tell Moses to do?** (Lead the people out of Egypt.) **Did Moses give up when it got hard? What did he do?** (He trusted God and kept trying.)

PRESCHOOL BIBLE STORY

Let the People Go! (Exodus 5:1—10:29)

Supplies: Bible, figure of Moses from the Exodus Stand-up Figures—Part 1 (from Lesson 9), flannel board, paper bag, old magazines

Preparation: Cut out pictures from old magazines of the following: a river, a frog, a fly, a cow and a horse, a sick person, a hailstorm, a grasshopper, darkness. Put all the pictures in the paper bag.

Show the children Exodus 5 in your Bible. **Our story today comes from the part of the Bible called Exodus. Sometimes in our story I will say, "Let the people go!" When you hear me say that,** you say, "But Pharaoh said, 'No!'" Practice this with the children a few times.

The Bible tells us about a man named Moses. Put the figure of Moses in front of you. **God sent Moses to the Pharaoh, king of Egypt. God wanted Pharaoh to let His people leave Egypt. Let's see what happened when Moses talked to Pharaoh.** Read the story with expression.

Moses and Aaron went to Pharaoh.
We have a message for you from God.
God says, "Let the people go!"
But Pharaoh said, "No!"

Pharaoh made the people work harder.
Back to Pharaoh Moses went.

Moses turned the river into blood and said, "There is no water for you to drink, so do what God says. Let the people go!"
But Pharaoh said, "No!"

But Moses trusted God and kept trying. Then God sent frogs to Egypt. They were everywhere!

Pharaoh told Moses to send them away. Then God said, "Let the people go!"
But Pharaoh said, "No!"

This time God sent tiny, pesky bugs and then many flies. They were everywhere—on animals, on people, and in their homes. Then God said, "Let the people go!"
But Pharaoh said, "No!"

Moses trusted God and kept trying. God sent another test to Egypt. Camels, horses, and cows, too, all got sick and died. When God said, "Let the people go!" what happened?
Pharaoh said, "No!"

Then came sores on the Egyptian people. And hail that covered all the ground. Again God said, "Let the people go!"
But Pharaoh said, "No!"

Moses had to trust God and keep trying. So God sent grasshoppers everywhere, to eat up all the trees and fruits and plants. But when God said, "Let the people go!"
Again Pharaoh said, "No!"

A big cloud of darkness came for three days. No Egyptian could see a thing. Still when God said, "Let the people go!"

Pharaoh said, "No!"

Finally, Pharaoh told Moses, "Don't come back again!" Moses knew to trust God and keep trying.

Use the pictures in the bag to review the Bible story. Have a child take a picture out of the bag and put it on the ground. Ask the following questions: **What did God send?** (Blood in the water, frogs, flies, sickness to the animals and people, hail, grasshoppers, darkness.) **What did Pharaoh say when God said, "Let the people go!"?** (No!) **What did Moses need to do?** (Trust God and keep trying.)

NOAH'S PARK PUPPETS
Whistling Wannabe

Lead the children to the puppet theater for today's puppet play, found on page RP-25 of the Noah's Park *Puppet Skits Book*. When everyone is ready, signal the Park Patrol to begin the skit.

BIBLE MEMORY
Circle Verse

Supplies: None

Preparation: Help the children learn a verse of your choosing, or reinforce today's Sunday school verse.

Have the children sit in a circle. Read the verse aloud from a Bible. Then read it one phrase at a time and have the children repeat it.

Have all the children crouch. Pick a child to pop up and say the first word and remain standing. The next child stooping next to him or her pops up to say the second word. Continue around the circle for the entire verse and reference, repeating until all are standing. Then play again, this time having the children sit on each word.

Once the verse is familiar, assign two children at different points in the circle to begin the verse so there are two verses going around the circle (without standing up). Ask Park Patrol members to help you keep track of each verse and to give help as needed.

It's hard to keep more than one verse going around the circle. But just like Moses, we can trust God and keep trying. Let's praise God now that we can trust Him to help us.

SINGING PRAISES TO JESUS

Supplies: Noah's Park CD and CD player, rhythm instruments

Sing the Unit 3 theme song, "God's Already There," from the Noah's Park Children's Church CD. Hand out rhythm instruments for the children to keep time and make music as they sing. As time allows, praise God through other songs you and the children know and love.

SHARE AND PRAYER
Group-created Prayer

Supplies: None

Moses heard Pharaoh say no over and over again. After every no, Moses went back to try again. He kept trusting God. We can trust God and keep trying too. And we can ask God to help us over and over again.

Let's create a prayer we can pray this coming week whenever we have to try again to do what we should do. How do we begin prayer? (Dear God, Heavenly Father, etc.) Write the class choice on the board. **What might we pray next when asking God for help to trust Him and to keep trying?** Let the children give their ideas. They might begin with thanks, or with admitting that we need God's help. **What else should we have in our prayer?** Encourage the children to suggest things that are important to them. Limit prayers to three sentences if possible. When finished, read aloud the prayer from the board in unison as you point to each word. Then have the children fold hands and close eyes to pray your class prayer together.

For the following activities, lead the preschool and elementary children to separate areas for age-appropriate activities that reinforce the lesson. You could have the Park Patrol members lead the children to their snack area with the puppets.

SNACK SHACK
Celery Frogs

The lesson-related snack suggestion for today is on page RS-25 in the Noah's Park *Snacks and Games Book.*

CAMPSITE CAPERS
"Keep Trying" Charades (Elementary)
Ball Test (Preschool)

The "Keep Trying" Charades for elementary and the "Ball Test" game for preschool will give the children opportunity to get actively involved in applying today's lesson focus. See pages RS-25 and RS-26 in the *Snacks and Games Book.*

COZY CAVE CRAFTS
One-Way Airplanes (Elementary)
T-Rings (Preschool)

The "One-Way Airplanes" will provide children the opportunity to think through and practice how to trust God and keep trying. Directions are on page RC-25 in the Noah's Park *Craft Book.* The preschool craft, "T-Rings," is on page RC-26.

CLOSING ACTIVITIES

Have children help clean up the room and then gather them into a circle. Stand up, say the first word of your memory verse and prompt the next ones to continue in turn around the circle. Briefly pray to close the lesson. Be sure the children have their crafts and belongings before leaving.

OVERTIME ACTIVITIES

For the children who are waiting for parents to arrive, play the unit song on the music CD and encourage children to sing along.

R11 Lesson God Gives Us a Way to Be Saved

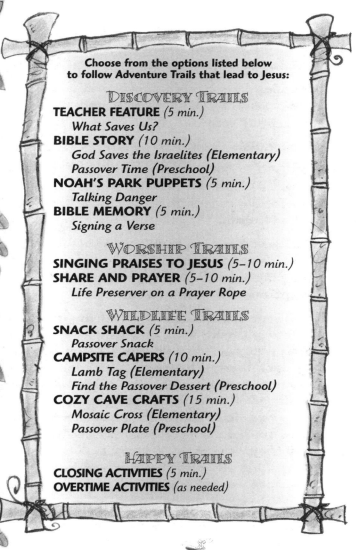

Choose from the options listed below
to follow Adventure Trails that lead to Jesus:

DISCOVERY TRAILS
TEACHER FEATURE *(5 min.)*
What Saves Us?
BIBLE STORY *(10 min.)*
God Saves the Israelites (Elementary)
Passover Time (Preschool)
NOAH'S PARK PUPPETS *(5 min.)*
Talking Danger
BIBLE MEMORY *(5 min.)*
Signing a Verse

WORSHIP TRAILS
SINGING PRAISES TO JESUS *(5–10 min.)*
SHARE AND PRAYER *(5–10 min.)*
Life Preserver on a Prayer Rope

WILDLIFE TRAILS
SNACK SHACK *(5 min.)*
Passover Snack
CAMPSITE CAPERS *(10 min.)*
Lamb Tag (Elementary)
Find the Passover Dessert (Preschool)
COZY CAVE CRAFTS *(15 min.)*
Mosaic Cross (Elementary)
Passover Plate (Preschool)

HAPPY TRAILS
CLOSING ACTIVITIES *(5 min.)*
OVERTIME ACTIVITIES *(as needed)*

DISCOVERY TRAILS

TEACHER FEATURE
What Saves Us?

Supplies: Raincoat, swim float, fire extinguisher, flashlight, bandage, sunscreen, hat, and other things that we use to save or protect ourselves

Show the children one of the items you brought that we use to help save or protect ourselves from something. **What is this?** Let the children name the object. **What is its job?** Let the children explain

what the object does. **Why would a person use it?** Reinforce how we use it to save ourselves from something bad happening, such as getting wet or cold, keeping things from burning up, and so on.

Repeat this discussion for the other objects. For each item, conclude that it helps save us from something.

There are many things that we want to save ourselves from, aren't there? That's what all these things are for. But sometimes there's very little we can do to save ourselves. One thing is sure, we can't save ourselves from our own sin—our own wrongdoing. Today's Bible lesson is about how God saves us.

If you are separating the children into two groups for the Bible story, have the Park Patrol lead the children to their story areas at this time.

ELEMENTARY BIBLE STORY
God Saves the Israelites

(Exodus 11:1—12:42)

Supplies: Bible, (optional: Bible-time clothes for Moses, Aaron, Pharaoh)

Preparation: Ask a Park Patrol member to play the role of Pharaoh, and go over his or her responsibility before class.

Show the children Exodus 11—12 in your Bible and say that today's Bible story comes from here. Ask two children to play the parts of Moses and Aaron; they will only have to imitate what you tell them. Moses, Aaron, and Pharaoh will begin at the front of the room. Have the remaining children play the role of the Israelites and wait near the back.

Moses and Aaron had been sent by God to go tell Pharaoh, "Let My people go!" Have Moses and Aaron echo this statement as they speak to Pharaoh. **But Pharaoh kept on saying no.** Have Pharaoh holler, "No!" and point to send Moses and Aaron away. **So God sent a terrible punishment on the Egyptians. With this plague, God also gave Moses and Aaron a message for the people of Israel.** Moses and Aaron go to the group of Israelites and pantomime what you're saying.

"You must get ready for a long trip!" they told the Israelites. "Pack your things!" Have the Israelites pretend to pack. "Put on your coats!" The Israelites pretend to put on coats. "We need to have some supper, but there's not even time to sit down and eat. We have to be ready when God says to move!" Have Moses and Aaron gather the Israelites around a table, standing, and pretend to eat. They tell the Israelites to hurry. Pharaoh is pacing and looking worried.

The Israelites knew something terrible was about to happen. They had already seen God send horrible plagues on the Egyptians. Would they be safe from this next one? Would God give them a way to be saved? Moses told them to take some of the blood from the lambs they had eaten for supper and smear it on their doorposts. Moses points. Let all the children go to the doorway and touch the door frames, then continue.

Suddenly, they heard Pharaoh shouting, "Oh, no! My people are dying!" Pharaoh shouts this as he rushes back and forth. God had sent an angel to punish the Egyptians by killing the first-born of all their families. But the Israelites who trusted God and put blood on their doorposts were safe. The angel passed over their homes. God saved them.

Pharaoh called Moses. Have Pharaoh holler to Moses to come back. Moses goes. Pharaoh told Moses to take all the Israelites and leave! He wanted them out of his country! Pharaoh urgently points away, and Moses returns to the Israelites. Then Moses led them out of Egypt. Have Moses lead the Israelites once around the room.

Have the Israelites be seated. God saved the Israelites. He gives us a way to be saved too. God saves us through Jesus, who shed His blood on the cross. His blood paid for the punishment for our wrongdoing, our sin. So instead of lamb's blood on a doorpost, God provided His Son's blood on the cross. If we believe in Him, He forgives us for all the wrong we've done and welcomes us into His family.

Use these questions to check comprehension: How did God save the Israelites? (the angel passed over their homes because of the blood of lambs on the doorpost.) What way has God given us to be saved? (Jesus Christ, His Son, who died on a cross to pay for our sins.)

PRESCHOOL BIBLE STORY
Passover Time (Exodus 11:1—12:42)

Supplies: Bible, a completed Passover Plate (*Craft Book*, p. RC-28), scissors, washable markers, plastic plate, plastic cup

Preparation: Color and cut out the Passover Meal pieces from page RC-28 of the *Craft Book*.

Show the children Exodus 11 in the Bible. **Our story today comes from the part of the Bible called Exodus.**

God sent Moses to lead the people out of Egypt. But Pharaoh, the king, wouldn't let the people go. God sent terrible tests to the Egyptians, and still Pharaoh said no.

God sent one last test. But first the Israelites had to get ready for a long trip. God had Moses tell the people to cook a lamb supper for each family. They were to paint around the outside of the door with the blood of the lamb. Pretend to brush with your hand. Then they were to quickly cook and eat the lamb meat, some special plants, and bread. Pretend to eat. And they were to do all this standing up with their shoes and coats on, ready to leave. Pretend to put on a coat.

Show children the empty plate. **Let's make a supper like the Israelites had. The first special food was parsley (a green plant) dipped in salt water.** Put the picture of the parsley on the plate. **The salt water reminded them of the tears the people cried because they worked so hard in Egypt. This is a spicy food called horseradish.** Put the horseradish on the plate. **It was a reminder of how bad life was in Egypt. This special bread is called matzo.** Put the picture of the matzo on the plate. **The people didn't have time to bake their bread the usual way that night. They ate matzo crackers instead. And there is the lamb.** Put the picture of the lamb on the plate. **The Israelites put lamb's blood on their doors so that no one died in their house.**

The same night that the people were eating this special meal, God sent the last test to Pharaoh and Egypt. An angel came to each house that didn't have the lamb blood on it. In those houses, the oldest child died—even in Pharaoh's palace. But the angel passed over the homes of God's people, because of the lamb's blood. So, they called that night *Passover.*

Pharaoh was so upset that he told Moses to take the people and leave Egypt right away. So Moses, all of God's people, and their animals left Egypt in a big hurry.

The Passover time reminds us that God gave a way for Moses and the people to be saved. God gives us a way to be saved too—Jesus!

Empty the plate and then invite volunteers to place the food pictures on the plate and remember how they are mentioned in the story. Close with the question, **How does God save us?** Put the picture of the cross on the plate. (Through Jesus.) **God gives us a way to be saved.**

NOAH'S PARK PUPPETS
Protection

Ask the children to form a line behind a Park Patrol member with a Noah's Park puppet and follow the leader to the puppet theater just as the Israelites followed Moses out of Egypt. You will find the puppet script for today's lesson on page RP-27 of the *Puppet Skits Book.*

BIBLE MEMORY
Signing a Verse

Supplies: (Optional: library book or website showing American Sign Language)

Preparation: Choose a Bible verse that teaches how we are saved. Choose key words from the verse and learn how to sign them in American Sign Language.

Show the class the signs for the verse words you chose. Teach the children how to properly make the signs. Then say the verse for the class while signing it. Then practice slowly saying the verse and signing while the children join you. Repeat several times so

the children can learn it well. Then let volunteers take turns standing at the front and say and sign the verse for the class until all know it well.

The fact that God gives us a way to be saved is a great reason to worship Him. Let's do that now.

WORSHIP TRAILS

SINGING PRAISES TO JESUS

Supplies: Noah's Park CD and CD player

Lead the children in singing the Unit 3 song, "God's Already There," from the Noah's Park CD. Select additional, familiar songs that praise God for saving us, especially those that lend themselves to actions and motions that reinforce the music.

SHARE AND PRAYER
Life Preserver on a Prayer Rope

Supplies: String, hard candies with a hole in the middle

Give each child a piece of string and a hard candy with a hole in the middle. Have the children tie one end of their string to the candy. Ask Park Patrol members to help as needed.

We just tied a little candy life preserver to a string. Does it remind you of a real life preserver on a rope at a swimming pool? When someone in water needs to be saved we throw them a life preserver on a rope. Our little life preservers on string can help remind us that God gives us a way to be saved.

How does God save us? Children's responses will let you know what they understand about the Gospel. **God sent His Son, Jesus, to die on a cross. But He didn't stay dead. He came back to life to save us from our sins and to always be with us. If we believe Jesus is God's Son and ask Him to forgive us, God saves us. Let's thank God now for giving us a way to be saved.**

Ask for volunteers who would like to lead the class in thanking God for sending Jesus to save us. Let the children pray. Conclude your prayer time.

Tie a knot in your life preserver string each time you thank God for Jesus, for forgiving you, or for loving you. Since we just prayed, let's each tie a knot right now.

What are some times during the week you can thank God for saving you? Let the children suggest ideas. Any time would be good! **All these are good times to thank God for saving you. And each time you do, tie another knot in your life preserver string.** Ask the children to note what color life preserver they have and where it will be so they can get it at the end of class.

The preschoolers and elementary-age children have separate snack, games, and crafts. Let the Park Patrol use Noah's Park puppets to help the children transition to their next areas.

SNACK SHACK
Passover Snack

Let the children experience a little of the Passover meal the Israelites ate on the night before they left Egypt. Explain the details of what God instructed them to eat—bread without yeast so it couldn't rise, lamb meat, and bitter herbs to remind them of their hard slavery. Tell the children that Jewish people still eat a Passover meal to celebrate the way God's angel passed over their homes so they were saved. You will find the Passover Snack suggestion on page RS-27 of the *Snacks and Games Book.*

CAMPSITE CAPERS
Lamb Tag *(Elementary)*
Find the Passover Dessert *(Preschool)*

Fun games help the children review the lesson content and remember it. The elementary "Lamb Tag" and the preschool "Find the Passover Dessert" will help reinforce today's lesson. You will find the

preschool game on page RC-28 of the Noah's Park *Snack and Games Book* and the elementary game on page RC-27 in the same book.

COZY CAVE CRAFTS
Mosaic Cross *(Elementary)*
Passover Plate *(Preschool)*

Crafts help children delve deeper into lesson content by getting "hands on." The finished project helps them remember the lesson through the week. The elementary "Mosaic Cross" and the preschool "Passover Plate" will help accomplish both objectives. You'll find the elementary project on page RC-27 in the *Craft Book* and the preschool project on page RC-28. The Mosaic Crosses will need drying time in a spot where they won't be disturbed.

CLOSING ACTIVITIES

When the children have completed the snack, games, and craft, play the unit song on the CD player as a signal for cleanup time. Encourage all the children to help straighten the room. You could use Noah's Park puppets (worked by the Park Patrol) to give suggestions of what could be straightened and to give encouragement for a job well done. When finished, gather the children back together for a wrap-up time.

Review the Bible memory verse with sign language. Close your Children's Church time in prayer. Be sure the children all have their Life Preservers on a Prayer Rope and their crafts before leaving.

OVERTIME ACTIVITIES

With extra time while waiting for parents, have Park Patrol members take turns naming different events in the story for the children to act out all together. Events might be: chase and catch a lamb, pack in a hurry, paint blood on doorposts, make matzo bread without yeast, and eat quickly. Take time to say good-bye to each child as they leave with their parents.

R12 Lesson: Celebrate God!

Choose from the options listed below
to follow Adventure Trails that lead to Jesus:

DISCOVERY TRAILS
TEACHER FEATURE *(5 min.)*
Celebration Charades
BIBLE STORY *(10 min.)*
The Israelites Celebrate God (Elementary)
Walking through the Water (Preschool)
NOAH'S PARK PUPPETS *(5 min.)*
Clap and Shout
BIBLE MEMORY *(5 min.)*
Verse Banner

WORSHIP TRAILS
SINGING PRAISES TO JESUS *(5–10 min.)*
SHARE AND PRAYER *(5–10 min.)*
Jumping Celebration Prayers

WILDLIFE TRAILS
SNACK SHACK *(5 min.)*
Celebration Snacks
CAMPSITE CAPERS *(10 min.)*
Red Sea Water (Elementary)
Through the Sea (Preschool)
COZY CAVE CRAFTS *(15 min.)*
Celebration Tambourines (Elementary)
Exodus Stand-up Figures—Part 2 (Pre.)

HAPPY TRAILS
CLOSING ACTIVITIES *(5 min.)*
OVERTIME ACTIVITIES *(as needed)*

DISCOVERY TRAILS

TEACHER FEATURE
Celebration Charades

Supplies: None

Have the children sit where all can see the front.
Pantomime listening to the "Happy Birthday" song,
making a wish, and blowing out candles on a birthday cake. If you'd prefer, let a Park Patrol member
do the pantomime. **Who can guess what I was
doing?** You may repeat the actions, humming the

tune this time, if the children don't guess correctly.
**That's right, I was acting out a birthday
celebration. Birthdays are a reason to
celebrate. Let's find out if you can guess
more reasons to celebrate.**

Act out applauding at the end of a performance (or
ask a Park Patrol member to act it out). Ask the
children to guess what was being pantomimed.
Reinforce that we celebrate good performances.

Continue acting out additional events and reasons to
celebrate, such as watching fireworks, watching a
sports game, opening a wrapped gift, receiving an
award at a school assembly, receiving a test or other
school assignment with a great grade, and so on. If
the children have difficulty guessing, use sound
effects. After each pantomime, talk briefly with the
children about why each is a reason to celebrate.

If you used the Park Patrol in the pantomimes, lead
the children in applauding and celebrating their help
and acting abilities. **We all look forward to the
special days throughout the year that we
have celebrations. But we also have a lot
more reasons to celebrate. God gives us
reasons to celebrate.**

At this time, divide the preschoolers from the
elementary-age children and have the Park Patrol
lead them to their separate Bible story areas. They
will come back together for the puppet skit.

ELEMENTARY BIBLE STORY
The Israelites Celebrate God
(Exodus 13:17—15:21)

Supplies: Bible, tambourine, sounds of water
(recorded waves crashing or river rushing or a table
fountain with running water, etc.), celebration music
and CD player

Preparation: If using taped sound effects, set up
the CD or tape player where it will be easy to use
during the story. If using a tabletop fountain, place it
where it won't get knocked over by children but
where it can be turned on during the story where

indicated. You might assign a Park Patrol member to work the fountain and recorded music.

Show the children that today's Bible story is found in Exodus 13—15. Ask volunteers to briefly tell what has happened in the three Bible stories leading up to today's lesson. (God called Moses to lead the people of Israel from Egypt; God sent many plagues to punish Pharaoh and convince him to let them go; the people ate the Passover meal in a hurry after God saved them by blood on the doorposts, etc.)

Invite children to help with sound effects for today's story. **The people of Israel were finally leaving Egypt! How they celebrated!** Shake the tambourine; encourage the children to clap and cheer. **It would be a long walk to their new country, but they were happy. How did the people know where to go? They didn't have a map. God led them. During the day He placed a tall pillar of cloud in front of them to follow.** Encourage all the children to make the sound of wind with you. **At night the pillar turned to fire so the people could see it.**

In time, they came to the Red Sea and rested there. Play water sounds or turn on the fountain. **Suddenly, they heard another sound.** Have everyone pat their legs to make the sound of horses' hooves. **It was the Egyptian army! Pharaoh had changed his mind. His soldiers were chasing them! The people got up to run away.** Let everyone stamp their feet on the floor quickly. **There was nowhere to go! The Red Sea blocked their way!**

But God was with them. He moved the pillar of cloud to stand in between them and the Egyptians. Everyone makes wind noise. **Then God told Moses to hold out his staff over Red Sea. Moses did, and guess what?** Play the water sounds while the children make wind sounds. **The wind blew and blew. It blew back the water until there were two walls of water and a dry path between!**

Now the people could walk safely across the Red Sea. Have the children tap their feet for walking sounds. **They all made it safely to the other side. Then the Egyptian army decided to follow them.** Have everyone pat their legs for horse trotting sounds. **But God kept protecting His people. He told Moses to stretch out his**

staff again. And all the water went back down into the Red Sea. It covered the Egyptians and destroyed their army. Have the children make wind noise. Play the water sounds.

Now the people were really safe from Pharaoh. He couldn't come after them any more. So the people of Israel had a big celebration! They sang and danced and played tambourines. Shake the tambourine and encourage the children to clap and shout, "Praise God!"

Discuss these questions to check the children's understanding of the Bible story: **Why did the Israelites have reason to celebrate?** (Because God parted the Red Sea to protect them from the Egyptian army.) **What reasons does God give us to celebrate?** (Because God loves us, helps us, cares for us, saves us, etc.)

PRESCHOOL BIBLE STORY
Walking through the Water
(Exodus 13:17—15:21)

Supplies: Bible, Exodus Stand-up Figures Part 1 (from Lesson 9) and Part 2 (*Craft Book*, p. RC-30), a box lid with rice or sand in it (to make a "stage" for the stand-up figures), blue construction paper

Preparation: Use the Exodus Stand-up Figures—Part 1 from Lesson 9, or make a new set from page RC-24 in the *Craft Book*, along with Part 2 from page RC-30.

Our story today comes from Exodus. Keep your Bible open to Exodus 13 as you tell the story.

We have learned that God told Moses to lead the people. Stand the figure of Moses in the box. **The people were called the Israelites.** Stand the figure of the Israelites to the right of Moses. **The Israelites had to work very hard for the king of Egypt. God wanted the Israelites to not work so hard. He wanted them to live in their own country. So God told Moses to lead them on a trip out of Egypt and to a new land.**

Moses and the Israelites walked and walked. Have the children pat their knees. **They had many farm animals that walked with them. They all walked until they came to the Red Sea.** Put the piece of paper to the left of Moses. **Where**

would they go now? They couldn't walk across the sea. They didn't have any boats. Then Moses and the Israelites heard the sound of horses and chariots. It was the Egyptians! They wanted the Israelites to come back and work for them. Put the Egyptian soldiers figure to the right of the Israelites.

The Israelites were afraid. "What will we do?" they asked Moses. "We can't get across the water. We can't fight the Egyptians."

But God gave them a reason to celebrate. He told Moses to stretch out his stick over the sea. Tape Moses' staff to his hand. Then God pushed the water apart. It stayed apart with a dry path in the middle! Tear the blue paper into two pieces. Put the pieces to the left of Moses with a path between them. Moses and the Israelites could walk on the dry land through the two walls of water. "Walk" the figures of the Israelites and Moses between the pieces of paper.

The Egyptians started to follow Moses and the Israelites between the walls of water. Move the Egyptians between the pieces of paper.

Moses and the Israelites reached the other side of the sea safely. God told Moses to hold out his stick over the water again. This time God closed the water over the Egyptians. Put the Egyptians down and put the two pieces of blue paper over it. They couldn't catch the Israelites.

Moses and the Israelites celebrated. God had brought them through the Red Sea. God had saved them from the Egyptians. God gives us reasons to celebrate too.

Why were the Israelites afraid? (They couldn't get through the Red Sea, the Egyptians were coming to catch them.) What did God do? (He pushed back the water so his people could walk across on dry land.)

NOAH'S PARK PUPPETS
Clap and Shout

Kids often hop, skip, jump, and clap their hands when celebrating. Invite children to do all these actions to celebrate God on the way to your Noah's Park puppet theater. You will find the puppet script for today on page RP-29 of the *Puppet Skits Book*.

BIBLE MEMORY
Verse Banner

Supplies: Bible, colorful construction paper or gift wrapping paper, scissors, marker, yarn, masking tape

Preparation: Choose a verse about celebrating God. The kids could probably use extra practice on today's Bible memory verse from Sunday school. Cut colorful construction paper or gift wrap into four- to six-inch shapes—squares, triangles, circles, stars, and so on—so that there is one for each word of the verse and the reference.

Read the verse aloud from the Bible. Explain any difficult words or concepts. As the children watch, print one word at a time on a paper shape, saying it aloud as the children repeat it. Let the children lay the papers out in order on the floor.

Stretch out a length of yarn or ribbon longer than the line of verse papers. Let the children help you tape the paper shapes in order to the yarn to make a banner. Have the children help you hold it up as you stretch it out across a wall and tape it up. Then read the verse together, clapping on each word. See who can turn their back to the banner and say the whole verse.

God gives us many reasons to celebrate. We can celebrate by hanging up our memory verse banner. We also celebrate by singing. Let's celebrate God with our voices.

SINGING PRAISES TO JESUS

Supplies: Noah's Park CD, CD player, rhythm instruments

Encourage the children to celebrate God with you through song, clapping, rhythm instruments, and motions. You might consider doing the Wildlife Trails segment before Worship Trails so the elementary children can use their tambourines during this time.

Sing together the Unit 3 theme song, "God's Already There," from the Noah's Park CD or sheet music in the back of this *Leader's Guide*. As time permits, ask the children to suggest other songs that help them celebrate God.

SHARE AND PRAYER
Jumping Celebration Prayers

Supplies: None

What are reasons God gives us to celebrate?
(Jesus, salvation, food, family, friends, pets, abilities for sports and games, our church, etc.) **What do we like about God that makes us want to celebrate Him?** (He is loving, powerful, awesome, He helps us.)

God gives us many more reasons to celebrate. Let's thank Him for them. We'll all crouch down here in the middle. I'll start off with a sentence prayer. Then you each can finish the sentence to praise or thank God for something. Any of you can pop up at any time and call out a word or two to finish the prayer sentence, and then stoop back down again.

Gather the children to crouch in an open space. Begin by praying: **Dear God, we want to praise You because You are...** Then let the children randomly pop up and call out short ways to complete the sentence. When the popping up is winding down, begin a second sentence prayer: **And God, we want to thank You for giving us these reasons to celebrate...** Again, encourage the children to call out things and people they are thankful for. When everyone has had a chance to pray, close the prayer time by praising God for being awesome and giving us reasons to celebrate.

When it's time for crafts and games, divide the preschoolers from the elementary-age kids for separate activities. You may have snack time together or separately. Utilize the Park Patrol to help with transitions and organizing the children and supplies.

SNACK SHACK
Celebration Snacks

We have many different foods that go along with our celebrations. The Celebration Snacks suggestion on page RS-29 in the *Snacks and Games Book* is one idea. Feel free to substitute your own celebration snack if you wish.

CAMPSITE CAPERS
Red Sea Water (Elementary)
Through the Sea (Preschool)

You will find the elementary "Red Sea Water" on page RS-29 of the Noah's Park *Craft Book.* The preschool game, "Through the Sea," is on RC-30.

COZY CAVE CRAFTS
Celebration Tambourines (Elem.)
Exodus Stand-up Figures—Part 2
(Preschool)

The crafts get the children actively involved in the Bible lesson through a hands-on celebration. See page RC-29 for the elementary craft, "Celebration Tambourines." The preschool craft, "Exodus Stand-up Figures—Part 2," is on page RC-30.

CLOSING ACTIVITIES

We can even celebrate clean up chores when we make them fun by doing them in rhythm to music, such as the unit song from the Noah's Park CD. After clean up, ask the children to join you in celebration. Have the children stand up and spread out. Ask a volunteer to tell everyone a reason God gives us to celebrate. Let the children jump up and down, clap, and shout to celebrate until you clap your hands three times in a row. Repeat with another volunteer suggesting a reason God gives us to celebrate. Be sure the children have their projects from the day and any personal belongings before leaving.

OVERTIME ACTIVITIES

While waiting for parents, include the Park Patrol and act out reasons to celebrate for others to guess.

R13 Lesson Using Our Talents for God

Choose from the options listed below
to follow Adventure Trails that lead to Jesus:

DISCOVERY TRAILS
TEACHER FEATURE (5 min.)
Myself at My Best
BIBLE STORY (10 min.)
The Israelites Use Their Talents for God (Elem.)
A Worship Tent for God (Preschool)
NOAH'S PARK PUPPETS (5 min.)
Talking Danger
BIBLE MEMORY (5 min.)
Rhythmic Verse

WORSHIP TRAILS
SINGING PRAISES TO JESUS (5–10 min.)
SHARE AND PRAYER (5–10 min.)
Prayers That Stick

WILDLIFE TRAILS
SNACK SHACK (5 min.)
Snacks from Our Talents
CAMPSITE CAPERS (10 min.)
Talent Races (Elementary)
Offering Relay (Preschool)
COZY CAVE CRAFTS (15 min.)
Talent Tracker (Elementary)
Talent Banner (Preschool)

HAPPY TRAILS
CLOSING ACTIVITIES (5 min.)
OVERTIME ACTIVITIES (as needed)

DISCOVERY TRAILS

TEACHER FEATURE
Myself at My Best

Supplies: Drawing paper and pencils

Give each child a piece of paper and a pencil. **Think about one thing you are really good at doing. Draw a picture of yourself doing that thing.** Let the children draw. Many will draw favorite school subjects or hobbies they like. The children may not think of anything unique at this age.

Ask volunteers to show their pictures and tell what they are good at doing. **These are talents God has given you. Each of us has talents, because each of us is good at something.**

We can use our talents for ourselves, for others, and especially for God. How do people use talents in our church? Let the children think this through and suggest ideas. (Musicians, teachers, food preparers, greeters, sound system operators, etc.)

You also have talents that you can use for God. Our Bible story tells us how some people in Old Testament times used their talents. I think you might get some ideas from that. Have the children add their names to their drawings. Set them aside until the end of class.

Have the Park Patrol assist you by taking the preschool children to their story area. They will return to the large group for the puppet skit and Bible memory verse. If you choose to keep the groups together for the Bible story, use the Elementary Bible Story to teach the lesson.

ELEMENTARY BIBLE STORY
The Israelites Use Their Talents for God (Exodus 25:1-9; 35:4—36:7)

Supplies: Bible

Preparation: Copy each part below onto its own index card or slip of paper. Ask children who can read (or Park Patrol members) to play a role and read their part when you cue them during the Bible story.

See if any children can find Exodus in your Bible. Turn to chapters 25 and 35 to show the class where today's story is found. If not already assigned, ask for volunteers to read parts on the index cards during the story.

The people of Israel were on a long journey through the desert to the country God had promised them. During this time, they needed a place to worship God. The people were very grateful that God had rescued

them from slavery in Egypt. And they were amazed at God's awesome power in all the miracles He did for them. They wanted to worship God with all their hearts!

God gave Moses the plan for a place of worship. It had to be something the people could carry with them, so it couldn't be a building, like our church. And it had to be easy to set up and take down whenever they stopped for their days of rest. So God planned a large tent called a tabernacle. God planned it to have long, wooden tent poles and large, beautiful pieces of cloth on the top and sides. He planned many special tools and decorations for the inside.

God told Moses to ask the people for an offering to make the tabernacle. Let's see what happened. Have the readers line up across the front of the room and begin.

Israelite 1: **God is awesome! We were so happy to bring offerings to Him. Everyone in the whole community gave something. My family gave gold and silver coins and jewelry. These were melted down to make important things for the tabernacle.**

Israelite 2: **My family gave beautiful fabric and hides that could be used in the tabernacle. Our neighbors gave oil for the lamps, and someone else gave gemstones for decorations. But most importantly, we all gave from our hearts. You could almost say that God gave us a talent for giving!**

Israelite 3: **We were happy to make a beautiful place for God's house. Some of us were good at weaving. I helped to weave the curtains and other cloth that the tabernacle needed. We used our sewing talent.**

Israelite 4: **Some of us were good at metalwork. I helped to hammer out the metal and make it into lamp stands and bowls and all kinds of things used to worship God.**

Israelite 5: **I carved the wood for the tent poles. My friends worked on the tools used in worshiping God. People used their talents for God.**

Bezalel: **My name is Bezalel. God gave me a talent to do all kinds of fancy craft work. I make artistic designs in gold, silver, and bronze. I cut gemstones and set them into metal. I do wood carving too. I am glad that I can use my talents for God.**

Oholiab: **My name is Oholiab. God gave me the talent of teaching. He gave me skill to do the tabernacle design work. I can teach others to do this work too.**

All: **We are happy to use our talents for God.**

Thank the readers and let them be seated. Use these review questions to check the children's understanding of the story: **What talents did the people of Israel use for God?** (Giving, woodworking, weaving, sewing, metal working, wood carving, teaching, etc.) **What talents could you use for God?** (Reading a Bible story to a younger child, giving, helping, encouraging, being a friend, praying, making music, doing artwork, serving, etc.)

PRESCHOOL BIBLE STORY
A Worship Tent for God
(Exodus 25:1-9; 35:4—36:7)

Supplies: Bible, baskets filled with gold and silver costume jewelry, skeins of blue, purple, and red yarn, white cloth, colorful stones, and bottles of olive oil

Preparation: Set the baskets with the various objects in different parts of the area where you are telling the story.

Show the children Exodus 25 in your Bible. **Our story today is from the part of the Bible called Exodus.**

Moses and the Israelites were on their way to their new land. They had a very long walk ahead of them.

God knew that the Israelites needed a place to worship Him as they traveled. So God told Moses how to build a worship building. But this worship building had to be able to move with the people as they walked to their new land. The building God told Moses how to build was like a tent. God promised to stay with the people in the worship tent.

Moses talked to the people about helping build the worship tent. He needed people to help get materials. He needed people to use their talents to make the worship tent. The Israelites used their talents for God.

Moses asked the people to bring gifts to God called *offerings*. **First, he asked for things made of gold and silver. Can you find baskets filled with gold and silver things?** Have the children bring the baskets. **The next offering Moses asked for was blue, purple, and red yarn.** Have the children bring those baskets. **Moses asked for an offering of fabric.** Have the children bring the basket of fabric. **Then Moses asked for pretty stones.** Have a child bring the stones. **And Moses asked for an offering of olive oil.** Have the children bring the last basket. **Moses thanked the people for bringing the offerings.**

When everything was gathered, **Moses asked people to use the offerings to make a worship tent just as God had told them to. People who could weave used the yarn and fabric to make the tent.** Point to those baskets. Have the children pretend to sew. **People who could work with metal and stones made the things to go inside the tent.** Point to those baskets. Have children pretend to hammer metal.

Moses and the Israelites used their talents for God to make a worship tent. We can use our talents for God too.

These questions will help you review the Bible story. **What did God ask the Israelites to build?** (A worship tent.) **What did they use?** (The people brought offerings of gold and silver, yarn, material, stones, and olive oil.) **How did they make the worship tent?** (People used their talents to put these things together for God.)

NOAH'S PARK PUPPETS
Talking Danger

Signal the Park Patrol members who will perform today's puppet skit to get ready. You will find the puppet script in the Noah's Park *Puppet Skits Book* on page RP-31. Bring all the children together for this part of your lesson. When all are seated where they can see, begin the puppet show.

BIBLE MEMORY
Rhythmic Verse

Supplies: None

Preparation: Select a Bible verse the children can memorize that encourages us to use our talents for God. Practice ahead of time figuring out a rhythm or familiar tune for the verse.

Learning Bible verses is a talent we can use for God. One way to memorize is to sing a verse to a melody or say it in rhythm. The musical rhythm helps us remember the words. Let's memorize today's verse this way.

Read the Bible memory verse aloud. Invite the children to think of a natural rhythm to use with the words. Begin by focusing on just the first phrase or two. Once a likely rhythm is found, help the children lightly clap or pat their legs on the beats as they say the words in rhythm.

The rhythm may suggest a familiar children's tune that the words would fit to. If so, you may try fitting in the verse words to the tune.

Once you have a rhythm or tune established, add the rest of the verse, phrase by phrase. Repeat each phrase several times before moving on. When the whole verse has been set to a rhythm, let the class stand and either clap or tap their feet as they say the verse together.

SINGING PRAISES TO JESUS
Supplies: Noah's Park CD and CD player

Let the children use their music talent to praise God. Lead in the singing of the Unit 3 song, "God's Already There," from the Noah's Park CD or the music in the back of this *Leader's Guide*. Sing additional fun praise songs as time allows.

SHARE AND PRAYER
Prayers That Stick

Supplies: Pad of large and colorful self-adhesive notes, pencils, half sheets of plain paper

Sometimes we need help remembering to stop and pray, and sometimes we need help remembering something we want to pray about! Today we'll make ourselves little reminders so those prayer requests "stick" in our minds during the week.

Ask volunteers to tell about something they would like God's help with or would like to thank Him for. Encourage the children to be specific and personal. Jot the children's requests on the board by printing their first name and then just one or two simple words that sum up the request.

We want these prayer concerns to stick in our minds so we can keep praying about them during the week. Let's write them on sticky notes. Give each child a half sheet of paper, a pencil, and two or three self-stick notes. The children should stick their notes to the paper so they are easy to carry home. Have the children choose a prayer request from the board to copy down on each sticky note. Guide the children's choices so that all the requests get chosen by at least one person. Park Patrol can help younger elementary children.

Once the children have their requests copied, open a prayer time where the children can talk to God about the requests on their notes. The children may simply pray sentence prayers.

You may want the keep the groups together for snack time. Afterwards, Park Patrol members can lead the different groups to their activities and help as you have assigned them.

SNACK SHACK
Snacks from our Talents

Let the children wash up before enjoying the refreshments. You can find the lesson-related snack suggestion on page RS-31 in the Noah's Park *Snacks and Games Book*. As the children eat, let the Park Patrol work the Noah's Park puppets and wander around the room to chat with different children.

CAMPSITE CAPERS
Talent Races (Elementary)
Offering Relay (Preschool)

Today's games will give the children opportunity to actively reinforce that God gives them many different abilities. You will find directions for the elementary "Talent Races" on page RS-31 in the Noah's Park *Snacks and Games Book*. The preschool game, "Offering Relay," is on page RS-32 of the same book.

COZY CAVE CRAFTS
Talent Tracker (Elementary)
Talent Banner (Preschool)

The elementary craft, "Talent Tracker," is explained on page RC-31 in the Noah's Park *Craft Book*. The preschool "Talent Banner" is on page RC-32. Both crafts will reinforce the application of the Bible story.

CLOSING ACTIVITIES

Near the end of your Children's Church time, ask the children to use their talents to help clean up the room. Play music from the Noah's Park CD as they work. Then gather the children back together.

Invite volunteers to use their talents to lead the others in saying the Bible memory verse. Ask other children to lead in singing the unit song one more time. Close your Children's Church time with prayer, thanking God for all the talents He has given us to use for Him.

Be sure the children have their crafts, prayer sticky notes, and belongings before leaving,

OVERTIME ACTIVITIES

To fill extra time while waiting for parents to come for their children, let the children tell Noah's Park puppets, worked by the Park Patrol, what talents they would like to use in a career when they grow up. Don't worry about unrealistic suggestions; just let the children share from their imaginations.

R14 Lesson: Strong and Brave

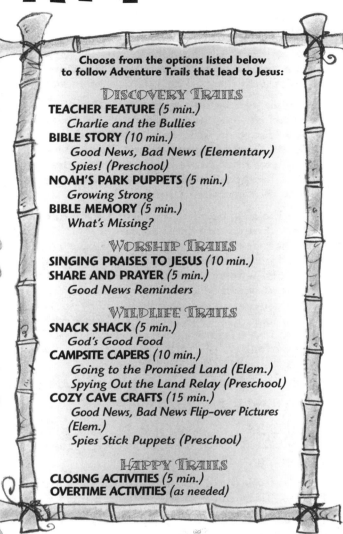

Choose from the options listed below
to follow Adventure Trails that lead to Jesus:

DISCOVERY TRAILS
TEACHER FEATURE (5 min.)
Charlie and the Bullies
BIBLE STORY (10 min.)
Good News, Bad News (Elementary)
Spies! (Preschool)
NOAH'S PARK PUPPETS (5 min.)
Growing Strong
BIBLE MEMORY (5 min.)
What's Missing?

WORSHIP TRAILS
SINGING PRAISES TO JESUS (10 min.)
SHARE AND PRAYER (5 min.)
Good News Reminders

WILDLIFE TRAILS
SNACK SHACK (5 min.)
God's Good Food
CAMPSITE CAPERS (10 min.)
Going to the Promised Land (Elem.)
Spying Out the Land Relay (Preschool)
COZY CAVE CRAFTS (15 min.)
*Good News, Bad News Flip-over Pictures
(Elem.)*
Spies Stick Puppets (Preschool)

HAPPY TRAILS
CLOSING ACTIVITIES (5 min.)
OVERTIME ACTIVITIES (as needed)

DISCOVERY TRAILS

TEACHER FEATURE
Charlie and the Bullies

Supplies: None

With the children in a large group, begin with a brief discussion. **What is a bully?** (A mean person, someone who picks on other kids, etc.) **Listen to this story about Charlie and the bullies.**

Charlie looked around his new house. The movers had just left and boxes were everywhere. It felt strange and lonely, and he missed his dad. Dad would be coming soon, but for now it was just Mom and him.

Charlie settled into the new school. He liked his teacher and had made a new friend, but he dreaded the bus ride home with the older boys yelling and pushing each other. And the worst part of it was, they got off at his bus stop. One day they stopped him. "What's your name?" they demanded.

"Charlie," he said. "I'm new here."

"Hi, I'm new here," the biggest boy, Raymond, mimicked in a squeaky voice as the others laughed. "Well, we don't want anyone new here!" he said in Charlie's face. "We'll be waiting for you tomorrow. We'll show you what the neighborhood is really like."

All the next day Charlie worried about the boys waiting for him after school. He slinked onto the after-school bus with his head down and his heart heavy. "Hi Charlie!" Raymond and the other boys yelled, laughing.

"I guess this is the end of me," Charlie thought nervously on the ride home.

As he stepped off the bus he heard a friendly voice, "Hey, Charlie!" His dad was lifting him off the ground. "I'm so glad to see you!" his dad said. "Let's go home!"

Charlie took his dad's hand, and with his head high, he walked past Raymond and the big bullies, grinning. "Hi, guys, this is my dad." And they walked happily home.

How was Charlie feeling at school, thinking about meeting Raymond? (Scared.) **How was he feeling holding his dad's hand?** (Brave and strong.) **God is like Charlie's dad in this story. When God is with us, we can feel strong and brave to do the things God wants us to do.**

Age-appropriate Bible stories are provided for preschool and elementary-age children. Let the Park Patrol lead the groups to their different areas. The groups will join back together for Noah's Park puppets. If you are keeping the groups together, use the Elementary Bible Story.

ELEMENTARY BIBLE STORY
Good News, Bad News
(Numbers 13:1—14:45)

Supplies: Bible, one sheet of cardboard or construction paper

Preparation: Draw a smiley face with "Good news!" on one side of the cardboard and a sad face with "Bad news!" on the other.

Show the children in a Bible where today's Bible story is found: Numbers 13—14. **Our Bible story is full of good news and bad news.** Show the sign you made. **Can you figure out which is which?**

In the Book of Numbers in the Old Testament, we read more about Moses leading the people of Israel to the land God had promised them. They had walked a long way to get there. Finally, they reached the border. Was this good news or bad news? (Good news!) When the children choose "good news," hold up that side of the sign.

God told Moses to send out 12 men with these instructions: "Sneak through the land and secretly explore it. Find out about the people. What are their cities like? Is the soil good for crops?"

So the 12 spies went and explored the land for 40 days and found many good things there. They brought back a bunch of grapes so big that two men had to carry it on a pole between them. They told Moses, "This land is full of good things. Just look at these grapes!" Would this be good news or bad news? (Good news.) **Why?** (Because it would be easy to grow delicious food and live there.)

But 10 of the men weren't happy. They added, "But the people are big and powerful. They look like giants and their cities have strong walls around them." Would this be good news or bad news? (Bad news.) **Why?** (Because the people would chase them out.)

Two men named Caleb and Joshua said, "Don't worry. We can take this land that God has promised us. God will go with us!" Good news or bad news? (Good news.) **Why?** (Because God would go with them.)

But the other 10 men answered them back, "We can't go into that land. We're as small as grasshoppers next to them. They will beat us!" Good news or bad news? (Bad news.)

Moses joined in, saying, "Don't be afraid, because God promised to go with us and help us. He has sent us here. Believing in God will make us strong and brave." Good news or bad news? (Good news.) **Why?** (Because God would go with them and help them.)

Who do you think the people listened to? Joshua and Caleb with their good news or the 10 spies with the bad news? Let children share.

Well, the people became afraid. They believed the bad news and doubted that God would take care of them. If they had believed God, like Joshua and Caleb, they would have been brave enough to take the land. So God punished them by not letting them go into that promised land for 40 years.

Review the main points of the Bible story: **What was the good news and the bad news?** (The new land was a great place to live but the people who already lived there were big and powerful.) **What happened when the people believed the bad news and doubted God?** (They became afraid and didn't trust God, so they were punished by not being allowed to go to the promised land.) **What can we believe about God when we are afraid?** (That God will be with us.)

PRESCHOOL BIBLE STORY
Spies! *(Numbers 13:1—14:45)*

Supplies: Bible, one set of Spies Stick Puppets from preschool craft *(Craft Book, p. RC-34)*, a long piece of foam as a stand for the puppets.

Preparation: Make a complete set of Spies Stick Puppets *(Craft Book, p. RC-34)*

Our story today comes from the part of the Bible called Numbers. Show the children Numbers 13 and keep it open as you tell the story.

The people of Israel had traveled to a land God promised them. God told Moses to send some men into that part of the country. They were to find out what the land was like.

So Moses sent 1-2-3-4-5-6-7-8-9-10-11-12 men to spy on the promised land. Put the puppets in the foam one at a time as you count. Have the children count with you. **This man was named Caleb.** Point to Caleb. **This man was named Joshua.** Point to Joshua.

Caleb, Joshua, and the other 10 men spent many days finding out what the land was like. Take the puppets away. **They looked to see if they could grow food.** Put your hand over your eyes as if looking. **They looked to see if there were a lot of people.** Hold up your fingers and wiggle them. **And they looked to see if the people were strong.** Show your muscles.

When the 1-2-3-4-5-6-7-8-9-10-11-12 spies came back to the people of Israel, they told the people what they had found. Put the puppets in the foam one at a time as you count with the kids. **They showed a bunch of grapes that was so big it took two men to carry it on a pole.** Spread your arms out wide. **The land was good for growing food. But the people there were big and strong.** Show your muscles.

Take down the Caleb and Joshua puppets. **Ten of the spies said, "The people there are too big and strong. We are afraid of them. We can't live in this land."**

Remove the 10 puppets. Put up the Caleb and Joshua puppets. **But Caleb and Joshua told the people, "This is good land. If God wants us to live here, He will help us.** Point up. **Don't be afraid. God will make us strong and brave."** Make muscle arms.

What did the people choose? They listened to the 10 spies who were afraid. They didn't believe God would make them strong.

Point up. **God talked to Moses. Even though God was very angry that His people didn't believe Him, He forgave them. But the people wouldn't be able to go to the land God had promised them.** Shake your head "no." **They would have to stay in the desert for many years. Only Caleb and Joshua would get to go into the promised land. They believed in God. Believing in God makes us strong and brave.**

Use the puppets to review the Bible story. Lay them on the floor or table in front of you. Have the children pick the puppets that answer the questions. **Who went to Canaan?** (12 spies.) **Who said the land was good and God would make them strong and brave?** (Caleb and Joshua.) **Who said the people were too big and strong for them to fight?** (The other 10 spies.) **Who did the people believe?** (The 10 who were afraid.)

NOAH'S PARK PUPPETS
Growing Strong

Have the children move to the puppet stage area. Today's puppet skit is on page RP-33 in the *Puppet Skits Book*. You might lead the children to the puppet stage by quietly tiptoeing, like the spies in the promised land.

BIBLE MEMORY
What's Missing?

Supplies: None

Preparation: Choose a Bible verse for the children to memorize that supports the lesson. The verse memorized in Sunday school might be a good choice. Print the verse and reference in large letters on the board.

Read the memory verse together two or three times. When the children are familiar with it, erase one word. Have the class read the verse, including the missing word. Erase another word, and again have the class repeat the verse. Continue in the same way until there are no more words left on the board. Then ask for individual volunteers to "read" the verse.

WORSHIP TRAILS

SINGING PRAISES TO JESUS

Supplies: CD player and Noah's Park CD.

Begin by having the children listen to the new Unit 4 song, "Glory to You." Encourage them to sing along as you play it two or three times. If you have strong readers, you may want to project the song words on a screen or wall. Lyrics for the Unit 4 song are on page R-248 of this *Leader's Guide*. As time permits, sing additional praise songs the children know.

SHARE AND PRAYER
Good News Reminders

Supplies: Card stock or poster board, hole punch, yarn, crayons or markers

Preparation: Cut two- to three-inch circles, one for each child, and punch one hole in top. Cut a 12-inch piece of yarn per child.

In our opening story, when Charlie walked by the bullies holding his dad's hand, how did he feel? (Brave and strong.) **When Moses and Joshua and Caleb believed the good news that God would go with them to the promised land, how did they feel?** (They felt strong and brave.) **When the people of Israel doubted God and believed the bad news, how**

did they feel? (They were afraid.) **It is important for us to remember the good news that God will go with us, too. Believing in God makes us strong and brave.**

What are some times when we might be afraid? (Going to a new place, standing up in front of the class, going to bed when it's dark, etc.) **Let's make Good News Reminders to help us remember that we don't need to be afraid. We can ask God to go with us and He will. You can hang these reminders on the doorknob of your room or put them on the lamp by your bed. Remember the good news that God will be with you.**

Give each child a circle and a piece of yarn. Have the children make a smiley face on both sides and tie the string through the hole. Then gather the children together for prayer. If your group is large, divide into small groups with a Park Patrol helper in each.

Encourage the children to each thank God for a time when they are happy that God is with them. You might suggest that the children hold onto their circle as they pray, as a reminder.

The preschoolers and elementary-age kids have separate snack, games, and crafts. Let the Park Patrol use Noah's Park puppets to help the children transition to their different areas.

SNACK SHACK

God's Good Food

Today's lesson-related snack is on page RS-33 of the Noah's Park *Snacks and Games Book*. Ask someone to thank God for the good food. While the children are eating they may want to share other favorite foods that God gives us.

CAMPSITE CAPERS

Going to the Promised Land (Elem.)
Spying Out the Land Relay (Pre.)

Games are a great way for the children to become actively involved in learning. The elementary game

instructions for "Going to the Promised Land" are on page RS-33 of the *Snacks and Games Book*. The preschool game, "Spying Out the Land Relay," is described on page RS-34 of the same book.

COZY CAVE CRAFTS

Good News, Bad News Flip-over Pictures (Elementary)
Spies Stick Puppets (Preschool)

The elementary children will be making "Good News, Bad News Flip-over Pictures." Directions are found on page RC-33 of the *Craft Book*. The "Spies Stick Puppets" for the preschoolers are on page RC-34. Both crafts will help the children remember and apply today's lesson.

CLOSING ACTIVITIES

After completing the activities, have the children help with cleanup. The Noah's Park puppets can work with the children to offer ideas and encouragement. When finished, gather the children together to close out the time.

Give out the children's crafts and Good News Reminders from the Share and Prayer time. Ask the children to share with someone next to them a time this week when they will want to remember that believing in God makes us strong and brave. The crafts and Good News Reminders might help them remember some times. Then close out your time with a group prayer and the singing of the Unit 4 theme song again.

As children leave, remind them that believing in God can make them strong and brave.

OVERTIME ACTIVITIES

While waiting for parents to come and pick up their children, use some of the Noah's Park books to help the children become familiar with the Noah's Park characters. You can read to the children or let the children look at the books in small groups together.

R15 Lesson Obey God Even When It Doesn't Make Sense

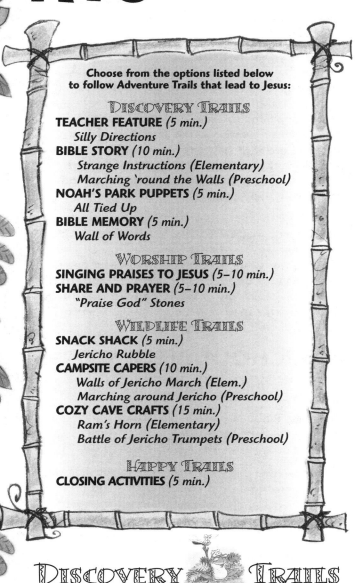

Choose from the options listed below
to follow Adventure Trails that lead to Jesus:

DISCOVERY TRAILS
TEACHER FEATURE *(5 min.)*
  Silly Directions
BIBLE STORY *(10 min.)*
  Strange Instructions (Elementary)
  Marching 'round the Walls (Preschool)
NOAH'S PARK PUPPETS *(5 min.)*
  All Tied Up
BIBLE MEMORY *(5 min.)*
  Wall of Words

WORSHIP TRAILS
SINGING PRAISES TO JESUS *(5–10 min.)*
SHARE AND PRAYER *(5–10 min.)*
  "Praise God" Stones

WILDLIFE TRAILS
SNACK SHACK *(5 min.)*
  Jericho Rubble
CAMPSITE CAPERS *(10 min.)*
  Walls of Jericho March (Elem.)
  Marching around Jericho (Preschool)
COZY CAVE CRAFTS *(15 min.)*
  Ram's Horn (Elementary)
  Battle of Jericho Trumpets (Preschool)

HAPPY TRAILS
CLOSING ACTIVITIES *(5 min.)*

DISCOVERY TRAILS

TEACHER FEATURE
Silly Directions
Supplies: None

Have the children stand apart from one another so that they can move around. **I am going to give you some directions that I want you to follow exactly. Here we go: Put your left arm all the way around your back. Put your right elbow on your left knee. Now walk in a circle, quacking like a duck. Stand up. Now I want you to jump up and down while wiggling your ears, blinking your eyes, and saying the**

alphabet. Give other silly directions as time allows.

After they are seated and quiet, ask them: **Did the directions I gave you make sense?** (No, they were silly.) **Why did I give them to you?** (To have fun.) **Sometimes people give us directions that don't seem to make sense to us. I wanted you to have fun this morning, but sometimes our parents ask us to do something that may not make sense to us—like when LaTonya's mother told her to wear a jacket to school.**

"Aw, Mom," she said, "Yesterday I was so hot at school! I'm going to wear a T-shirt and shorts!" Was she ever sorry! Right after lunch a big storm blew in with freezing, drizzly rain. "Why didn't I listen to Mom," LaTonya thought, as she shivered at recess.

What are some directions you have gotten that did not make sense at the time? Allow sharing.

Jesus gave us some directions in the New Testament that sometimes don't seem to make sense. He said things like:

"When someone does something bad to you, do something good in return."

"When you go into a room, look around and take the worst seat there, not the best."

"Don't wait to be served. Get up and serve others."

"Try to not always be first. Instead, be last."

"Don't try to hurt your enemies. Love them."

Most of these directions don't make sense to us, but we will be wise if we listen and follow them. In today's Bible lesson we will learn about some strange instructions that God gave to Joshua and the people of Israel.

If you are separating the elementary and preschool children for the Bible story, have your Park Patrol members lead them to the appropriate class area. After the Bible stories the children will come back together for the puppet skit.

ELEMENTARY BIBLE STORY
Strange Instructions *(Joshua 5:13—6:27)*

Supplies: Five or six cereal boxes about the same size and shape (or hardback books, such as hymnals)

Preparation: If you have time, cover the cereal boxes or books with brown paper.

Set the boxes or books upright, several inches apart, on a table or on the floor (as you would dominos). Allow space for the children to walk around them without knocking into them.

Show the children today's Bible passage from Joshua 5. **Today's story takes place almost 40 years after last week's story. Who remembers what happened in that Bible story?** (Moses sent 12 men to explore the promised land; Joshua and Caleb came back with a good report, but the people of Israel believed the 10 who came back with a bad report.) **After the 40 years, Moses died and God made Joshua the leader of the people of Israel.**

Now was time for Joshua to lead the people of Israel into the new land. But Jericho, a big city with strong walls, was in the way! God had a plan. He told Joshua, "Have the people march around the city walls for seven days."

Joshua probably wondered, "What is God thinking? We can't knock down a wall by walking around it?" But he believed God anyway and told the people of Israel, "We are going to march around Jericho each day for seven days. The last time around we will shout and the walls will come down."

Can you imagine what the people were thinking? "Joshua must be crazy! He wants us to do what?!"

But this time they believed God and did exactly what Joshua told them. We are going to be the people of Israel. We will pretend that these boxes (or books) **are the walls of Jericho and march around them.** Line the children up to march around the boxes. **Joshua told the people, "Don't shout or even talk as you march around until you hear the horns blowing on the seventh day, the seventh time around. Then shout as loudly as you can."**

The first day the people of Israel marched once around the city without saying a word. Have children march around the boxes, without speaking, and then sit off to the side. **On the second day the people of Israel marched once around the city without saying a word.** Have the children repeat their silent march. Repeat this four more times.

On the seventh day, the people of Israel marched around the walls seven times. If time permits, have the children march around seven times. If

they get giggly, remind them that God's instructions were that they should march silently. If you don't have time to march the class seven times, have them march around once and then count to seven on their fingers in unison.

After seven times, the priests blew their horns. Have the kids blow imaginary horns. **And the people shouted!** Have the children shout, "Praise God! He has given us this city!" Knock down the first box and the rest will tumble down. **And the walls of Jericho came tumbling down, just as God had said they would. The army of Israel went in and took the city of Jericho. They were now in the wonderful land God had promised them!**

Discuss the main points of the Bible story to check for comprehension. **Did the instruction that God gave Joshua make sense?** (No.) **Did God's plan work when the people of Israel listened and obeyed?** (Yes.) **What happened?** (The walls came down.) **What can we learn from this lesson?** (That we need to obey God even when it doesn't make sense.)

PRESCHOOL BIBLE STORY
Marching 'round the Walls
(Joshua 5:13—6:27)

Supplies: Bible, classroom chairs, several toy trumpets or party noisemakers, a box wrapped in gift wrap, a blanket, a marker, seven pieces of paper

Preparation: Create a large circle with the chairs, seats facing the center. This will be the city of Jericho. Lay the blanket on the floor a little bit apart from the city. Label the pieces of paper with the numbers 1–7.

Have the children sit on the blanket. Show the children Joshua 5, and keep it open as you tell the story. **Our story today comes from the book of the Bible called Joshua.**

Today's Bible story tells of how Joshua and the people of Israel followed God's directions when they didn't make sense. Let's pretend to be with Joshua and the people of Israel. This blanket is our army camp. The chairs are the big city of Jericho. It is a very strong city with strong walls surrounding it. The people of Israel need to break down the walls. But how can they? The walls are too strong, and the army of Jericho is too strong for them.

One day the Lord appeared to Joshua. "I will

help you win the land I promised you. Start with the city of Jericho. I'll tell you what you need to do."

God told Joshua to have the people make a parade. "Half of the army needs to go first," God explained. "Have seven men, each carrying a trumpet, go second. After the trumpet players should walk men carrying the special box from the worship tent. At the end of the parade will be the other half of the army."

Let's form the parade. Have one child carry the gift box to symbolize the ark of the covenant (the "special box"). In front of that child, put seven trumpeters (or fewer if your class is small). Divide the rest of the children into the two halves of the army with half in front and the rest in the back. **Now let's march around the city. We have to be very quiet.** March the children around the city one time; then go back to the blanket and be seated, staying in order. Have a Park Patrol member hold up the "1" sign. **That was the first day.**

The next morning, Joshua led the parade around the city again. They were very quiet, as God had told them. Have a Park Patrol member hold up the "2" sign as the children march around the city again.

Every day for six days, Joshua and the parade marched quietly around the city. Lead the children in marching around the city four more times. Each time the Park Patrol should hold up a different sign as the children count. After the "6" sign has been used, go back to the blanket.

On the seventh day, the parade was a little different. This time the quiet parade went around the city six times. Have the children march around the city six times. Use the signs to help count. **Then, on the seventh time they marched around, the trumpets played and the army shouted.** March the kids around the city one last time with the trumpets playing and the army cheering. Then lead them back to the blanket.

With all that noise going on, the walls of the city came tumbling down! Joshua and the people of Israel made the city their own. Joshua and the people of Israel obeyed God even when it didn't make sense. We can obey God even when it doesn't make sense.

Put all the props in a bag except for the blanket. Have the class sit on the blanket to review the Bible story. Ask a child to pull out an item from the bag.

As a class, talk about what happened in the story with that prop. The last question you should ask is, **What can we do even when it doesn't make sense?** (Obey God.)

NOAH'S PARK PUPPETS
All Tied Up

The assigned Park Patrol children should be ready to begin the puppet presentation just as soon as the Bible stories are both completed. Have kids stand and move to the puppet theater while you play the Unit 4 song from the CD. Today's puppet skit is found on page RP-35 of the Noah's Park *Puppet Skits Book.*

BIBLE MEMORY
Wall of Words

Supplies: Index cards, marker, masking tape

Preparation: Choose a Bible verse for the children to memorize. Use one from the Sunday school curriculum or one that supports today's lesson. Print each word in large letters on an index card. Tape the words to a wall in order.

Have all the children gather around the verse on the wall. Read the verse aloud as you point to each word. Scramble the words around. Choose a few volunteers to come up and, as a team, put the scrambled verse in the right order. When the wall of words is correct, read the verse together again.

Scramble the words again, and let another small team try. Repeat until all the children have been on a team. Then let the teams turn their backs to the wall and say the whole verse together from memory.

SINGING PRAISES TO JESUS

Supplies: CD player and Noah's Park CD

Sing together the Unit 4 song, "Glory to You," that was introduced last week. The sheet music and lyrics are provided on page R-248 of this Leader's Guide. Allow the children to sing along while "marching around the walls of Jericho." As time permits, sing additional songs about trusting God for wisdom.

SHARE AND PRAYER
"Praise God" Stones

Supplies: Brown or gray construction paper, markers

Preparation: Cut brown paper into stone shapes about 4" x 6" in size.

Today we are going to make "Praise God" Stones to help us remember to praise God for all He does for us.

In our story today we heard how God helped the people of Israel get into the city of Jericho. After the seventh day of marching around the city, the people shouted and the walls of Jericho fell. As the people looked at the stones lying on the ground, they were probably reminded of God's powerful help.

Pass out the paper stones. **We are going to make paper stones to help us remember to praise God for what He does for us.** Instruct the children to write "Praise God" on their stones. You may need to write it on the board for younger children to copy.

Let's share some things we have to praise God about. Allow time for volunteers to share. The kids might mention family, friends, school, church, and so on, but encourage them to name specific items as well. If time permits, let the children write some of these praises on their stones.

Let's thank God for each of these things. Anyone who wishes to pray aloud may read from his or her stone in a sentence prayer. Allow time for all the children to pray; then close the prayer asking God to help the children to trust and obey Him, even when it doesn't make sense.

Have the children write their names on their stones and put them in a special place to take home at the end of the activities. **Remember during the week to thank and praise God for His help.**

WILDLIFE TRAILS

The following age-appropriate activities work best by separating the older and younger children. The groups could be in the same room at different tables (for crafts) and different areas (for games). Or you could arrange to use separate rooms for the two groups. Let the Park Patrol lead the different groups to their activities and help as you have assigned them.

SNACK SHACK
Jericho Rubble

Today's snack will remind the children that the city of Jericho was a pile of rubble after the people of Israel followed God's instructions. Instructions for the snack are on page RS-35 of Noah's Park *Snacks and Games Book.*

CAMPSITE CAPERS
Wall of Jericho March (Elem.)
Marching around Jericho (Preschool)

The game for today, "Wall of Jericho March," can be found on page RS-35 in the *Snacks and Games Book.* You may play this game outside if the weather is good. The preschool game, "Marching around Jericho," is on page RS-36.

COZY CAVE CRAFTS
Ram's Horn (Elementary)
Battle of Jericho Trumpets (Preschool)

The elementary children will be making a Ram's Horn, called a shofar, similar to what Joshua and the priests blew as they walked around the walls of Jericho. The instructions can be found on page RC-35 of the *Craft Book.* You may want the elementary children to begin their craft earlier in the lesson so the glue for the first part has time to dry before doing the second part of the gluing. The preschool "Battle of Jericho Trumpets" is found on page RC-36.

HAPPY TRAILS

CLOSING ACTIVITIES

As you close out the activities, encourage the children to help with cleanup. Then gather them together and play "Pop Up." Ask for a volunteer to tell one thing he or she learned today. It could be something from the lesson or the memory verse. After he or she shares something say, **Anyone else who also learned that can "pop up"** (stand up) **with them.** Then have everyone sit down and repeat with another volunteer and "pop ups."

R16 Ask God What to Do

Lesson:

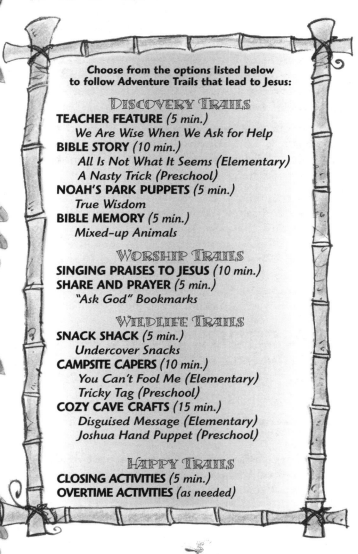

Choose from the options listed below
to follow Adventure Trails that lead to Jesus:

DISCOVERY TRAILS
TEACHER FEATURE *(5 min.)*
    We Are Wise When We Ask for Help
BIBLE STORY *(10 min.)*
    All Is Not What It Seems (Elementary)
    A Nasty Trick (Preschool)
NOAH'S PARK PUPPETS *(5 min.)*
    True Wisdom
BIBLE MEMORY *(5 min.)*
    Mixed-up Animals

WORSHIP TRAILS
SINGING PRAISES TO JESUS *(10 min.)*
SHARE AND PRAYER *(5 min.)*
    "Ask God" Bookmarks

WILDLIFE TRAILS
SNACK SHACK *(5 min.)*
    Undercover Snacks
CAMPSITE CAPERS *(10 min.)*
    You Can't Fool Me (Elementary)
    Tricky Tag (Preschool)
COZY CAVE CRAFTS *(15 min.)*
    Disguised Message (Elementary)
    Joshua Hand Puppet (Preschool)

HAPPY TRAILS
CLOSING ACTIVITIES *(5 min.)*
OVERTIME ACTIVITIES *(as needed)*

DISCOVERY TRAILS

TEACHER FEATURE

We Are Wise When We Ask for Help

Supplies: Suitcase

Preparation: Write a complicated math formula on the board, such as:

$$f(z)=14/z(2\underline{PI})/49x+(45000x16)/45^2$$

This morning before we begin, I need to solve this math problem. Stand in front of the problem, looking perplexed. Attempt to solve it. **I need you to help me solve this math problem. Just raise your hand when you have the answer.** Allow time for kids to explain that that they just can't do it.

We don't know how to solve this problem without help, do we? And we are smart enough to know that we need help. This is a silly problem that I wrote here to remind us that it is wise to ask for help when we don't know how to do something.

Hold up a suitcase. **Now I need you to help me plan my trip to Alaska. I think I'll just get in my car and start driving. Will I get there eventually?** (No, you need to ask for directions; you need a map, etc.)

Again, I would be wise to ask for help or directions before I start out on my trip. These are both examples of how others can help us when we need it. What kinds of things have you needed help with? Let kids respond.

There are times in our lives when others can't help us with our decisions or plans. These are the times when we would be wise to ask God what to do. There may be other times when we think we know what to do, so we try to solve our problems on our own. Later we find out that we should have asked God for help or directions.

Our Bible story today is about someone who didn't ask God for help. Let's find out what happened.

Have the Park Patrol lead children to their Bible story areas. If you are keeping the groups together, use the Elementary Bible Story.

ELEMENTARY BIBLE STORY

All Is Not What It Seems *(Joshua 9:1–27)*

Supplies: Bible, worn-out shoes, clothes with holes, old bread or a crust of bread, empty water bottle, worn-out bag or backpack

Let a volunteer find Joshua chapter 9 in a Bible. Leave the Bible open as you tell the story.

Display the rest of the items from the supply list on the table or floor near you. **What happened in** our Bible story last week? (The people of Israel believed God, followed His instructions and the walls of Jericho tumbled down.) **Now the people of Israel are settling into the land God promised them. In today's story, they meet some of their neighbors, from an area called Gibeon.**

The story about the walls of Jericho spread throughout the land. All the people who lived there were talking about the people of Israel and their God who made the walls fall down without even a fight! The people of Gibeon heard the story and said to themselves, "We are afraid of their God, and we are living on the land that their God will give to them. Let's play a trick on them so they won't know the truth about us."

So they put on worn-out shoes (hold up shoes) **and ragged clothes** (hold up clothes). **They filled their bags with moldy, dried-up bread and empty bottles.** (Put the bread and empty bottle in the bag or backpack.) **When Joshua and the people of Israel saw the men of Gibeon, what do you think was going through their minds?** (The people look like they have been traveling a long, long time; maybe they were poor and harmless; etc.)

That is exactly what the men from Gibeon wanted Joshua to think. They told Joshua they had been on a long trip from their home. "Let's be friends," they said. "We live so far away that we could never hurt you. See? Our clothes are worn out from the long trip and our food is used up. That proves it."

Then the men from Gibeon made a suggestion. "Let's sign a peace agreement to promise that we'll never fight. Besides, we live so far away, you'd never have to fight us anyway." Joshua and his men examined the old shoes and clothes, the dry bread and empty bottles and said, "It must be true that these men have come a long way. These old things wouldn't have worn out on a short trip. We can sign the promise." But, the Bible says, they forgot to ask God about it.

Three days later the truth came out: The Gibeonites had tricked them! They actually did live nearby—on the same land that God had promised to His people! These were enemies that God had wanted them to fight. The people of Gibeon did not worship the one true God. But since the promise had been signed, the people of Israel couldn't change their minds.

They had to let these tricky enemies stay. God's people couldn't break their promise.

The people of Israel were very angry with the men of Gibeon. Joshua and the leaders kept their promise to let the people of Gibeon stay, but only if they became the servants of the people of Israel. The people of Gibeon were given the job of bringing wood and water for the house of God, where the people of Israel worshiped.

So Joshua and the other leaders learned to always ask God about a decision. God wants us to ask Him when we are not sure what to do. He will help us and make us wise.

Review the main facts of the Bible story with a few comprehension questions. **What decision did Joshua and the people of Israel have to make?** (Whether or not to trust the men from Gibeon.) **What did the Bible say the Israelites forgot to do?** (To ask God for help in deciding.) **What happened when they forgot to ask God?** (They were tricked by the men from Gibeon.)

PRESCHOOL BIBLE STORY
A Nasty Trick (Joshua 9:1-27)

Supplies: Bible, a completed Joshua Hand Puppet (*Craft Book*, p. RC-38)

Preparation: Make a Joshua Hand Puppet from page RC-38 *Craft Book*.

Our story today comes from the part of the Bible called Joshua. Show the children Joshua 9, and keep it open as you tell the Bible story.

There was a man named Joshua. Put the Joshua puppet on your hand and pretend to "walk" it up a staircase in front of you. Then turn the puppet to face the children. **God chose Joshua to lead the people of Israel. God was helping them win the land He had promised them. Many enemies lived in that land, and God was helping the people of Israel win their fights against their enemies.**

Move your hand to make the puppet talk as you speak for it. **"God showed His power as we moved into the promised land. Some of the people who lived there were scared of God's power. One day, these people played a trick on us. We learned to ask God what to do.**

One day some men came to see me. They said they lived far away. Their food was stale. Their

clothes and sandals were dusty and falling apart. They must have come from far away. The men said they had heard how powerful God was. They wanted us to promise that we wouldn't fight with them."

Hold the puppet off to the side. **What do you think Joshua and the other leaders of Israel should do? Should they go ahead and make a promise? Should they ask God what to do?** Let volunteers gives their ideas.

Again, have the puppet talk. **"We looked at the men. They didn't look like enemies. So we didn't ask God what to do. We made a promise to not fight with the men.**

Three days later we found out that the men had played a nasty trick on us. They hadn't come from far away. They lived right nearby! And because of our promise, we couldn't fight them and get their land as God would have led us to do. Now we would always have enemies living near us.

"But because they had tricked us, they had to serve us in God's worship tent, bringing wood for the fires and water." Set puppet aside.

The enemies played a nasty trick on Joshua and the people of Israel. Joshua and the people didn't ask God what to do. That wasn't wise. We are wise when we ask God what to do.

Ask a few review questions to make sure the children understood the main points of the Bible story. **What did the tricky enemies ask Joshua to do?** (Make a promise to not fight them.) **Why did Joshua and the other leaders believe them?** (The enemies dressed in worn-out clothes and had stale food, so it looked like they traveled from far away.) **What did Joshua and the people of Israel not do?** (They didn't pray and ask God what to do.)

NOAH'S PARK PUPPETS
True Wisdom

Bring out the Noah's Park puppets for today's puppet show, found on page RP-37 of the *Puppet Skits Book*. The Park Patrol members should be ready to begin the puppet presentation when you have finished the Bible story. If your puppet theater is set up in a different location, have the children stand and move to the puppet theater while you play the unit song from the CD.

BIBLE MEMORY
Mixed-up Animals

Supplies: Index cards, marker or animal stickers

Preparation: Pick a Bible memory verse that supports the lesson, or choose one the children are learning from Sunday school. Begin by dividing the verse into phrases of two or three words each. Write each phrase on a separate index card. Make three identical sets of the verse cards. Next, draw a duck on each card in the first set. Draw a dog on each card of the second set, and draw a cat on each card of the third set. (You may use animal stickers or stamps instead of drawing the animals.) Shuffle the cards all together.

Say the verse one time for the children so they have an idea of what it says. Give one prepared card to each child. At your signal, the children walk around making the noise of their animal. They try to find their team by listening to the animal noises. When they identify another animal like theirs, they begin forming a group. Once the groups have gathered, the team members try to arrange their cards in the correct order of the verse.

When a team is ready, they signal by making their animal noise. Listen to them read the verse, and if they don't have it right, they try again. Continue until each team has read the verse in the correct order. Then collect the cards, reshuffle them, and play again.

SINGING PRAISES TO JESUS
Supplies: CD player and Noah's Park CD

Sing together the Unit 4 song, "Glory to You," found on the Noah's Park CD and in the back of the Leader's Guide. You may also sing additional worship songs the children know.

SHARE AND PRAYER
"Ask God" Bookmarks

Supplies: Card stock or construction paper, markers or crayons

Preparation: Cut paper into bookmark-size strips.

Have the kids draw a big question mark on one side of the bookmark and write "Ask God" on the other.

There are many times in our lives when we

don't know what to do. We may have a big question mark in our mind about something. Sometimes we think we can solve a problem by ourselves and we forget to ask God for help—as Joshua did. Your bookmark will help you remember to ask God for help. The question mark side will remind you that we don't always know what to do. The "Ask God" side reminds you to stop and pray to God for help.

Ask the children to share a time when they might need to ask God for wisdom or help. When all are finished sharing their ideas, model how someone would pray to ask for wisdom and help. Then ask if any children would like to pray too. Allow time for children to pray; then close by thanking God that He will give us wisdom when we ask.

Be sure the children have their names on their bookmarks. Set them aside until the end of class.

Use this time to focus on the differing abilities of your preschoolers and elementary-age children. Enlist the Park Patrol to help with the crafts, games, and snack, assigning their responsibilities ahead of time. You may choose to have the snack time together before dividing up the two groups.

SNACK SHACK
Undercover Snacks

Today's Undercover Snacks reinforce the Bible lesson and are found on page RS-37 of the Noah's Park *Snacks and Games Book*. Be sure to have the kids wash their hands, or use a disinfectant liquid, before snack. Let the Noah's Park puppets, worked by the Park Patrol, circulate and visit with the children as they eat. If you are using the same tables for crafts, have the Park Patrol members wipe off the tables after snack time is finished.

CAMPSITE CAPERS
You Can't Fool Me (Elementary)
Tricky Tag (Preschool)

The elementary game, "You Can't Fool Me," can be found on page RS-37 of the *Snacks and Games Book*. The preschoolers will be playing "Tricky Tag," with directions on page RS-38 of the same book. Invite the Park Patrol to play along if they have no other responsibilities at this time.

COZY CAVE CRAFTS
Disguised Message (Elementary)
Joshua Hand Puppet (Preschool)

The elementary children will be working on trying to find the message that is disguised on the page. This "Disguised Message" craft can be found on page RC-37 of the Noah's Park *Craft Book*. The preschool craft, "Joshua Hand Puppet," is found on page RC-38. Be sure all children have their names on their crafts.

CLOSING ACTIVITIES

A few minutes before class time is over, play the unit song on the CD player to signal that it is time to finish up activities. Have all the children help straighten the room and gather supplies. Encourage the children to sing along as they work.

Then gather the children together for closing activities. Ask for a volunteer to tell about the Bible story. **Why did the people of Gibeon bring old clothes and food when they talked with Joshua?** (To trick him into thinking they were from far away.) **What should Joshua have done?** (Ask God before making a decision.) Also review the Bible memory verse. Be sure children have their crafts and "Ask God" Bookmarks, along with any belongings, as they leave.

OVERTIME ACTIVITIES

While you are waiting for parents to pick up the children, play a Bible story cassette for them.

R17 Lesson: God Can Help in Big or Small Ways

Choose from the options listed below to follow Adventure Trails that lead to Jesus:

DISCOVERY TRAILS
TEACHER FEATURE *(5 min.)*
Big and Little Problems
BIBLE STORY *(10 min.)*
The Longest Day Ever (Elementary)
The Day the Sun Stood Still (Preschool)
NOAH'S PARK PUPPETS *(5 min.)*
Big and Small
BIBLE MEMORY *(5 min.)*
Memory Verse Partners

WORSHIP TRAILS
SINGING PRAISES TO JESUS *(5–10 min.)*
SHARE AND PRAYER *(5–10 min.)*
Big and Small Wristbands

WILDLIFE TRAILS
SNACK SHACK *(5 min.)*
Big and Small Snacks
CAMPSITE CAPERS *(10 min.)*
The Day the Kids Stood Still (Elem.)
Go! The Sun Is Shining (Preschool)
COZY CAVE CRAFTS *(15 min.)*
The Promised Land News (Elementary)
Sun-stopper Sunglasses (Preschool)

HAPPY TRAILS
CLOSING ACTIVITIES *(5 min.)*
OVERTIME ACTIVITIES *(as needed)*

DISCOVERY TRAILS

TEACHER FEATURE
Big and Little Problems

Supplies: A pencil, a pair of prescription eyeglasses, a self-adhesive bandage, some type of hospital equipment (crutches, IV bag, etc.), a watch, a stuffed cat or dog, a shoe that ties, construction paper, marker

Preparation: Fold a piece of construction paper in half so that it can stand up on a table. Label it "Big." Do the same with a second piece, labeling it "Little."

Lay out the items from the supply list, except for the two signs, where all the children can see them. You may pass the items around as you talk about them, if safe. **We all face problems every week. Some of our problems are big.** Set up the "Big" sign. **And some of our problems are little.** Set up the "Little" sign. Point to the things spread out on the table or floor. **These things remind of us problems we might have. Help me think of the kinds of problems each of these things could be about, and then we'll decide if each is a big or little problem.**

Hold up the eyeglasses. **What are these used for?** (Seeing clearly.) **What if the person who needs them lost them? Would that be a big problem or a little one?** (Big because the person might get hurt walking into things and couldn't drive, etc.) If the class agrees, place the glasses by the "Big" sign.

Hold up the pencil. **What is this used for?** (Writing.) **What if someone lost a pencil? What might happen?** (They wouldn't be able to finish writing until they found another pencil.) **Would that be a big problem or a little one?** (A little one.) If the children agree, place the pencil by the little sign.

Repeat for each of the items you brought. A bandage could symbolize getting a scrape; the hospital item could represent a serious injury or illness. A watch could mean not having enough time to finish homework or being late to something like school. The stuffed animal could represent a lost pet (children will probably view this as serious). The athletic shoe could represent not being able to tie a shoe (little). Be aware that children this age will view most problems relating to them as "big."

When finished categorizing the items as "big" or "little," let the children give a few examples of their own. **What are some little problems you've had this week? What big problems do you face?**

Here's one more problem: Sometimes when it gets dark and we are still having fun playing outside, we wish we could make it stay "day" a little longer. Is that a little problem or a big one? (A little one.) **There is nothing we can do to keep it daylight longer. But in our story today it was a big problem. A grown-up asked God to make the day stay longer! That is a**

very big thing to ask God for.

As we go to our Bible story areas, let's think of big and small ways God helps us. If you are separating the children into two groups for the Bible story, ask the Park Patrol members to lead the children to their respective areas. If all the children will stay together for the Bible story, use the Elementary Bible Story to teach the lesson.

ELEMENTARY BIBLE STORY

The Longest Day Ever (Joshua 10:1-14)

Supplies: Bible, microphone or a cardboard tube covered with foil to resemble a microphone, Bible-time clothes

Preparation: Ask a Park Patrol member to play the part of the reporter. Make a copy of the script for him or her. Practice the lines ahead of time. Dress in Bible-time clothes.

Reporter: **I'm here today with the Promised Land News, investigating the late-breaking news that everyone is talking about. We have Joshua here to tell us the details. Joshua, what happened yesterday?**

Joshua: **Thank you. Yes, I am Joshua, and God has given me the job of leading His people, the Israelites. As you may remember, the people of Gibeon tricked us into promising them we wouldn't fight. So when they called for help, we had to help them. That is what God wanted us to do. I marched my entire army down to help Gibeon fight off five bad kings who had come to take over their land.**

Reporter: **How could you fight off five kings? Weren't you outnumbered, Joshua?**

Joshua: **Yes, we were outnumbered, but God told me not to be afraid. He said we would win the battle. We traveled all night and surprised them. God threw them into a panic so that we won that battle.**

Reporter: **But what about the terrific hailstorm we heard about?**

Joshua: **Some of them tried to escape, but God sent a terrible hailstorm that killed the ones who were running away. Still, there were more bad guys to fight and we were running out of daylight. We knew we could not see to fight at night.**

Reporter: **So what did you do?**

Joshua: **I knew that I had to ask God for help in a big way. I asked Him to cause the sun to stand still until we could win the battle.**

Reporter: **Yes, that is what everyone is talking about. The sun actually stood still, making it daylight when it should have been night. You heard it here, folks!**

Joshua: **God helped us in a very big way. There has never been a day before or since when God answered such a prayer as mine. We won the battle and all the people knew that it was God who helped us. We all need to remember to ask for God's help—whether it is for big things or small things.**

Reporter: **That's our news for today.**

Take time to review the main points of the Bible story presentation with the children. **What problem did the army of Israel have?** (They were fighting an army and running out of daylight.) **What did Joshua do about it?** (He asked God to make the sun stop so there could be more hours of daylight.) **How did God answer that prayer?** (He stopped the sun.)

PRESCHOOL BIBLE STORY

The Day the Sun Stood Still
(Joshua 10:1-14)

Supplies: Bible

Preparation: None needed

Show the children Joshua 10 in the Bible, and keep it open. **Today's story is in the part of the Bible called Joshua.** As you do the actions in the story, encourage the children to do them with you.

Point up. **God had helped Joshua and the people of Israel fight off the people who lived in the land He had promised them. God also promised to help keep their neighbors safe. Then they would live in a peaceful land.**

Five kings were not happy about this promise. Hold up five fingers. **They said they would fight the neighbors of the people of Israel. The neighbors sent a message to Joshua.** Cup your hands around your mouth. **"Come quickly and help us!"**

Point up. **God told Joshua not to be afraid. God would help fight the five kings. So Joshua took the best men in his army, and they marched.** Pat knees in a walking pattern. **They marched uphill. They marched all night. They marched until they got to the five kings.**

Point up. **God made the army of the five kings afraid of Joshua and his army, and they started to run away from the army of Israel.** Pat knees. **But the army of Israel marched right after them.** Point up. **God sent a big hailstorm to hurt the army of the five kings.** "Rain" your fingers down in front of you.

But the soldiers from the enemy armies were still there. Joshua and the army of Israel needed more time. Joshua asked God to help them fight in a big way. Fold your hands. **"Please make the sun stand still so we can fight the five kings."** Make a circle above your head with your arms. **And the sun stayed up! It stood still in the sky all day and all night until Joshua and his army were done fighting the five kings.**

God helped Joshua and the army of Israel fight against the five kings by stopping the sun in the sky. God helped them in big and small ways. God can help us in big and small ways.

Review the main points of the Bible story with the kids. **What did the neighbors of the people of Israel ask them to do?** (Help fight the five kings.) **How did God help Joshua?** (God made the enemy afraid so they ran away; then He sent a hailstorm on them; then He made the sun stand still in the sky so the army of Israel could finish the fight.)

NOAH'S PARK PUPPETS

Big and Small

Have the Park Patrol member playing the "reporter" announce that it is time to go to the puppet show area for the puppet skit. Today's skit is found on page RP-39 of the Noah's Park *Puppet Skits Book.* For help in training your Park Patrol volunteers, see the *Park Patrol Training Book.*

BIBLE MEMORY

Memory Verse Partners

Supplies: Index cards, pens or makers

Preparation: Choose a Bible verse for the children to memorize. It may be one the children learned in

Sunday school or another one related to the unit theme: Conquering the Promised Land. Print the verse on index cards, one card for every two children.

Read the verse a couple of times to all the children. Then have them pair up. Pair non-reader with readers. Encourage them to help each other memorize the verse. When a pair thinks they have the verse memorized, they find another pair. The four of them make two new teams and each say the verse to their new partner. When the newly formed partners have the verse memorized, they look for another team to pair up with and go through the process again until everyone knows the verse and has recited it to at least two other partners.

SINGING PRAISES TO JESUS

Supplies: Noah's Park CD and CD player

Let the children sing along with the Unit 4 song, "Glory to You," from the CD. As time permits, sing additional praise songs that the children enjoy. Encourage the children to stand up and clap and move where appropriate.

SHARE AND PRAYER

Big and Small Wristbands

Supplies: Cardboard, scissors, colorful paper, hole punch, yarn or ribbon, crayons

Preparation: Make circles from cardboard for the children to trace around. Make one pattern about 2" to 3" in diameter and one about 1". Make several so children don't have to wait long to use the pattern. Cut yarn or ribbon in six-inch lengths, one for each child.

We learned in our stories today that God can help us in big and small ways. When have you asked God for help with something big or small? Let the children share things they have prayed about.

Let's make wristbands to remind us this week to ask for God's help with everything—big or small. Set out the cardboard circle patterns and construction paper, and let each child choose colors to trace one large and one small circle on. Encourage the children to patiently wait their turn to use the pattern and to share well. Have the kids cut out their circles. Let the children punch a hole near the top of each circle.

Show the children how to string their circles on a length of yarn or ribbon. Help the children tie their wristbands on (loosely enough that they can slide over their hands). Let the Park Patrol help.

Think about some big and small things you might want to pray about this week. Then share with someone near you what you want to ask God about. After briefly sharing, let the pairs pray together. Encourage the children to pray for the requests of their partners. If any kids are too shy to pray aloud, let a Park Patrol member join that pair and pray for them. Remind the children that they can talk to God about "small" problems too.

Remember this week to ask for God's help for everything in your life—whether it is big or small.

Divide the class into age-appropriate groups. Have Park Patrol take the preschool group to their part of the classroom to continue with snack, crafts, and games. Direct the elementary children to where they will begin their activities.

SNACK SHACK

Big and Small Snacks

The snack suggestion for today reinforces the concept that God can help us in big and small ways. The snack can be found in the Noah's Park *Snacks and Games Book* on page RS-39. You may keep the preschoolers with the elementary-age children for refreshments before separating them for games and crafts.

CAMPSITE CAPERS

The Day the Kids Stood Still
(Elementary)
Go! The Sun Is Shining *(Preschool)*

The preschoolers will be playing a game called "Go! The Sun Is Shining," described on page RS-40 of the *Snacks and Games Book.* The elementary children will be playing "The Day the Kids Stood Still," from page RS-39. Both games can be played indoors or out.

COZY CAVE CRAFTS

The Promised Land News (Elem.)
Sun-stopper Sunglasses (Preschool)

The elementary-age children will be illustrating a picture for the Promised Land News to go along with the news report of today's Elementary Bible Story. Instructions are in the *Craft Book* on page RC-39. The preschoolers will be making "Sun-stopper Sunglasses," described on page RC-40 of the same book. The Park Patrol may help with handing out supplies, and giving the children ideas. Check to see that children have their names on their crafts before moving on to the next activity.

CLOSING ACTIVITIES

When the children have finished with the crafts, games, and snack, play the unit song, "Glory to You," on your CD player while everyone helps with cleanup. When finished, gather the children back into one large group to wrap up the lesson.

Ask for volunteers to say the Bible memory verse for the class. Give out the crafts, and ask for volunteers from the elementary group to share the pictures of the story they illustrated. Then give the preschoolers a chance to explain their craft to the group.

Close by praying to thank God for being so awesome that He can help us with any problem, big or little. As children leave, be sure they have their Big and Small Wristbands, their crafts, and any belongings.

OVERTIME ACTIVITIES

As the children wait to be picked up, let them try to find the Bible passage from today in their Bibles. Children old enough to read can be shown the table of contents. Children might also find the memory verse from today.

R18 Pay Attention to God's Directions

Lesson

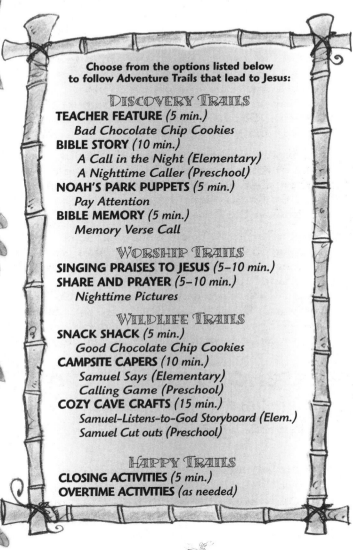

**Choose from the options listed below
to follow Adventure Trails that lead to Jesus:**

DISCOVERY TRAILS
TEACHER FEATURE *(5 min.)*
Bad Chocolate Chip Cookies
BIBLE STORY *(10 min.)*
A Call in the Night (Elementary)
A Nighttime Caller (Preschool)
NOAH'S PARK PUPPETS *(5 min.)*
Pay Attention
BIBLE MEMORY *(5 min.)*
Memory Verse Call

WORSHIP TRAILS
SINGING PRAISES TO JESUS *(5–10 min.)*
SHARE AND PRAYER *(5–10 min.)*
Nighttime Pictures

WILDLIFE TRAILS
SNACK SHACK *(5 min.)*
Good Chocolate Chip Cookies
CAMPSITE CAPERS *(10 min.)*
Samuel Says (Elementary)
Calling Game (Preschool)
COZY CAVE CRAFTS *(15 min.)*
Samuel-Listens-to-God Storyboard (Elem.)
Samuel Cut outs (Preschool)

HAPPY TRAILS
CLOSING ACTIVITIES *(5 min.)*
OVERTIME ACTIVITIES *(as needed)*

DISCOVERY TRAILS

TEACHER FEATURE
Bad Chocolate Chip Cookies

Supplies: A recipe for chocolate chip cookies, a mixing bowl and wooden spoon, measuring cups and spoons, salt, vinegar, dry beans of some sort, marshmallows, dish detergent, unpopped popcorn kernels, pickles, parsley flakes, or any assortment of things from your kitchen

Preparation: Set out the ingredients on the table beside you. Give the recipe to one of the good readers in the group or a Park Patrol helper to silently read through ahead of time.

Let's make some chocolate chip cookies today. I brought a recipe and some things from my kitchen. As the recipe is read, I'll follow the directions and mix the ingredients.

Have your chosen reader begin to read the ingredients (adjust to fit the actual recipe): "Two cups of flour." **Hmmm. I don't have flour. I'll just use salt. It's white, too.** Pour some salt into your bowl. **It doesn't matter if I measure... Go ahead and read the next ingredient.** "One teaspoon of baking powder." **No baking powder here, so I'll just use some vinegar. What's next?** "One cup of butter." **Hmmm. I guess I forgot the butter so I'll just use this liquid soap.** Continue in this fashion, substituting the ingredients any way you want to, making it as yucky as possible.

Now we are ready to bake our cookies. Uh-oh. I don't have cookie sheets or an oven, so let's just eat them this way. Who wants some of my cookies? Let the children respond. Some children may try to be silly by offering to taste it, but instead let them sniff the dough. **Why will these cookies taste terrible? Was it because** (name of reader) **didn't read the directions correctly?** (No, they were read right.) Get the children to tell you that *you* didn't follow the directions.

How important do you think it is to follow directions? I was being silly today, but God has given us directions in His book, the Bible. What should we do with the directions He has given us? (We need to listen to them and follow them.) **Yes, God's directions are very important for our lives. God wants us to pay attention to them. Where do we find God's directions for us?** (In the Bible.)

In our Bible story today we will read of a boy who learned to follow God's directions.

Divide the children into two groups—preschool and elementary—and have the Park Patrol lead them to their Bible story areas. The groups will come back together after their Bible stories.

ELEMENTARY BIBLE STORY
A Call in the Night (1 Samuel 3:1–20)

Supplies: Bible

Show the children where 1 Samuel is in a Bible. **Our Bible story today is from the book of 1 Samuel. It is about the person this book is named after—Samuel. When Samuel was a young boy, he lived in a building where people worshiped God. It's where all the priests and their families lived. Samuel helped a very old priest named Eli.**

As I tell the story, all of you will be Samuel. Our story takes place at night so pretend to be sleeping. Have the children lie down where they are or simply fold their arms over their knees and rest their heads. **When you hear a voice call** Samuel, **you sit up and answer, "Here I am, Eli. You called me." I'll tell you when to say this during the story.** Be sure the kids understand, and then begin the Bible story.

Eli the priest was very old and was almost blind. He had just gone to bed. Samuel was sleeping in another room when he heard a voice call, "Samuel! Samuel!"

Samuel jumped up and ran into Eli's room. Have the children sit up and join you: **"Here I am, Eli. You called me."**

"I didn't call you, my boy," said Eli. "Go back to bed. You must have been dreaming." So they both went back to their beds. Have the children rest their heads again.

Soon Samuel heard the voice again calling, "Samuel, Samuel!" And again Samuel ran into Eli's room. Have the children sit up and say: **"Here I am, Eli. You called me." Again Eli said, "I didn't call you, Samuel. Go back to bed." So he did.** Have the children rest their heads again.

It happened a third time. Samuel was asleep and he heard a voice, "Samuel! Samuel!" The children sit up. **Samuel ran into Eli's room again and said, "Here I am, Eli. You called me."**

This time Eli said to Samuel, "I think it is the Lord who is calling you. The next time He calls say, 'Lord, I am Your servant and I'm listening.'"

So Samuel went back to bed. When he heard the voice again, what did he say this time? Help the children repeat the new sentence with you: **"Lord, I am Your servant and I'm listening." It was the Lord calling to Samuel.**

He had a message, and Samuel listened to all that the Lord said to him that night.

Now, Eli had some very bad grown-up sons. God's message to Samuel said that He was going to punish those sons very soon. The next morning, Eli asked Samuel to tell him all that God had said. Samuel was afraid to tell Eli what God said about his bad sons. But Samuel knew it was important to pay attention to God's directions. So Samuel told Eli all that God had said. And Eli knew that God was doing the right thing.

Samuel paid attention to God's directions, and he did that for his whole life. He became a great prophet who served God. We also can follow God's directions. He gives us His directions in the Bible.

Check the children's comprehension with some brief review questions: **How did Samuel please God?** (By listening carefully and obeying.) **How can we please God?** (By paying attention to God's directions.) **What are ways we can learn God's directions?** (By reading the Bible, listening to Bible stories, going to Sunday school and children's church where we can learn what the Bible teaches, etc.)

PRESCHOOL BIBLE STORY
A Nighttime Caller (1 Samuel 3:1–20)

Supplies: Bible, a bath or beach towel for each child

Lay the towels out in a circle, and let each child sit on a towel. Show the children 1 Samuel 3 in your Bible. **Our story today comes from the book of the Bible called 1 Samuel.** Keep your Bible open to 1 Samuel as you tell the story.

Samuel was a boy who lived with Eli, a very old priest, at the building where people went to worship God. Samuel helped the priest with his job of serving God. One night Eli went to bed, and Samuel went to his bed in another part of the building. Let's lie down on our beds. Have the children lie down on their towels.

Then God called, "Samuel! Samuel!" Have the kids sit up. **But Samuel didn't know it was God's voice. He thought it was Eli calling him. So he ran to Eli's room.** Pat your knees to make a running sound. **"Here I am," said Samuel. "You called me."**

"I didn't call you," Eli said, surprised. "Go back to bed." So Samuel went back to his bed and lay back down. Have the children lie down. **Again God called, "Samuel! Samuel!"** Have the children sit up.

Again Samuel ran to Eli. Pat your knees. **"Here I am. You called me." Again Eli said, "I didn't call you. Go back to bed." So Samuel went back to his place and lay back down.** Have the children lie down.

A third time God called, "Samuel! Samuel!" Have the children sit up. **Again Samuel ran to Eli.** Pat your knees. **"Here I am. You called me."**

This time Eli figured out that it was God calling Samuel. Eli said, "I'm not calling you. God is. If He calls you again, say, 'Lord, I'm listening.'"

So Samuel went back to his bed and lay back down. Have the children lie down. **And God called Samuel another time, "Samuel! Samuel!"**

This time Samuel sat up and said, "Lord, I'm listening." Have the children sit up for the rest of the story. **God told Samuel many things that were going to happen. God had chosen Samuel to be His special helper.**

In the morning, Samuel told Eli everything that God had said. Samuel paid attention to God's direction. We can pay attention to God's direction too.

Go over a few review questions to be sure the kids understood the main points of the story: Have the children lie down on the towels. Those children who know the answers should sit up. **Who did Samuel think was calling him?** (Eli.) **Who called Samuel?** (God.) **Did Samuel pay attention?** (Yes.)

NOAH'S PARK PUPPETS
Pay Attention

Let a Noah's Park puppet lead the children in standing and stretching. The puppet skit for today can be found on page RP-41 of the *Puppet Skits Book*. When the Park Patrol is ready, let the children settle themselves quietly to be good listeners for the puppet presentation.

BIBLE MEMORY
Memory Verse Call

Supplies: None

Preparation: Choose a verse from today's lesson or one that the children are learning from Sunday school. Print the verse on the board in short phrases.

Divide the children into two groups, and have them stand facing each other. Read a phrase to the group and have both groups call it back to you. Continue through the whole verse this way.

Then have the group on one side say one of the phrases to the group across from them. That group calls the phrases back to the first group. Then the first group calls the second phrase while the second group echoes it. When the verse has been "called" completely by one side, let the other side be the callers.

Try to remember the verse we are learning through this next week. Share it with someone at home. It is important to learn God's Word this way so that we can pay attention to God's directions.

SINGING PRAISES TO JESUS

Supplies: Noah's Park CD and CD player

Today you will introduce the song for the new unit. The lyrics are on page R-249 of this Leader's Guide. You may want to project the words on a screen using an overhead projector. Play the song, "Take a Stand," from the Noah's Park CD on the CD player, and have the children listen. Clarify any vocabulary they do not know. Play it again and let the children sing along. As time permits, sing the song again, and then add more worship songs the children love to sing.

SHARE AND PRAYER
Nighttime Pictures

Supplies: Black paper, yellow or white crayons, star stickers

Nighttime, just before you fall asleep, is a good time to talk to God. We can ask Him to

help us at school or to know how to follow His directions for our lives. Or we can pray about anything we are worried about or happy about. **What kinds of things do you want to pray about?** Let the children share.

We are going to make night pictures to put by our beds to help us remember that God is watching over us, just as He was watching over Samuel in our Bible story.

Give each child a piece of black paper, a white or yellow crayon, and star stickers. **Use the crayons and star stickers to make a night picture. As you work, think of all the things you can pray about when you go to bed. Be sure to put your name on the back of your picture.**

When the children are finished, take time to pray with them about the things they think about at bedtime. Let volunteers pray aloud; then close the prayer time, thanking God for being with each child at nighttime, daytime, and anytime!

Remember to put this picture beside your bed to help you remember that God is listening and watching over you, just as He was Samuel. Collect the pictures until the end of class.

The following age-appropriate activities work best by separating the older and younger children.

SNACK SHACK
Good Chocolate Chip Cookies

The children will enjoy eating good chocolate chip cookies, not the terrible ones from today's opening segment. See details in the Noah's Park *Snacks and Games Book* on page RS-41. You may have the preschoolers and elementary-age children eat together before separating for games and crafts.

CAMPSITE CAPERS
Samuel Says (Elementary)
Calling Game (Preschool)

Two fun games support this week's lesson. The

preschoolers will play a "Calling Game" from page RS-42 of the Noah's Park *Snacks and Games Book*. The elementary game is called "Samuel Says" and is explained on page RS-41 of the same book.

COZY CAVE CRAFTS
Samuel-Listens-to-God Storyboard
(Elementary)
Samuel Cut outs (Preschool)

Today's elementary craft, "Samuel-Listens-to-God's Storyboard," can be found in the **Craft Book** on page RC-41. The preschoolers will make "Samuel Cut-outs." Complete instructions are found on page RC-42. Be sure the children put their names on their crafts and put them in a safe spot.

CLOSING ACTIVITIES

A few minutes before class time is over, tell the kids that you (or the Noah's Park puppets) are going to give them "directions" to pay attention to. Give them cleanup jobs to do, such as putting the crayons in the box, picking up paper scraps, and pushing the chairs in.

Then gather the children together in a group to review the new unit song and today's memory verse. Be sure each child remembers to take their Nighttime Picture from the Share and Prayer activity and their craft.

OVERTIME ACTIVITIES

While waiting for parents to come for their children, let the children share their crafts with each other. The elementary students can tell today's story to the preschoolers using their storyboards. The preschoolers can tell elementary children what they remember about their craft.

R19 Lesson: Let Your Choices Show That You Follow God

Choose from the options listed below
to follow Adventure Trails that lead to Jesus:

DISCOVERY TRAILS
TEACHER FEATURE (5 min.)
Choices Story
BIBLE STORY (10 min.)
A King for Israel (Elementary)
The First King (Preschool)
NOAH'S PARK PUPPETS (5 min.)
The Right Choices
BIBLE MEMORY (5 min.)
It's the King's Turn

WORSHIP TRAILS
SINGING PRAISES TO JESUS (5–10 min.)
SHARE AND PRAYER (5–10 min.)
Prayer Partner Cards

WILDLIFE TRAILS
SNACK SHACK (5 min.)
Choices
CAMPSITE CAPERS (10 min.)
The King Wants to Know (Elementary)
Donkeys or a Crown? (Preschool)
COZY CAVE CRAFTS (15 min.)
Magnetic Picture Frame (Elementary)
A Crown for a King (Preschool)

HAPPY TRAILS
CLOSING ACTIVITIES (5 min.)
OVERTIME ACTIVITIES (as needed)

DISCOVERY TRAILS

TEACHER FEATURE
Choices Story

Supplies: None

Gather the children together for a story. **What are choices?** Let volunteers describe choices in their own words. **What are some of the choices you get to make each day?** (What cereal to eat for breakfast, what clothes to wear, when to do my chores, etc.) Different children may be allowed to make different choices. **Let's listen to a story**

about choices. Listen for what kinds of choices the kids get to make.

Ellie was heading out the door for school when her mother called, "Come straight home today. I need you to watch Tommy while I work at home."

"Oh, Mom," Ellie sighed. "Why do I always have to watch Tommy?"

"You know I have to get this project done for my boss this week," Mom replied.

Ellie shrugged her shoulders and left to meet Abby for the walk to school. The first thing Abby said was, "I'm so excited! Jenna has a new puppy and we are all going over to her house after school to play with him!"

"I can't go," said Ellie, glumly. "I have to watch Tommy."

"You always have to watch Tommy! Can't you go just this once?" said Abby. "Everyone is going. Jenna's mom is baking cookies."

Jenna's mom was always baking cookies and doing fun stuff. Not like Ellie's mom who was always working. One day won't matter, Ellie thought. My mom is always working. She can do her project later. Besides, I won't stay that long."

"Okay, count me in," Ellie said.

"Great," said Abby. "Let's meet after school."

But all afternoon Ellie was miserable. She kept thinking about what Miss Baker had said in Sunday school class. "Our choices really matter to God. We show by our choices that we follow God."

"I *do* want to follow God," Ellie said to herself. So after school she told Abby she had changed her mind. "Whatever!" said Abby, walking away. Sadly, Ellie started home.

As she walked into the house, Tommy toddled toward her, grinning. Her mom was at her desk, working. "Why don't you take Tommy for a walk?" Mom called through the doorway. "You could walk over to Jenna's house. I hear her mom baked cookies for everyone." Mom came out of her office room, smiling. "I talked to Jenna's mom today," she said with a wink. Ellie was so happy!

What was Ella's choice that she had to make? (Whether or not to go home after school to watch her brother as her mother had said.) **Ellie made a good choice. How did it turn out for her?** (Good, because she got to go see the puppy anyway.) **Will all good choices turn out good for us?** Let the kids discuss this with you. Make sure they know that we need to make good choices, regardless of the outcome.

Divide the children into two groups—preschool and elementary—and have the Park Patrol lead them to their Bible story areas.

ELEMENTARY BIBLE STORY
A King for Israel (1 Samuel 8–10)

Supplies: Bible

Let a volunteer find 1 Samuel in a Bible, and show the class where today's story comes from. **Today you are going to be the people of Israel. During the story, you have a line to say. Whenever I point to you, chant, "We want a king! We want a king!"** Practice with the children. Briefly review last week's Bible story. **Who was Samuel?** (He was a boy who listened to and obeyed God.)

Many years have past since last week's story when Samuel was a boy. He is now a very old man and has been leading the people of Israel for many years as their prophet. He did a great job and always led the people to obey God. But now the people of Israel said to him, "We want a king like everyone else!" Point to children so they may chant, "We want a king!"

There had never been a king in Israel before. God ruled over them through His prophet Samuel. Samuel was sad as he prayed to God about what the people had said. God told Samuel to warn the people that a king would take their sons for his army and make their daughters cook and bake for him. But the people said, (signal children the chant) "We want a king! We want a king!

Then Samuel told them that a king would take all their best land and make them his unpaid servants. But the people said, (signal the children) "We want a king! We want a king!" **Then God told Samuel, "Alright, I will give them a king. I will send a young man to you.**

You are to make him their king."

In place far away a young man named Saul was looking for his father's donkeys, which had wandered off. As he searched high and low for them he wandered a long way from home. His friend said, "Let's go ask Samuel the prophet where the donkeys are. He is a wise man and will tell us what to do. As they walked to Samuel's house, God spoke to Samuel saying, "I have sent this young man to you. He is the king I have chosen for Israel."

Samuel met Saul on the road and anointed him to be the king. Samuel took Saul to the people of Israel and said, "This is what God has told me. 'I, the Lord, have taken good care of you but you still say: (point to children) 'We want a king! We want a king!' Therefore, I have told Samuel to crown Saul to be your king.'"

And the people said, "Long live the king! Long live the king!" Point to children to chant this now: "Long live the king! Long live the king!"

God did not want a king for Israel, but they demanded one anyway. God let the people choose, and they got their king. We'll find out in our next lessons how King Saul did as a king.

Ask a few questions to make sure the kids understood the Bible story. **Did the people of Israel show by their choices that they followed God?** (No.) Samuel did not want to crown a king over Israel but God told him to. Did his choice show that he followed God? (Yes.) **How do our choices show that we follow God?** Let the kids offer ideas or examples.

PRESCHOOL BIBLE STORY
The First King (1 Samuel 8—10)

Supplies: Bible

Preparation: None

Open your Bible to 1 Samuel 8 and keep it open. **Our story today is in the part of the Bible called 1 Samuel.**

Show the children how to make a crown with their fingers by touching pinkies and thumbs together, then extending their fingers upward. Then they should put their finger crowns on their heads. **Listen carefully to our story. Whenever I say the word "king," make a crown with your fingers.**

Samuel had led the people of Israel for many years. He was getting old. The people came to him and said, "We want you to give us a king." Make a crown with your hands. **This made Samuel sad. God had always led His people through special leaders called prophets or judges. It would be a big change for the people of Israel to have a king.** Make a crown with your hands.

Samuel prayed to God. God said, "Samuel, don't be sad. The people are forgetting that I am in charge. Go back and tell them what they would give up if they had a king." Make a crown with your hands.

Samuel warned the people how bad it could be. But they still wanted a king. Make a crown with your hands. **So God told Samuel, "Listen to them and give them a king."** Make a crown with your hands.

A man named Saul lived in Samuel's country. One day, some of Saul's father's donkeys ran away. Saul and a servant looked all over for them. After three days, the servant said, "Let's go ask Samuel about the donkeys. He knows a lot. Maybe he can tell you where the donkeys are." So off they went to find Samuel.

When Samuel saw Saul and his servant coming down the road, he knew that Saul was the man who would be king. Make a crown with your hands. **God had told him the day before.**

Samuel told Saul not to worry about the donkeys. They had been found. Instead, Samuel invited Saul to come to his house to eat. After supper, Samuel took out some special oil and put it on Saul's head. This was very special. Samuel told Saul, "God has chosen you to be the king." Make a crown with your hands.

Days later, the people of Israel gathered together. Samuel had Saul stand before them. "Do you see this man?" he asked. "This is the man God has chosen to be your king." Make a crown with your hands.

Samuel let his choices show that he followed God. We can let our choices show that we follow God.

Ask the children some review questions: **What did the people want?** (A king.) **Who did God choose to be their king?** (Saul.)

NOAH'S PARK PUPPETS
The Right Choices

Lead the children over to the puppet skit area. Ask them to make a good choice by being seated quietly and listening respectfully to the puppet skit. Today's skit is found in the *Puppet Skits Book* on page RS–43.

BIBLE MEMORY
It's the King's Turn

Supplies: Paper crown or toy crown (more than one if your group is large), CD player, Noah's Park CD

Preparation: Choose a verse for the children to memorize. Pick one from the Sunday school lesson or a verse that supports this lesson: "Let Your Choices Show That You Follow God."

Arrange the children in a circle, either on chairs or on the floor. Read the verse aloud with the children several times.

In our Bible story today, the people of Israel wanted a king. We are going to let a "king" help us memorize our verse. Pass the crown from head to head while the music plays. When it stops, whoever is wearing the crown will be the king and will tell us the verse.

Play a song on the CD player as the children pass the crown around. When you stop the music, the person holding the crown must say the verse. At first, let a Park Patrol whisper help to the child if needed. As the children get more familiar with the verse, let each one try it without help. Be generous with praise and encouragement.

SINGING PRAISES TO JESUS

Supplies: Noah's Park CD and CD player

Sing together the song for this unit, "Take a Stand." Sing the song at least twice. You might also review the song from the first unit. Choose additional praise songs as time allows.

SHARE AND PRAYER
Prayer Partner Cards

Supplies: Index cards, marker

Preparation: Print each child's name on a card. Put all the name cards in the center of the group, face down. If the group is large, divide into smaller groups but be sure the name cards are divided with the groups. Let the children each pick a name card. If they pick their own, they should pick a different one.

In all areas of our lives, we have to make choices. In our families, with our friends, when we play, when we are at school—just as Ellie did in our opening story. God tells us in the Bible that if we need wisdom to make good choices we can ask Him. Today we are going to pray for wisdom to make good choices for ourselves and for each other.

As we think about some times when we need to decisions, let's ask God to help us make good, wise choices. Then pray the same thing for the person on your name card. Like this: "Dear God, help me make good and wise choices in my family (allow time for the children to repeat after you) **and help _____ make wise choices in his (or her) family too."** Allow time for the children to pray for the names on their cards, either aloud or silently. Go through each area of their lives: home, school, play, church, and so on.

Take these name cards home with you so you can pray for these friends. Remember to ask God for wisdom to make good choices this week, and pray the same thing for your name-card friend.

At this time have the Park Patrol lead the preschoolers and elementary-age children to their separate activities. Be sure the Park Patrol helpers have their assignments before class so they know how to help and where supplies are found.

SNACK SHACK
Choices

The children will be making choices for their snack today, to reinforce the lesson theme. The directions for the snacks can be found in the *Snack and Games Book* on page RS-43.

CAMPSITE CAPERS
The King Wants to Know (Elementary)
Donkeys or a Crown? (Preschool)

The elementary game, "The King Wants to Know," is on page RS-43 in the *Snacks and Games Book*. The preschool game, "Donkey or a Crown?" is on page RS-44 of the same book.

COZY CAVE CRAFTS
Magnetic Picture Frame (Elementary)
A Crown for a King (Preschool)

Today's crafts will give the children a reminder about making wise choices. Instructions for the preschool craft, "A Crown for a King," are on page RC-44 of the Noah's Park *Craft Book*. The elementary kids will be working on "Magnetic Picture Frames," found in the *Craft Book* on page RC-43.

CLOSING ACTIVITIES

When the children have completed their crafts, start the Unit 5 song on the CD player to signal time for cleanup. The Park Patrol can encourage the children to make good choices as they straighten and help.

Gather everyone together and ask someone to stand and tell what his or her favorite activity was today and why. As one shares the favorite activity, ask for anyone else who also enjoyed that activity to stand too. Send the children off with a hug, being sure they have their crafts and Prayer Partner Cards.

OVERTIME ACTIVITIES

While waiting for parents to pick up their children, let the children play with the Noah's Park puppets and make up scenarios where the puppets have a choice to make.

R20 Lesson: God's Power Is Greater Than Our Biggest Problems

Choose from the options listed below to follow Adventure Trails that lead to Jesus:

DISCOVERY TRAILS
TEACHER FEATURE *(5 min.)*
  Powerful Help
BIBLE STORY *(10 min.)*
  David and Goliath (Elementary)
  A Giant of a Fight (Preschool)
NOAH'S PARK PUPPETS *(5 min.)*
  God's Power
BIBLE MEMORY *(5 min.)*
  Word by Word

WORSHIP TRAILS
SINGING PRAISES TO JESUS *(5–10 min.)*
SHARE AND PRAYER *(5–10 min.)*
  Smooth Stone Prayer Reminders

WILDLIFE TRAILS
SNACK SHACK *(5 min.)*
  Power Snacks
CAMPSITE CAPERS *(10 min.)*
  What Time Is It, Goliath? (Elementary)
  What Should I Take to Fight? (Preschool)
COZY CAVE CRAFTS *(15 min.)*
  David's Five Stones (Elementary)
  David and Goliath Stick Puppets (Pre.)

HAPPY TRAILS
CLOSING ACTIVITIES *(5 min.)*
OVERTIME ACTIVITIES *(as needed)*

DISCOVERY TRAILS

TEACHER FEATURE
Powerful Help

Supplies: Small scraps of paper, a vacuum cleaner hose and attachment, a hair dryer

Preparation: Scatter scraps of paper on the floor around where you will be sitting. (Be sure a helpful child doesn't go ahead and pick them up!)

Gather the children around and have them be seated on the floor. **I've made a mess here! Luckily, I have my vacuum cleaner.** Attempt to vacuum up the scraps using only the hose. Look perplexed. **Oh well, I have my hair dryer. I will just blow the scraps away.** Try blowing the scraps away without plugging in the hair dryer. Again, look perplexed.

What is the problem? Why aren't these things working? Lead children to tell you that you need electric power for the hair dryer and that you need the whole vacuum cleaner to work.

Sometimes we have big problems that we are powerless to solve. We are like a hose without a vacuum cleaner or a hair dryer without power. We can't solve the problem on our own. But God is all-powerful. When we plug into His help, we can have courage and power to solve our problems.

What kinds of problems do kids face that you need help with? Let the children share. (Some tough homework problems, dealing with a friend, getting some chores done, a problem with a teacher.) **In our Bible story today we are going to hear about a young boy with a grown-up problem! How did he solve the problem? Let's find out!**

If you are separating the elementary and preschool children for the Bible story, have your Park Patrol lead them to the appropriate class areas at this time.

ELEMENTARY BIBLE STORY
David and Goliath *(1 Samuel 17)*

Supplies: Bible, measuring tape, long dowels or 2'x 4' board, or masking tape

Preparation: On dowels or boards, measure nine feet long and cut the dowels or boards to that length. *Or* measure nine feet on the wall in the center of the room and mark it with tape. Use tape to make the outline of a person nine feet tall.

Have the children stand on one side of the room to be the Israelite army. Have all the Park Patrol helpers stand on the other side and be the Philistine army. Keep the nine-foot dowel or wall mark near you.

The army of the Philistines kept invading Israel. So the Israelite army went to fight them. But the Philistines had an idea. They sent a message to the Israelites. Have one of the Philistines walk over to the Israelites. **"We'll send our best warrior to fight with your best warrior. If your guy wins, we'll all become your servants. But if our guy wins, you become our slaves!"** Send the Philistine back.

When the Philistine warrior stepped out everyone was amazed! Have a Philistine step up. Help this child hold the nine-foot tall dowel upright or stand next to the marking on the wall. **His name was Goliath, and he was nine feet tall!** Point out to the children how tall nine feet is. **His helmet and armor weighed 125 pounds, and he carried a huge spear. He even had a helper walk in front of him to carry his heavy shield. The Israelite army shook with fear. Everyone said, "I'm not fighting him!"**

Every day the Philistine army sent Goliath to shout to the army of Israel, "Send out a man to fight me! If he wins, we will serve you. But if he loses, you will serve us!"

King Saul and his army were terrified. They didn't trust that God was powerful enough to help them. No one was brave enough to fight Goliath. This was a big problem.

A young shepherd boy, named David, had come to the army camp to visit his brothers, who were soldiers. David heard Goliath's shouts and was angry. "Who is this Philistine that shouts against the armies of the living God?" he said. "Someone should stop him!" The soldiers looked at David as if he were crazy and took him to King Saul.

David told King Saul, "Don't worry. I will kill Goliath. I have killed a lion and a bear to protect my sheep. The Lord will help me."

Saul said, "You're just a boy. You must wear my armor." He dressed David in his own armor, put a helmet on his head and a sword on his belt. David tried to move but the armor was too heavy. He gave it back to the king. Instead, David put a slingshot and five

smooth stones in his pouch and set off to fight Goliath. Pick one of the "Israelites" to step forward and move to "Goliath."

Goliath saw David coming toward him and laughed. "I asked for a warrior and you sent me a boy!" he shouted. "I will feed this boy to the birds!"

David shouted back, "You come at me with a sword and shield, but I come to you in the name of the Lord!" He put the first stone in his sling, spun it around, and let it fly. The stone hit Goliath on his bare forehead, and Goliath fell down at David's feet. Help the child with the dowel carefully lay it down.

The Philistines ran away, afraid, with the army of Israel chasing them. The people of Israel learned by watching David that God's power was greater than their biggest problems.

Take time to review the main points of the story. **What was the big problem the army of Israel had?** (The Philistines sent a giant warrior named Goliath to fight their best man, but everyone was afraid to fight.) **Was David strong enough on his own to kill a giant?** (No.) **How did David win the fight?** (He trusted in God's power; God helped him.) **God's power gave David courage and strength. He will do the same for us, too.**

PRESCHOOL BIBLE STORY
A Giant of a Fight (1 Samuel 17)

Supplies: Bible, completed set of David and Goliath puppets *(Craft Book,* p. RC-46)

Preparation: Make a set of David and Goliath puppets from page RC-46 of the *Craft Book.*

Show the children 1 Samuel 17 in your Bible. **Our story today is from 1 Samuel.**

Show the Goliath puppet. **This is a big soldier named Goliath. He was a giant in an enemy army. His army wanted to fight against King Saul and the people of Israel. Goliath was very big and strong. When you see this puppet, hold up your arms to show your strong muscles.** Make muscle arms.

Show the David puppet. **This is David. He is a boy and is much smaller than Goliath. David** belonged to the people of Israel, God's people. David trusts in God's power. When you see this puppet, point up. Point up.

Show the David puppet. Point up. **David's job was to take care of his family's sheep. His brothers were soldiers with King Saul, fighting the enemy. One day, David went to the army camp where his brothers were. He heard a loud voice calling out. It was Goliath, the giant.** Show the Goliath puppet. Make muscle arms.

Every day Goliath would yell to King Saul and his soldiers. "Choose one man to come and fight me. If he wins the fight, we will obey your king. But if he loses, you all will obey our king."

Show the David puppet. Point up. **"Why doesn't anyone fight Goliath?" David asked. "Why doesn't anyone stand up for God?" But the men were too scared to fight Goliath.** Show the Goliath puppet. Make muscle arms.

Show the David puppet. Point up. **"I will fight Goliath," David said. King Saul heard what David had said. He said to David, "You are only a boy. What makes you think that you can fight a giant?"**

Show the David puppet. Point up. **"I have fought a lion and a bear while protecting my father's sheep. God's power was in those fights. God will keep me safe from Goliath."**

So King Saul agreed. David took his own things to fight—his shepherd's staff, five smooth stones, and a sling. Point to the sling on the David puppet. **But most importantly, David took his trust in God's power.** Point up.

Show the Goliath puppet. Make muscle arms. **When Goliath saw David coming to fight him, he laughed. "You're only a boy! It will be easy to beat you."** Show the David puppet. Point up. **"I don't need a sword and a spear to fight you," said David. "I come in the name of God." Then David put one of his smooth stones in his sling and let the stone go. The stone hit Goliath so hard that he fell down and died.**

Show the David puppet. Point up. **David won the fight over Goliath. He knew that God's power would win the fight. God's power is greater than our biggest problems.**

Review the story with these questions to be sure the children understood the main points. **Who wanted to fight the army of Israel?** (Goliath.) **Who said he would fight Goliath?** (David.) **How did David win the fight?** (With God's power.)

NOAH'S PARK PUPPETS
God's Power

Today's puppet presentation, "God's Power," is found in the *Puppet Skits Book* on page RS–45. While the Park Patrol is getting ready, let each child name a problem that God can give them courage and strength to face.

BIBLE MEMORY
Word by Word

Supplies: Index cards

Preparation: Choose a verse from today's lesson or from the Sunday school curriculum. Print each word on a separate index card. If the group is large, divide the children and make a set of cards for each group.

Place the verse cards face down in the center of the group. Say the verse to the group several times. Children should come up one at a time to pick a card. Let them read their word and stand in a line in approximate word order (with the word facing out). Park Patrol may help young readers with words and whisper advice about where to stand. When all the cards are used, children should say the verse, word by word, each one saying only the word he or she holds.

Play again by mixing up the cards and letting different children choose cards this time.

SINGING PRAISES TO JESUS

Supplies: Noah's Park CD and CD player

Begin with the unit song, "Take a Stand," by having the children sing along with the CD. Then choose some other songs about God's power and help.

SHARE AND PRAYER
Smooth Stone Prayer Reminders

Supplies: Brown construction paper, markers, resealable plastic bags

Preparation: On brown construction paper draw smooth stone shapes, about two to three inches wide. Cut them out. Prepare five for each child.

David picked up five smooth stones to fight Goliath. With God's help the first stone went right to the mark and the giant fell dead. These paper stones will remind us of God's power in our lives. Each one of you has five stones. On each stone, write a word to remind you of times when you might need courage and God's help.

Encourage the children to share times or places when they need courage and God's help. Print these on the board. The children might suggest *school, sports, bullies, alone, friends, teacher,* and so on. Give each child five stones and let them choose words to write on their stones.

Have children suggest words of courage. Print these on the board. Remind them that God is greater than their biggest problems. They might suggest *loves me, powerful, Father,* etc.. Let the children choose words from this list to write on the other side of their stones.

Open a prayer time where the children can pray off their stones. They may either ask God for help with something or praise God for a way He gives them courage. Model how you would pray for help or courage in your life.

Give out resealable plastic bags for the children to keep their stones in. **This week use these stones to remind you to ask for God's help and courage when you have a big problem.**

WILDLIFE TRAILS

The following activities are geared for either preschool or elementary children. These two groups could be in the same room in different spaces or in separate rooms. Let the Park Patrol lead the different groups to their activities and help as you have assigned them.

SNACK SHACK
Power Snacks

Today's snack will reinforce our lesson on God's power. The snack suggestion is found on page RS-45 of the *Snacks and Games Book.*

CAMPSITE CAPERS
What Time Is It, Goliath? (Elem.)
What Should I Take to Fight? (Pre.)

You will need an open area to play the elementary game. Play outdoors if the weather is nice. The game is found in the *Snacks and Games Book* on page RS-45. The preschoolers will play "What Should I Take to Fight?" from on page RS-46.

COZY CAVE CRAFTS
David's Five Stones (Elementary)
David and Goliath Puppets (Pre.)

Preschool children will be making "David and Goliath Stick Puppets," found in the *Craft Book* on page RC-46. Elementary children will be making a Bible story reminder called "David's Five Stones." The directions are on page RC-45 of the *Craft Book.*

HAPPY TRAILS

CLOSING ACTIVITIES

Have all the children participate in cleanup time. Use the Park Patrol to help with directions and encouragement. Then gather together to sing the Unit 5 song. Review the memory verse again. Ask for volunteers to say it from memory.

Give out the children's crafts and Smooth Stone Prayer Reminders. As children leave, remind them to ask God for help and courage to solve big problems.

OVERTIME ACTIVITIES

While waiting for the parents, you may want to have one of the Park Patrol read to the children from a Bible storybook about David and Goliath.

R21 Lesson: Don't Be Jealous—Trust God Instead

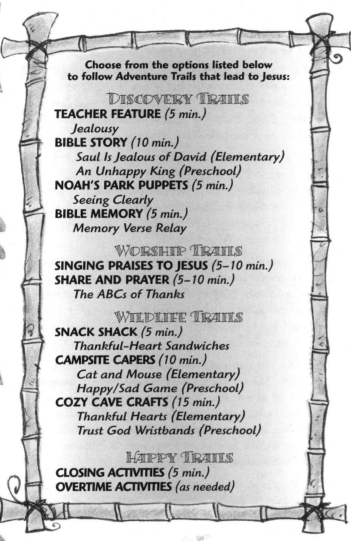

Choose from the options listed below
to follow Adventure Trails that lead to Jesus:

DISCOVERY TRAILS
TEACHER FEATURE *(5 min.)*
Jealousy
BIBLE STORY *(10 min.)*
Saul Is Jealous of David (Elementary)
An Unhappy King (Preschool)
NOAH'S PARK PUPPETS *(5 min.)*
Seeing Clearly
BIBLE MEMORY *(5 min.)*
Memory Verse Relay

WORSHIP TRAILS
SINGING PRAISES TO JESUS *(5–10 min.)*
SHARE AND PRAYER *(5–10 min.)*
The ABCs of Thanks

WILDLIFE TRAILS
SNACK SHACK *(5 min.)*
Thankful-Heart Sandwiches
CAMPSITE CAPERS *(10 min.)*
Cat and Mouse (Elementary)
Happy/Sad Game (Preschool)
COZY CAVE CRAFTS *(15 min.)*
Thankful Hearts (Elementary)
Trust God Wristbands (Preschool)

HAPPY TRAILS
CLOSING ACTIVITIES *(5 min.)*
OVERTIME ACTIVITIES *(as needed)*

DISCOVERY TRAILS

TEACHER FEATURE
Jealousy

Supplies: Jar with a neck small enough for a child to squeeze a hand in but can't pull it out when a fist is made, piece of wrapped candy for each child plus one extra (a slippery wrapper would be best)

Preparation: Ask two Park Patrol members to practice the skit. Place the extra piece of wrapped candy in the jar; leave the rest of the candy in the bag. Have all the children sit where they can see the

skit. **This is a skit about two kids meeting after school.**

Kid 1: Hi, (name of other actor)**.**

Kid 2: Hi, (name of first actor)**. Did you hear? I'm going to be on the All-Star Soccer Team. I guess they heard about all the goals I've made.**

Kid 1: (Hesitates.) **Uh, congratulations.**

Kid 2: And I just heard from my art teacher that I won the art contest. She thought my picture was the best of the whole class.

Kid 1: (Sounds insincere and jealous.) **Oh, that's great.**

Kid 2: I've gotta go. I'm having friends over to play my new video game. It's really cool. (Hurries off.)

Kid 1: (Mimics.) **It's really cool.** (Grumbles.) **He (she) thinks he's is so special. Always bragging.** (Walks off grumbling.)

Thank your actors and invite them to be seated. **In the skit, how was this first kid feeling about the friend that had all the great things happen?** (Jealous.) Children will recognize the feeling, but may not be familiar with the word. **Jealousy is a feeling that all of us have had. But it is a sin. It keeps us from enjoying what we have because we're focusing on things that we don't have.**

Pass out candy to all but tell them not to eat it yet. Show the extra piece in the jar and ask, **"Who would like another piece?"** Pick a child.

Let a child reach into jar to retrieve the one candy. The child should be able to touch the candy but not grasp it to pull it out. (Child's name) **can't pull her (his) hand out as long as she (he) is holding onto the candy. That is like jealousy. We can't enjoy what we have unless we let go of our jealousy. One way to get rid of jealous feelings is to be thankful for what we have. When** (child's name) **lets go of the candy she already has, she can enjoy the candy.** Let all the children eat their candy.

Our Bible story is about jealousy and how it makes us feel bad if we don't let go of it by being thankful for what we already have.

At this time, have the Park Patrol members take the children to the appropriate areas for the Bible story. If all the children are staying together, use the Elementary Bible Story to teach the lesson.

ELEMENTARY BIBLE STORY

Saul Is Jealous of David (1 Samuel 15— 16; 18:5—19:18)

Supplies: Bible, washable marker

Preparation: Use washable marker to draw a happy face on the palm of one of your hands and an angry face on your other palm.

Show the children in a Bible where today's story comes from—1 Samuel. Let children practice making happy, thankful faces and jealous, mean faces. Signal the class which face to make by pointing the hand with that face at the class during the story.

Our Bible story today is about the King Saul of Israel. King Saul loved being king. (Signal children to make a happy face.) **He loved being popular.** (Happy face.) **He loved being rich and ruling over everyone.** (Happy face.) **But he wasn't very happy.** (Signal a mean face.) **He wanted things done his own way and he worried when they weren't.** (Mean face.) **Sometimes he got so worried that he stopped trusting and obeying God.** (Mean face.)

In last week's lesson someone beat the big, bad giant, Goliath. Who was it? (David.) **David turned out to be a very good warrior.** (Happy face.) **King Saul liked his army to always win, so he put David in charge of his army. David's army always won.** (Happy face.) **David trusted God, and God always helped David and the army of Israel win.** (Happy face.)

Wasn't that good news? You'd think King Saul would be happy that his army always won. But King Saul wasn't happy. (Mean face.) **He heard some celebration songs that his people were singing. Their song went like this:**

"Saul has killed thousands of enemy soldiers, but David has killed *tens* of thousands."

Every time David and the army came back from a battle, everyone celebrated David, dancing and singing about what a great job he was doing. (Happy face.)

Saul became very jealous. (Mean face.) **He thought maybe David wanted to be king instead of him.** (Mean face.) **Maybe the people of Israel wanted David to be their king!** (Mean face.) **Saul decided that David would have to go.** (Mean face.)

Saul often got into bad moods and would call for David to play the harp for him. One day Saul called for David to play. As David began to play, Saul threw a spear at him! David jumped out of the way in time. (Mean face.)

Since that didn't work, Saul gave David a tiny army instead of a large one and sent him to battle. Maybe David would be killed. (Mean face.) **But God helped David win many tricky battles.** (Happy face.) **This made Saul even more jealous.** (Mean face.)

Saul thought of another trick. He promised David could marry his beautiful daughter if he would kill 100 Philistines. For sure David would be killed, he thought. (Mean face.) **But instead he killed 200 Philistines!** (Happy face.) **Saul became even more jealous.** (Mean face.)

Then Saul sent soldiers to David's house to get him. (Mean face.) **But David heard about it ahead of time. He stuffed something in his bed and put some goat's hair on his pillow to look like he was sleeping. When Saul tried to kill David, he found it was only a pillow. David had escaped.** (Happy face.)

Saul stopped being a good king. (Mean face.) **All he could think about was getting rid of David. That is what jealousy does to us. It takes over.** (Mean face.) **But David had learned to be thankful to God for everything, and God rewarded him.** (Happy face.) **Even though Saul tried to kill him, David knew God would take care of him.** (Happy face.) **We can also trust God and not be jealous.** (Happy face.)

Review by asking these questions: **What was Saul like?** (Jealous of David.) **What was David like?** (Thankful for everything.) **What should we do when we feel jealous?** (Trust God; be thankful.)

PRESCHOOL BIBLE STORY

An Unhappy King (1 Samuel 15— 16; 18:5—19:18)

Supplies: Bible, two colors of construction paper, marker, craft sticks, glue sticks

Preparation: Make happy/sad face puppets for each child: Cut out a circle from each color of construction paper. Draw a happy face on one circle and a sad face on the other. Glue them back-to-back on either side of a craft stick.

Give each child a happy/sad face puppet. **In our story today we will meet some people who are happy. If they are happy, show me the happy face. Some people will be sad. Then you show me the sad face.**

Show the children 1 Samuel 18, and keep it open as you tell the story.

Last week we learned that a boy named David fought a giant named Goliath and won. King Saul was very happy about that. Show the happy face. **He had David come and live with him.**

King Saul gave David many things to do. David played the harp for King Saul. He was especially good at fighting enemies with the army. David did everything very well. This made King Saul very happy. Show the happy face.

One day King Saul, David, and the soldiers were coming back from fighting a battle. The people from the towns were dancing and singing. As they danced, they sang, "Saul has won many fights. But David has won many more." This probably made David happy. Show the happy face. **But King Saul was not happy.** Show the sad face.

***They like David more than me!* thought King Saul. This made Saul even sadder. From then on Saul didn't like David.** Show sad face.

The next day, at Saul's house, David was playing music to help King Saul feel better. But Saul became angry at David. Show sad face. **He threw things at David to hurt him. But David stayed safe.**

Then King Saul sent David off to fight another battle. David won the fight. This made the people happy. Show the happy face. **But it made King Saul sad.** Show the sad face.

King Saul's daughter loved David. They wanted to get married. Show happy face. **But before they could get married, Saul gave**

David a job to do. If he finished the job, he could marry the king's daughter. When David came back, he married the daughter. They were very happy. Show happy face. **But King Saul was sadder and sadder each day.** Show the sad face. **He knew that God was helping David.**

King Saul was jealous of David. He wanted to be as good as David. That made King Saul sad. Show the sad face. **David trusted God. That made David happy.** Show the happy face. **Don't be jealous—trust God instead.**

Use the puppets to review the story: **How did King Saul feel when David did everything well?** (Sad face.) **Show me how David felt when he trusted God.** (Happy face.)

NOAH'S PARK PUPPETS
Seeing Clearly

When the Park Patrol is ready to present the skit, lead the children to the puppet stage. When the children are settled, have the Park Patrol present the skit found on page RP-47 of the *Puppet Skits Book.*

BIBLE MEMORY
Memory Verse Relay

Supplies: Index cards, marker

Preparation: Select a verse from the Sunday school curriculum or one that supports today's lesson. Print the verse on the cards, one for each team and one for each helper.

Read the verse to the children several times until it's familiar. Divide the children into even teams, placing readers and non-reader equally. Give each team a card with the verse on it. Line teams up behind a starting point. Place a Park Patrol helper on the other side of the room, opposite each team. Let the teams practice the verse together until they're ready.

At your signal, each team sends someone across to recite the verse to the Park Patrol helper. The helper listens to the verse. When the verse is said correctly, that player runs back and tags the next player. Repeat. The team that completes the relay first is the winner. The first time through, the Park Patrol members may give help to the players. You might let the teams do the relay in pairs and help each other.

SINGING PRAISES TO JESUS

Supplies: Noah's Park CD and CD player

Sing together the Unit 5 song, "Take a Stand." As time allows, sing other songs the children request or that fit with today's lesson.

SHARE AND PRAYER
The ABCs of Thanks

Supplies: None

Today we learned that we should not be jealous of what others have or do. Instead, be thankful for what we have. Let's practice that now. We're going to pray through the alphabet, thanking God for as many things as we can think of that begin with each letter.

Lead children in prayer this way: **Dear God, You're so awesome! Thank You for these things that begin with A...** Let children call out one- or two-word prayers in random order. Allow 10 seconds for each letter, and don't worry if kids call out things with a different letter. After each letter, pray to begin the next one: **And God, thank You for these letter B things...**

When the group has prayed through the alphabet, close the prayer time by thanking God for loving each child and asking His help to not be jealous when others have things or opportunities we'd like.

This week, if you start to feel jealous of what someone else has or gets to do, remember to thank God for what you already have instead.

The following age-appropriate activities work best by separating the older and younger children. You might use separate rooms or separate tables for them. Let the Park Patrol lead the different groups to their activities and help as you have assigned them.

SNACK SHACK
Thankful Heart Sandwiches

Refer to page RS-47 in the *Snacks and Games Book* for today's lesson-related snack suggestion. Be aware of any food allergies.

CAMPSITE CAPERS
Cat and Mouse (Elementary)
Happy/Sad Game (Preschool)

The elementary game, "Cat and Mouse," can be played indoors or out. The instructions for this game are in the *Snacks and Games Book* on page RS-47. The preschool game, "Happy/Sad Game," can be found on page RS-48.

COZY CAVE CRAFTS
Thankful Hearts (Elementary)
Trust God Wristbands (Preschool)

The preschoolers today will make "Trust God Wristbands." You can find the directions on page RC-48 of the *Craft Book*. The directions for the elementary craft, "Thankful Hearts," are found on page RC-47.

CLOSING ACTIVITIES

A few minutes before class time is finished, play the unit song to signal cleanup time. Encourage the children to help pick up the room and put away supplies. You might bring out the Noah's Park puppets to help give cleanup directions. When cleanup is complete, gather the children together.

OVERTIME ACTIVITIES

To keep the children occupied as they wait for their parents, you might play the Noah's Park CD and let the children sing along with any songs they know.

R22 Lesson: Unselfish Friends

Choose from the options listed below
to follow Adventure Trails that lead to Jesus:

DISCOVERY TRAILS
TEACHER FEATURE *(5 min.)*
A Friendship Dilemma
BIBLE STORY *(10 min.)*
*Jonathan and David—Unselfish Friends
(Elementary)*
Really Good Friends (Preschool)
NOAH'S PARK PUPPETS *(5 min.)*
The Best Kind of Friend
BIBLE MEMORY *(5 min.)*
Find a Friend

WORSHIP TRAILS
SINGING PRAISES TO JESUS *(5–10 min.)*
SHARE AND PRAYER *(5–10 min.)*
Prayer Chains

WILDLIFE TRAILS
SNACK SHACK *(5 min.)*
Friendship Snack
CAMPSITE CAPERS *(10 min.)*
Smiles, Handshakes, or Hugs (Elem.)
Elbow to Elbow—Friend to Friend (Pre.)
COZY CAVE CRAFTS *(15 min.)*
Simple Friendship Wristbands (Elem.)
David and Jonathan Action Figures (Pre.)

HAPPY TRAILS
CLOSING ACTIVITIES *(5 min.)*
OVERTIME ACTIVITIES *(as needed)*

DISCOVERY TRAILS

TEACHER FEATURE
A Friendship Dilemma

Supplies: Four wooden rulers or dowels, masking tape, roll of toilet paper, bowl of popcorn

Preparation: Pick two friends who are good sports or two Park Patrol helpers for this skit. Tape the rulers to their arms above and below the elbows so that they cannot bend their arms. Roll toilet paper around each arm to resemble a cast. Set the bowl of goodies between them on a table or chair.

These two good friends have a problem. It looks like they both have broken arms and can't bend their elbows. Now they want to enjoy this snack but can't. Can you help them figure out what to do? Let the children offer ideas, except taking off the bandages. If no one comes up with this suggestion say:

What if _____ and _____ (names of participants) help each other? How could they do that? Let the children suggest more ways. Once suggested, let the participants feed each other the snack. **Can they both enjoy the snack now?**

Thank your helpers and let them remove their "bandages." If there is enough, let each child have a small handful of popcorn.

The best way to be friends is to help each other. That is what friendship is all about. Being a friend means being unselfish and putting the other person first. What are some ways we can be unselfish with our friends? Encourage children to offer ideas or examples. (Share our things with them, help them solve problems, stand up for them when others are mean to them, let them go first or choose the activity, etc.) **Can you tell about a time a friend did something unselfish for you?** Let a few volunteers share.

In our Bible story today we are going to hear about a very famous friendship. It is between Jonathan, who was King Saul's son, and David. What do you remember about David? (He killed Goliath, King Saul was jealous of him, etc.) **Let's see what happens with David and Jonathan in our story today.**

If you are separating the elementary and preschool children for the Bible story, have your Park Patrol members lead them to the appropriate class areas now. If not, use the Elementary Bible Story.

ELEMENTARY BIBLE STORY
Jonathan and David—Unselfish Friends *(1 Samuel 20)*

Supplies: Bible-time clothes; bow and arrows, if available

Preparation: Recruit a Park Patrol helper to wear

Bible-time clothes and play the role of the passerby. Plan on playing Jonathan yourself. Practice the skit together ahead of time.

(Jonathan looks sad—almost crying. Passerby walks past and notices.)

Passerby: **Aren't you King Saul's son Jonathan? Why are you so sad?**

Jonathan: **Yes, I am the son of King Saul. I've just said good-bye to my best friend.**

Passerby: **Why did he leave you?**

Jonathan: **It's a long story. But my father, the king, has become obsessed with killing my friend, David.**

Passerby: **You mean David, the one who killed Goliath?**

Jonathan: **Yes, *that* David. My father is jealous of David because God promised to make David the next king. David was worried that my father wanted to kill him. So he asked me to find out the truth. I thought David was wrong. We came up with a plan. There was an important feast at my father's palace. Instead of coming, David hid in this field. We made up a signal so I could secretly let him know what my father said during dinner.**

Passerby: **Sounds risky. What if you got caught?**

Jonathan: **Well, then I'd be in big trouble. But David was my best friend. Our secret signal was that I would come out to this field, shoot arrows into the air, and then send my servant to find them. If I yelled to my servant, "Go to that side," that would mean my father didn't want to kill David and he could come home. If I yelled, "Keep going. The arrows are beyond you," David would know for sure my father wanted to kill him.**

Passerby: **What happened?**

Jonathan: **At dinner, my father became very angry when David was missing. It turns out my father had planned to kill David. He almost killed me instead! I knew I was risking my life to help David, but we had made a promise of friendship. I ran to this field with my bow and arrows and shot them into the air. I yelled to my servant, "Keep going. The arrows are beyond you." While my servant looked for the arrows, David came out of hiding. We hugged each other and cried. We knew it might be the last time we ever saw each other. Then David ran off to a faraway land to hide from my father.**

Passerby: **You risked your life to save your friend. That is really unselfish. You are really a good friend.**

Thank your fellow actor for helping, and be seated with the children.

Jonathan was a young man who knew that he needed to obey God rather than the evil king. What did Jonathan do that was unselfish? (He risked his life to help David.) **We may not need to risk our lives for our friends, but we always need to be unselfish to our good friends. What are unselfish ways we can help our friends?** (Share, stand up for them, etc.)

PRESCHOOL BIBLE STORY
Really Good Friends (1 Samuel 20)

Supplies: Bible, David and Jonathan Action Figures (*Craft Book*, p. RC-50)

Preparation: Make a completed set of action figures from page RC-50 of the *Craft Book*.

Our story today comes from the book of the Bible called 1 Samuel. Show the children 1 Samuel 20 in your Bible. Keep the Bible open as you tell the story to show that this story is from the Bible.

Stand the figure of David in front of you. **This is David.** Stand the figure of Jonathan in front of you. **This is Jonathan. David and Jonathan are best friends. Jonathan's father is King Saul. King Saul doesn't like David.**

Turn the figures to face each other. **One day David asked Jonathan, "What have I done to make your father so angry? I know that he wants me to go away and never, ever come back."**

Jonathan was sad. "My father has never said anything to me about not liking you. It can't

be true! But tell me how I can help you. I'll do it for you."

Jonathan and David went out to a field to talk where no one else could hear them. Move the figures to hide behind the grass. **They came up with a plan. David was supposed to go to a special dinner at the king's house. Only Jonathan would go. If the king was angry that David was missing, Jonathan would know that the king wanted David to go away and never, ever come back. The next day Jonathan would tell David what had happened.**

Take away the David and grass figures. Stand the Jonathan figure in front of you. **Jonathan went to the dinner. The king asked Jonathan, "Where is David?"**

Jonathan answered, "He needed to have dinner with his family. I told him that it would be fine to miss dinner with us." The king was so mad that David wasn't there that he threw things at Jonathan. Then Jonathan knew that the king wanted David to go away and never, ever come back.

The next morning, David hid in the field. Set up the grass figure. Lay the David figure behind it. **Jonathan came and shot an arrow so that it would go far beyond where his helper was.** Set up the Jonathan figure. Put the bow with him. **This was the signal that Jonathan knew that David would have to leave.**

The servant took the bow and arrows home. David and Jonathan met to talk in secret again. Put the David and Jonathan figures next to each other. **David and Jonathan hugged each other. They promised to always help each other and their families. Then David went away.**

David and Jonathan were best friends. The best friend is an unselfish friend.

Be sure to check the children's comprehension of the Bible story. **Who were friends?** (David and Jonathan.) **How was Jonathan a good friend to David?** (He found out that the king wanted David to go away and never, ever come back and warned David about this.)

NOAH'S PARK PUPPETS
The Best Kind of Friend

It is time for the Park Patrol to present today's puppet skit, "The Best Kind of Friend." It is found in the *Puppet Skits Book* on page RP-49. Let the children link arms with a friend on the way to the puppet stage. As soon as the children are settled the presentation can begin.

BIBLE MEMORY
Find a Friend

Supplies: Construction paper of a variety of colors, markers, scissors, tape

Preparation: Choose a Bible verse for the children to memorize that supports today's lesson or choose one from the Sunday school lesson. Cut heart shapes in a variety of colors, about 5"–6" tall. Print the selected verse on a heart—one for every two children. Cut each heart in two in a jagged manner, each heart cut apart differently.

Read the verse to the children. Discuss any unfamiliar words or concepts with them. Pass out the heart halves randomly. **Each of you has half of the verse for today. You need to find the friend that has the other half of your heart. When you find him or her, you can tape your heart together. Then help each other memorize the verse. When you think you *both* can say the verse from memory, find another friendship team and say the verse to each other.**

On your signal, let the children find their partners with the matching hearts. Allow time for the children to practice the verse in pairs. As time permits, let pairs recite the verse for the rest of the class.

SINGING PRAISES TO JESUS

Supplies: Noah's Park CD and CD player

Begin teaching the Winter Quarter, Unit 6, song, "Trust Him and Obey." You may want to project the words on a wall or screen so that the children can follow along. The lyrics are in the back of this *Leader's Guide.*

SHARE AND PRAYER
Prayer Chains

Supplies: Colored construction paper, scissors, markers, tape, glue or stapler

Preparation: Cut strips of paper in a variety of colors about 1" x 8".

We have been learning about friendships from our Bible story. One way to be a friend is to pray for our friends. I've set out markers and strips of paper. Write the name of a friend on a strip of paper. You can use more strips to write more names, if you want to. Park Patrol helpers can help children with spelling.

Glue your strips of paper together on the ends, looping one into the next to make a chain. Demonstrate how to make a chain. **Then pick other colors to make your chain longer. This week hang your chain in your room to remind you to pray for your friends every day.**

When finished, divide children into small groups to pray for their friends. Model how to pray for a friend with phrases such as: "Thank You, God, for _____. Help him/her at school" or "Thank You, God, that You love _____" or "Dear Jesus, help me be a good friend to _____ this week."

Be sure the children write their names on their chains and put the chains in a safe place until the end of the activities.

The following age-appropriate activities work best by separating the older and younger children. Let the Park Patrol lead the different groups to their activities and help as you have assigned them.

SNACK SHACK
Friendship Snack

Today's lesson-related snack, "Friendship Snack," continues the theme of friendship and is found on page RS-49 in the *Snacks and Games Book*. Have the Park Patrol help get the children settled for snack time, and lead a prayer thanking God for the food.

CAMPSITE CAPERS

Smiles, Handshakes, or Hugs (Elem.)
Elbow to Elbow—Friend to Friend (Pre.)

The elementary game, "Smiles, Handshakes, or Hugs," can be found in the *Snacks and Games Book* on page RS-49. The preschool game, "Elbow to Elbow—Friend to Friend," is found on page RS-50 in the *Snacks and Games Book*.

COZY CAVE CRAFTS
Simple Friendship Wristbands (Elem.)
David and Jonathan
Action Figures (Preschool)

The directions for making "Friendship Wristbands," the elementary craft, can be found on page RC-49 in the *Craft Book*. Some Park Patrol members will be needed to help with this craft. The preschoolers will make "David and Jonathan Action Figures," found on page RC-50.

CLOSING ACTIVITIES

Play the unit song as a signal for children to begin cleanup. Use one of the puppets to encourage everyone's participation in straightening up the area. The Park Patrol can help by setting a good example and leading the others to help.

When everyone is back in the group, recite the memory verse together again. Remind the group to take home their Prayer Chains from Share and Prayer and remember to pray for a friend. Ask for volunteers to share ways to be a good friend this week.

OVERTIME ACTIVITIES

While waiting for parents, encourage the children to share the Bible story with the Noah's Park puppets.

R23 Lesson: God's Way Is Better

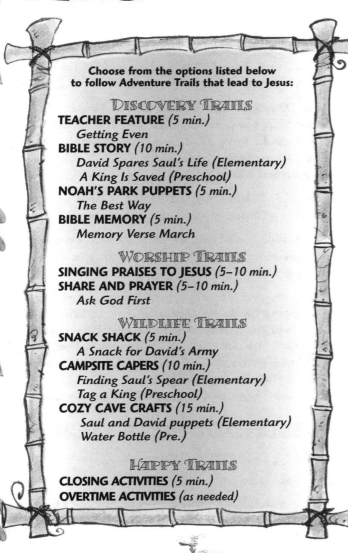

Choose from the options listed below to follow Adventure Trails that lead to Jesus:

DISCOVERY TRAILS
TEACHER FEATURE *(5 min.)*
Getting Even
BIBLE STORY *(10 min.)*
David Spares Saul's Life (Elementary)
A King Is Saved (Preschool)
NOAH'S PARK PUPPETS *(5 min.)*
The Best Way
BIBLE MEMORY *(5 min.)*
Memory Verse March

WORSHIP TRAILS
SINGING PRAISES TO JESUS *(5–10 min.)*
SHARE AND PRAYER *(5–10 min.)*
Ask God First

WILDLIFE TRAILS
SNACK SHACK *(5 min.)*
A Snack for David's Army
CAMPSITE CAPERS *(10 min.)*
Finding Saul's Spear (Elementary)
Tag a King (Preschool)
COZY CAVE CRAFTS *(15 min.)*
Saul and David puppets (Elementary)
Water Bottle (Pre.)

HAPPY TRAILS
CLOSING ACTIVITIES *(5 min.)*
OVERTIME ACTIVITIES *(as needed)*

DISCOVERY TRAILS

TEACHER FEATURE
Getting Even

Supplies: None

Read the following story to the children. **A silly old man lived with his silly old wife in a tiny house. They were always quarreling and were never happy. They played tricks on each other and were always trying to get even.** Discuss what "getting even" means.

One cold, gray day the old woman felt particularly bad-tempered. She watched her husband throw logs on the fire and said to herself, "Does he think we are made of money? He wastes so much of our wood to keep himself comfortable." Then she watched him heap porridge into his bowl and said to herself, "He is eating up all our food." And as she watched him pour water into the kettle for tea, she grumbled, "Hmmp! We will soon be out of water."

When the old man left to work in the fields, the old woman thought about it and became more and more cranky. "I will get even with him," she thought. "I will burn up all the logs, and throw out all the food, and boil up all the water." And she did.

That day, the weather grew so cold that icicles formed inside the windows. "I will make a fire," she thought. But when she went to the wood box, what do you suppose she found? (Nothing.) "Oh well," she thought, "I will have some bread. That will warm me up." But when she looked into the bread box, what was there? (Nothing.) "Some hot tea will warm me up," she said. But what do you think she found when she poured the kettle? (Nothing.)

Just then her husband came home. She called out, "I got even with you for burning up all our wood and eating up all our food and drinking up all our water! Ha, Ha!"

The old man looked at his silly old wife, shivering in the cold, and said, "I think you got even with yourself!"

Did "getting even" make the silly old woman happy? (No, she made herself more unhappy.) **In our Bible story today we will learn that God's way is better than getting even.**

At this time, you can have one or two Park Patrol members help you by taking the preschool children to the area where they will listen to their Bible story.

ELEMENTARY BIBLE STORY
David Spares Saul's Life (1 Samuel 26)

Supplies: Bible, a water jug, a "spear" (tinfoil point on the end of a pole)

Preparation: Ask Park Patrol members to play roles in this skit: Saul, Abner (Saul's general), David, Abishai (David's friend), two spies. Go over their roles with them. Tell the children that they will be armies in today's Bible story. **Today's story is found in 1 Samuel 26.** Show the children this passage in a Bible.

Divide the children in two groups—a bigger group to be Saul's army and a smaller group to be David's army. Pick two children to be David's spies. David's army should camp on one side of the room, Saul's on the other side.

In last week's story, Jonathan helped David escape from King Saul. However, Saul continued to chase David. Each time, the Lord helped David escape. Once again, Saul got word that David and his men were camped in the wilderness, hiding. David and men pretend to hide. **Saul and his general, Abner, took their best men to go find David.**

Saul's army moves halfway toward David's camp. They get ready for the night, lying on floor. Abner places Saul's water jug and spear near Saul and him.

David heard that Saul was coming after him, so that night he sent out spies to find out if Saul was nearby. David's spies sneak over to Saul's camp. **The spies found Saul's army sleeping! They went back to tell David.** Spies sneak back and whisper to David.

David and his friend Abishai sneaked into Saul's tent. David and Abishai sneak over to Saul. **The Lord helped David by causing Saul's army to fall into a deep sleep. David and Abishai found Saul sleeping.**

Abishai said, "Let's get even. I'll kill him for you, David." Abishai motions this.

David said, "No, I will not kill the man God made king. Instead, take his jug and spear." David motions no. David picks up the water jug and spear, and he and Abishai return to their camp.

When they got back to their camp, David yelled across the valley to Saul's camp, **"Wake up, Saul!"**

Saul sits up. **"Is that you, David?"** Saul hollered back. David called, **"Yes, it is me! Hey Abner, aren't you the strongest man in Saul's army? Look around for Saul's spear and water jug. Do you see them?"** Saul and Abner look for the jug and spear.

Then David called, "I have them! This is proof that I was so close to you last night that I could have killed you. But I won't kill God's king. Stop chasing me. Let me come back to my home."

Saul said, "I have sinned, David. Come back home. I will not try to hurt you again."

David said, "Send one of your men to come and get your spear. The Lord rewards us for doing good."

Ask the children a few review questions. **What was Saul trying to do to David?** (Kill him.) **What did David have the chance to do?** (Sneak into Saul's camp and kill him first.) **Why was it better for David to trust God and not kill Saul when he had the chance?** Allow time for discussion. **God's way is always better than getting even.**

PRESCHOOL BIBLE STORY
A King Is Saved (1 Samuel 26)

Supplies: Bible

Show the children 1 Samuel 26 in your Bible. **Our story today is from the part of the Bible called 1 Samuel.** Encourage the children to copy your actions as you tell the story.

Pat your knees quickly. **David had run away from King Saul. He knew that King Saul was very mad at him—mad enough to hunt for him.**

Pat your knees with your fists in a marching rhythm. **One day King Saul and his army came to the same area where David was. It was nighttime so they lay down to rest.** Put your hands together by your cheek as if resting. **King Saul put his water jug** (pretend to drink) **and his spear** (pretend to hold a spear) **near his head. He could get them quickly if he needed them.**

David heard that King Saul and his army

were camping nearby, looking for him. Pat your fingers on your knees. **He quietly went to their camp. Everyone was sleeping!** Put your head on your hands. **David's friend told David that now was his chance. He could get rid of the king and not have to hide anymore.**

David said, "The king doesn't like me and wants to hurt me. But God chose him to be king. I can't hurt him." Shake your head no. **So David quietly picked up the king's water jug and spear and walked away. He borrowed these things to prove that he had been close enough to hurt the king but didn't.**

Pat your knees. **David climbed to the top of a hill nearby.** Cup your hands around your mouth. **He called out to King Saul's army, "Why didn't you guard the king better? Someone could have hurt him. Where is his water jug? Where is his spear?" King Saul saw that his things were missing. He knew David had been nearby.** Tap your finger against your head.

David called out, "What have I done to get the king so angry at me?"

King Saul knew that David could have hurt him but had not gotten even. The king knew that he had done the wrong thing to David. Cup your hands around your mouth. **The king called across to David, "I am sorry, David. I will not try to hurt you again."**

David called back, "Send someone to get your spear and water jug from me. God put you in my hands today, but I wouldn't hurt you because God chose you to be the king." Make a crown with your hands.

King Saul promised he wouldn't try to hurt David any more. Pat your knees. **David went on his way. King Saul returned home.**

David could have gotten even with King Saul. But he knew that God's way is better. Ask the children a few review questions. **Who wanted to hurt David?** (King Saul.) **Who had the chance to hurt King Saul?** (David.) **Why didn't David hurt King Saul?** (Because God had chosen Saul to be king and David knew that God's way was better than getting even.)

NOAH'S PARK PUPPETS
The Best Way

Have the Park Patrol use one of the Noah's Park puppets to call the children to the puppet stage. Today's puppet skit is provided on page RP-51 in the *Puppet Skits Book.*

BIBLE MEMORY
Memory Verse March

Supplies: Two index cards, markers

Preparation: Select a verse that supports today's lesson or one the children are memorizing from Sunday school. Print the verse on index cards, one for each team.

Read over the verse with the children several times, phrase by phrase. Take time to discuss any unfamiliar words or concepts with them.

You will need an open area for this activity. Divide the group into two groups. Have them line up opposite each other at the sides of the room, spread out. (You might have them pretend to be Saul's army and David's army.) Give each team a card. Give them a few minutes to practice the verse together.

When both teams are ready, have them march toward each other to the opposite side of the room. Explain that they may not touch another person as they march, even though they will be passing through the other team's line. They may only march while saying the verse. If they can't remember what comes next in the verse, they need to stop until they do. When they reach the other side, they turn around as a group and "march" the verse back. If some on a team reach the opposite wall before others, they must wait until all have arrived before turning around. Remind the children that they can only march while reciting the verse so they may have to repeat the verse several times if it is a short one.

SINGING PRAISES TO JESUS
Supplies: Noah's Park CD and CD player

Begin with the Unit 6 song, "Trust Him and Obey,"

found on the Noah's Park CD. Song lyrics can be found in the back of this *Leader's Guide*. Let the children clap along or play rhythm instruments, if available.

SHARE AND PRAYER
Ask God First

Supplies: Construction paper, craft sticks, markers, glue, resealable plastic bags

Preparation: Make spearheads (simple triangles will do) to fit on the craft sticks.

Print the words "Ask God first" on the board. Have the children each copy the words on a triangle spearhead and glue the spearheads on the craft sticks.

In today's Bible story, David had a chance to kill Saul with his own spear. But David chose to follow what he knew God wanted. David knew that getting even was not God's way. If we feel like getting back at someone, we need to remember to pray and ask God first. He will show us a better way.

When are some times that you feel like getting even? Let volunteers briefly share. **Let's pray together that God will help us remember that getting even is not the best way.** Ask for volunteers to pray for God's help in not getting even and for any other prayer requests.

Have the children put their spear reminders in their plastic bags, labeled with names, and put them in a designated place to pick up at the end of class.

Put your spear reminder beside your bed or use it as a bookmark to remind you to ask God first when you feel like getting even. God will show you a better way.

Use the Park Patrol to help the children in the different age groups do their crafts, games, and snack.

SNACK SHACK
A Snack for David's Army

The children will pretend to be part of David's army

as they eat this snack found in the Noah's Park *Snacks and Games Book* on page RS-51. Let the children wash their hands or use a disinfectant liquid before eating. Ask for a volunteer to thank God for the food.

CAMPSITE CAPERS
Finding Saul's Spear (Elementary)
Tag a King (Preschool)

The elementary game, "Finding Saul's Spear" can be found on page RS-51 of the *Snacks and Games Book*. See page RS-52 for the preschool game, "Tag a King."

COZY CAVE CRAFTS
Saul and David Puppets (Elementary)
Water Bottle (Preschool)

The elementary children will be making "Saul and David Puppets." These will remind the children of today's Bible story. The directions can be found on page RC-51 in the *Craft Book*. The preschool craft, "Water Bottle," can be found on page RC-52 of the same book. Ask the Park Patrol to wipe off the craft tables when the children finish.

CLOSING ACTIVITIES

A few minutes before class time is over, ask the children to finish up their activities and help with cleanup. Remind children to gather their "Ask God First" reminders and their crafts for going home.

Then gather together and review the memory verse. You may also use this time for singing songs from the Noah's Park CD. Let the elementary children retell the Bible story to the preschoolers using their puppets made during Cozy Cave Crafts.

OVERTIME ACTIVITIES

While the children are waiting for parents you might have them play another round of one of the Campsite Capers games. This will free you to greet parents and collect children's things.

R24 Lesson: When Life Gets Tough

Choose from the options listed below
to follow Adventure Trails that lead to Jesus:

DISCOVERY TRAILS
TEACHER FEATURE *(5 min.)*
A Lemon's Lament
BIBLE STORY *(10 min.)*
Tough Times for David (Elementary)
A King Who Prays (Preschool)
NOAH'S PARK PUPPETS *(5 min.)*
Muddy Days
BIBLE MEMORY *(5 min.)*
One Step at a Time

WORSHIP TRAILS
SINGING PRAISES TO JESUS *(5–10 min.)*
SHARE AND PRAYER *(5–10 min.)*
Cloudy Days

WILDLIFE TRAILS
SNACK SHACK *(5 min.)*
Lemonade and Donuts
CAMPSITE CAPERS *(10 min.)*
David and the Amalekites (Elementary)
Can You Help Me Find My Brother? (Pre.)
COZY CAVE CRAFTS *(15 min.)*
"Helping David" Maze (Elementary)
Prayer Journal (Preschool)

HAPPY TRAILS
CLOSING ACTIVITIES *(5 min.)*
OVERTIME ACTIVITIES *(as needed)*

DISCOVERY TRAILS

TEACHER FEATURE
A Lemon's Lament

Supplies: A lemon, marker

Preparation: Draw a sad face on the lemon.

Hold up the lemon and read this story, sadly, as if the lemon were talking. **Hi, I'm a lemon. Sure, I look pretty, all yellow and shiny, but let me tell you, the life of a lemon is tough. First of** all, no one really likes me—just me for who I am. People only like me when they put me with lots of sugar and water. Lemonade. But no one likes me just for me. And when I am made into lemonade—oh, the squeezing I go through! You think that's fun? It hurts to be a lemon!

Everyone likes oranges. Kids like to take oranges to school in their lunch boxes, but does anyone ever take a lemon to school? No! And have you ever seen someone take a bite out of me? They make the most awful faces. How do you think that makes me feel?

I tell you, no one really understands how tough the life of a lemon is!

Set the lemon aside and speak to the children: **I was being silly with that lemon, but there are times in our lives when things get tough for us, too. Someone in our family gets very sick—or even dies. We may lose a pet. Our family could move to a new place and we might have to start out in a new school and make new friends. Have any of you had times like that in your life?** Allow time for the children to share their own experiences. Sometimes it feels like no one understands what we are going through, so it's good for children to hear about one another's tough times.

There is someone we can talk to who understands all about us and what is happening in our lives. Who is that? (God.) **Yes, God is always there to listen and help.** You might want to briefly share a time in your life that was tough and how God helped you through it.

In today's Bible story, David goes through a very tough time. But he remembers to turn to God for help.

If you are separating the children into two groups (preschool and elementary) for the Bible story, ask the Park Patrol to lead the children to their respective areas. If all the children will stay together for the Bible story, use the Elementary Bible Story to teach the lesson.

ELEMENTARY BIBLE STORY
Tough Times for David (1 Samuel 30:1–20)

Supplies: Bible

Show the children 1 Samuel 30 in a Bible and explain that today's Bible story comes from there. Let volunteers briefly explain what they remember about David from the previous weeks' lessons.

Tell the children that they will help tell today's story. Have them practice crying, showing anger on their faces, looking sad, acting worried, looking scared, acting tired, and laughing to show happiness. Have the children stomp their feet where they are sitting to make the sound of marching in unison. When they have practiced all these at your direction, begin the story.

How would you feel if you came home from a trip and everything in your house was gone, including your pets? (Very angry.) Have the children demonstrate being angry. **That is just how David and his army felt when they came home from a long battle. Some very bad people, called the Amalekites, had invaded their town. The Amalekites had taken everything, including their wives and children! As you can imagine, the men were very sad and cried for days.** Have the children pretend to cry.

Then the men became very angry. Children show anger. **Who do you think they were angry with?** Let children suggest. **They were angry with David.** Children show anger still. **The men said, "If you hadn't taken us out to battle, we would have been here to fight off the Amalekites. We could have protected our families." The men wanted to throw stones at David.**

This was a tough time for David. Children act sad. **He had also lost his family, and now all his men were mad at him. David felt like giving up.** Children show sadness again. **But instead he went to the priest to ask God for help. David asked God, "What should I do? Should I chase them? If so, will I catch them?"** Children look worried. **God said, "Yes, go after them. I will help you get back everything and everyone that you have lost."** Children smile.

So David and his men marched out after the Amalekites. Children make marching sound on their legs. **On the way, some of the men**

became so tired they could not go on. Children act tired. **David told them to stay behind to protect their supplies, and he and the rest marched on.** Children make the marching sound.

On the way, they found a hurt man by the road. "Who are you?" David asked him. "And why are you here?"

The man was scared. Children act scared. **He told David, "Please don't hurt me and I will tell you. I was a slave of the Amalekites. They dumped me here when I got sick. The Amalekites just finished capturing the families of your town, and they are on their way back to their camp."**

David and his men rushed to the Amalekite camp. They fought the Amalekites for that night and the whole next day. And they rescued their families! Not one family member was hurt. Everyone rejoiced. Children act happy, clap, and cheer. **They also brought back all of their things that had been stolen.**

David was happy that he had talked to God when things got tough. We also should talk to God when life gets tough for us.

Why do you think David felt like giving up? (His men were angry with him and he had lost his family too.) **What did he do instead of giving up?** (He asked God for help.)

PRESCHOOL BIBLE STORY
A King Who Prays (1 Samuel 30:1–20)

Supplies: Bible

Show the children 1 Samuel 30 in your Bible. **Our Bible story comes from the book of the Bible called 1 Samuel.** Keep your Bible open as you tell the story.

Pat your knees to show walking. **David and his men were on their way home. They had been fighting for their country. They were happy to be going home.**

But when they got home, they saw something very sad. Pretend to cry. **All their houses were gone. Some bad people had taken their families to a faraway land.**

What should they do? Lift your hands in question. **The men wanted to hurt David for taking them away when their families needed them. But David knew he should pray.** Fold your hands. **David asked God what to do.**

God told David, "Go after your families. You will rescue them."

Pat your knees. **David and his men traveled after their families. They looked for their families and the bad people who took them. But they couldn't find them.** Put your hand over your eyes as if looking for something.

Along the way they found a man in a field. He was hungry and thirsty. They gave him food and water. Pretend to eat and drink. **The man knew where the families were. He took David and his men to where the bad people were camped. Their families would be there too.**

David and his men rescued their families! Not one family member was hurt. God had answered David's prayers.

Pat your knees. **David and his men took their families, animals, and things back home.**

David was sad when he found that his family had been taken. He talked to God when his life got tough. God helped him. We can talk to God when life gets tough.

Discuss a few review questions with the children. **What happened to David and his men?** (Their families were taken.) **How did David know what to do?** (He prayed to God.)

NOAH'S PARK PUPPETS
Muddy Days

Let any Park Patrol members not involved in the puppet presentation lead the children to the puppet stage by marching. Today's puppet skit can be found in the *Puppet Skits Book* on page RP-53. Encourage the children to be good listeners during the show.

BIBLE MEMORY
One Step at a Time

Supplies: Poster board, scissors, marker, masking tape, (optional: clear self-adhesive paper)

Preparation: Choose a Bible memory verse that supports today's lesson or one the children are working on in Sunday school. Cut poster board into large squares. Print one word on each square. (Cover with clear self-adhesive paper, if desired.) Tape each square in order on the floor, making a stepping-stone path. Wind the path throughout the room. If your group is large, you may want to make more word square sets in other colors so that the children can tell them apart. Tape the squares firmly to the floor so that they won't slip when the children step on them.

Say the verse together a few times. Discuss any unfamiliar words or concepts. Have the children form a line and take turns walking down the memory verse path. The others can recite the verse together as the child walks the path while they wait their turn, or you may want to have more than one on the path, if your group is large.

SINGING PRAISES TO JESUS

Supplies: Noah's Park CD and CD player

Have the children join together in singing the Unit 6 song, "Trust Him and Obey," from the Noah's Park CD. If you have strong readers, you might project the words on a wall or the board for the children to sing along with. As time permits, let the children suggest other songs they would like to sing to worship God.

SHARE AND PRAYER
Cloudy Days

Supplies: Gray construction paper, scissors, markers

Preparation: Cut out little gray clouds about 4" x 6," one for each child. Print on the board: "Talk to God when life gets tough."

In our Bible story lesson today we learned about a time when life was tough for David. He was discouraged and sad and confused. What did he do? (He talked to God.)

Pass out the clouds—one for each child. **Each of you has a little gray cloud today for our Share and Prayer time. The little gray cloud is a** picture of how we feel when life gets tough or we feel discouraged—kind of like a gray cloud is hovering over us. On one side of your cloud write, "Talk to God." Then turn your cloud over and write on the other side, "When life gets tough." Pass out markers, and give the children time to write.

Use these little gray clouds to remind you to talk to God when you are discouraged. Pray a short, simple prayer, showing how the children might talk to God about feeling discouraged. Ask if anyone else would like to pray aloud, and let these children do so. Close by thanking God for hearing and answering the children's prayers.

When you are feeling sad at school or at home, think of this little gray cloud that reminds you to talk to God. Remember we can talk to God anywhere and anytime. Be sure the children have their names on their clouds, and set them aside until the end of class.

Let the Park Patrol guide the preschoolers and elementary-age children to their separate areas for crafts, games, and snacks. You might let them use Noah's Park puppets to tell the children what they will do next. If you prefer, you can keep all the children together until after Snack Shack. Then have the Park Patrol lead the children to their areas.

SNACK SHACK
Lemonade and Donuts

Today's snack suggestion supports the opening "lemon story" from Teacher Feature. It is found on page RS-53 of the Noah's Park *Snacks and Games Book.* As the children enjoy their snack, let them tell Noah's Park puppets, worked by the Park Patrol, what they remember about the Bible story.

CAMPSITE CAPERS
David and the Amalekites (Elem.)
Can You Help Me Find My Brother (or Sister)? (Preschool)

The elementary game, "David and the Amalekites," is best played outdoors or in a large indoor area, such as a gym. The directions can be found on page RS-53 in the Noah's Park *Snacks and Games Book.* The preschoolers will play "Can You Help Me Find My Brother (or Sister)?" described on page RS-54.

COZY CAVE CRAFTS
"Helping David" Maze (Elementary)
Prayer Journal (Preschool)

The craft for the elementary children, "'Helping David' Maze," can be found on page RC-53 of the Noah's Park *Craft Book.* The children will be helping David through a maze to find his family. The preschool craft, "Prayer Journal," can be found on page RC-54 of the same book.

CLOSING ACTIVITIES

When today's activities are completed, have the Park Patrol use the Noah's Park puppets to direct the children to clean up the craft area. Then gather everyone together again in a group. Ask for volunteers to stand and tell which activity they enjoyed the most. All who also enjoyed that same activity can stand with them. Then call on another volunteer with another favorite activity.

Take a moment to review the Bible memory verse as a class. Then close in prayer. Be sure the children have their crafts, gray clouds from Share and Prayer, and any belongings.

OVERTIME ACTIVITIES

While the children are waiting for their parents, let them tell today's Bible story to the Noah's Park puppets, worked by the Park Patrol, or listen to the Noah's Park music CD.

R25 Lesson Give God Credit

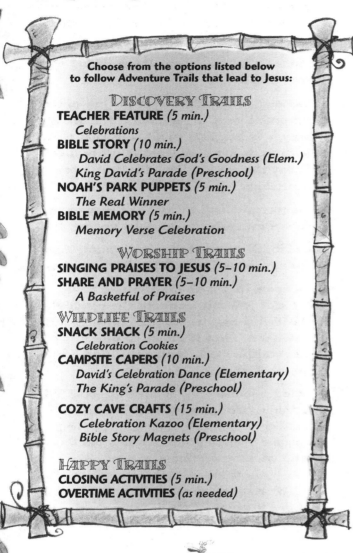

Choose from the options listed below
to follow Adventure Trails that lead to Jesus:

DISCOVERY TRAILS
TEACHER FEATURE (5 min.)
Celebrations
BIBLE STORY (10 min.)
David Celebrates God's Goodness (Elem.)
King David's Parade (Preschool)
NOAH'S PARK PUPPETS (5 min.)
The Real Winner
BIBLE MEMORY (5 min.)
Memory Verse Celebration

WORSHIP TRAILS
SINGING PRAISES TO JESUS (5–10 min.)
SHARE AND PRAYER (5–10 min.)
A Basketful of Praises

WILDLIFE TRAILS
SNACK SHACK (5 min.)
Celebration Cookies
CAMPSITE CAPERS (10 min.)
David's Celebration Dance (Elementary)
The King's Parade (Preschool)
COZY CAVE CRAFTS (15 min.)
Celebration Kazoo (Elementary)
Bible Story Magnets (Preschool)

HAPPY TRAILS
CLOSING ACTIVITIES (5 min.)
OVERTIME ACTIVITIES (as needed)

DISCOVERY TRAILS

TEACHER FEATURE

Celebrations

Supplies: Pictures of different holidays and celebrations

Preparation: Gather pictures of families celebrating a variety of holidays and special days, such as Thanksgiving, Christmas, birthdays, and Independence Day. Picture books from the children's section of the public library would be a good place to find these.

Hold up a picture of a family celebrating Thanksgiving. **What is this family celebrating?** (Thanksgiving Day.) **What does your family do on Thanksgiving Day?** Allow time for children to share about their traditions and experiences.

Hold up the picture of Christmas. **What is this celebration?** (Christmas.) **Why do we celebrate Christmas?** (Because Jesus was born.)

Hold up the picture of a birthday party. **How many of you like to go to birthday parties?** Let the children raise their hands. **Birthday parties are fun even if they're not for our birthday, aren't they? What are we celebrating at a birthday party?** (Turning a year older.)

Hold up the picture of an Independence Day celebration. **What is this celebration?** (Independence Day.) **What do we celebrate on this day?** (Our country became a nation.) **How do we celebrate?** Let children respond.

There are more times than these that we celebrate—baby showers, Valentine's Day, weddings, and many more. For many of the celebrations, we sing special songs like Christmas carols and "Happy Birthday." Every celebration is different.

In our Bible story today, we will learn about a big celebration. David even writes a special song for the occasion, and there is music and dancing. David and all the people celebrate God's goodness to them. It makes God happy when we remember to thank Him for all the good things He gives us and does for us.

Divide the children into their preschool and elementary groups, and have them follow the Park Patrol to their Bible story areas. They will come back together into a large group for the puppet skit.

ELEMENTARY BIBLE STORY

David Celebrates God's Goodness

(1 Samuel 31; 2 Samuel 2:1-7, 11; 5:1—6:19; Psalm 21)

Supplies: Bible, Bible-time clothes, microphones (or

something to serve as microphones), two clipboards with copies of the skit

Preparation: Ask a Park Patrol helper to play the part of the Announcer. Plan to play the role of Adibadab yourself. Place two chairs in front, facing each other. You and your helper should wear Bible-time clothes and sit facing each other, each holding a microphone and a clipboard with the script. Read with dramatic expression.

Before beginning, show the children the books of 1 and 2 Samuel in the Old Testament and explain that today's skit is based on these factual accounts. You may need to explain that the ark of the covenant was a large box that represented God's presence because it held special items that proved God's power.

Announcer: This is radio station KSAM coming to you *live* from Jerusalem. We are in the middle of what appears to be a huge celebration. There is music and dancing; I see tambourines and harps. Everyone is eating cakes with dates and raisins. Adibadab is here with me. Tell us, Adibadab, what is the celebration about?

Adibadab: Haven't you heard? David has been crowned king of all Israel!

Announcer: I thought David was king of only one part of the country.

Adibadab: Yes, he used to be—until now. When the old king, Saul, and his son Jonathan died in a battle, part of the country asked David to be the king. Now the rest of the country wants him to be their king too!

Announcer: What a happy day for David! Tell us, Adibadab, what has David been doing to help this whole country?

Adibadab: God helped David conquer the Philistines. They are people who kept attacking us. Then David made this great city, Jerusalem, our capital.

Announcer: Adibadab, hasn't David waited a long time to become king?

Adibadab: Yes! God told the prophet Samuel to anoint David king when he was just a young man! Now he is 30 years old. He

has been patiently waiting for God to keep His promise to make him king all these years. Now David has planned this celebration to give God credit for the good things that happen.

Announcer: Tell me about this parade I see over there.

Adibadab: David has brought the ark of the covenant here to Jerusalem. The ark is a very holy box that reminds us that God is with us. It has been kept in other towns. Today the ark has been brought into Jerusalem.

Announcer: Adibadab, what else is going on there? Everyone seems to be singing, too.

Adibadab: David wrote a song praising God for all He has done. It's called a Psalm.

Announcer: That is all the time we have, folks. If you can, come to the celebration. David is giving everyone cakes with raisins and dates. Now it's back to our celebration music here on station KSAM in Jerusalem.

Check for understanding with these questions. **What good things had happened to David?** (He became king after waiting many years, God helped him conquer the Philistines, etc.) **How did David respond when good things happened to him?** (He had a celebration to thank God and give Him credit.) **What were some of the special things David did to celebrate?** (He planned a parade, he gave out cakes, he brought the ark of the covenant to Jerusalem, etc.) **We need to remember to thank God when good things happen to us, too.**

PRESCHOOL BIBLE STORY
King David's Parade (1 Samuel 31; 2 Samuel 2:1-7, 11; 5:1—6:19; Psalm 21)

Supplies: Bible, completed set of Bible Story Magnets (*Craft Book*, p. RC-56), a metal baking sheet that magnets stick to

Preparation: Copy and color a set of Bible magnets from page RC-56 of the *Craft Book*. Add a piece of magnetic tape to the back of each figure.

Open your Bible to 1 Samuel 31. **Our story today comes from the Bible 1 and 2 Samuel in the Bible.** As you tell the story, hold the baking sheet in front of you, being sure all the children can see it.

King Saul had died. Who would be king next? God chose David to be king. Hold up the David figure. **All the men from one part of the country came to the town. There they made David their king.** Put the robe and crown on David. **David was king of that part of the country for 1-2-3-4-5-6-7 years.** Hold up your fingers.

Take off the robe and crown. **One day, men from another part of the country came to David. "You have always fought for our country. It is time for you to be king over the whole country instead of just part of it. God has said you will be the king." So David became king over the whole country.** Put the robe and crown on David.

David was a good king. He prayed to God for help in knowing the right things to do. Fold hands. **And God blessed David.** Point up.

After David had chased out the people who wanted to hurt the country, he chose one city to be the center of the country. This city was called Jerusalem.

Then David brought God's ark to the city. God's ark was a special box. It showed the people that God was with them. What a wonderful parade! The people were shouting. Wave your hands in the air and shout, "Praise God! Yea for King David!" **The trumpets were blowing.** Hold your fists in front of your mouth as if blowing a trumpet. **King David was leaping and dancing before God.** Move the David figure back and forth. **Then David gave gifts of food to everyone. The food was like raisin cookies.**

With everything he did, David gave God credit for the good things that happened. We can give God credit for good things too.

Use the figures to review the Bible story. **Who became king?** (David.) **How did David celebrate?** (He brought God's ark to the city, he planned a parade, etc.) **What did David do when he brought God's ark to the city?** (He danced.)

NOAH'S PARK PUPPETS
The Real Winner

When the Bible story time is over, have the children move to the area for the puppet presentation. You might have them pretend to be in a parade, with the Noah's Park puppets at the head. Today's skit can be found in the *Puppet Skits Book* on page RP-55. When the children are ready, begin the skit.

BIBLE MEMORY
Memory Verse Celebration

Supplies: Index cards, markers, Noah's Park CD and CD player

Preparation: Select a Bible verse from the Sunday school curriculum or one that supports today's lesson about praise or thanksgiving. Divide the verse into phrases. Print each phrase on a separate card, and number the cards. Make as many sets as you need so that each child gets one phrase card. Make sure that the phrases are numbered the same way—the first phrase is on card 1 in all sets, the second phrase is on card 2 in all the sets, and so on. Place chairs in a circle touching each other.

Read the verse to the children. Discuss with them any unfamiliar words. Then read the verse a few times, and have the children repeat it.

Have the children take a seat in the circle. Pass out a card to each child in random order. Start the music on the CD player. While the music plays, the children slide around the circle from chair to chair without standing up. When the music stops, call out, "Number 1." All the children holding cards numbered 1 stand up and read their phrase loudly in unison. Everyone cheers. The music begins again, briefly. Proceed like this until all the phrases have been read. Repeat as time allows.

WORSHIP TRAILS

SINGING PRAISES TO JESUS
Supplies: Noah's Park CD and CD player

Play the Unit 6 song, "Trust Him And Obey," from the *Noah's Park Children's Church CD*, and have the children sing along. You might let the children make up motions for this song and then sing it again.

SHARE AND PRAYER
A Basketful of Praises

Supplies: Butcher paper, masking tape, self-stick notepads, pencils

Preparation: Draw a large basket on butcher paper and tape it on a wall. (Or you may draw the basket on the board.) Set out several self-stick notepads and pencils so that everyone can reach them.

Today we are all about celebrating and praising God and giving Him credit for the good things that happen! On the sticky notes, write or draw something you want to thank God for. Then bring it up and stick it on the basket. You can write as many sticky notes as we have time. At the end we will read some of them and thank God together.

After a few minutes, read some of the sticky notes and thank God together. Let individual children say sentence prayers. For example, **"Thank You, God, for our families."**

Remember to thank God and give Him credit this week for the good things in your life. Each night thank Him for the good things that day.

Divide the class into age-appropriate groups of preschoolers and elementary-age children. Have Park Patrol members lead each group in a parade to their activity area.

SNACK SHACK
Celebration Cookies

Today's snack suggestion, "Celebration Cookies," can be found on page RS-55 of the *Snacks and Games Book.* As the children eat, let the Noah's Park puppets visit with them and ask about parades and celebrations the children have been to.

CAMPSITE CAPERS
David's Celebration Dance (Elementary)
The King's Parade (Preschool)

The elementary game is called "David's Celebration Dance" and is described on page RS-55 of the Noah's Park *Snacks and Games Book.* The preschoolers will be playing "The King's Parade," found on page RS-56 of the same book.

COZY CAVE CRAFTS
Celebration Kazoo (Elementary)
Bible Story Magnets (Preschool)

The elementary children will be making "Celebration Kazoos." The directions can be found on page RC-55 of the *Craft Book.* This craft will need a little drying time. The preschool craft, "Bible Story Magnets," will reinforce the Bible story. Instructions can be found in the same book on page RC-56. Be sure all the children have their names on their crafts.

CLOSING ACTIVITIES

When the children have completed their snack, games, and crafts, start the unit song on the CD player as a signal for cleanup. Let the Park Patrol set a good example by joining in.

When finished, gather the class together to review the memory verse. Also review the praise suggestions in the Basketful of Praises. Remind the children to give God credit for the good things in their lives. If you have time, sing the Unit 6 song.

OVERTIME ACTIVITIES

While waiting for parents to pick up their children, play the Noah's Park CD and let the children sing along and even march in a parade. They may be familiar with several songs by now. The children may enjoy using the puppets to sing and march with.

R26 Lesson: Ask God for Wisdom

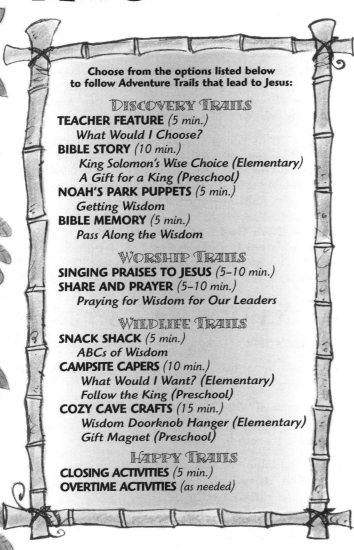

**Choose from the options listed below
to follow Adventure Trails that lead to Jesus:**

DISCOVERY TRAILS
TEACHER FEATURE *(5 min.)*
What Would I Choose?
BIBLE STORY *(10 min.)*
King Solomon's Wise Choice (Elementary)
A Gift for a King (Preschool)
NOAH'S PARK PUPPETS *(5 min.)*
Getting Wisdom
BIBLE MEMORY *(5 min.)*
Pass Along the Wisdom

WORSHIP TRAILS
SINGING PRAISES TO JESUS *(5–10 min.)*
SHARE AND PRAYER *(5–10 min.)*
Praying for Wisdom for Our Leaders

WILDLIFE TRAILS
SNACK SHACK *(5 min.)*
ABCs of Wisdom
CAMPSITE CAPERS *(10 min.)*
What Would I Want? (Elementary)
Follow the King (Preschool)
COZY CAVE CRAFTS *(15 min.)*
Wisdom Doorknob Hanger (Elementary)
Gift Magnet (Preschool)

HAPPY TRAILS
CLOSING ACTIVITIES *(5 min.)*
OVERTIME ACTIVITIES *(as needed)*

DISCOVERY TRAILS

TEACHER FEATURE
What Would I Choose?

Supplies: Gift bag with several items inside: chocolate candy bar, popular kids' DVD, action figure or doll, bottle of vitamins, money, the word "wisdom" printed on an index card

Everyone loves gifts, and today I have brought in some gifts to show you. One by one, take each gift out of the gift bag, except for the "wisdom" card. Pass around each item and let the children comment on what a nice gift that would make.

When all of the items have been returned, hold up each item, talk about it, and let the children vote on whether or not they would like to receive that gift.

I like your choices. Now let's talk about how helpful or long lasting these gifts might be. A candy bar is a good choice if you are hungry, but it doesn't last long and then you would be hungry again. A DVD is fun to watch but you get bored after watching it a few times. Action figures are fun, but they sometimes break or you outgrow playing with them. Vitamins help us keep healthy, but no one can live forever. Money is a great gift, but it gets spent quickly. These are all good gifts, but there is one gift left in my bag that we all could use over and over. Ask a child to reach into the bag, remove the card, and read the word.

Let volunteers offer definitions for "wisdom."
Wisdom is more than being smart or getting good grades. It's more than having common sense. Not everyone learns wisdom, not even people who have lived a very long time. Wisdom is knowing from God what is the right thing to do. Some wise people are smart and have common sense, too, but being wise is being able to tell right from wrong and being able to make tough choices.

Why do you think wisdom would make a good gift for you? (You could make good choices using wisdom, help you learn your schoolwork, use wisdom to please God, etc.) **Wisdom is a wonderful gift that comes from God. We don't have to take a test or pay money to get wisdom. All we have to do is ask God to teach us to be wise. God loves when we ask Him for wisdom! Let's learn more in our Bible story.**

Now is the time for Park Patrol helpers to lead preschoolers to their own area for the preschool Bible story. If all of the children stay together for Bible story time, use the Elementary Bible Story.

ELEMENTARY BIBLE STORY
King Solomon's Wise Choice
(1 Kings 3:5-15; 4:29-34)

Supplies: Bible, resealable plastic bag filled with sand

Today we are going to learn about a man who had something really amazing happen to him. We can read about it in the book of 1 Kings in our Bible. Show the children 1 Kings in your Bible. **As I tell you about this man, listen for a special word—wisdom. Whenever you hear me say "wisdom," stand up and point to your head and then quietly sit back down. Let's practice that right now as I say our special word, "wisdom."** Thank the children for following your directions and quietly being seated again.

A new king, named Solomon, was ruling over the people of Israel. Solomon had gone to a special place to give offerings to God. That night while King Solomon slept, God spoke to him in a dream. God asked Solomon a question. What do you think the question was? Let the children suggest questions.

God asked Solomon, "What would you like to get if you could have anything?" Solomon could ask for anything at all and God would give it to him! King Solomon knew this was the opportunity to get whatever he wanted. Since it was such an important question, he thought carefully about his answer. What do you think Solomon could have asked for? Let the children speculate. Encourage them to name several good possibilities, even if they know the answer already.

Finally Solomon replied, "I'm new to this job of being king and I'm pretty young. To be able to rule over these people, I really need wisdom. (Pause for the children to stand and do their motion.) **To know right from wrong, I need wisdom."** (Pause for the motion.)

God was so happy that King Solomon chose wisdom. (Pause for the motion.) **Solomon could have asked to be the richest person in the world, to live a long time, or to be really popular. God gave King Solomon so much wisdom** (pause for the motion) **that it couldn't be measured, just like the amount of sand on a beach can't be measured.** Hold up the sand and start to count the grains of sand. **Solomon had**

amazing wisdom (pause for the motion) **about plants, animals, birds, reptiles, and fish. People from all over the world heard about Solomon's wisdom** (pause) **and came to learn from him.**

God gave King Solomon a bonus—riches and glory. Solomon hadn't even asked for those, but God blessed him because of his wise choice of wisdom. (Pause.) **We also can ask God for wisdom.** (Pause.)

Ask a few review questions to be sure the children understood the important facts. **What was the question that God asked Solomon?** (What do you want Me to give you?) **What were some of the topics that Solomon taught people?** (About plants, animals, birds, reptiles, and fish.) **Why do you think God was so happy with Solomon's choice of wisdom?** (Answers might include: it wasn't selfish, he wanted to lead God's people well, etc.)

PRESCHOOL BIBLE STORY
A Gift for a King (1 Kings 3:5-15; 4:29-34)

Supplies: Bible, two boxes wrapped as gifts, paper, toy money

Preparation: Write "wisdom" on a piece of paper and put it in one of the wrapped boxes. Put the toy money in the other.

Keep your Bible open to 1 Kings as you tell the story. **Our story today comes from the book of the Bible called 1 Kings.**

The Bible tells us about a king named King Solomon. He loved God and worshiped Him. One night while he was sleeping, Solomon heard God speak to him. "I will give you whatever you ask Me for."

Solomon could have anything he wanted! What do you think Solomon should ask for? Put the box with the "wisdom" paper in front of you. Let children give ideas of what a king might ask for.

A king could ask for money. He could ask to be king for a long time. He could ask that other countries wouldn't fight his country. But Solomon didn't ask for any of these.

Solomon prayed, "God, You have made me the king over all Your people. So I know what

I need. As a king, I have to make many choices. Please give me the gift of wisdom. That way I can make good choices."

Wisdom doesn't mean that you know lots of things. It means that you know the right things to do.

Let the children open the box. Take out the piece of paper and read the word "wisdom" to the children. **God was pleased with Solomon's choice. "I will give you the gift of wisdom," God said. "You will know the right things to do. That is a good thing to ask for." So God made Solomon wise. He was the wisest man on earth!**

"Because you made such a good choice," God said, "I will give you other gifts—things like money and honor." Have the children open the box containing money.

God made Solomon a great and wise king. Solomon showed his love for God by making good choices and asking God for wisdom. We can ask God for wisdom too.

Ask a few review questions: **What did God offer Solomon?** (Solomon could ask for anything.) **What did Solomon ask for?** (Wisdom—knowing the right things to do.)

NOAH'S PARK PUPPETS
Getting Wisdom

Have the children line up and walk regally, like kings, over to the puppet stage. When the Park Patrol helpers are ready to present the skit, let the class be seated. Today's skit is found in the *Puppet Skits Book* on page RP–57.

BIBLE MEMORY
Pass Along the Wisdom

Supplies: Resealable plastic bag filled with sand (from the Elementary Bible Story), CD player, Noah's Park CD

Preparation: Choose a Bible verse relating to the topic of wisdom or use the verse the children learned in Sunday school to reinforce it. Print the verse on the board.

Help the children read the verse together as you point to each word. Say it together several times. Remind the children that it is *wise* to memorize Bible verses.

Ask the children to sit in a large circle. Hand a child the bag of sand. Explain to the children that the bag of sand reminds us of the amazing amount of wisdom that God gave Solomon because it was so much wisdom it couldn't be measured.

Be sure the sand bag is tightly sealed. While the CD is playing the unit song, the children will pass the bag of sand around the circle like a "hot potato." Remind them to carefully pass the bag of sand. When the music stops, the child holding the bag of sand gets to say the Bible memory verse. Continue playing until everyone has said the verse. If you have a large group, you might want to have two or three bags of sand to pass around at the same time.

Solomon asked God for wisdom, and God gave him as much wisdom as the sand on a beach. When we see God do amazing things like that in Solomon's life or in our own lives, we just want to praise Him!

SINGING PRAISES TO JESUS
Supplies: CD player and Noah's Park CD.

Since this is the first week of this unit, take a few minutes to talk about the meaning of the words in the Unit 7 song, "Living for You." You might want to project the song words (found on page 250 of this *Leader's Guide*) on a screen for the children who can read well. Encourage the children to sing along with the music. Play the song a second time. As time permits, sing more familiar songs that praise God for His wisdom.

SHARE AND PRAYER
Praying for Wisdom for Our Leaders
Supplies: None

We can ask God for wisdom for ourselves or for others. King Solomon wanted wisdom so that he could use it to be a good leader. Today many leaders need wisdom as they

lead and serve others. On the board, let's list people who could really use some wisdom to be good leaders. Have the children call out names of world leaders, leaders in your state or city, leaders at school and sports, etc., and leaders of your church. Also point out that parents are leaders and need prayer for wisdom.

All of these people could be better leaders if they used wisdom from God. Some of these leaders may not have a friendship with Jesus or may not even have heard of Him. But God still wants them to lead wisely. So today let's pray for God to give these leaders wisdom to make wise choices.

Break into small groups of both older and younger children. Ask each group to pray through the list of leaders. Have a Park Patrol helper read the names for the younger children.

The following age-appropriate activities work best by separating the older and younger children. The two groups could be in the same room at different tables (for crafts) and different areas (for games). Or you could arrange to use separate rooms for the two groups.

SNACK SHACK
ABCs of Wisdom

Today during snack time, the children will think about foods they could ask for that would be wise choices. Ask a member of the Park Patrol to set up the snack according to the directions found on page RS-57 in the *Snacks and Games Book*.

CAMPSITE CAPERS
What Would I Want? (Elementary)
Follow the King (Preschool)

Today's games reinforce the teaching about asking God for wisdom. Directions for the elementary game, "What Would I Want?" are on page RS-57 in the *Snacks and Games Book*. The preschool game, "Follow the King," is found on RS-58 in the same book.

COZY CAVE CRAFTS
Wisdom Doorknob Hanger (Elem.)
Gift Magnet (Preschool)

The elementary craft, "Wisdom Reminder," is designed to be a visual reminder that the children can and should ask God for wisdom. The directions are on page RC-59 in the *Craft Book*. The preschoolers have their own age-appropriate craft, "Gift Magnet," found on page RC-60. After all of the children have completed their crafts, place them where the children can get them as they leave the room to go home.

CLOSING ACTIVITIES

Encourage the children to make a wise choice to help put away all of the materials that were used and straighten up the room. Thank each child for choosing wisely and being part of the cleanup team.

King Solomon asked God for wisdom and so can we! As we end our time together, let's ask God to give us wisdom so that we can know how to love and treat others in a way that makes God happy. Gather the children in a large circle and hold hands (or two circles if your group is large). Begin by saying your own sentence prayer out loud and then continue around the circle.

Briefly review today's Bible memory verse. Pass out crafts and any other papers that need to be taken home. As the children leave, remind them to pray this week for God to give them wisdom.

OVERTIME ACTIVITIES

While waiting for parents to arrive, have the children talk about who they think is the wisest person they know and tell what makes that person seem so wise. You could make a "Top Ten Wisest People" list. Use any extra time to practice singing the new unit theme song.

R27 Lesson: Knowing What to Do

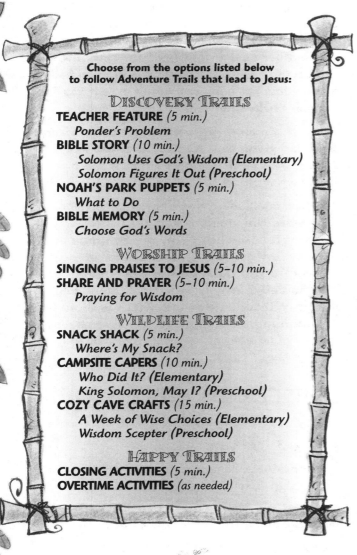

**Choose from the options listed below
to follow Adventure Trails that lead to Jesus:**

DISCOVERY TRAILS

TEACHER FEATURE (5 min.)
   Ponder's Problem
BIBLE STORY (10 min.)
   Solomon Uses God's Wisdom (Elementary)
   Solomon Figures It Out (Preschool)
NOAH'S PARK PUPPETS (5 min.)
   What to Do
BIBLE MEMORY (5 min.)
   Choose God's Words

WORSHIP TRAILS

SINGING PRAISES TO JESUS (5–10 min.)
SHARE AND PRAYER (5–10 min.)
   Praying for Wisdom

WILDLIFE TRAILS

SNACK SHACK (5 min.)
   Where's My Snack?
CAMPSITE CAPERS (10 min.)
   Who Did It? (Elementary)
   King Solomon, May I? (Preschool)
COZY CAVE CRAFTS (15 min.)
   A Week of Wise Choices (Elementary)
   Wisdom Scepter (Preschool)

HAPPY TRAILS

CLOSING ACTIVITIES (5 min.)
OVERTIME ACTIVITIES (as needed)

DISCOVERY TRAILS

TEACHER FEATURE
Ponder's Problem

Supplies: Ponder the puppet

Ponder wants you to help him to make a wise choice. Today his friends are going to a park and they asked him to go along. The problem is that Ponder's mom gave him a list of chores to do today and he hasn't even started to do
them. **Can you give Ponder some advice to help him make a wise choice?** Let the children tell Ponder their advice. Guide the children to see the importance of thinking about the consequences of not obeying his mother.

It sounds like you kids have lots of wisdom and have made wise choices. What are some wise choices you have made? Encourage children to share their choices with the group. As each child shares, let him or her speak to the Ponder puppet. Have the group applaud the wise choices.

Not everyone makes wise choices. You can probably think about some choices that you or other people made that weren't very smart. Let the children talk about some not-so-smart choices, like disobeying, cheating, hurting someone, taking without permission, lying, being mean, and so on.

Every day we make choices. Today at church you've made choices. You chose to come to our class; you chose to sit and listen. Thank you for your wise choices. Wouldn't it be great if everyone had wisdom to make wise choices every time? Let children comment. **Where can people go to get wisdom to help them make good decisions?** (Asking parents, reading the Bible, listening to the pastor or Sunday school teacher, studying books or taking classes, asking God, etc.)

There are many places where we can go to get wisdom to help us make a good choice, but the best way to get wisdom is to go to God. Our heavenly Father loves us and wants us to make wise choices. He promises to give us wisdom when we ask Him for it. Today we will learn about how He helped someone in the Bible to make a wise decision.

At this time, let the preschoolers and elementary children go to their separate Bible story areas. If you are keeping the groups together, use the Elementary Bible Story.

ELEMENTARY BIBLE STORY
Solomon Uses God's Wisdom
(1 Kings 3:16–28)

Supplies: Bible, baby doll, Bible-time clothes, toy sword (one cut from cardboard is fine)

Ask three Park Patrol helpers to act out the roles of Solomon and the two women as you read the Bible story. Turn to 1 Kings 3 to help the children understand that today's story is from the Bible.

Last week we talked about Solomon. Have the Solomon actor come. **God asked Solomon what gift he wanted. Who can tell me what Solomon asked God for?** (Wisdom.) **Yes, Solomon wanted wisdom so he could be a good leader of God's people.**

Not long after, two women came to Solomon with a problem. Have the two women actors come before Solomon. **Both women had lived in the same house and each woman had just given birth to a baby boy. Instead of being happy, the women were crying and only one woman was holding a baby.** Stop and let the children watch the women crying.

Have one actor pantomime telling her story to Solomon. **The first woman explained that during the night the other woman's baby had died. The other woman switched the babies, so this first woman now had a dead baby that wasn't hers.**

Solomon listened carefully. Then he asked the second woman to come and tell her side of the story. Have the other actor come. **This woman told Solomon that no way was the dead baby hers. The living baby was hers.**

Then the two women began to argue in front of Solomon. Let the actors display the rest of the scene for the group. **Finally, Solomon asked for a sword. "Cut the baby in two—give half to each woman," said Solomon. Everyone was shocked at Solomon's words.** Ask all the children to act shocked of hearing Solomon's answer.

Then the first woman cried and begged Solomon to let the second woman have the baby so that the baby would live. The other woman said to kill the baby because if she couldn't have the baby she didn't want the other woman to have it either.

Solomon wisely figured it out. "Give the baby to the first woman because she is the real mother," he said. Solomon figured out that the real mother would want her baby alive, even if she couldn't keep it. The second woman had already lost her baby and didn't care if the first woman's baby died too.

All of the people were amazed at the wisdom God had given that helped Solomon make such a wise choice. God's wisdom can help us know what to do too.

Ask these questions to check for comprehension. **Why were the women arguing?** (Each claimed the living baby was hers.) **Why did Solomon ask for a sword?** (He said he was going to cut the baby in half.) **Do you think he was really going to kill the baby? Why or why not?** Let children share their thoughts. **How did God's wisdom help Solomon in his decision?** (Solomon could see that only one woman really loved the child so it must be hers.)

PRESCHOOL BIBLE STORY
Solomon Figures It Out
(1 Kings 3:16–28)

Supplies: Bible, completed Wisdom Scepter (*Craft Book,* page RC-60)

Preparation: Make a Wisdom Scepter following the directions on page RC-60 of the *Craft Book.*

Our story today comes from the part of the Bible called 1 Kings. Show the children 1 Kings is in your Bible, and keep it open as you tell the Bible story.

God gave Solomon the gift of wisdom. He knew the right things to do. He knew how to figure out hard problems.

One day two women came to see King Solomon. Hold up one finger on each hand. **The two women lived in the same house.** Put your hands together with the two fingers showing. **They brought a baby boy with them.** Pretend to rock a baby.

One of the women had a problem to tell King Solomon. Hold up one finger on one hand. **She**

said that she had a baby boy. Hold up another finger on the hand. **A few days later the other woman also had a baby boy.** Hold up two fingers on your other hand. **But the second baby boy got hurt and died.** Take down one finger. **So now there was only one baby in the house but two mothers. The woman telling the story said that the other woman wanted the baby boy as her own.** Take down your hands.

The other woman had a story to tell too. She told King Solomon that the baby boy was hers. Hold up two fingers on one hand.

The two women each thought her story was right, but one of them was lying. What would King Solomon do? How would he decide which woman was the real mother of the baby boy?

Then King Solomon held up his scepter. Hold up the scepter. You may need to briefly explain that a king would hold this to show he was in charge. **"You both say the baby is your own," the king said. "What would happen if the baby boy got hurt?"**

The real mother of the baby boy didn't want that to happen. So she told King Solomon that the other woman could have her baby if the boy wasn't hurt. The other woman didn't care what happened to the baby boy.

Hold up the scepter again. **King Solomon knew that the woman who cared about the baby was the mother. She would keep the baby.** Hold up two fingers.

When the people of Israel heard what had happened, they knew that God's wisdom helped King Solomon know what to do. God's wisdom helps us know what to do.

Now discuss some review questions to be sure the children understood the Bible story: **What was the problem the two women had?** (They both said they were a baby's mother.) **What did Solomon's wisdom help decide?** (Which woman was the baby's mother.)

NOAH'S PARK PUPPETS
What to Do

Bring out a Noah's Park puppet and have it lead the children to the puppet stage. See page RP-59 in the

Puppet Skits Book. for today's skit. Have the puppet encourage the children to be "wise" listeners as they watch the puppet play.

BIBLE MEMORY
Choose God's Words

Supplies: Index cards

Preparation: Choose a Bible verse that enforces the idea of God's wisdom helping us know what to do. You may want to use a memory verse learned during Sunday school time. Print each word of the Bible verse on a separate index card. Make three to five extra cards with words that are clearly not part of the verse.

Hold up each card as you read it. Put the cards in the correct order on the floor or a table where all of the children can see them. Have the children practice reading the words as you point to them.

Seat the children in groups of three or four. Be sure that each group has a mature reader. Mix all of the cards and spread them out on the floor. Call a group of children to come and gather up the words from the verse and put them in the correct order. Congratulate them for wisely choosing God's words and leaving the others. Continue mixing cards and calling groups until all the groups have had a turn. You may want to use a stopwatch to time the groups.

God loves to help us know what to do. Every time we ask, God gladly shares His wisdom with us. This makes me want to praise Him!

SINGING PRAISES TO JESUS
Supplies: Noah's Park CD and CD player

Begin your praise time by reviewing the words to the unit song, "Living for You," from the Noah's Park CD. If you have a class of strong readers, copy the lyrics from the back of this *Leader's Guide* and project them on a wall for the children to follow along with. (See page 250.) Sing through the song a couple of times. Ask a child to choose a favorite worship song to sing next. If time allows, ask another child to suggest a song.

SHARE AND PRAYER
Praying for Wisdom

Supplies: Slips of paper, pencils

Pass out slips of paper, and have each child write his or her name on one. Ask a Park Patrol helper to collect the names, mix them up, and hand each child a name. Be sure no one receives his or her own name.

King Solomon asked God for wisdom, and we learned that God gave him wisdom. Solomon wanted wisdom so that he would know what to do as he ruled God's people. We all want to know the right thing to do during our week, so we are going to pray for each other to have God's wisdom and know what to do, just like King Solomon.

Choose a child to come to where you are and read the name he was given. That child can come and join you. Let the first child pray for the other child to seek God's wisdom and for God to help him to know the right things to do. Both children can return to their seats. Continue until each child has been prayed for by another child. End the prayer time by asking God to help each child know the wise thing to do.

The following age-appropriate activities work best by separating the older and younger children. The two groups could be in the same room at different tables (for crafts) and different areas (for games). Or you could arrange to use separate rooms for the two groups.

SNACK SHACK
Where's My Snack?

Today's healthy choice of a snack will be hidden under a bowl. Each child will have fun wisely choosing which bowl is concealing his or her snack. Even though the choice is really just a guess, it helps the children realize that they do make choices all the time. The instructions for the snack are found on page RS-59 of the *Snacks and Games Book*.

CAMPSITE CAPERS
Who Did It? (Elementary)
King Solomon, May I? (Preschool)

Preschoolers and elementary students will both play games that tie in with the theme of making wise choices. The preschool game, "King Solomon, May I?" is found on page RS-60 of the *Snacks and Games Book*. The elementary game, "Who Did It?," is found on RS-59.

COZY CAVE CRAFTS
A Week of Wise Choices (Elementary)
Wisdom Scepter (Preschool)

The elementary-age craft is a wonderful reminder to ask God for wisdom during the coming week. You will find this craft on page RC-61 of the *Noah's Park Craft Book*. Preschoolers have their own craft, "Wisdom Scepter," shown on RC-62. Look over the supply list and be sure to have everything prepared before the children begin craft time.

CLOSING ACTIVITIES

A few minutes before class time is over, give a signal to clean up the activities. Encourage each child to make the wise choice of helping to clean up the activity areas. Ask the Park Patrol helper who played the role of Solomon to walk around pointing out children who are being wise by helping.

After inspecting each area, have the children gather their crafts and anything else they brought with them. Have the Park Patrol help preschoolers get their things and sit together in a large group. As time permits, let the preschoolers explain their crafts to the elementary children, and vice versa. Close the class time with a prayer thanking God for wisdom and asking Him to help the children do the right thing during the week.

OVERTIME ACTIVITIES

As the children wait for their parents to come, write the word "wisdom" vertically down the white board. Have the children write ideas of wise choices they could make that start with one of the letters in the word. For example, you might write W—wait my turn; I—invite someone to church; and so on.

R28 Lesson Jesus Opens the Way to God

Choose from the options listed below to follow Adventure Trails that lead to Jesus:

DISCOVERY TRAILS
TEACHER FEATURE (5 min.)
Group Charades
BIBLE STORY (10 min.)
Solomon Builds the Temple (Elementary)
A Place to Praise God (Preschool)
NOAH'S PARK PUPPETS (5 min.)
Secret Valley
BIBLE MEMORY (5 min.)
Bible Verse Leapfroggers

WORSHIP TRAILS
SINGING PRAISES TO JESUS (5–10 min.)
SHARE AND PRAYER (5–10 min.)
Praise Prayers

WILDLIFE TRAILS
SNACK SHACK (5 min.)
Build a Snack
CAMPSITE CAPERS (10 min.)
Temple Workers Mix-up (Elementary)
Building the Temple (Preschool)
COZY CAVE CRAFTS (15 min.)
Stand-up Temple (Elementary)
Worship Doorknob Hanger (Preschool)

HAPPY TRAILS
CLOSING ACTIVITIES (5 min.)
OVERTIME ACTIVITIES (as needed)

DISCOVERY TRAILS

TEACHER FEATURE
Group Charades

Supplies: None

When we want to celebrate someone, there are many different ways we can do that. Let's play a game of Group Charades to figure out some of those ways.

Divide into groups of four or five. Call up each group

and whisper a scenario to them from the list below. If necessary, quietly talk through how they could briefly portray the scene. It's okay if they use sounds and words to act out their scene. Let each group act out at least one scene. Make up more as needed.

Use scenarios like these:

1. A birthday party (the kids might sing "Happy Birthday" to one child)
2. Applauding a child who has just won an event (perhaps cheering her on first)
3. Eating out at a restaurant (which could be something like Mother's Day or rewarding a good report card)
4. Giving hugs to someone they haven't seen in a long time, such as a grandparent
5. A teacher giving out stickers to students with good work
6. Giving an award or trophy

When finished, discuss celebrations of people with the class. **What are ways your family or friends have celebrated *you*?** Let volunteers share.

In our Bible story today, King Solomon wanted to help his people celebrate Someone very special—and that was God. Let's see what the people did to show God that He was special and deserved their praise.

Let the Park Patrol lead the children to the preschool and elementary Bible story areas. If you are keeping the groups together, be sure to use the Elementary Bible Story.

ELEMENTARY BIBLE STORY
Solomon Builds the Temple
(1 Kings 5:1—9:9; 1 Chronicles 29:1-9;

Hebrews 9; Matthew 27:51)

Supplies: Bible, (optional: large appliance box)

Show the children 1 Kings in your Bible. Then show them the books of Hebrews and Matthew, and explain that parts of the New Testament help us understand parts of the Old Testament.

King Solomon wanted to do something **special for God. And the king wanted his people to be able to praise God in a special place. Solomon decided to build a temple—a place where all the people could come to praise God that would be so spectacular it would be like no other building.** A temple is like a huge, beautiful church or cathedral.

Building the temple would be a huge job for about 180,000 workers! Let's pretend to be some of those workers and build a temple. Place the large box in the center of your area. Have groups stand a little ways off from the box, one group on each side.

Many kinds of workers were needed. One kind was the stonecutters. Ask a fourth of the class to go stand where you direct them. **Stonecutters cut huge stone blocks that formed the outside walls.** Have this group act out cutting the blocks. **They cut the blocks far away from the temple site and then hauled them back. This was so there would be no loud and annoying noises in the place of God's temple. Even though it was hard work, the people remembered that they were doing it to build a special place to praise God.**

Woodcutters cut the wood to make the inside beams and the boards for the walls. Choose another fourth of the class to go stand opposite the stone cutters. **The woodcutters took a very beautiful kind of wood called cedar and cut it to the right size and shape.** Have this group act out cutting long beams and boards and sanding.

Next, wood-carvers put on the details. Have another fourth of the class stand in a third spot. **Wood-carvers cut designs—of fruits and flowers—onto the cedar wood walls. The cedar doors had carvings of angels, palm trees, and flowers.** Let this group act out carving with chisels and gouges. You may need to demonstrate this.

The temple of God was decorated with lots of gold to show that God was worthy of the most expensive things. Gold workers put gold everywhere! Have the last portion of the class stand and pretend to hammer and press gold. **They put gold on the walls, the ceiling, the floor,** and the altar. **It was beautiful, like artwork.**

Have groups pretend to do their crafts. Then ask the stonecutters to "carry" stones to the box and stack them up. Next, the woodcutters place the "wood" around the "stones." Have the wood-carvers carve into the wood. Then let the gold workers press and hammer their gold on the "temple."

What did they do for furniture and utensils in the temple? A really good artist named Hiram made bronze furniture and statues for the temple. The people worked for seven years building the temple! Solomon had been wise to build a place where the people could come and praise God. The temple was a great place to celebrate the Lord. Let the children be seated around the pretend temple they just built.

Inside the temple were rooms. One very special room was called the "Most Holy Place." It was to remind people that God was so special and holy and perfect that no one was good enough to see Him or be with Him. Only once a year, one person—the high priest—was allowed to go into the Most Holy Place. He brought special offerings to God. There was a huge, thick curtain in the doorway so people couldn't even see in.

But all of that changed when Jesus came to earth. He knew that God wanted His people to talk directly to Him—even outside of the temple or any building. When Jesus died on the cross for our sins, the curtain in the temple was torn in two. God did that to show that Jesus opened the way to Him. Now we can pray and talk to God whenever we want.

Review the key facts of the Bible story. **Why did Solomon want to build a temple?** (To give the people a place to come and praise God.) **What kinds of workers built the temple?** (Stone-cutters, wood-cutters, wood-carvers, and gold workers.) **What was the Most Holy Place for?** (It showed that God was holy.) **Why can we talk directly to God now?** (Because Jesus died on the cross for our sins—He opened the way to God.)

PRESCHOOL BIBLE STORY
A Place to Praise God (1 Kings 5:1—9:9; 1 Chronicles 29:1-9; Hebrews 9; Matthew 27:51)

Supplies: Bible, three rectangular boxes of three different sizes, fabric, cross

Preparation: Keep the smallest box intact. Tape fabric to one side to represent the Most Holy Place. Cut the top and bottom off the other two boxes—middle-sized box=the Holy Place; large box=the outside perimeter of the temple. Put bookmarks in 1 Chronicles 29, Hebrews 9, and Matthew 27.

Show the children the different places in the Bible you have marked. **Our story today comes from many books of the Bible. One of the parts of the Bible is 1 Kings.**

King Solomon wanted to build a special church building for God. The building would be called a temple. God would have a place where people could come and pray to Him.

When Solomon became king, it was time to build the temple. Hammer with your fists. **Many people worked many years to build a wonderful temple. First some workers cut white stone into large blocks. They built the outside walls with these. Then other people cut beautiful wooden boards for the inside walls. Once the walls were up, some people carved designs and pictures into the wood. And then some people made gold decorations to cover the walls. It was a wonderful sight!**

In the middle of the temple was a room called the Most Holy Place. Put the smallest box in front of you. **A special curtain covered the door. Only one man was allowed to go into the Most Holy Place.**

Next was the Holy Place. Put the middle-sized box around the Most Holy Place. **This was where the priests did many of their jobs to serve God. The people couldn't go there, but some of them could see what the priests did.**

Then there was the outside part of the temple. Put the largest box around the other boxes. **This part was where all the people could go to praise God.**

When the temple was finished and everything was in its place, a huge cloud filled the temple. It was the glory of the Lord. God was in the Most Holy Place.

When Jesus died on the cross, the curtain covering the door of the Most Holy Place

ripped into two pieces. Fold the fabric up. Put the cross in its place. **Because Jesus died for our sins, we can go to God and worship Him. We don't need priests to do the work as they did in King Solomon's time. Jesus opens the way to God so we can praise Him.**

Ask a few review questions: **Who built the temple?** (King Solomon and many workers.) **What happened when Jesus died on the cross?** (He opened the way so we can praise God.)

NOAH'S PARK PUPPETS
Secret Valley

After the Bible story time, let any Park Patrol helpers not involved in the skit lead the groups to the puppet stage. When ready, present the skit found on page RP-61 in the *Puppet Skits Book.*

BIBLE MEMORY
Bible Verse Leapfroggers

Preparation: Choose a Bible verse that supports today's lesson. A verse the children have been learning in Sunday school may be a good choice.

Print the Bible memory verse on the board. Say the verse together as you point to each word. Repeat the verse a few times until it is familiar to the class.

Have children line up. Choose one child to say the verse. Then that child crouches down on the floor. The next child in line says the verse and then goes up and "leapfrogs" over the crouching child. To leapfrog, the child runs up, puts his or her hands on the crouching child's back, and jumps over the child. Continue until all of the children have had a chance to say the verse and leapfrog over someone.

When the temple was finished, King Solomon led all the people to praise and worship God. We can praise God right now too.

SINGING PRAISES TO JESUS
Supplies: Noah's Park CD and CD player

Begin worship time by playing the unit song, "Living

for You." Remind the children that singing is a great way to praise God.

SHARE AND PRAYER
Praise Prayers

Supplies: None

King Solomon built a beautiful temple to praise God. Then Jesus opened the way to God, showing us that God doesn't really live in a temple and that we can praise and pray to Him any time and anywhere.

Let's talk about all the wonderful things that God has done that we could praise Him for. Let volunteers share. Encourage the children to tell about ideas specific to their lives rather than just general ones.

Let's have some prayer time and tell God how great He is. You may call out your prayers to God and begin your sentence like this, "God, I praise you because You . . ." Then you can finish the sentence by naming some of the wonderful things He has done. You may want the children to stand in a circle and take turns going clockwise around the circle. Model the first prayer for the kids and then let them take turns praising God through their prayer. Encourage the children to pray several things. For example: "God, I praise You because You helped my dad get a job."

Let the Park Patrol members help you divide the preschoolers from the elementary-age kids for games, crafts, and snack.

SNACK SHACK
Build a Snack

The children will use a variety of snack items to build a small-scale temple that they will then eat. Read the instructions on RS-61 of the *Snacks and Games Book.*

CAMPSITE CAPERS
Temple Workers Mix-up (Elementary)
Building the Temple (Preschool)

The preschoolers will play "Building the Temple." Directions are on RS-62 in the Noah's Park *Snacks and Games Book.* The elementary game is called "Temple Workers Mix-up" and is found on RS-61 in the same book. Be sure to include Park Patrol helpers in these activities to assist you and the children.

COZY CAVE CRAFTS
Stand-up Temple (Elementary)
Worship Doorknob Hanger (Preschool)

Today's crafts will help the children remember that Jesus opened the way to God so that we can praise Him. "Stand-up Temple," the elementary craft, is found on RC-61 of the *Craft Book.* The preschool craft, "Worship Doorknob Hanger," is provided on page RC-62 of the *Craft Book.*

CLOSING ACTIVITIES

Encourage the children to help you straighten the room after they have finished their snacks, games, and crafts. You may want to quietly play the unit song, "Living for You," as the children are working. They might pick up scraps from the floor and put away pencils, crayons, or craft items. Praise them as they get the room cleaned up.

When they have finished cleaning, gather the children into a large group on the floor for closing activities. Make sure each child has his or her craft. Let the elementary-age children take turns showing their mobiles to the group and explaining how Jesus opened the way to God. Give the preschoolers an opportunity to share their crafts with the group as well. End the time with a review of the memory verse and a closing prayer.

OVERTIME ACTIVITIES

While waiting for parents to pick up their children, you could sing one of the songs from the Noah's Park CD. In addition, you may ask one of the Park Patrol members to read to the children from a Bible storybook.

R29 Lesson: Don't Let Anything Turn You from God

Choose from the options listed below to follow Adventure Trails that lead to Jesus:

DISCOVERY TRAILS
TEACHER FEATURE (5 min.)
What Changes Your Mind?
BIBLE STORY (10 min.)
Solomon Turns from Obeying God (Elem.)
The King Who Left God (Preschool)
NOAH'S PARK PUPPETS (5 min.)
U-Turn
BIBLE MEMORY (5 min.)
Pass It Along

WORSHIP TRAILS
SINGING PRAISES TO JESUS (5-10 min.)
SHARE AND PRAYER (5-10 min.)
Worldwide Worshippers

WILDLIFE TRAILS
SNACK SHACK (5 min.)
Be Wise Snack
CAMPSITE CAPERS (10 min.)
Come, Be Wise (Elementary)
Jereboam Tag (Preschool)
COZY CAVE CRAFTS (15 min.)
Turn-around King Solomon (Elementary)
King Solomon Stand-up Figures (Pre.)

HAPPY TRAILS
CLOSING ACTIVITIES (5 min.)
OVERTIME ACTIVITIES (as needed)

DISCOVERY TRAILS

TEACHER FEATURE
What Changes Your Mind?

Supplies: Plate of cookies

Preparation: Ask Park Patrol members to prepare the two short skits.

Have two Park Patrol members perform this skit for the class:

Actor 1 carries plate of cookies.

Actor 2: **Yum! Cookies!**
Actor 1: **I'm sorry, you can't have any. There's only just enough for my sister's class.**
Actor 2: **They sure look good.**
Actor 1: **And smell good too. I've really been wanting one.**
Actor 2: **Aw, come on. It's just one cookie. You deserve one for helping your mom.**
Actor 1: (*Thinks it over.*) **Well, I guess just one would be okay.** (*Takes a cookie, breaks it in half for Actor 2, walks off with Actor 2.*)

Have another pair come right on and perform this skit:

Friend 1 & 2 enter from opposite sides.

Friend 1: **Hi! Are you coming to watch my game tomorrow? You promised!**
Friend 2: **I can't. I forgot I have Sunday school.**
Friend 1: **But that's not important! You'd have more fun at the game.**
Friend 2: **I'm sorry. But I really shouldn't miss church. It's where I learn about God.**
Friend 1: **My game is going to be really fun. And there are snacks afterward. You really should come.**
Friend 2: **Let me ask my dad if I can skip Sunday school.** (*Both exit.*)

Thank the actors for their great performance. **What was the first kid supposed to do in the first skit?** (Deliver some cookies.) **What turned this kid from what was right?** (Wanting to eat one.) **What was the problem in the second skit?** (The friend wanted to go watch a game instead of going to Sunday school.) **What turned this kid from doing what was right?** (The friend making him think the game would be more fun.)

Sometimes when we know the right thing to do, we don't do it anyway. We let something turn us from God's way. Our Bible story today is about someone who loved God very much, but he let some things and some people turn him from God.

Let the Park Patrol lead the preschoolers and the elementary-age children to their respective Bible story areas. The children will rejoin for the puppet skit.

ELEMENTARY BIBLE STORY
Solomon Turns from Obeying God
(1 Kings 11—12)

Supplies: Bible, poster board, marker, two large cardboard boxes, (optional: toy crown for Solomon)

Preparation: Make two large signs, one reading "Yes! Yes!" and one reading "No! No!" Recruit three Park Patrol members to help—one to play the silent role of Solomon and two to hold cue cards. Draw lines on one box to represent the temple. On the other box draw a decorative, idol-looking face. Place the boxes at opposite sides of the story area.

Show the children where to find today's story in your Bible. Point out the temple box. Point to the box with the face and say that it will represent an idol— a statue that people would pray to.

When Solomon first became king, he was a very good king. "Solomon" should stand in the middle. **He cared very much about being a good leader for God's people, and he prayed only to God.** Hold up the "Yes! Yes!" sign. Encourage the children to cheer this at Solomon.

As the years went by, King Solomon wanted to get married to a woman from a foreign country. In her country the people prayed to idols. God had said not to marry those women. Solomon walks toward the idol box looking like he's thinking hard and looking back and forth between the temple and the idol. Have the helper hold up the "No! No!" sign as he walks to the idol. Let children shout no! **But Solomon married the woman anyway. He let his feelings for her turn him from God. King Solomon was not wise to disobey God's laws.**

God had another law. He said that a man should marry only one woman. Solomon walks toward the temple box. Hold up the "yes" sign and let children cheer him. **But Solomon decided he didn't like that rule either. He married hundreds and hundreds of women from other countries.** Solomon walks slowly toward the idol box. Hold up the "no" sign for children to shout, but Solomon keeps going. **The new wives brought their idols with them to Israel. He let his**

wives turn him from God. It wasn't wise of Solomon to break this law of God's either.

God had given the people of Israel another very important law. He said that the people should pray only to Him. Solomon walks toward the temple box with hands in prayer. Hold up the "yes" sign and children shout to encourage him. **Solomon loved God. Wouldn't this be an easy rule to follow? But Solomon wanted to make his wives happy.** Solomon walks toward the idol box. Hold up the "no" sign. **Solomon started praying to the idols the women had brought from their countries. He let the idols turn him from God. Solomon disobeyed God. He wasn't using his wisdom.**

The Bible tells us that God became angry with Solomon. God decided that for punishment, Solomon's country would be split apart after he died. His son and grandsons wouldn't get to be kings over all Israel. Have Solomon look sad and sit down in the middle.

This is what happened. A servant of the king, named Jeroboam, was walking in the countryside. God sent a prophet to him. The prophet took off his new cloak and tore it into 12 pieces. He gave 10 pieces to Jeroboam and explained, "God says that after Solomon dies of old age, the country will divide into 12 parts. Ten of the parts will follow you as king!" Later on, when Solomon's son became king, he was very mean. Ten parts of Israel formed their own country with Jeroboam as their king.

It was all because Solomon let things and people turn him from God. We shouldn't let anything turn us from God either.

Ask some review questions to check that the children grasped the main concept. **In what ways did Solomon turn from God?** (He married many foreign women and prayed to idols.) **What was his punishment?** (The kingdom of Israel would be divided.)

PRESCHOOL BIBLE STORY
The King Who Left God (1 Kings 11—12)

Supplies: Bible, King Solomon figures (*Craft Book,* p. RC-64)

Preparation: Make a complete set of Solomon figures from page RC-64 of the *Craft Book*.

Our story today is from the book of the Bible called 1 Kings. Show 1 Kings in your Bible.

King Solomon ruled the kingdom of Israel for many years. Put the figure of King Solomon in front of you. **But he didn't make wise decisions. He didn't follow God's rules. Solomon married many women. Those women didn't love God. They worshiped pretend gods. King Solomon built statues of these pretend gods for people to worship. He didn't keep his promise to worship only God.**

So God punished him. God told King Solomon that his country would be split apart after he died. His son wouldn't have the great kingdom that Solomon had enjoyed.

One day, a helper of Solomon's, named Jeroboam, was walking in the country. Remove the figure of Solomon. Put the figure of Jeroboam in front of you. **Jeroboam met a man wearing a new coat.** Put the figure of Ahijah next to Jeroboam. **The man ripped his new coat into 12 pieces. He asked Jeroboam to take 10 of the pieces. "God will split apart the kingdom of Israel," the man told Jeroboam. "King Solomon's son will rule over only two groups of people. You will rule over the rest."** Remove the figures of Jeroboam and Ahijah.

After King Solomon died, his son became king. Put the figure of Rehoboam in front of you. **But this son was a mean king. So Jeroboam and most of the people made their own country.** Set Jeroboam next to Rehoboam. **Because the kings didn't listen to God, He split the country apart. That was what happened because Solomon let things turn him from God.**

Discuss these review questions: **Who stopped worshiping God?** (King Solomon.) **What happened because of his sins?** (God split his country.)

NOAH'S PARK PUPPETS
U-Turn

Have Ponder the puppet lead the children over to the puppet skit area. On the way, have the children stretch and hop to help them sit quietly during the puppet skit. Today's puppet presentation is found in the Noah's Park *Puppet Skit Book* on page RP-63.

BIBLE MEMORY
Pass It Along

Supplies: Balloon or ball

Preparation: Choose a Bible verse for the children to memorize that supports today's lesson. You may want to take the verse the children learned in Sunday school and further practice it.

Have the children form a long line. If your group is very large, you might want to break the class into two groups. Say the verse for the class and have them repeat each phrase after you. Do this a few times so that it becomes familiar.

Give the balloon or ball to the first child in the line. Have the whole class say the first word of the verse as the child hands the ball over his head to the person behind him. That child takes the ball and passes it between her legs to the next child as the whole class says the second word of the verse. The third child passes the ball over her head when the class says the third word. Continue with each child passing the ball in an over, under pattern as the class says each word of the verse.

When the ball reaches the end of the line, continue saying the verse and pass the ball forward through the line. If the children learn the verse quickly, have only the child passing the ball call out the word as it is passed.

If we want to make sure that nothing turns us from God, we need to stay focused on Him, praying to Him and worshiping Him. Let's worship Him now as we sing our praises.

WORSHIP TRAILS

SINGING PRAISES TO JESUS
Supplies: Noah's Park CD and CD player

Since this is the last week of the "Wise to Advise" unit, be sure to give the children an opportunity to sing the unit song. If available, let the children play rhythm instruments along with it. Take time to sing another song or two from the Noah's Park CD.

SHARE AND PRAYER
Worldwide Worshippers

Supplies: World map or globe, (optional: pictures of missionaries your church supports)

Gather the children around the globe. Let a volunteer find North America. Some children may be able to find your state.

All around the world there are many people who don't know the one true God or worship Him. Solomon knew the one true God but let himself be turned from following Him.

Let's pray for people around the world that they might learn about Jesus. If using the map, toss a coin onto the map. If using the globe, spin the globe and place your pointer finger on the globe. Lead the children in praying for the people of the country under the coin or finger. Be sure to give volunteers a chance to pray for these people too. (For example: Ecuador—"Dear God, please help the people of Ecuador learn about You and worship only You. Amen.")

Repeat as you have time, choosing different spots around the world. If you have pictures of missionaries, show the children where they work and pray for the people in those countries.

The preschoolers and elementary-age children have separate activities for this part of the lesson. Ask the Park Patrol to help the children transition to their separate areas.

SNACK SHACK
Be Wise Snack

Today's snack will reinforce that children need to make wise choices. Turn to page RS-63 of the *Snacks and Games Book* to find the list of ingredients and directions.

CAMPSITE CAPERS
Come, Be Wise (Elementary)
Jeroboam Tag (Preschool)

Elementary students will enjoy playing the fun game "Come, Be Wise" that is found on page RS-63 of the *Snacks and Games Book*. The preschool game "Jeroboam Tag" is found on page RS-64 of the same book. Have the Park Patrol members help guide children to the game area and cheer their game.

COZY CAVE CRAFTS
Turn-around King Solomon (Elem.)
King Solomon Stand-up Figures (Pre.)

Crafts are a wonderful visual reminder of the lesson focus and can be used as a family discussion starter. You will find directions for the elementary craft, "Turn-around King Solomon," on page RC-63 of the *Craft Book*. Preschoolers will enjoy their craft, "King Solomon Stand-up Figures," with directions on page RC-64 of the *Craft Book*. Be sure to label the crafts with the children's names.

CLOSING ACTIVITIES

Give the children time to clean up and put away all materials used in today's activities. Remind the children to make a wise choice and help clean up. Choose an appropriate place for the children to set their crafts and any other items they need to take home.

When the room is cleaned, have the children say the Bible memory verse together, or let volunteers say it for the class. You may also choose two or three older children to give a quick summary about the life of King Solomon over the past four weeks.

OVERTIME ACTIVITIES

With any leftover time, the children can act out scenes from King Solomon's life and let the other children guess what scene is being portrayed. If you have Bible-time clothes in the room, let the kids use them and put them away when they're finished.

R30 Lesson: Sin Always Has Consequences

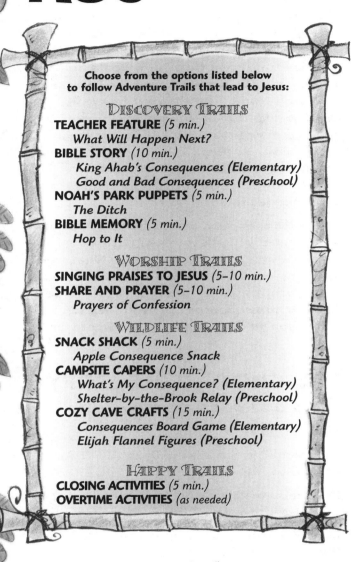

Choose from the options listed below to follow Adventure Trails that lead to Jesus:

DISCOVERY TRAILS
TEACHER FEATURE *(5 min.)*
　What Will Happen Next?
BIBLE STORY *(10 min.)*
　King Ahab's Consequences (Elementary)
　Good and Bad Consequences (Preschool)
NOAH'S PARK PUPPETS *(5 min.)*
　The Ditch
BIBLE MEMORY *(5 min.)*
　Hop to It

WORSHIP TRAILS
SINGING PRAISES TO JESUS *(5–10 min.)*
SHARE AND PRAYER *(5–10 min.)*
　Prayers of Confession

WILDLIFE TRAILS
SNACK SHACK *(5 min.)*
　Apple Consequence Snack
CAMPSITE CAPERS *(10 min.)*
　What's My Consequence? (Elementary)
　Shelter-by-the-Brook Relay (Preschool)
COZY CAVE CRAFTS *(15 min.)*
　Consequences Board Game (Elementary)
　Elijah Flannel Figures (Preschool)

HAPPY TRAILS
CLOSING ACTIVITIES *(5 min.)*
OVERTIME ACTIVITIES *(as needed)*

DISCOVERY TRAILS

TEACHER FEATURE
What Will Happen Next?

Supplies: Inflated balloon, small ball, tall clear glass, baking soda, vinegar

We are going to play a game today that lets you guess what will happen next. Hold up an inflated balloon. **I'm going to start with this balloon. Guess what will happen when I sit on it**. Let the children call out answers. Sit on the balloon until it pops, or let a volunteer from the class do it. **How did you know that the balloon would break?** Let the children explain.

Well, maybe you were just lucky guessers. Let's try another one. Hold a ball up high. **You may think you know what will happen when I let go of the ball, but I'm wearing my lucky shoes and it will change what happens to the ball. Go ahead and guess what will happen when I let go of the ball.** (The ball will fall.) Drop the ball. **Why didn't my lucky shoes change what happened to the ball?** (Nothing changes gravity except going into outer space.)

How did you know what would happen each time? (It was obvious because for every action there is always a reaction.) **Each time you knew what would happen because you could predict the consequence. What does the word "consequence" mean?** Let volunteers try to put this in their own words. Most children know a consequence as a punishment for disobeying. Help the children to see that a consequence is a result of an action and can be good or bad.

Okay, I have one last thing to show you and you might not know the consequence. Put a teaspoon of baking soda in a clear glass. Hold up the vinegar. **What will happen when I pour in this vinegar?** Let the children guess. Pour in the vinegar (about half a glass full) and let it foam. **The foaming might have surprised you, but scientists know the chemical reactions and it wouldn't have surprised them. Sometimes people act surprised by the consequences of their actions, but we can be sure of one thing—what we do has consequences!** Print the word "consequences" on the board.

There are consequences for the good things and the bad things we do. The bad things we do are called sin. This was true back in Bible times also. In fact, today we will talk about a man who broke God's laws and the consequence for this sin.

Have your Park Patrol members lead the children to the age-appropriate class areas at this time.

ELEMENTARY BIBLE STORY
King Ahab's Consequences

(1 Kings 16:29—17:1)

Supplies: Bible, crown, Bible-time clothes, two large pieces of paper or poster board

Preparation: Today's Bible story will be presented as a melodrama. Gather a crown and Bible-time clothes for the roles of King Ahab and Elijah. Make two signs, "Boo" and "Cheer."

Today you will help me as I tell the Bible story. Long ago, there were plays called melodramas. A melodrama has lots of emotion and the audience would help by booing the bad guy, who was called the villain. The audience would cheer loudly for the good guy who was the hero of the story. So as I tell the Bible story, I want you help me by booing and cheering at the correct times. Let's practice together. Designate two Park Patrol helpers to hold up the signs when you point to them. Have the helper hold up the "Boo" sign and let the children practice booing. Then have the other helper hold up the sign "Cheer" and encourage the kids to cheer.

Turn to 1 Kings 16 and show the children where the story is located in the Bible. **There was a king over Israel named Ahab.** Signal for the "Boo" sign to be held up. **We read in the Bible that King Ahab did more evil in the eyes of the Lord than any other king before him.** ("Boo" sign.) **Would you like that to be said about you?** Let the children respond.

But the Bible tells us that Ahab copied the sins of other bad kings. ("Boo" sign.) **But that wasn't all—he married a wicked woman named Jezebel.** ("Boo" sign.) **God was the only true God and He wanted His people to pray to only Him.** ("Cheer" sign.) **But Ahab prayed to a god called Baal.** ("Boo" sign.) **Things got even worse when Ahab built a temple for worshiping Baal.** ("Boo" sign.) **He did many other bad, bad things.** ("Boo" sign.) **Now, God is a very patient God.** ("Cheer" sign.) **But Ahab was so bad that he made God angrier than all the previous kings put together.** ("Boo" sign.)

God sent someone to talk to Ahab. His name was Elijah. ("Cheer" sign.) **Elijah was God's special messenger. Elijah told King Ahab that God was angry and that there would be consequences! God would not send any rain to Ahab's country for the next few years. What would happen if there was no rain?** Let the children suggest answers, such as crops couldn't grow, animals and people might die, and so on. **So Elijah told Ahab that there were consequences for his sins.** ("Cheer" sign.) **There are consequences for our sins too.**

Review the main points of the Bible story: **Why did God send Elijah talk to Ahab?** (God was angry with Ahab because he sinned so badly.) **What were the consequences for Ahab's sins?** (God would send a drought and there would be no rain.) **What kinds of consequences have you seen for things you've done wrong?** Let volunteers briefly share.

PRESCHOOL BIBLE STORY
Good and Bad Consequences

(1 Kings 16:29—17:6)

Supplies: Bible, Elijah flannel figures (*Craft Book*, page RC-66), flannel board

Preparation: Make a set of Elijah flannel figures from page RC-66 of the *Craft Book*.

Our Bible story today is from the book of the Bible called 1 Kings. Show the children where 1 Kings 16 is in your Bible. **The Bible tells us about King Ahab.** Put the figure of King Ahab on the board. **He was a very bad king. He did many things that God said not to do. He married a woman who didn't believe in God. King Ahab didn't pray to God. Instead he built statues and prayed to them. King Ahab sinned. King Ahab made God very angry.**

At that time lived a man named Elijah. Put the figure of Elijah next to King Ahab. **Elijah loved God. God told Elijah things to tell King Ahab. God wanted King Ahab to know that his sins had consequences—that is what**

happens because of his sins. Elijah told King Ahab, "I worship God. I serve God. But you have sinned. Because of your sins, there will not be any rain for the next few years."

King Ahab was mad at Elijah. King Ahab didn't want to know what was going to happen to his country because of his sins. After all, he didn't even believe in God. How could God punish him?

Then God told Elijah to leave where Ahab was and go to a hiding place. Remove the figure of King Ahab. **He needed to get away from angry King Ahab.** Walk the king figure back and forth at the bottom of the board.

So Elijah hid by a brook. Be sure the children know what a brook is. Put the figure of the brook next to Elijah. **He drank water by the brook.** Have the figure pretend to drink. **Every morning birds brought Elijah meat and bread to eat.** Move the bird figure down to Elijah and then back to a top corner of the flannel board. **Every evening the birds brought Elijah meat and bread to eat.** Again move the bird figure down to Elijah and then back to a top corner of the flannel board.

King Ahab sinned. Because of his sins, there was no rain in his country. That was a consequence. Elijah obeyed God, and God took care of him. That was a consequence. Our actions always have consequences. Sin always has consequences.

Discuss a few review questions: **What did King Ahab do that was wrong?** (He didn't pray to or believe in God.) **What did Elijah say would happen?** (There wouldn't be any more rain.) **How did God take care of Elijah?** (God sent him food by a brook.)

NOAH'S PARK PUPPETS
The Ditch

Have Park Patrol helpers get ready for the puppet skit found on page RP-65 of the *Puppet Skits Book.* Use the puppets to guide the children over to the puppet skit area. As you hold up each animal, have the children do the action of that animal. Explain that just as consequences are a natural result of an action, each animal is designed by God to do a certain movement. Hold up Ponder the Frog and have the kids hop. Do this with your other puppet as well.

BIBLE MEMORY
Hop to It

Supplies: Index cards, masking tape

Preparation: Choose a memory verse that supports the lesson focus. Print each word of the verse on an index card. Tape the cards to the floor in a hopscotch pattern.

Lead the class in reciting the verse several times by saying a few words and having the class repeat after you. Be sure that all of the children understand the verse.

Have the children stand in a line behind the hopscotch pattern on the floor. Explain that as they hop on each square they say or read the word. (They should land with a foot on either side of the index card so they don't actually step on the word.) Let the children take turns doing the hopscotch pattern. As time permits, let the children each have several turns. Then encourage the children to hop the verse from memory without looking at the words.

Just as sin has consequences, so does obeying God. If we want to have God's blessings in our lives, then we need to make wise choices and obey Him. One thing we can do right now is to worship God. When we worship God, we have a better relationship with Him and we give glory to Him. Those are great consequences, so let's all worship God together now.

SINGING PRAISES TO JESUS

Supplies: Noah's Park CD and CD player

Begin teaching the new song for Unit 8, "I Wanna Live God's Way," by having the children listen to it on the CD. If you have strong readers in your class, you might project the lyrics (found in the back of this *Leader's Guide*) on a screen or wall to help the children learn the words.

SHARE AND PRAYER
Prayers of Confession

Supplies: Collection of red things (red ball, red pencil, can of tomato sauce, red shirt, red paper, etc.), one per child

We know that sin means we have broken one of God's rules and disobeyed Him. How do you feel when you sin? Let volunteers share. (Sad, guilty, miserable, afraid that someone will find out)

The Bible sometimes says that sin is like the color red. I have a collection of red things. These red things remind me of the blood that Jesus shed on the cross to forgive my sins. Sometimes we sin and forget to ask God to forgive us. For our prayer time, each of you may hold a red item. Hold that item as you pray to remind you that because Jesus died on the cross, we can tell God we are sorry for our sins and ask Him to forgive us.

Let each child quickly choose a red item and sit quietly. Open a prayer time and then allow a minute for silent prayers. You may want to model a prayer for forgiveness that the children may pray in their hearts.

At this time, have a Noah's Ark puppet invite the preschoolers to their area to participate in games, snack, and craft that are geared for younger learners. Another puppet may lead the elementary-age children to their activities.

SNACK SHACK
Apple Consequence Snack

The snack for today relates to consequences—the consequence of smashing apples. You will find the directions for this lesson-related snack on page RS-65 of the *Snacks and Games Book*.

CAMPSITE CAPERS
What's My Consequence? (Elem.)
Shelter-by-the-Brook Relay (Pre.)

Lesson-supportive games are found in the Noah's Park *Snacks and Games Book*. The elementary game is on page RS-65 and the preschool game on page RS-66.

COZY CAVE CRAFTS
Consequences Board Game (Elem.)
Elijah Flannel Figures (Preschool)

The elementary project "Consequences Board Game" can be found on page RC-65 in the **Craft Book**. The preschool project, "Elijah Flannel Figures," is on page RC-66 in the same book. Be sure the children have their names on their projects.

CLOSING ACTIVITIES

A few minutes before class time is over, have the children stop their activities and help clean up the room. Have Park Patrol members take the Noah's Ark puppets around to thank each child for his or her helpfulness. Then gather the children back together for closing activities.

Have the children practice saying the Bible memory verse. Let confident volunteers offer to say the verse alone. Review the Bible story by letting the children retell the story in their own words. Be sure to let preschoolers share their Bible story with the whole group.

Ask a child to volunteer to close the time in a prayer. Then pass out the crafts. As the children leave, encourage each to make good choices this week and watch to see what good consequences happen because of obeying God.

OVERTIME ACTIVITIES

While children are waiting for their parents, let them play their "Consequences Board Game." Have Park Patrol members help read the spaces on the game board. Preschoolers may want to tell the story with their flannel figures.

R31 Trust God for the Help You Need

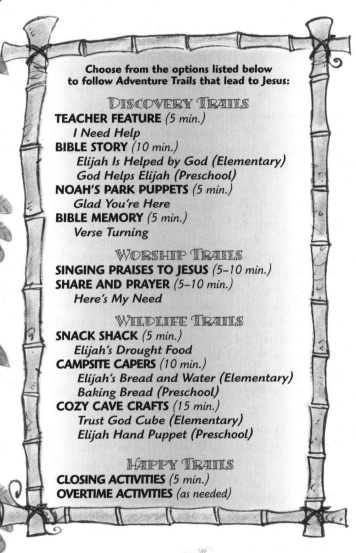

Choose from the options listed below
to follow Adventure Trails that lead to Jesus:

DISCOVERY TRAILS
TEACHER FEATURE (5 min.)
I Need Help
BIBLE STORY (10 min.)
Elijah Is Helped by God (Elementary)
God Helps Elijah (Preschool)
NOAH'S PARK PUPPETS (5 min.)
Glad You're Here
BIBLE MEMORY (5 min.)
Verse Turning

WORSHIP TRAILS
SINGING PRAISES TO JESUS (5–10 min.)
SHARE AND PRAYER (5–10 min.)
Here's My Need

WILDLIFE TRAILS
SNACK SHACK (5 min.)
Elijah's Drought Food
CAMPSITE CAPERS (10 min.)
Elijah's Bread and Water (Elementary)
Baking Bread (Preschool)
COZY CAVE CRAFTS (15 min.)
Trust God Cube (Elementary)
Elijah Hand Puppet (Preschool)

HAPPY TRAILS
CLOSING ACTIVITIES (5 min.)
OVERTIME ACTIVITIES (as needed)

DISCOVERY TRAILS

TEACHER FEATURE
I Need Help

Supplies: Paper, marker, yarn, props for actors (clown wig, health textbook, cash register, etc.)

Preparation: Make signs labeled "clown," "teacher," and "clerk." Attach yarn so they can be hung around the neck. Gather props/costumes for these people:

clown (funny wig), teacher (health text book), store clerk (cash register). Ask three Park Patrol helpers to play the parts of the clown, teacher, and store clerk. Briefly practice with them ahead of time. They should each wear a name tag and carry their props.

Begin the group time talking about how you hurt your leg. Get up and limp around. **I really need some help for my leg. I wish there was someone I trust for help!** The "clown" walks over to you.

Clown: **I know how to help! You should just smile and have fun!** *(Exit.)*

Ask the children if that was good advice or not for your hurt leg. **My leg still hurts. I wish there was someone I could trust for help!** The teacher walks up to you.

Teacher: **I know how to help! You should read this book about staying healthy!** *(Hands you the book and exits.)*

Was that good advice or not? Let the children tell why or why not. **But my leg still hurts! I wish there was someone I could trust for help!** The store clerk walks up to you.

Clerk: **I know how to help! Just take some pain medicine and then you won't feel what's wrong with your leg!** *(Presses buttons on the cash register and exits.)*

Was that good advice or not? Let the children share how that would or wouldn't help your leg get better.

My leg still hurts and I have asked three people, but none of them seems to know how to help me. Can you think of someone I could ask for help? (Doctors or nurses.) **Why would they be good to trust for help?** (They are trained in medicine, etc.)

I think you're right. I need to ask someone who really knows about my problem. Every day, people choose to trust other people for help. What would our world be like if people trusted God for the help they needed?

Children may say: We wouldn't have so many wars, people would get the help they need, wouldn't need so many jails, people would spend more time talking to God, and so on.

We all have times when we need help. We can turn to people for help, but first we should turn to God and ask for His help. In the Bible story today, we will learn about someone who really needed help.

Have the assigned Park Patrol helpers lead the elementary and preschool children to their separate Bible story areas.

ELEMENTARY BIBLE STORY
Elijah Is Helped by God
(1 Kings 17:2-16)

Supplies: Bible, Bible-time clothes

Preparation: Ask two Park Patrol members to put on Bible-time clothes and play the roles of Elijah and the widow.

Open your Bible to 1 Kings 17 and show the children where today's story is found. **Last week we met a man named Elijah.** Have Elijah enter and act out the scene you describe. **He has just told wicked King Ahab that God was angry at his sin and Ahab's sin had a big consequence—a drought! A drought means no rain, and that made King Ahab really angry. Elijah needed to trust God for help. He had to run for his life. God told him where to go—to a special little brook.** Have Elijah run to a different area of the room.

Let's go join Elijah and see what happens. Have the children follow you over to Elijah. **When Elijah got there, he saw that God would help him have water because of the brook. And God sent ravens, big black birds, to bring him meat and bread. Even though there was a drought, every day Elijah got water from the brook and food from the birds.**

One day Elijah found the brook had dried up. What would he do now? Elijah trusted God for the help he needed. God told him where to go next. Have Elijah go to a different area and let the children follow him. **This time**

God sent Elijah to a village, where he met a poor woman whose husband had died. Have the widow enter. **Elijah asked her for a drink and some food. She sadly shook her head and explained that her tiny bit of flour and oil was all she had left to make one last piece of bread for herself and her son. This would be their last meal and they would probably die.** Have the widow cry.

Elijah trusted God for help. He told the woman that if she made a small biscuit for him first, God would make it so the flour and oil wouldn't run out during the drought.

If you were the widow, what would you have done? Let the children respond. **Well, the woman hurried home.** Have her hurry to another area of the room; lead the children to join her. **Immediately, she made Elijah a biscuit. Then she couldn't believe what she saw—the jar still had flour and oil in it! She could make more bread. God did exactly what He had promised to do! For the rest of the drought the woman had flour and oil to make bread. Elijah was glad that he had trusted God for the help he needed. We also can trust God for the help we need.**

Be sure to discuss some review questions with the children: **What happened when Elijah trusted God when King Ahab was mad at him?** (God told Elijah to hide by a brook where he could get water; God sent ravens to bring bread and meat.) **What happened when Elijah trusted God with the widow?** (God made the woman's flour and oil not run out so there was always bread.) **God wants us to trust Him for the help we need.**

PRESCHOOL BIBLE STORY
God Helps Elijah *(1 Kings 17:7-16)*

Supplies: Bible, Elijah hand puppet (*Craft Book,* page RC-67)

Preparation: Make a completed Elijah hand puppet from page RC-67 of the *Craft Book.*

Today's story comes from the book of the Bible called 1 Kings. Show the children where 1 Kings is found in the Bible.

The Bible tells us about a man named Elijah. Use the Elijah puppet and pretend to "walk" it up a staircase to bring it in front of you. Then turn the puppet to face the children. **Elijah was a prophet. He told people special messages from God. He had told bad King Ahab that there wouldn't be any rain because of the bad things King Ahab had done.**

Move your hand to make the puppet talk as you speak for it. **"God had me hide near a brook. But when the water in the brook dried up, He told me to go to Zarephath. A woman there would help me find food and water."**

"Walk" the puppet back and forth in front of you. **Elijah walked and walked until he came to the town gates.** Hold the puppet off to the side. **How do you think Elijah would know who would help him? I'll let Elijah tell you about how he found the woman.**

Have the puppet talk as before. **"When I got to the town gates, I was hot and thirsty and hungry. A woman was there picking up sticks. I asked her if she could please bring me a little water so I could have a drink. While she was going to get it, I called, 'Would you please also bring a little bit of bread to eat?'**

"The woman told me, 'Your God knows this: I don't have any bread. I have only a little oil and a little flour. I was picking up sticks so I could make a fire and use the oil and flour to bake one last loaf of bread. Then my son and I won't have any more food.'

"I told the woman to make the bread and bring me a piece. God would not let the oil or flour go away until after it rained.

"She did what I said. The woman, her son, and I had food to eat that day . . . and the next day . . . and the next day. We had food every day just like God said." Set aside the puppet.

Elijah trusted God for the help he needed. You can trust God for the help you need too.

Discuss a few review questions: **What help did Elijah need?** (He needed food and water.) **How did God help him?** (He had Elijah go to a woman's house; God provided food for the woman's family and Elijah.)

NOAH'S PARK PUPPETS
Glad You're Here

Lead the children to the puppet stage When all the children are seated, let the Park Patrol present the skit. Today's puppet skit is found on page R-67 of the *Puppet Skits Book*.

BIBLE MEMORY
Verse Turning

Supplies: Newsprint paper or poster board, marker

Preparation: Choose a Bible verse for the children to memorize that supports the lesson. Print the verse on a sheet of newsprint or poster board.

Hold up the verse and read it to the children. Talk about the meaning of the verse and why it is such an important verse to learn. Have the children read it with you several times.

Ask the children to form a line. Hand the memory verse card to the first child in the line and have that child shout out the first word of the verse. Then the child quickly turns around and hands the verse card to the child standing behind him. That child then calls out the next word in the verse and turns to give the card to the next person. Encourage children to quickly turn and say the next word of the verse. Continue until you reach the end of the line. If you have time, repeat the process back up the line to the starting child.

Just as you turned to give the memory verse card to the person behind you, we can get in the habit of quickly turning to God. One way we can show God we trust Him is through our worship. Let's sing to Him now.

SINGING PRAISES TO JESUS
Supplies: Noah's Park CD and CD player

This is the second week to work on "I Wanna Live God's Way," the unit song. You will find the lyrics listed in the back of this *Leader's Guide*. Let the children sing with the CD a couple of times.

SHARE AND PRAYER
Here's My Need

Supplies: Paper, markers or crayons

We have learned today how important it is to turn to God for help with our needs. Each one of us has needs. Some of our needs may be very serious right now, like a parent who needs to get a job or a family member who is in the hospital. Let the children share any needs like these that they or their family are going through.

We also have everyday needs like understanding our schoolwork, obeying our parents, and getting along with friends or family members. Encourage the children to talk about help they need that might not seem very "big" or important. Remind the children that God wants us to come to Him with all of our needs—big or small.

Ask the children to think of something they need help with. Using paper and crayons or markers, let the children draw a picture of their need. On the paper write "I will trust God for the help I need."

Ask the children to stand in a large prayer circle holding their pictures. Go around the circle and let each child pray and ask God's help with the problem they drew on the paper. Collect the pictures and pass them out at the end of class. Be sure children's names are on their papers.

Let the Park Patrol members use Noah's Park puppets to lead preschool and elementary-age children to their different areas for a snack, games, and crafts.

SNACK SHACK
Elijah's Drought Food

A lesson-related snack is provided on page RS-67 of the *Snacks and Games Book*. Allow time for hand washing before and after the snack. Park Patrol members may set up the snack during hand-washing time. Let a volunteer thank God for the snack before the class begins eating.

CAMPSITE CAPERS
Elijah's Bread and Water (Elementary)
Baking Bread (Preschool)

Today's elementary game, "Elijah's Bread and Water," is found on page RS-67 of the *Snacks and Games Book*. Preschoolers will enjoy playing "Baking Bread," located on RS-68 of the *Snacks and Games Book*.

COZY CAVE CRAFTS
Trust God Cube (Elementary)
Elijah Hand Puppet (Preschool)

Elementary children will make a "Trust God Cube" to remind them to turn to God in any situation. You will find craft and directions on page RC-67 of the *Craft Book*. Preschool children will make "Elijah Hand Puppets" as their age-appropriate craft. Directions for this craft are located on page RC-68.

CLOSING ACTIVITIES

Encourage all of the children to take part in cleaning up spills, putting away supplies, straightening chairs, and so on. You could divide the children into work groups and assign a Park Patrol helper to direct and assist each group.

When cleaning is finished, let the elementary children tell the group about some of the things they drew on their cube. Let preschool volunteers retell the Bible story using the Elijah hand puppet.

Ask for volunteers to pray, asking God help them remember to trust Him for help with their needs.

OVERTIME ACTIVITIES

While you wait for parents to come and pick up the children, the children can play "Charades." Choose one child to act out a person that someone turns to for help (pastor, teacher, policeman, doctor, firefighter, etc.). The rest of the group guesses, and the child who correctly identifies the person becomes the new actor.

R32 Lesson: God Listens When We Pray

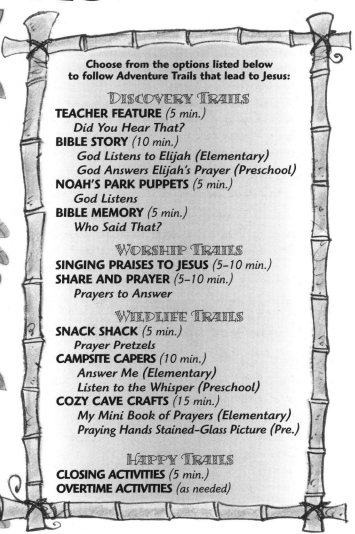

Choose from the options listed below
to follow Adventure Trails that lead to Jesus:

Discovery Trails
TEACHER FEATURE (5 min.)
Did You Hear That?
BIBLE STORY (10 min.)
God Listens to Elijah (Elementary)
God Answers Elijah's Prayer (Preschool)
NOAH'S PARK PUPPETS (5 min.)
God Listens
BIBLE MEMORY (5 min.)
Who Said That?

Worship Trails
SINGING PRAISES TO JESUS (5–10 min.)
SHARE AND PRAYER (5–10 min.)
Prayers to Answer

Wildlife Trails
SNACK SHACK (5 min.)
Prayer Pretzels
CAMPSITE CAPERS (10 min.)
Answer Me (Elementary)
Listen to the Whisper (Preschool)
COZY CAVE CRAFTS (15 min.)
My Mini Book of Prayers (Elementary)
Praying Hands Stained-Glass Picture (Pre.)

Happy Trails
CLOSING ACTIVITIES (5 min.)
OVERTIME ACTIVITIES (as needed)

Discovery Trails

TEACHER FEATURE
Did You Hear That?

Supplies: Box full of items that make a noise (musical instrument, timer, stapler, party noisemaker, bell, etc.)

Preparation: Ask some Park Patrol members at the appropriate time to make a noise from the box of items. Be sure the class cannot see what is making the noise. You might want to have the helpers stand behind the class or behind a file cabinet.

If you listen carefully, you will hear something. I want you to raise your hand and I'll ask someone to tell what you heard. Have a Park Patrol helper take an item and make its noise. Have the children listen and then raise a hand to give an answer. Continue with each item that you brought. Affirm the children for being good listeners.

You were able to hear each of those sounds and know what the sound was. Now let's see what happens when all of the sounds make noise at the same time. Have all of the Park Patrol helpers take items and make noise together. Signal them to stop making the noise. **Were you able to hear just the stapler?** Children might respond that there was too much noise at once, they couldn't hear the one item, and so on.

It is very difficult to hear something when lots of different noises are going on at the same time. Let's do an experiment. When I give the signal, we'll all talk in our normal, indoor voices. See if you can pick out my voice or the voice of a friend. Give the signal and let the class talk for 10 seconds. **Were you able to just focus on one voice or was it difficult?** Let the children respond.

I would get a headache if I had to listen to all of that noise at once. My ears aren't designed to hear all of those noises and pick out one noise or one particular voice to listen to. But I know someone who can hear me when I talk, no matter where I am or how many other people are talking. Do you know who that might be? (God.)

Aren't you glad that God can hear each one who talks to Him? When we talk to God, we call that prayer. I know that God will hear our prayers and answer them. He listens to each one of you whenever you pray. Today we will learn about someone in the Bible who prayed to God. Listen carefully to learn what happened when he prayed.

Divide the children into preschool and elementary groups, and have them follow a Park Patrol helper to their Bible story areas. If you are keeping all the children together, be sure to use the Elementary Bible Story.

ELEMENTARY BIBLE STORY
God Listens to Elijah (1 Kings 17:17–24)

Supplies: Bible

We have been learning about a man named Elijah. Show the children 1 Kings 17 in a Bible.

You get to help me tell the story today by showing on your faces how different people felt at different points in the story. The first time we met Elijah, he told evil King Ahab that sin had consequences and there would be a drought because of Ahab's sins. Well, that made King Ahab mad. Have the children show mad faces. **Elijah had to run away.** Have the children look scared. **Elijah trusted God for help, and God sent Elijah to live near a brook where he would have water, and God sent ravens to bring Elijah food each day.** Have the children look happy. **Then God told Elijah to go to a village, where Elijah met a poor widow using her last bit of flour and water to make bread. God did a miracle when she made bread for Elijah and her flour and oil didn't run out.** Have the children look happy.

What happened to Elijah next? Elijah stayed in an extra room that belonged to the woman. One day the widow's son was very sick. In fact, he got worse until he finally stopped breathing. You can imagine how upset the widow was! Let the children show sadness and pretend crying.

The widow was so upset that she thought maybe Elijah's presence in her home made God look at her more closely. God might see her sins and punish her with her son's death. Have the children look mad. **That wasn't true, but what could poor Elijah do?** Have the children look worried.

Well, Elijah did the only thing that he could, he prayed to God. Have the children close their eyes and bow their heads for a moment. **He knew God would listen. The Bible tells us that Elijah carried the boy's body to a bed, and Elijah prayed a prayer from his heart. He prayed, "O Lord, have you brought this terrible tragedy to this kind, poor woman I am staying with? Please let this boy's life return to him!"** Have the children look hopeful.

God listened to Elijah's prayer and answered it. God put breath back into the boy's body—he was alive again! Elijah picked up the boy and carried him to his mother. What do you think the mother did when she saw her son alive? Let the children show this on their faces. **I'm sure she was excited and no longer upset that Elijah was staying at her home. Just think, this woman's son was dead and now he was alive because God listened to Elijah's prayer.**

God also listens to us when we pray. Show me on your face how that makes you feel.

Be sure to discuss a few questions to check for understanding: **What problem did the widow have?** (Her son died.) **What did Elijah do?** (He prayed and God listened; the boy came back to life.)

PRESCHOOL BIBLE STORY
God Answers Elijah's Prayer
(1 Kings 17:17–24)

Supplies: Bible, Elijah hand puppet (from Lesson 31, *Craft Book*, page RC–67), (optional: Bible-time clothes)

Preparation: Make an Elijah hand puppet from page RC–67 of the *Craft Book*. As an option, you could dress in Bible-time clothes and play the role of Elijah yourself instead of using a puppet.

Open your Bible to 1 Kings 17, and keep it open as you tell the story. **Our Bible story comes from the part of the Bible called 1 Kings.**

The Bible tells us many things about Elijah. He told people the messages that God told him. Use the Elijah puppet and pretend to "walk" it up a staircase to bring it in front of you. Then turn the puppet to face the children. **Elijah lived in the spare room of a poor woman and her son. Each day God provided food for Elijah, the woman, and her son.**

Move the mouth of the puppet with your hand for each word. **"I'd like to tell you what happened one day to the family I was staying with. The boy who lived at the house got very sick. He got sicker and sicker and sicker. Finally, he died.** Hold your other hand out flat.

"His mother was very sad. 'Why did he die?' she asked me. She thought that her sins might have caused the boy to die. But that wasn't true.

"I took the boy up to the room where I was staying." "Walk" the puppet in front of you as if it were carrying your other hand. **I put the boy on my bed and prayed, 'Dear God, let this boy live.'"**

"I knew God would listen to my prayer. The boy started breathing. He was alive again! I picked him up and took him to his mother." Again "walk" the puppet in front of you as if it were carrying your other hand.

"The boy's mother told me that now she knew I was a man of God. She could believe God's Word." Put the puppet aside.

Elijah knew that God listened when he prayed. We can know that God listens when we pray.

Ask a few Bible review questions: **What happened to the boy?** (He got very sick and died.) **What happened?** (Elijah prayed and God listened; the boy came back to life.)

NOAH'S PARK PUPPETS
God Listens

Signal the Park Patrol helpers to prepare the puppet skit that is found on page RP-69 of the *Puppet Skits Book*. While they are getting ready, have the children listen very carefully to hear your instructions. Give some fun commands in different voices. For example, in a gruff voice tell the children to pat the back of the person to their left; in a high voice tell them to stomp your feet; in a British accent tell them to tickle the knee of the person on their right. Lead the children to the puppet stage and remind them to listen to the puppets message.

BIBLE MEMORY
Who Said That?

Supplies: Tape recorder

Preparation: Choose a Bible memory verse that applies to today's lesson focus. Record several people

in the church saying the memory verse. If possible, choose people who are familiar to the children.

Print the Bible memory verse on the board. This will help children who are visual learners as they memorize the verse. Read the verse together and talk about the meaning of the verse and any words that may be unfamiliar to the children.

Tell the children that they will hear several people say the verse and they are to guess who the people are. Play the first recording and let the children guess who said the verse. If they can't name the person, they can identify the type of person, such as a "teenager" or a "grandmother." Continue through the entire recording. Then, play the tape again, and this time have the children say the verse along with each person on the tape.

God listens when we pray and He listens when we say Bible verses. God always listens to us. Let's give God something really great to listen to—our worship. As we worship God together, let's sing in a way so that God hears our love for Him.

SINGING PRAISES TO JESUS
Supplies: Noah's Park CD and CD player

Play the unit song, "I Wanna Live God's Way," from the CD and invite the children to sing along. If you have musical instruments available, pass them out and let the children use them to accompany the singing. After playing a song, have all the children with instruments give the instrument to a child that hasn't played one yet.

SHARE AND PRAYER
Prayers to Answer

Supplies: None

Just like God listened when Elijah prayed, God listens when you pray. Can you think of a prayer that you prayed and God answered? Let the children share experiences they have had with answered prayers.

We always like it when God answers our prayer with a yes and does what we ask Him. But there are times when God answers our prayers with a no. Sometimes God says, "Not right now." Sometimes we think that God didn't hear our prayer or answer it, but He always answers our prayers. We might need to be patient and wait to see what answer He gives us. Can you think of a time when God might have answered you with a no or said, "Later"? Give volunteers an opportunity to answer. Encourage the children to see that God always answers, but it might not be the answer we want.

Have the children stand in a large circle. If your class is large, you may want to make two circles. **When we talk to God, first let's thank Him for hearing our prayers and answering them. Then you can talk to God about whatever you want.** Begin the prayer time by modeling a prayer of thanks to God for listening and answering, and then ask God to help you with something. Encourage each child to take a turn and pray.

Separate activities are provided for elementary and preschool children at this time. Have the Park Patrol workers (previously assigned) lead the groups to their areas and help as necessary. This separation of the children may occur before Snack Shack or after, depending on your facilities and the number of children involved in your program.

SNACK SHACK
Prayer Pretzels

Have the Park Patrol set up the snack area. See page RS-69 in the *Snack and Games Book* for a snack that reinforces today's Bible lesson.

CAMPSITE CAPERS
Answer Me (Elementary)
Listen to the Whisper (Preschool)

Today's elementary and preschool games will give the kids an opportunity to have fun reinforcing the lesson focus. Turn to page RS-69 in the *Snacks and Games Book* to find the elementary game, "Answer Me." The preschool game, "Listen to the Whisper," is on page RS-70 in the same book.

COZY CAVE CRAFTS
My Mini Book of Prayers (Elementary)
Praying Hands Stained-Glass Picture (Preschool)

The crafts for both elementary and preschool children will help them remember that God listens when they pray. The preschool craft, "Praying Hands Stained-Glass Picture," is on page RC-70 of the *Crafts Book*. The elementary craft, "My Mini Book of Prayers," is on page RC-69.

CLOSING ACTIVITIES

When the children have finished their crafts, games, and snacks, play the unit song to signal time for cleanup. Allow a few minutes at the end of your class time for all the children to help with some straightening up. You might want to have the children sing with the CD as they clean. Be sure to affirm children who are working hard and helping others.

Let the preschoolers tell the group about their Bible story. Give the elementary students an opportunity to tell the preschoolers about their Bible story. Review the memory verse together. End with a prayer thanking God for listening to prayers.

OVERTIME ACTIVITIES

As you wait for parents, gather the remaining children together. Use the tape recorder to let the kids record their own voices saying the memory verse.

Set out several of the books and Bible storybooks. Encourage the children to look for books or stories about prayer or about the story of Elijah. Ask the Park Patrol members to be available to read a book or to help the younger children as needed.

R33 Lesson: There's Only One God

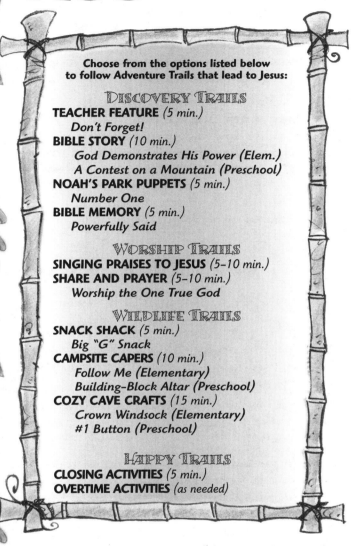

Choose from the options listed below
to follow Adventure Trails that lead to Jesus:

DISCOVERY TRAILS
TEACHER FEATURE (5 min.)
  Don't Forget!
BIBLE STORY (10 min.)
  God Demonstrates His Power (Elem.)
  A Contest on a Mountain (Preschool)
NOAH'S PARK PUPPETS (5 min.)
  Number One
BIBLE MEMORY (5 min.)
  Powerfully Said

WORSHIP TRAILS
SINGING PRAISES TO JESUS (5–10 min.)
SHARE AND PRAYER (5–10 min.)
  Worship the One True God

WILDLIFE TRAILS
SNACK SHACK (5 min.)
  Big "G" Snack
CAMPSITE CAPERS (10 min.)
  Follow Me (Elementary)
  Building-Block Altar (Preschool)
COZY CAVE CRAFTS (15 min.)
  Crown Windsock (Elementary)
  #1 Button (Preschool)

HAPPY TRAILS
CLOSING ACTIVITIES (5 min.)
OVERTIME ACTIVITIES (as needed)

DISCOVERY TRAILS

TEACHER FEATURE
Don't Forget!

Supplies: None

Pretend you are trying to remember a list of things and tick them off on your fingers. Suddenly notice the children. **Are you good at remembering things? I have a lot of things to remember today and need some help so I don't forget anything.**

What are some ways that people remember what's important? (They make a list, practice, repeat it, etc.) **Those are very good ideas. Do you think they work? What works for you when you have to remember something important?** Let volunteers share ideas.

Let's play a game to see how well you remember. Ask for a volunteer and say that you will give *four* commands which he or she must complete in the order they were given. You may use classroom items in your commands. For example, you might suggest: **Bring me a tissue, turn off the light, put the Bible on the table, hop on one foot.** If the child is able to do all four in order, praise him and let him sit down. Ask for another volunteer. Give her *five* different commands to remember. If she completes them successfully, praise her and let her sit down. Keep playing the game with a new volunteer and adding a new command each time until a child forgets one of the commands.

Other possible commands are: eat a cracker, bounce a ball, pat your head, turn on the lights, put on the hat, take off the hat, clap your hands, sneeze, take off your shoe, hug a friend.

Praise all volunteers for doing a good job. **Those things are fun, but if we forget them, it's not really important, is it? What are some things that *are* important for you to remember?** (Addresses, phone numbers, birthdays, homework assignments, etc.)

You're right. Those things are very important. But the Bible tells us that there is something even *more* important that we must never forget. We must never forget there is only one true God. In our Bible story today, the people of Israel are reminded about the one and only God in a very amazing way. At this time, have Park Patrol helpers take the preschoolers and elementary-age children to their separate Bible story areas to continue the lesson.

ELEMENTARY BIBLE STORY
God Demonstrates His Power
(1 Kings 18:16-40)

Supplies: Bible, paper, marker

Preparation: Make two signs labeled "god" and "God."

Give the signs to Park Patrol helpers to hold up when you point to them. Explain to the class that "God" with a capital G refers to the one mighty and true God. When the "God" sign is held up, the children should stand and flex their muscles for God's might. Have them practice.

Then discuss that "god" with a little "g" means something that people worship that they made themselves, like a statue. When the "god" sign is held up, have the kids crouch as small as they can get. Practice this a few times.

Today I am going to open my Bible to 1 Kings 18 because I want to tell you about an exciting contest. Show the children 1 Kings 18 in a Bible. **The people watching this contest were the people of Israel. They were known as God's people because they followed God** (God sign)**, but for many years they followed other gods** (god sign)**. King Ahab worshiped gods** (god sign) **and because of his sin, there was a drought.**

One day Elijah told Ahab to gather all of the people and meet him at the top of Mount Carmel. Elijah told the people they had to choose who they would follow—the god Baal (god sign) **or the real God** (God sign)**. Elijah asked for a contest between Baal and God. King Ahab had 450 prophets of the god Baal** (god sign) **along with 400 prophets of another god** (god sign)**. But the one true God** (god sign) **had only one prophet there, Elijah. Those numbers don't sound like a fair contest—850 to 1!—but Elijah wasn't worried because he followed the one true God** (God sign)**.**

So the Baal prophets got a bull sacrifice and prayed to the god Baal (god sign) **to set fire to the sacrifice. All day long the people cried out to Baal, but nothing happened. Elijah laughed and asked if their god** (god sign) **was sleeping. The people tried all the harder to get Baal's attention, but still, nothing happened.**

Finally, Elijah got his turn. The people were amazed as they watched him pour bucket after bucket of water on his sacrifice. Then he prayed to God—the one true God (God sign)**. Immediately, fire came down and burnt up the offering and all the water! When the people of Israel saw this they remembered the one and only God** (God sign) **and worshiped him. We should never forget that there's only one God.**

Discuss a few review questions: **How many prophets of Baal and the other god were there?** (850.) **How many prophets of God were there?** (One.) **How did God prove that He is the one true God?** (The other god didn't answer the prayer but God sent fire from heaven to burn up the altar and water.) **What is it important to never forget?** (There's only one real God.)

PRESCHOOL BIBLE STORY
A Contest on a Mountain (1 Kings 18:16-40)

Supplies: Bible, a large shallow plastic container, several sponges, crumpled orange tissue paper, a pitcher of water

Our story today comes from the book of the Bible called 1 Kings. Show the children 1 Kings 18 in your Bible.

After three long years of no rain, Elijah went back to talk to bad King Ahab. King Ahab was still mad at Elijah. But Elijah asked King Ahab to be part of a contest. Elijah needed King Ahab to have all the people of the country and all the prophets of the false gods to come to a mountain.

When everybody gathered at the mountain, Elijah asked the people, "When will you choose who is God? You can't follow the real God and the false gods. There is only one God."

The people didn't answer Elijah. So Elijah told about the contest. "I am the only one of God's prophets here. But there are many for the false god. They will make an altar and a sacrifice and then pray to their god. I will do the same thing. The god that answers by sending fire—He is God."

The people agreed to the contest. The false god's prophets built an altar, put on the sacrifice, and then prayed. They danced. They hit themselves. But nothing happened.

Then Elijah took stones and built an altar. Use the sponges to build an altar in the shallow pan. Elijah put on the sacrifice. But then he poured water all over the sacrifice and the altar. Pour a third of the water on the sponges. Then Elijah poured some more water on everything. Pour another third of water on the sponges. Again Elijah poured water on everything. Pour the rest of the water on the sponges.

Then Elijah prayed, "God, let the people know that You are the only God. Please answer my prayer and send fire on this altar. Then people will know that there's only one God."

God sent fire down. Put the crumbled tissue paper on top of the altar. The fire burned up everything. Then all the people knew that there is only one God.

Ask some Bible review questions: What happened when Elijah prayed? (God sent fire down to burn up Elijah's altar.) What did the people know? (There's only one God.)

NOAH'S PARK PUPPETS
Number One

Have the Park Patrol members set up and prepare for the puppet skit found on page RP-71 of the *Puppet Skits Book*. In the meanwhile, lead the children to the puppet stage and then let them demonstrate their "power" by showing strong arm muscles. Ask volunteers to tell how God showed His power in the Bible story. Then have the group be seated to enjoy the puppet show.

BIBLE MEMORY
Powerfully Said

Supplies: None

Preparation: Choose a Bible verse for the children to memorize that reinforces today's lesson. The verse the children have been learning in Sunday school may be a good choice.

Say the verse for the class, one phrase at a time, and have them repeat it. Do this a few times for the verse to become familiar. Then have the whole class say the verse with you in a whisper. Tell the kids that they can increase in power each time they say the verse. So the second time they say it, they should use a loud whisper. The third time, they should use a soft voice. The fourth time, they should use their regular speaking voice. The fifth time they should say it loudly. And the last time, the children may use "full power" and shout the verse.

To further practice, have the children watch you for signals of how loud or soft to say the verse. Use your hands to direct ("up" means get louder, "down" means get softer) as the children repeat the Bible verse.

We can worship the one and only God just as the people of Israel did the day of the contest with Elijah. Let's get ready now to worship and sing our praises to God.

WORSHIP TRAILS

SINGING PRAISES TO JESUS
Supplies: Noah's Park CD and CD player

Set up the CD player and be ready to play the unit song, "I Wanna Live God's Way." Divide the class in two. Have a contest between the two groups to see which group knows the unit song and can do the best job singing it. Play the song twice, with one group singing along each time. Applaud both groups for doing a great job and declare the contest a tie. Remind the children that there is no "tie" with God—He is the all-powerful, one true God.

SHARE AND PRAYER
Worship the One True God

Supplies: None

God is the one true God. Let's brainstorm some reasons we can worship Him this morning. Help the children think of things from Bible stories and from their own lives. Write their answers on the board. If children can't think of reasons to worship God, ask them leading questions along the way. The children might suggest answers such as *God made everything, He is stronger than fake gods and idols, He loves us, He did miracles, He answers our prayers, He helps us,* and so on. Encourage the children to suggest many reasons to worship God.

When finished brainstorming, have the children sit in a circle, either in one large group or divided into smaller groups with a Park Patrol helper in each. Begin a prayer time by letting each child pray, "God, I worship You because . . ." and finishing the sentence with something from the brainstorming time. Encourage the children to pray from their hearts as they worship the Lord. When finished, close by praising God for being the one true God.

Let the Park Patrol use puppets to lead the preschoolers and elementary-age children to their separate snacks, games, and crafts. The puppets could call each child by name to line up and move to their next activity. If you prefer, all the children can stay together for snack time and then divide into their groups when they have finished eating.

SNACK SHACK
Big "G" Snack

Today's snack suggestion is found on page RS-71 of the *Snacks and Games Book*. Give the children a chance to wash their hands before and after the snack. Ask the Park Patrol members to wipe off the tables and set out everything needed for the snack. Be sure to let a volunteer thank God for the food before beginning.

CAMPSITE CAPERS
Follow Me *(Elementary)*
Building-Block Altar *(Preschool)*

The elementary-age children will need an open space to play their game, "Follow Me." Directions are on page RS-71 of the Noah's Park *Snacks and Games Book*. The preschoolers will enjoy playing "Building-Block Altar" from page RS-72 of the *Snacks and Games Book*.

COZY CAVE CRAFTS
Crown Windsock *(Elementary)*
#1 Button *(Preschool)*

Today's crafts will reinforce the Bible story. The preschoolers will make "#1 Buttons." Instructions are on page RC-72 of the Noah's Park *Craft Book*. The elementary craft, "Crown Windsock," is found on page RC-71. This craft may need a little drying time before it can be sent home. Prepare a safe spot for the windsocks to set while drying before sending them home. Be sure children's names are on their crafts.

CLOSING ACTIVITIES

A few minutes before class time is over, play the unit song from the Noah's Park CD as a signal that it is time to finish up activities and begin cleaning up the room. Be sure the children understand the jobs that need to be done. You might assign a Park Patrol member to lead a small group of children in "Follow the Leader" to go to a certain part of the room to clean up there.

When the room is ready, gather the class back together. Ask for volunteers to stand and say the Bible memory verse for the class. Give out the children's crafts, and let each child turn to someone next to him or her and explain how their craft will remind them that there's only one God. Close the time in a word of prayer.

OVERTIME ACTIVITIES

With any extra time, let the children retell today's Bible story. Other children may want to interact with the puppets, acting out puppet skits they've seen.

R34 Lesson: God Cares When We Feel Bad

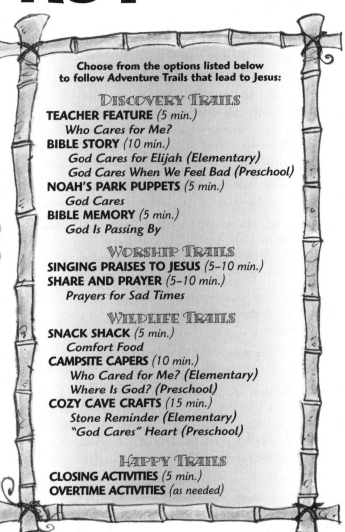

Choose from the options listed below
to follow Adventure Trails that lead to Jesus:

Discovery Trails
TEACHER FEATURE *(5 min.)*
Who Cares for Me?
BIBLE STORY *(10 min.)*
God Cares for Elijah (Elementary)
God Cares When We Feel Bad (Preschool)
NOAH'S PARK PUPPETS *(5 min.)*
God Cares
BIBLE MEMORY *(5 min.)*
God Is Passing By

Worship Trails
SINGING PRAISES TO JESUS *(5–10 min.)*
SHARE AND PRAYER *(5–10 min.)*
Prayers for Sad Times

Wildlife Trails
SNACK SHACK *(5 min.)*
Comfort Food
CAMPSITE CAPERS *(10 min.)*
Who Cared for Me? (Elementary)
Where Is God? (Preschool)
COZY CAVE CRAFTS *(15 min.)*
Stone Reminder (Elementary)
"God Cares" Heart (Preschool)

Happy Trails
CLOSING ACTIVITIES *(5 min.)*
OVERTIME ACTIVITIES *(as needed)*

Discovery Trails

TEACHER FEATURE
Who Cares for Me?

Supplies: None

Preparation: Have your whole Park Patrol group practice showing these feelings on their faces: happy, worried, excited, sad, angry, and relieved.

There are all kinds of different feelings that we feel. What could these feelings be? Have the Park Patrol line up and motion to them to show happiness on their faces. Let the class guess what they're feeling. Do the same for each feeling you had them practice. (You may need to whisper or hold up a sign to show which feeling to demonstrate.)

Can you show me on your faces how you feel during bad times? I'll name a problem, and you all show me how you would look if you had that problem. Name situations like these:

· A good friend doesn't want to play with you
· Your team didn't win a game
· Your grandpa is in the hospital
· You lost your favorite stuffed animal
· Your bike got stolen
· Your dad doesn't have time to play with you all weekend

It's not fun to have days when we're feeling bad, but those times do happen. What are things that you sometimes feel bad about? Let volunteers briefly share. Children may mention big or little things, such as not getting along with a sibling, having a sick family member or pet, not getting something they want, worrying about something that might happen, and so on. Listen and empathize with what each child feels and has experienced.

Those are really sad things, and sometimes they happen to all of us. Who helps you when you feel bad? What do they do to help you feel better? Let volunteers tell who helps them and what they do. Answers might include listening, hugging, giving a special treat, helping solve the problem, spending time, and so on. Focus the lesson not on the bad feelings but on ways people help us feel better.

There's one more person who helps us. God cares when we feel bad. Our Bible story today shows us some ways God cared for Elijah when he felt really bad.

At this time, separate the preschoolers from the elementary children and have the Park Patrol lead them to their separate Bible story areas.

ELEMENTARY BIBLE STORY
God Cares for Elijah (1 Kings 19:1-18)

Supplies: Bible, scroll with this message on it: *"Dear Elijah, By this time tomorrow you will be dead. Your Queen, Jezebel."* Plan on a Park Patrol helper to read it when cued.

Show the children 1 Kings 19 in your Bible. **Tell me what you remember about Elijah.** Let volunteers answer. Briefly review the past lessons.

What an exciting time for Elijah! In last week's lesson he had just seen a huge miracle of God in front of all Israel. The contest between Baal and God proved that God is the one true God. How do you think Elijah might have felt after that contest? Let the children give their thoughts. (Cheerful, like celebrating, relieved, etc.) **How do you think King Ahab might have felt?** (Angry, scared, grumpy, etc.)

King Ahab went back to his palace and told his wife, Jezebel that God had won over their false prophets and had proven that their gods weren't real at all. Have all the kids clap their hands together once and shout, "Boom!" **But Jezebel was super mad! In fact, she was so mad that she sent a message to Elijah.** Have the Park Patrol messenger enter, unroll the scroll, and read the message: "Dear Elijah, By this time tomorrow you will be dead. Your Queen, Jezebel." The messenger rolls up the scroll and exits. **How do you think Elijah felt now?** (Scared, confused, etc.)

Poor Elijah—he had just been so excited about God's greatness and now he was running for his life! Have the kids pretend to be Elijah and run in place, looking around scared. **Elijah was scared to death. He was discouraged. He was confused. And he finally was so exhausted that he lay in the shade of a bush and just wanted to die.** Kids can act that out.

Elijah fell asleep, but he woke up when an angel shook him. The angel brought him bread and water. God cared that Elijah felt bad. He knew that Elijah was discouraged and He sent the angel to bring comfort to Elijah. Elijah ate the food and fell asleep again. Have the kids act out eating and then sleeping. **A second time the angel came with** more food and water. **Now Elijah felt much better and traveled for forty days and nights to get away from Jezebel.**

Elijah arrived at a cave and fell asleep. But God had something to say to Elijah. Have the children cup their ears as if listening. **"Elijah! What are you doing here?" God said.**

Elijah said to God, "I've been working hard for You with all my heart, and look what I get for it! The people of Israel still don't follow You. They've killed all Your prophets except me. And now they're trying to kill me, too!"

God only replied, "Go out of this cave; stand on the mountain. I'm going to pass by you."

Suddenly, there was a huge, powerful, noisy wind, like a tornado! Have the children act out cowering against a huge wind. **But God was not in the wind.**

Then there was an earthquake! Act out shaking in an earthquake. **But God was not in the earthquake.**

Then a huge fire hit the mountain! Fall to the floor; cover heads. **But God was not in the fire.**

Then Elijah heard a gentle whisper. Have all the children whisper at once. **Elijah went and stood at the entrance of the cave. He knew that was God. And God said, "Elijah, what are you doing here?"**

Elijah told God that he was all alone. But God had news for Elijah. God had saved 7,000 people in Israel who still followed Him. That really comforted Elijah. And God gave Elijah instructions of where to go next, and the plan would help Elijah be safe.

Elijah was no longer discouraged because God cared when he felt bad. God cares when you feel bad too. He may not show up with a big display of His power, but He might encourage you with a quiet whisper to remind you of His love.

Why was Elijah discouraged and running away? (Jezebel wanted to kill him.) **How did God comfort Elijah?** (He sent an angel to bring food; later God spoke to him in a whisper.) **What helped Elijah to stop feeling bad?** (He learned that God cared for him.)

PRESCHOOL BIBLE STORY
God Cares When We Feel Bad

(1 Kings 19:1-18)

Supplies: Bible

Our story today comes from the book of the Bible called 1 Kings. Show the children 1 Kings 19 in your Bible. Keep your Bible open as you tell the story.

In our Bible story today, I will need you to make some sounds. When there is a big, strong wind, you have to blow really hard. Have the children blow as hard as they can. **When there is an earthquake, stomp your feet.** Have the children stomp feet for a few moments. **When there is a fire, you need to rub your hands together really fast.** Let the children quickly rub their hands together. Practice each motion a couple more times.

Bad King Ahab had a wife. Her name was Jezebel. When she heard that all the false prophets were gone from the country and the people were worshiping the one true God, she was very, very angry. She wanted to hurt Elijah.

Elijah was scared for his life. He ran to hide. Pat your knees quickly. **He traveled into the desert. There he sat under a tree. "I can't go any further, God,"** he prayed. **God cared that Elijah felt bad. God sent an angel to feed Elijah. Elijah ate and slept. Again God sent an angel to Elijah. Again the angel fed Elijah. When Elijah felt better, he traveled a long way to get away from Jezebel.** Pat your knees.

After many days, Elijah came to a nice, dry cave. He climbed into the cave and went to sleep. Put your head on your hands.

God talked to Elijah. "What are you doing here, Elijah?"

Elijah told God, "I love God very much. But the people don't love You or serve You. Now they want to kill me."

God told Elijah that He was going to pass by. Have the children stand. **First a big, strong wind came past Elijah.** Have the children blow as hard as they can. **But God was not in the wind.**

Then there was an earthquake. Have the children stomp their feet. **But God was not in the earthquake. Then there was a fire.** Have the children rub their hands together. **But God was not in the fire. Then there was a gentle whisper. God was in the whisper. Elijah went to the doorway of the cave.**

God asked, "What are you doing here, Elijah?"

Elijah told God, "I love You very much. But I feel bad and all alone. And the people are trying to kill me."

God said, "It's okay. You are not alone. I have a plan for you, and I care for you when you feel bad."

Make sure the children understood the main points of the Bible story: **Why did Elijah run away?** (Jezebel was trying to kill him.) **How did God come to Elijah?** (In a gentle whisper.)

NOAH'S PARK PUPPETS
God Cares

Let the Noah's Park puppets lead the children to the puppet stage. When everyone is ready, let the Park Patrol present today's skit, found on page RP-73 of the *Puppet Skits Book*.

BIBLE MEMORY
God Is Passing By

Supplies: none

Preparation: Choose a verse that supports today's Bible story. Divide it into four parts, and write them on the board. Draw a box around each part.

Tell the class that while they say the verse, they will act out the four things Elijah experienced—wind, earthquake, fire, and a quiet whisper. Each section of the verse can correspond to one of the actions.

Practice together. Say the first section of the verse and have kids act out "wind." For the second part they act out an earthquake. When they say the third part of the verse they act out fire. And for the fourth part they whisper it.

If the verse is too short to divide into four parts, have the kids do each action as they say the whole verse.

Repeat until the children are confident with the verse.

Sometimes we do feel discouraged or sad. God wants to comfort us. He cares when we feel bad. We can praise God for caring for us, and praising Him will help us feel better too. So let's sing to God!

WORSHIP TRAILS

SINGING PRAISES TO JESUS

Supplies: Noah's Park CD and CD player

Begin by singing the unit song, "I Wanna Live God's Way." Encourage the children to sing with smiles to show that they are not discouraged when they are praising God.

SHARE AND PRAYER
Prayers for Sad Times

Supplies: None

There are many people all around us who feel bad. Maybe you can think of someone who is having a tough time. When we think of some-one who is unhappy, we can be reminded to pray for that person. Ask the children if they know someone who is having a hard time. Let volunteers briefly share. After each child shares, pause and pray aloud for that person to know that God cares. For example, "Lord, Jordan's Uncle Bob just lost his job; please help him to know You care and help him find a new job." The child who mentions the request could pray, or another volunteer, if your children are confident. Allow time for all who wish to name someone to pray for and pray. When finished praying, encourage the children to pray throughout the week for themselves and others who may be feeling bad. Knowing that God cares can really help!

WILDLIFE TRAILS

At this time, separate suggestions are provided for preschoolers and elementary-age children. Arrange different areas of your space for the two groups.

SNACK SHACK
Comfort Food

Today's snack is found on page RS-73 of the *Snacks and Games Book*. Signal Park Patrol members when it is time to set up the snack. They should wipe off tables and get all of the items ready.

CAMPSITE CAPERS
Who Cared for Me? (Elementary)
Where Is God? (Preschool)

Directions for the preschool and elementary games are found in the *Snacks and Games Book*. The preschool game, "Where Is God?" is on page RS-74, and the elementary game, "Who Cared for Me?," is on page RS-73. Remind the children that having fun playing a game is a good way to feel better.

COZY CAVE CRAFTS
Stone Reminder (Elementary)
"God Cares" Heart (Preschool)

Preschoolers will enjoy their craft, "'God Cares' Heart," found on page RC-74 of the *Craft Book*. The elementary craft, "Stone Reminder," is found on RC-73 of the *Craft Book*.

HAPPY TRAILS

CLOSING ACTIVITIES

A few minutes before class is over, play the unit song to signal time for everyone to help clean up.

When finished, gather the children together to wrap up the session. Review the Bible memory verse and Bible story. Let the children use their crafts to tell how they will remember that God cares when they feel bad.

OVERTIME ACTIVITIES

While you are waiting for parents to arrive, play another round or two of one of the Campsite capers games. You might also have books and puppets for children to play with.

R35 Lesson: Learn from People Who Follow God

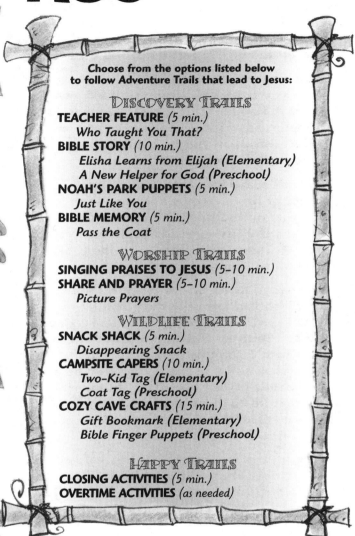

Choose from the options listed below
to follow Adventure Trails that lead to Jesus:

Discovery Trails
TEACHER FEATURE *(5 min.)*
  Who Taught You That?
BIBLE STORY *(10 min.)*
  Elisha Learns from Elijah (Elementary)
  A New Helper for God (Preschool)
NOAH'S PARK PUPPETS *(5 min.)*
  Just Like You
BIBLE MEMORY *(5 min.)*
  Pass the Coat

Worship Trails
SINGING PRAISES TO JESUS *(5–10 min.)*
SHARE AND PRAYER *(5–10 min.)*
  Picture Prayers

Wildlife Trails
SNACK SHACK *(5 min.)*
  Disappearing Snack
CAMPSITE CAPERS *(10 min.)*
  Two-Kid Tag (Elementary)
  Coat Tag (Preschool)
COZY CAVE CRAFTS *(15 min.)*
  Gift Bookmark (Elementary)
  Bible Finger Puppets (Preschool)

Happy Trails
CLOSING ACTIVITIES *(5 min.)*
OVERTIME ACTIVITIES *(as needed)*

taught you to ride a bike, to cook a certain dish, a foreign language, to fish, to do your job, and so on.

I'd like to tell you about some of the people I have learned from over the years. I've had many teachers, and not always at school. Hold up one of the pictures so that all the children can see it. Tell who it is and what he or she taught you. You might tell how old you were and why you were grateful for what you learned. Perhaps the *way* that person taught was what made a difference in your life. Continue in this manner with other pictures you brought for a couple of minutes.

I know that you have teachers at school and are learning a lot from them. Let a few kids name some things they learned last week in school.

You've also been taught things outside of school, just as I was. Let's play charades and guess what you learned. Let volunteers act out something they've learned. Once the class guesses, have the child tell who helped them learn it. If you have time, give each child an opportunity to go.

Wow, you kids have learned a lot of things from a lot of different people. Isn't great to have good teachers and people who help us? In our Bible story we will meet someone who wanted to learn about God and had an awesome teacher. Let's find out more.

Age-appropriate Bible stories are provided for both the elementary and preschool age-groups. If you are separating the children, have your Park Patrol helpers lead them to the appropriate areas. When the Bible story is completed, bring the children back together for the puppet skit and other activities.

Discovery Trails

TEACHER FEATURE
Who Taught You That?

Supplies: Photos of people who taught you something

Preparation: Bring pictures of people who have taught you things throughout your life. You could use a yearbook, family photo album, church directory, newspaper clippings, or whatever you have on hand. Besides school experiences, include people who

ELEMENTARY BIBLE STORY
Elisha Learns from Elijah
(1 Kings 19:19-21; 2 Kings 2:1-15)

Supplies: Bible, coat, newsprint paper or poster board, marker

Preparation: Make two signs labeled "EliJah" and "EliSHa," being sure to emphasize the "J" and the "SH." You could write those letters in a different color or simply capitalize them as shown. This will help kids visualize and hear the difference between the similar names. Under Elijah's name write "teacher" in parentheses. Under Elisha's name print "student" in parentheses. Choose two Park Patrol helpers to hold the signs at the right time during the story.

See if a volunteer can find 1 Kings 19 in a Bible. Explain that today's Bible story comes from there and you are continuing the story of Elijah.

Elijah certainly saw God do many amazing things! Ask the class to name some of them. (Elijah saw God send fire from heaven, take care of him when bad kings and queens wanted to kill him, make the widow's flour and oil never run out, and bring the widow's son back to life.) **Last week, we learned that when Elijah was feeling bad, God took care of him and whispered to him.**

Who can spell Elijah's name? Let a volunteer spell it. Then signal the helper with the "EliJah" sign to hold it up. Point to each letter as you spell it for the class. **In today's story, we learn about a friend of Elijah's named Elisha.** Have that helper hold up the sign. Spell it as you point to each letter. From this point on, each time you say *Elijah* or *Elisha*, have the helper hold up the appropriate sign.

Elijah knew it was time for him to find and train the next prophet of God. Elijah went where workers were plowing a field with oxen. He went up to a young man named Elisha. Elijah put his coat around the shoulders of Elisha. This showed that he was choosing Elisha to take over his job as a prophet for God. Elisha understood. Right away he sacrificed his own plow and oxen to God. Then he followed Elijah and learned from him.

Elisha spent all of his time with Elijah. He learned everything he could from Elijah. Wherever Elijah went, Elisha went.

Then Elijah knew that God was going to take him up to heaven. Other prophets of God knew this too. So in every town they walked through, some prophets came up and said to Elisha, "Do you know the Lord is going to take your teacher from you today?" And Elisha said, "I can't talk about it!" And he stuck close to Elijah wherever they went.

Finally, they stopped at the Jordan River. Elijah went down to the water and did something unusual. He took off his coat and rolled it up. Then he smacked the water with the coat. Immediately the river parted and they walked on dry ground to the other side!

Elijah asked his student Elisha, "What can I do for you before the Lord takes me away?" And Elisha simply said, "I want to be as good a prophet as you. Ask the Lord to give me a double portion of the spirit He gave you." "That's a hard job!" Elijah told him.

Suddenly something that looked like a chariot of fire pulled by horses of fire appeared on the road. The chariot drove between the two men and Elijah was picked up by it. Then a powerful whirlwind took Elijah up to heaven.

Elisha stood alone on the road. He noticed that Elijah had left something behind—his special coat. Elisha picked it up and walked over to the river. When he touched the water with Elijah's coat, it parted! That meant that God had chosen Elisha to be a prophet like his teacher, Elijah. Elisha was glad that he had learned from Elijah, who followed God. We also can learn from people who follow God.

Discuss a few review questions to check children's comprehension: **How did Elijah pick Elisha as his student?** (Elijah put his coat on Elisha.) **What did Elisha do?** (He offered God a sacrifice and then followed Elijah everywhere, learning from him.) **What did Elisha ask for before the Lord took Elijah away?** (To have a double portion of his spirit—to be as good a prophet as he had been.)

PRESCHOOL BIBLE STORY
A New Helper for God
(1 Kings 19:19–21; 2 Kings 2:1–15).

Supplies: Bible, set of Bible finger puppets (*Craft Book*, p. RC-76)

Preparation: Make a complete set of Bible finger puppets from page RC-76 of the *Craft Book*. (You may use a piece of fabric instead of the paper cloak for telling this story.)

Our Bible story today comes from the books of the Bible called 1 and 2 Kings. Show the children 1 and 2 Kings in your Bible.

Put the Elijah puppet on a finger. Add the cloak. **It was time for Elijah to find a helper. One day he saw a man named Elisha.** Put the Elisha puppet on the other hand. You might point out that the two names sound similar yet are different people. **Elisha was plowing in a field. Elijah put his coat around Elisha's shoulders.** Put the cloak on the Elisha puppet. **This was Elijah's way of picking a helper. So Elisha said goodbye to his family and went with Elijah.** Move the Elisha puppet next to the Elijah puppet. Put the cloak back on Elijah.

From then on Elisha followed Elijah everywhere he went. Elisha learned everything he could from his teacher and wanted to be just like him once he had learned enough. Show the two puppets "walking" around together.

One day, Elijah and Elisha traveled a long time. Finally they came to the Jordan River. Elisha knew that it was time for Elijah to leave, so he made sure they stayed together. Have the Elisha puppet move closer to Elijah.

When they got to the river, Elijah took off his coat and rolled it up. Then he hit the water with it. Put the cloak on another finger and tap it in front of you. **The water divided and Elijah and Elisha walked across the river on dry ground! Then Elijah asked Elisha something very special. "Is there anything I can do for you before the Lord takes me up to heaven?" the prophet asked his student. "Yes," Elisha said. "I would like to have God's power like you so I can be a good prophet like you." "That's a hard job!" Elijah told him.**

Then something strange and special happened—a chariot of fire pulled by horses of fire suddenly appeared! It separated the two men. Bring the chariot puppet down from above and set it between Elijah and Elisha. **In a whirlwind, the chariot carried Elijah up to heaven.** Have the chariot puppet carry the Elijah puppet up and away; set them aside. Wear the Elisha puppet, and set the cloak in front of you.

Elisha was sad that his teacher had gone. Then he saw something on the road. It was Elijah's special coat. Elisha picked it up and walked to the river. Pick up the cloak with the hand wearing Elisha. **Elisha parted the water with the coat and walked on dry ground.** Tap the cloak in front of you. **That meant that God had chosen Elisha to be a prophet! Elisha was happy because he had Elijah as a teacher.**

- **Elisha learned from Elijah who followed God. We can learn from people who follow God.**

Discuss some Bible review questions: **Who became Elijah's helper and learned from him?** (Elisha.) **How did Elisha learn from his teacher, Elijah?** (He followed him everywhere.) **What happened to Elijah?** (He went up to heaven in a fiery whirlwind.)

NOAH'S PARK PUPPETS
Just Like You

After the Bible story, have the Park Patrol members assigned to the puppet skit get set up. Today's skit is found on page RP-75 of the *Puppet Skits Book*.

BIBLE MEMORY
Pass the Coat

Supplies: An oversized cloak or coat

Preparation: Choose a Bible verse for the children to memorize. Draw an outline of a coat or cloak on the board. Print the verse and reference on the inside of the coat.

Read the verse to the children, and have them practice reading the verse together. Talk about the meaning of the verse.

Remind the children that Elijah passed his coat on to Elisha as a way of giving Elisha the job of being God's prophet. Have the children be seated in a large circle. Choose a child and place the coat on his or her shoulders. The child stands and walks around the outside of the circle saying the memory verse. When finished, the child places the coat on the shoulders of another child. That child stands and walks around the circle saying the verse. Continue until all of the children have the opportunity to say the verse.

Elisha learned a lot about God from Elijah, who followed God. We also can learn from people who follow God. The more we learn about God, it makes us want to praise Him.

SINGING PRAISES TO JESUS

Supplies: Noah's Park CD and CD player

Play the unit song, "I Wanna Live God's Way," from the CD and let the children sing along with it. If available, let the children play rhythm instruments in time with the music.

SHARE AND PRAYER

Picture Prayers

Supplies: Butcher paper, crayons or colored pencils

Preparation: Hang some butcher paper on a wall.

Elisha learned about God from Elijah. It's wonderful that people can help us learn about God. Who are some of the people who have helped you learn about God? Let the children call out people who teach them about God, such as family members, Sunday school teachers, pastor, TV and radio preachers or singers, and so on.

Have the children come to the butcher paper. They should draw a small picture on the butcher paper of anyone they mentioned. Encourage the children to fill the paper with lots of people. If time permits, let the children color their people. Across the top, print: "Learn from people who follow God."

Gather the class around the butcher paper. Begin a prayer time, letting the children thank God for the people on the butcher paper. Encourage the children to say something special the person taught them about God.

The elementary and preschool children have separate activities for this part of the lesson. Play music from the Noah's Park CD as the children transition.

SNACK SHACK

Disappearing Snack

Today's snack idea is found on page RS-75 of the *Snacks and Games Book*. Choose a volunteer to thank God for the food before beginning.

CAMPSITE CAPERS

Two-Kid Tag (Elementary)
Coat Tag (Preschool)

Instructions for the elementary game, "Two-Kid Tag," are on page RS-75 of the *Snacks and Games Book*. The preschoolers will be playing "Coat Tag," with the directions on page RS-76 of the same book.

COZY CAVE CRAFTS

Gift Bookmark (Elementary)
Bible Finger Puppets (Preschool)

The preschool craft, "Bible Finger Puppets," is on page RC-76 of the *Craft Book*. Elementary-aged children will make "Gift Bookmarks." See directions on page RC-75 of the *Craft Book*. Be sure all the crafts have the children's names on them.

CLOSING ACTIVITIES

Gather the kids. Review the memory verse. Do a quick review of the Bible story by pointing to a child to begin retelling the story. Point to another child to pick up the story at that point and continue telling what happened next. Point to other children until the story has been told. It's okay if they get some of the facts out of order as long as they emphasize that Elisha learned from Elijah, who followed God.

Pass out the children's crafts. As each child leaves, remind elementary-age students to give their Gift Bookmark to someone and remind all the children to learn from people who follow God.

OVERTIME ACTIVITIES

With leftover class time, let the children retell today's story of Elijah and Elisha using two Noah's Park puppets.

R36 Lesson: Help with Any Problem

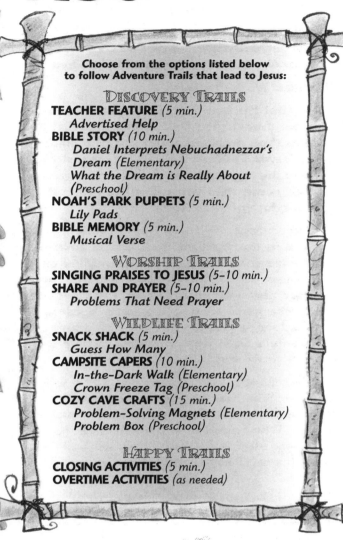

Choose from the options listed below
to follow Adventure Trails that lead to Jesus:

DISCOVERY TRAILS
TEACHER FEATURE (5 min.)
  Advertised Help
BIBLE STORY (10 min.)
  Daniel Interprets Nebuchadnezzar's Dream (Elementary)
  What the Dream is Really About (Preschool)
NOAH'S PARK PUPPETS (5 min.)
  Lily Pads
BIBLE MEMORY (5 min.)
  Musical Verse

WORSHIP TRAILS
SINGING PRAISES TO JESUS (5–10 min.)
SHARE AND PRAYER (5–10 min.)
  Problems That Need Prayer

WILDLIFE TRAILS
SNACK SHACK (5 min.)
  Guess How Many
CAMPSITE CAPERS (10 min.)
  In-the-Dark Walk (Elementary)
  Crown Freeze Tag (Preschool)
COZY CAVE CRAFTS (15 min.)
  Problem-Solving Magnets (Elementary)
  Problem Box (Preschool)

HAPPY TRAILS
CLOSING ACTIVITIES (5 min.)
OVERTIME ACTIVITIES (as needed)

DISCOVERY TRAILS

TEACHER FEATURE
Advertised Help

Supplies: Large brown paper grocery bag filled with a variety of objects that "help" people in some way (whitening toothpaste, bike helmet, first aid kit, map, portable CD player, dictionary, picture of a new car, etc.)

Place the bag where the children can't see into it. **Today we're going to talk about our problems. But it won't make us sad. I have all the help you need right in this bag. I've seen on TV and in magazines that certain things can help us with our problems. So I decided to help you with all of your problems, using these things. Let's give it a try.**

Ask a volunteer to name a problem he or she is facing. (Children might name things such as trouble in school, sibling issues, not liking their chores, etc.) Express sympathy for the problem. Then continue like this: **I bet something in this bag will help you with your problem. Reach in there and pull something out.** Don't let them look and whatever they pull out, exclaim how that is certain to help. For example, if the volunteer pulls out the toothpaste say, **I saw on TV that this whitening toothpaste will make you happy. Don't you think using this toothpaste would help you with your problem?** Let the volunteer or another child in the class explain why it wouldn't help.

Oh, well, maybe that wasn't the best choice. Let's try again. Continue to ask volunteers to come up, name a problem, and reach into the bag for "help." Each time, exclaim that whatever they grabbed is perfect and let the children explain why it's not.

You know, I don't think we're getting much help here for our problems. All these things I saw advertised don't really help at all! What *should* we do when we need help with a problem? Let the children suggest a variety of useful solutions, like going to a parent/teacher and praying.

Those are much better ideas than mine. Today we'll learn about a king in the Bible who needed help with a problem. But he didn't know about God—the one true God. Let's find out how he got help.

After dividing the elementary and preschool, have the Park Patrol lead them to their Bible story areas.

ELEMENTARY BIBLE STORY
Daniel Interprets Nebuchadnezzar's Dream (Daniel 2:1-49)

Supplies: Bible, Bible-time clothes for as many children as possible, crown

Preparation: Ask Park Patrol helpers to play the roles of Nebuchadnezzar, Daniel, and the wise man with the speaking part. Encourage them to act with drama and enthusiasm.

Show the class Daniel 2 in a Bible. Explain that today's story has all the action needed for an exciting play, so everyone will help act it out. Ask three children to play Daniel's three friends: Shadrach, Meshach, and Abednego. Ask the rest of the class to play wise men or court guards.

Have Nebuchadnezzar wear a crown and sit in a central chair. Daniel and the three friends wait in another part of the room (where they can see the play). Guards may stand behind the king, and the wise men wait by the door.

Nebuchadnezzar: *(Stands up and shouts.)* **Guards! Wise men! Everyone, come here!** *(Wise men come running. Nebuchadnezzar paces back and forth in agitation.)* **I had a dream! A very bad dream! I need to know what it means. Someone help me with my problem!**

Wise Man: **O great king Nebuchadnezzar, you need to chill. Just tell us your dream and we'll make up, er, I mean, we'll use our magic powers to tell you what it means.**

Nebuchadnezzar: **You're just trying to fool me. I want you to tell me what I dreamed. THEN you can tell me what it means. That way I'll know you're telling the truth.**

Wise Man: **O great king Nebuchadnezzar, no one on this whole planet can do that.**

Nebuchadnezzar: *(Points and shouts.)* **I'll have you all killed if you don't tell me my dream!** *(All the wise men run to side of room. Wise Man goes to Daniel, whispers the news, and leaves.)*

Daniel: *(Turns to his friends.)* **Shadrach, Meshach, Abednego—bad news! The king is going to have all us wise men killed if we don't tell him what he dreamed. Only God can do that. So let's pray.** *(Daniel and three friends kneel down and pray.)* **Lord God, please help us with this big problem.** *(After several moments Daniel jumps up.)* **I've got it! God told me what the king dreamed and what it means!** *(Looks up and raises arms.)* **Thank You, God!**

Nebuchadnezzar: *(Seated on chair.)* **I want all my wise men—Here!—Now!** *(All wise men, Daniel, and his friends go to the king and bow.)*

Daniel: *(Steps forward.)* **O great king Nebuchadnezzar, no one on this whole planet can tell you what you dreamed.**

Wise Man: **We told you so.**

Daniel: **But the Lord God in heaven sent you your dream. And He has told me what it was. You dreamed about a statue made of several different things. It means that you are a great king, and other kingdoms will come after yours. But the greatest kingdom of all is God's.**

Nebuchadnezzar: *(Falls to his knees.)* **Daniel, you're exactly right. Your God is amazing! He alone solved this problem.** *(Stands and announces.)* **The God of Daniel is the Lord God above all gods! Daniel, I will put you in charge of my whole country because God made you so wise. Let's all praise Daniel's God! He knows how to help with our problems!** *(All cheer.)*

Ask the children to be seated, and discuss a few review questions: **What was King Nebuchadnezzar's problem?** (He had a dream and didn't know what it meant.) **Who helped him?** (Daniel, because he prayed and asked God for help.) **How did God help?** (He told Daniel what the dream was and what it meant.)

PRESCHOOL BIBLE STORY
What the Dream Really Meant

(Daniel 2:1-49)

Supplies: Bible

Preparation: Practice saying the Bible story in rhythm while patting your knees, each line getting four beats (and each echo getting four beats).

Our story today is from the book of the Bible called Daniel. Show the children Daniel 2.

This is an echo story. I'll say a line and you say it back to me. Begin the rhythm—not too fast—and start the story. If the children's echo gets badly off the beat, simply beat a measure or two without speaking and then pick up where you left off.

King Nebuchadnezzar **King Nebuchadnezzar**
Had a very bad dream. *had a very bad dream.*
What did it mean? *What did it mean?*
"Tell me what I dreamed," he said. *"Tell me what I dreamed," he said.*
"Then tell me what it means." *"Then tell me what it means."*

All the king's wise men *All the king's wise men*
Didn't know the answer. *Didn't know the answer.*
"That's impossible, O king!" *"That's impossible, O king!"*
And the king was mad! *And the king was mad!*

Daniel heard the news. *Daniel heard the news.*
What did Daniel do? *What did Daniel do?*
He hurried home, told his friends, *He hurried home, told his friends,*
And kneeled down in prayer. *And kneeled down in prayer.*

For Daniel knew the Lord, *For Daniel knew the Lord,*
And God knows everything. *And God knows everything.*
God alone knows *God alone knows*
How to help us with our problems. *How to help us with our problems.*

When Daniel prayed to God, *When Daniel prayed to God,*
He learned about the dream. *He learned about the dream.*
So Daniel went to see the king. *So Daniel went to see the king.*
He told him about God. *He told him about God.*
"The Lord has told me everything." *"The Lord has told me everything."*
"And now I can tell you." *And now I can tell you.*

Daniel told about the dream *Daniel told about the dream*
And what it really meant, *And what it really meant,*
But most of all he showed the king *But most of all he showed the king*
That God knows everything. *That God knows everything.*

Nebuchadnezzar was amazed! *Nebuchadnezzar was amazed!*
He bowed down very low. *He bowed down.*

"Now I know the one true God." *"Now I know the one true God."*
"There is no god like Him!" *"There is no god*

like Him!"

God solved the mystery. *God solved the mystery.*
The king gave Daniel gifts. *The king gave Daniel gifts.*
And God can help each one of us *And God can help each one of us*
With each and every problem. *With each and every problem.*

Review the Bible story: **What did the king want?** (For his wise men to tell him about a dream and what it meant.) **Who told Daniel what the dream meant?** (God.)

NOAH'S PARK PUPPETS
Lily Pads

Lead the children to the puppet stage and have them be seated where all can see. Today's puppet skit is found on RP-77 of the *Puppet Skits Book.*

BIBLE MEMORY
Musical Verse

Supplies: None

Preparation: Choose a Bible memory verse that helps the children think about God's helping them with their problems. Think of a familiar tune that would fit the verse. Some ideas are "Row, Row, Row Your Boat," "Mary Had a Little Lamb," "Are You Sleeping," or "London Bridge." Plan to teach the verse using that melody.

Teach the memory verse by singing it for the class with the tune you chose. Sing it several times, and invite the children to begin singing along as it becomes familiar. When the children know it fairly well, divide the class in half and have each half sing every other line to each other. End by singing the whole verse in unison.

It's great that God knows how to help us with any problem! He deserves our praise. Let's worship God right now!

SINGING PRAISES TO JESUS
"It Pays to Obey"

Supplies: Noah's Park CD and CD player

Play the new song for Unit 9, "It Pays to Obey," for the children from the Noah's Park CD. If you have strong readers in your class you may want to project the lyrics on a wall. (Songs are in the back of this *Leader's Guide*.) Sing the song at least twice. Then sing other songs that will remind the children that God can help them with their problems.

SHARE AND PRAYER
Problems That Need Prayer

Supplies: Paper, crayons

God knows how to help you with any problem. This is our chance to talk with Him about a problem. First we'll draw the problem to help us think it through. Then you'll get to talk to God about that problem.

Have the children gather at tables to each draw a picture about a problem they need help with. When finished, divide the children into small groups. If possible, have a Park Patrol helper in each group.

Encourage the children in the groups to go around their circle, giving each child a chance to pray aloud about the problem in the picture they drew. If some children don't want to pray aloud, they could ask the Park Patrol helper or you to pray for them. When all the groups are finished, close the prayer time by thanking God for knowing how to help the children with their problems. Be sure children have their names on their pictures. Set them in a safe spot.

Enlist the Park Patrol to help, assigning their responsibilities ahead of time.

SNACK SHACK
Guess How Many

Ask Park Patrol helpers to set up for the snack found on page RS-77 of the *Snacks and Games Book*. They may need to wash the tables before and after the snack. Be sure to ask a volunteer to thank God for the food before beginning.

CAMPSITE CAPERS
In-the-Dark Walk (Elementary)
Crown Freeze Tag (Preschool)

Today's elementary game, "In-the-Dark Walk," needs a room that can be darkened. See ideas for this game on page RS-77 of the *Snacks and Games Book*. The preschool game, "Crown Freeze Tag," is found on RS-78 of the same book.

COZY CAVE CRAFTS
Problem-Solving Magnets (Elementary)
Problem Box (Preschool)

Today's crafts will give the children something to take home and remind them of the truth that God knows how to help them with any problem. The elementary craft, "Problem-Solving Magnets," is found on page RC-77 of the *Craft Book*. The preschool craft, "Problem Box" is on page RC-78.

CLOSING ACTIVITIES

A few minutes before class time is over, play the unit song as a signal that the children need to finish their activities and begin cleaning up. Allow a minute for all the children to help pick up part of the classroom. Then gather everyone together. Ask for volunteers to say the Bible memory verse. Review the Bible story by letting each child say one sentence of the story; another child says what happened next; another child adds a sentence to that; and so on. Have Park Patrol members hand out the crafts and pictures. As each child leaves, remind him or her that God knows how to help with any problem.

OVERTIME ACTIVITIES

If you have leftover time, get out the Bible-time clothes and let the children reenact the Bible story.

R37 Lesson: Trust God and Do What's Right

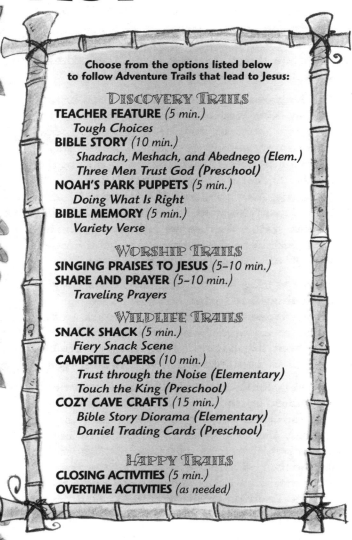

Choose from the options listed below to follow Adventure Trails that lead to Jesus:

DISCOVERY TRAILS
TEACHER FEATURE (5 min.)
Tough Choices
BIBLE STORY (10 min.)
Shadrach, Meshach, and Abednego (Elem.)
Three Men Trust God (Preschool)
NOAH'S PARK PUPPETS (5 min.)
Doing What Is Right
BIBLE MEMORY (5 min.)
Variety Verse

WORSHIP TRAILS
SINGING PRAISES TO JESUS (5–10 min.)
SHARE AND PRAYER (5–10 min.)
Traveling Prayers

WILDLIFE TRAILS
SNACK SHACK (5 min.)
Fiery Snack Scene
CAMPSITE CAPERS (10 min.)
Trust through the Noise (Elementary)
Touch the King (Preschool)
COZY CAVE CRAFTS (15 min.)
Bible Story Diorama (Elementary)
Daniel Trading Cards (Preschool)

HAPPY TRAILS
CLOSING ACTIVITIES (5 min.)
OVERTIME ACTIVITIES (as needed)

DISCOVERY TRAILS

TEACHER FEATURE
Tough Choices

Supplies: Index cards, pen, beanbag

Preparation: On separate index cards, write brief scenarios where children have a tough choice to make about right and wrong. Make enough cards so that every child in the class has one. If your class is large you may duplicate some. Turn the cards face down and spread them out on the floor in a

grid. Use" tough choices" like these for the index cards:

You broke a plate and are afraid you'll get in trouble when your mom finds out.

Your older brother just slugged you in the arm and you want to hit him back.

A mean kid on your street calls you names whenever you walk past her house; you'd like to get even.

All the kids are teasing one kid in your class; they might start teasing you if you don't join in.

You copied some answers on a test and now you think you should admit the truth.

You saw a friend take something from a store without paying for it. Do you turn your friend in?

Your whole team is cheering when the other team messes up. You're not sure that's being a good sport. Do you join in?

The other team was teasing you and then your team won. Do you say, "I told you so"?

One of the kids on your team is terrible, but you think you should pass the ball to her anyway. What if your team loses?

You want to hang out with your friends at church but the new kid looks lonely.

Your friend is trying to show you his new watch but the teacher is giving instructions.

You'd rather sleep in than go to Sunday school, but your mom is calling you. Do you get grumpy?

Sometimes we have tough choices to make. There are times when we know what would be the right thing to do—but we don't always feel like doing it. Sometimes we want to do the right thing but there may be a bad result. Let's look at some tough choices for you.

Have the children stand on one side of the grid of index cards. Ask for a volunteer to go first. Give that child the beanbag and have her take five steps back from the cards. The child tosses the beanbag onto an index card. Pick up that card and read it or let the child read it. That child must tell (1) if that would be a hard choice and (2) what she thinks she would honestly do in that situation. If a child admits she might not do the right thing, be accepting at this point, saying something like, "That would be a tough choice, wouldn't it?" Give each child in the class a chance to toss the beanbag and answer the situation on the card the beanbag lands on.

When everyone has had a turn, let the class be seated. **Our Bible story is about a really tough choice that three men had to make. Let's find out how God helped these men to trust Him and to do what was right.**

ELEMENTARY BIBLE STORY
Shadrach, Meshach, and Abednego Worship only God
(Daniel 3)

Supplies: Bible, Bible-time clothes, rhythm instruments

Preparation: Have Park Patrol helpers dress up as Shadrach, Meshach, Abednego, and Nebuchadnezzar.

Turn in your Bible to Daniel 3 and show the kids where today's Bible story is located. Have the Park Patrol helpers act out the story as you tell it. Give instruments to as many children as possible, but tell the kids to wait for the signal before playing them.

King Nebuchadnezzar built a huge statue of gold. He was so proud of the statue that he wanted all of the leaders of Babylon to bow down and pray to the statue like it was a god. There were many people from other countries living in Babylon and today we'll meet three of them: Shadrach, Meshach, and Abednego. Ask if the children remember these three friends of Daniel from last week's Bible story.

King Nebuchadnezzar said, "Whenever my special music is played on the instruments, everyone has to bow down and worship the statue. Anyone who doesn't bow down to my fabulous statue will be thrown into a fiery furnace!" And he made this the law.

So when the time came, the musicians began to play the music. Let the children play their instruments. **All of the people began to bow down. Shadrach, Meshach, and Abednego were from Israel, and they only worshiped the one true God. If they didn't bow down to the statue, they would die. If they did bow down, they could live but they would not be obeying God. They had a tough choice. They decided**

to trust God and do what was right.

The music sounded again. Let the children play the rhythm instruments again. **Everyone bowed low to the statue—everyone except Shadrach, Meshach, and Abednego. Suddenly someone shouted to the king, "Look, these men aren't bowing down to the statue!"**

The king was furious and had the men brought to him. King Nebuchadnezzar told them, "I'll give you one more chance. If you don't bow down to my marvelous statue, you will die!" The king signaled for the music to play again. Let the children play their instruments. **But Shadrach, Meshach, and Abednego did not bow down. They said, "We won't bow down to your statue because we only pray to the one true God. Even if you throw us in the furnace, we will trust God and do what's right."**

Now the king was furious! How dare they obey their God instead of him! King Nebuchadnezzar ordered the furnace to be made seven times hotter than normal. So Shadrach, Meshach, and Abednego were tied up and thrown into the fire in the furnace.

The king looked into the furnace—and then he looked again. Instead of three men, he saw four men walking around inside the fire. Quickly the king ordered for the men to come out. Everyone was amazed! Shadrach, Meshach, and Abednego didn't have any burn marks and they didn't even smell of smoke. The king cried, "Praise the God of these men!"

It took a lot of courage, but Shadrach, Meshach, and Abednego were happy they had trusted God and did what was right. We also need to trust God and do what's right.

What law did the king make? (When the music played, everyone had to bow down to a statue.) **Why wouldn't Shadrach, Meshach, and Abednego bow down to the statue?** (They only worshiped God.) **What should we do with a tough choice?** (Trust God and do what's right.)

PRESCHOOL BIBLE STORY
Three Men Trust God (Daniel 3)

Supplies: Bible, one complete set of enlarged

trading cards (*Craft Book*, p. RC-79)

Preparation: Use a photo copier to enlarge the trading cards from page RC-79 of the *Craft Book* as much as possible without being distorted. Make a set of the enlarged cards by copying them and coloring them with markers.

Our Bible story today is from the part of the Bible called Daniel. Keep your Bible open to Daniel 3 as you tell the story.

The Bible tells us about King Nebuchadnezzar. Show the card of the king. **He made a tall gold statue.** Show the card of the statue. **Then he called together all of his leaders and people. The king told them that when they heard the special music, all the people had to bow down and pray to the statue. Anyone who didn't would be in big trouble.**

There were three young men who worked for King Nebuchadnezzar. They were named Shadrach, Meshach, and Abednego. Set out each card as you say the name. **Shadrach, Meshach, and Abednego didn't believe in worshiping a statue. They only worshiped God. So they didn't bow down to the music. They trusted God and did what was right.**

When King Nebuchadnezzar heard about Shadrach, Meshach, and Abednego, he was very angry. He said to them, "I'll give you one more chance to pray to my statue! If not, I will throw you into the very hot furnace!"

Shadrach, Meshach, and Abednego told the king, "You don't have to give us another chance. We still won't bow down and worship your statue. We only worship God. We will trust God and do what's right."

So King Nebuchadnezzar had Shadrach, Meshach, and Abednego tied up and thrown into the very hot furnace. Set out the very hot furnace card. **As he was watching, he saw four men walking around in the furnace. One of them looked like an angel.**

The king told Shadrach, Meshach, and Abednego to come out of the furnace. He was amazed that they were not hurt at all. "You were right not to pray to my statue," the king said. **"Your God is the only God."**

Shadrach, Meshach, and Abednego trusted God and did what was right. You can trust God and do what's right too.

Discuss a few review questions to make sure they understood the story. **Why didn't the three men bow down and pray to the statue?** (They prayed only to God, the right thing to do.) **Who saved them from the very hot furnace?** (God.)

NOAH'S PARK PUPPETS
Doing What Is Right

Let a Noah's Park puppet lead the children to the puppet stage and get them seated. Today's puppet skit is found on page RP-79 of the *Puppet Skits Book*.

BIBLE MEMORY
Variety Verse

Supplies: None

Preparation: Choose a Bible memory verse that supports today's lesson. The verse the children are learning in Sunday school may be a good choice.

Say the verse a line at a time, and have the class repeat it after you. Do this until the verse is familiar.

Then let volunteers take turns leading the class in a different way to say the verse. They might have the class say it with their eyes closed, whispering, or while clapping on each word. Help each child to think of something different to do while saying the verse.

Shadrach, Meshach, and Abednego trusted God and did what was right. After God saved them in the furnace, I'm sure they felt like praising God. When God helps me do what's right, I want to praise Him too. Let's praise God now.

SINGING PRAISES TO JESUS
Supplies: Noah's Park CD and CD player

Lead the children in singing the unit song, "It Pays to Obey." You might use the rhythm instruments from the Bible story and let the children play along. If you don't have enough to go around, let the children hand their instruments to another child at the start of each verse. Feel free to sing other favorites.

SHARE AND PRAYER
Traveling Prayers

Supplies: Paper, marker

Preparation: Make signs labeled *School, Home, Sports, Church,* and *Store.* Hang each sign in a different spot in the room.

Why is it sometimes hard to do what's right? (Because sometimes bad things happen anyway.) **Shadrach, Meshach, and Abednego did what was right, and they were thrown in a furnace! If you do what's right, you still might lose a friend or be punished. But we have to do what we know is right. That shows our trust in God, and He sees our hearts. He is happy with us when we make good choices.**

Today we will do traveling prayers. Point out the five signs and read them with the children. **At each of these places, you often have to make choices.** Ask the children to give examples of a choice they might have to make in each place. **When you pray, go over to one of the signs and ask God to help you trust Him to do what's right when you're in that place. You can be specific and ask God to help you with something hard you know you have to do in that place this week. You can go in any order to any sign, so you all will be moving around at different times.** Ask the children to move quietly so as not to disturb those praying.

Let the children go and start praying, with kids going to all five places. Once children have prayed at all five signs, have them come back to a central spot and wait for the others to finish.

At this time, utilize the Park Patrol to help get the preschoolers and elementary-age kids to their separate areas for their age-appropriate games and crafts. You may combine the groups of children for snack time if you wish.

SNACK SHACK
Fiery Snack Scene

Today's lesson-related snack idea is found on page RS-79 in the *Snacks and Games Book.* Let the Park Patrol wear the Noah's Park puppets and chat with the children about their plans for this week.

CAMPSITE CAPERS
Trust through the Noise (Elementary)
Touch the King (Preschool)

Directions for today's elementary game, "Trust through the Noise," are on page RS-79 in the *Snacks and Games Book.* This game will be a noisy one, so consider playing it outside. The preschoolers will play "Touch the King," on page RS-80 in the same book.

COZY CAVE CRAFTS
Bible Story Diorama (Elementary)
Daniel Trading Cards (Preschool)

The elementary-age kids will be making "Bible Story Dioramas" to help them retell the Bible story. The art pieces and directions are found on page RC-79 of the *Craft Book.* The preschoolers will be making "Daniel Trading Cards," with directions on page RC-80.

CLOSING ACTIVITIES

Ask the children to help clean up the classroom. You may want to use Ponder the Frog to give them ideas of what they could straighten or pick up.

Gather everyone together. Let volunteers say the Bible memory verse. Pass out the crafts. You can let the elementary kids show their dioramas to the preschoolers and retell the Bible story.

OVERTIME ACTIVITIES

As you wait for parents to arrive, let elementary children share their dioramas with the preschoolers. Preschool children might show the older children their trading cards too!

R38 Lesson: A Nation That Disobeys God Is in Trouble

Choose from the options listed below to follow Adventure Trails that lead to Jesus:

DISCOVERY TRAILS
TEACHER FEATURE *(5 min.)*
   What Does That Mean?
BIBLE STORY *(10 min.)*
   Daniel Explains the Writing on the Wall (Elementary)
   Writing from Nowhere (Preschool)
NOAH'S PARK PUPPETS *(5 min.)*
   Big Trouble
BIBLE MEMORY *(5 min.)*
   Writing on the Balloons

WORSHIP TRAILS
SINGING PRAISES TO JESUS *(5–10 min.)*
SHARE AND PRAYER *(5–10 min.)*
   Prayers for Our Country

WILDLIFE TRAILS
SNACK SHACK *(5 min.)*
   Finger Writing
CAMPSITE CAPERS *(10 min.)*
   Following God through the Noise (Elementary)
   Party Relay (Preschool)
COZY CAVE CRAFTS *(15 min.)*
   Break the Code (Elementary)
   Obey God Mobile (Preschool)

HAPPY TRAILS
CLOSING ACTIVITIES *(5 min.)*
OVERTIME ACTIVITIES *(as needed)*

DISCOVERY TRAILS

TEACHER FEATURE
What Does That Mean?

Supplies: Books in foreign languages

Preparation: Gather books in foreign languages from the library or borrow some from people in the church. Set them out on a table for the children to look through before class.

Hold up a book. **I brought a book that I know**

you will enjoy. I'm going to ask someone to read part of it to you.** Ask an older child to read some of it aloud. If the child reads the words, ask another child to tell you what he or she said. **Why can't you tell me what it says?** (It's in a foreign language.) **How does it feel when you don't know what the words are saying?** (Frustrated, bored because I can't understand it, mad that I won't know the story, etc.) **How would you find out what the words mean?** (Ask someone who speaks the language, look it up in a dictionary, take time to learn the language, etc.)

Let's play a game. I'm going to say something in another language. First guess what language it is. Then guess what the phrase means. Read each phrase, one at a time. Encourage the children to raise their hands before answering.

Turkish: *Seni seviyorum* (I love you.)

Russian: *Gde tualet?* (Where's the toilet?)

French: *Je ne comprends pas* (I don't understand.)

German: *Schönen Tag noch!* (Have a nice day!)

Japanese: *Konnichiwa* (Hello.)

Hawaiian: *Mele Kalikimaka me ka Hau'oli Makahiki Hou* (Merry Christmas and Happy New Year.)

Italian: *Buon compleanno* (Happy Birthday.)

Spanish: *Quisiera comer como un rey?* (I want to eat like a king.)

Danish: *Hvor er den nærmeste rutsjebane?* (Where is the nearest roller coaster?)

(See: http://www.omniglot.com/language/phrases/index.htm)

It's fun to guess what someone in another language is saying. In today's Bible story there was a message that no one could figure out—and it was scary not to know what it meant. Let's find out who discovered the answer and what it said.

Have the Park Patrol lead the elementary and preschool children to their separate Bible story areas. If you choose to keep the children together for the Bible story, use the Elementary Bible Story to teach the lesson.

ELEMENTARY BIBLE STORY
Daniel Explains the Writing on the Wall (Daniel 5)

Supplies: Bible, paper, marker, goblet, party hat, blower, confetti, fake hand, magician's hat or wizard hat

Preparation: Before class, write each of these words on a separate sheet of paper: *Mene, Mene, Tekel, Parsin* (Note: the words differ slightly according to translations, please check your Bible and use those words in verse 25).

After King Nebuchadnezzar died, his son, King Belshazzar, was the new king. Belshazzar loved to throw big parties with lots and lots of drinking. Hold up the party hat, blow the party blower, and throw a handful of confetti over the kids' heads.

One night the king threw a party for a thousand people! Hold up the party hat, blow the party blower, and throw a handful of confetti. **King Belshazzar decided he wanted to drink wine out of some very special gold and silver cups that his father had stolen from God's temple in Jerusalem.** Hold up a goblet. **When the cups were brought, they were filled with wine and the king and his friends began to praise their own gods. That wasn't a very good idea!**

All of a sudden, fingers of a hand appeared— out of nowhere. Hold up the fake hand. **The fingers began writing something on the wall. The king saw this and turned as white as a ghost! His knees even knocked together.**

King Belshazzar called for his magicians and wise men to come. They were supposed to be the wisest people in the country. Hold up the magician's hat or wizard hat. **The king asked them to read what the hand had written on his palace wall.** Hold up the signs. **One by one they came and looked at the words, but not one single magician or wise man could read it or tell the king what it meant.**

Now the king was in a panic! The queen heard everyone going crazy and came to the banquet room. She calmly reminded the king that his father had had someone who had understood dreams and solved problems. Do you know who that person was? (Daniel.) **Yes, the queen told the king to ask for Daniel.**

So Daniel was brought before the king. He wasn't scared or panicked at the writing. He looked at it and God gave him the answer. Daniel explained to the king that God didn't like Belshazzar using the gold and silver cups that belonged in the temple. Hold up the goblet. **God really didn't like Belshazzar praising false gods for those cups. So God had put the message on the wall.** Hold up the fake hand.

Daniel said, "'Mene' (hold up the sign) **means that God says you don't have long left to live. 'Tekel'** (hold up the sign) **means the things you've done have been weighed on a scale and it doesn't add up to much. 'Parsin'** (hold up the sign) **means your kingdom will be taken from you and divided between two other countries."**

Daniel had done what none of the king's own wise men could do. Hold up the magician's hat or wizard hat. **They weren't so wise after all. The king rewarded Daniel and made him third-in-charge of the whole country. Daniel was glad that God had sent the answer he needed.**

That very night King Belshazzar was murdered. The nation was in huge trouble because of Belshazzar's sin. A foreigner became the new king and ruled the people. Any nation that disobeys God is in trouble.

Ask these questions to make sure the children understood the story. **Why was God angry with King Belshazzar?** (He used the cups from the temple and praised others gods.) **What made King Belshazzar so scared?** (A hand wrote a message on the wall.) **Why was Daniel able to know the meaning of the message?** (God gave him the answer.) **What happened to the nation?** (A foreigner came and ruled them.)

PRESCHOOL BIBLE STORY
Writing from Nowhere (Daniel 5)

Supplies: Bible

Our Bible story today is from the book of Daniel. Keep your Bible open to Daniel 5 as you tell the story.

The Bible tells us that the king gave a big party for a thousand people. They ate. Pretend to eat. They drank. Pretend to drink from a goblet. And the king asked that all the special gold and silver cups that had been stolen from God's temple be brought to the party. All the cups were brought in. The king and the people at the party started drinking from the special cups. As they drank, the king and the people praised false gods. It was not a good thing to do!

All of a sudden, a hand appeared out of nowhere and wrote on the wall. On the board write *Mene, Mene, Tekel, Parsin.* The king watched the hand write on the wall. He was so scared that he fell down. The party wasn't getting any better.

The king called for his wise men to find out what the words on the wall said. But none of the wise men knew what the words were. At this the king got even more scared.

The queen told the king to call for a wise man named Daniel. Since the king's father had trusted Daniel, maybe Daniel could help the king.

The king had Daniel come and look at the words. Point to the words on the board. "If you can tell me what the words say, I will give you expensive clothes and a special job," promised the king.

"I don't want those things," said Daniel. "Your father learned to not disobey God. But you have used the special cups from God's temple. You worship false gods. Here are what the words are: **Mene, Mene, Tekel, Parsin.** Point to each word as you say it. **The word** *mene* **means God has decided you won't live long. Your kingdom is over.** *Tekel* **means you have been judged. You don't live up to what God wants.** *Parsin* **means your kingdom will be divided and given to two kings from foreign countries."**

The king thanked Daniel and made him in charge of much of his kingdom. That very night, the king died. Another king came in and took over the kingdom. The king had disobeyed God and his country was in trouble.

Discuss a few Bible review questions: **What happened at the party?** (The king misused cups from God's temple and praised false gods, a hand wrote on the wall.) **What did the writing mean?** (The king had disobeyed God. His nation was in trouble.)

NOAH'S PARK PUPPETS
Big Trouble

Use Ponder the Frog to write a sign that says, "Follow me." Have Ponder hold up the sign and ask a child to read his message and explain it to the others. Then have Ponder lead the children around the room and to the puppet stage. Today's puppet presentation is on page RP-81 of the *Puppet Skits Book.*

BIBLE MEMORY
Writing on the Balloons

Supplies: Balloons, permanent marker

Preparation: Choose a Bible verse for the children to memorize that reinforces the unit theme, "A Time for Courage." You might want to use the memory verse from the Sunday school lesson. Inflate one balloon for each word in the verse. Write one word of the verse on each balloon with a permanent marker.

Place the balloons in the center of the group. Say the verse for the children. Have the children, one at a time, come and pick any balloon. That child reads the word on the balloon and then stands in line near where that word should go in the verse. Let Park Patrol members help non-reader with the word on their balloon and figure out where to stand. Continue until all the balloons are placed in the correct order. Then have the children say the verse together.

If you have more balloons than children, let the kids simply place their balloons on the floor in the proper spot in line. Ask Park Patrol helpers to help keep the balloons in place. As time permits, mix up the balloons and play again.

A nation that disobeys God is in trouble. Let's show God that we want to obey Him by praising Him now.

SINGING PRAISES TO JESUS

Supplies: Noah's Park CD and CD player

Tell the children that there is some writing on the wall for them to explain. Project the words to the unit 9 song, "It Pays to Obey," on a wall. (The words are provided on page 251 of this *Leader's Guide*.) Let volunteers explain the meaning of the song. Then play the song and let the class sing along. You may also let the children pick a few songs to sing together.

SHARE AND PRAYER
Prayers for Our Country

Supplies: None

We learned from our Bible story that a nation that disobeys God is in trouble. This would be a good day to pray for our country. What are some of the things we could pray for our country? List children's answers on the board. Encourage them to think of people who lead our country and cities, as well as opportunities for people to hear about Jesus.

When finished writing ideas of what to pray, read through the list again. Then ask for volunteers to each pray a sentence prayer about one of the items on the list. If needed, ask the Park Patrol to take turns to pray too. Then open a time of prayer. Allow time for those who wish to pray aloud. Close by thanking God for hearing our prayers and caring for our country.

For crafts and games, age-appropriate activities are provided for preschoolers and elementary-age children. Let the Park Patrol (previously assigned) lead the two groups to their separate areas and help them get started. The children may have their snack together or separately.

SNACK SHACK
Finger Writing

Today's snack suggestion is found on page RS-81 of the Noah's Park *Snacks and Games Book.* Have some of the Park Patrol helpers clean the tables and set up the snack for the group. Others in the Park Patrol may lead the children to a place where they can wash hands or use a liquid disinfectant.

CAMPSITE CAPERS
Following God through the Noise
(Elementary)
Party Relay *(Preschool)*

The elementary game, "Secret Message Relay," is found on page RS-81 of the *Snacks and Games Book.* The preschoolers will play "Party Relay," described on page RS-82 of the *Snacks and Games.*

COZY CAVE CRAFTS
Break the Code *(Elementary)*
Obey God Mobile *(Preschool)*

The elementary-age children will do a "Break the Code" project described on page RC-81 of the *Craft Book.* You will find directions for the preschool craft, "Obey God Mobile," on page RC-82 of the same book.

CLOSING ACTIVITIES

When the time comes for children to start cleaning up, play the unit song from the Noah's Park CD as a signal. Once the room is cleaned up, gather the children together to conclude today's session.

Review the memory verse together. Ask several children to tell something they remember from the Bible story. Give out crafts and let the children explain their craft to someone else.

OVERTIME ACTIVITIES

Sing along with the Noah's Park CD or read some Bible stories to the children.

R39 Lesson: Love God Every Day in Every Way

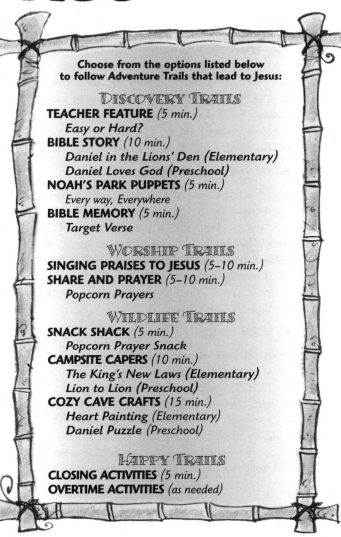

Choose from the options listed below
to follow Adventure Trails that lead to Jesus:

DISCOVERY TRAILS
TEACHER FEATURE *(5 min.)*
  Easy or Hard?
BIBLE STORY *(10 min.)*
  Daniel in the Lions' Den (Elementary)
  Daniel Loves God (Preschool)
NOAH'S PARK PUPPETS *(5 min.)*
  Every way, Everywhere
BIBLE MEMORY *(5 min.)*
  Target Verse

WORSHIP TRAILS
SINGING PRAISES TO JESUS *(5–10 min.)*
SHARE AND PRAYER *(5–10 min.)*
  Popcorn Prayers

WILDLIFE TRAILS
SNACK SHACK *(5 min.)*
  Popcorn Prayer Snack
CAMPSITE CAPERS *(10 min.)*
  The King's New Laws (Elementary)
  Lion to Lion (Preschool)
COZY CAVE CRAFTS *(15 min.)*
  Heart Painting (Elementary)
  Daniel Puzzle (Preschool)

HAPPY TRAILS
CLOSING ACTIVITIES *(5 min.)*
OVERTIME ACTIVITIES *(as needed)*

DISCOVERY TRAILS

TEACHER FEATURE
Easy or Hard?

Supplies: Paper for signs, masking tape

Preparation: Before class, make five signs: *Very easy, Easy, So-so, Hard, Very hard.* Hang them along one wall.

Let's find out if you think some things are hard or easy to do. I will read something to you; then you will go stand by the sign that answers how hard or easy you think it would be. **There are no right or wrong answers.** Read each sign to the children. Then read each phrase, and let the children stand by the sign that marks their answer.

You'd go with a friend to a movie.
You'd go with a friend to a movie, if they paid and bought popcorn.
You'd go with a friend to a movie, if you had to pay with your birthday money.
You'd go with a friend to a movie, if it was a movie you loved.
You'd go with a friend to a movie, if it was a movie you hated.

You'd obey your mom when she told you to come inside.
You'd obey your mom when she told you to come inside, or you'd be punished.
You'd obey your mom when she told you to come inside, if she gave you $5.
You'd obey your mom when she told you to come inside, if all the other kids stayed outside playing.

Gather the children back together. **What are some things that are very hard for you to obey?** (Go to bed, finish homework, be nice to my sister, etc.) **The Bible tells us to obey God because we love Him. But choosing to obey Him and do what is right isn't always easy. What if there would be punishment if we obeyed? Would it be easy or hard?** Let the children try to explain how they'd feel.

Today's Bible story is about someone who loved God every day in every way—but got in big trouble!

Divide the children into their two groups and have the Park Patrol lead them to their separate Bible story areas.

ELEMENTARY BIBLE STORY
Daniel in the Lions' Den *(Daniel 6)*

Supplies: Bible, poster board, marker, two classroom chairs

Preparation: Ask a Park Patrol member to play one of the parts and practice with you ahead of time. Set two chairs at the front of the Bible story area.

Host: *(Enters.)* **Welcome, friends at home and in our studio audience! Welcome to the best talk show ever! What a guest we have today—a real king! Are you ready to meet him?** *(Pauses to let children answer.)* **Let's give a warm welcome to King Darius!**

Darius: *(Enters and shakes hands with Host.)* **Thank you, thank you. It's great I can take time out of my busy kingship to stop by and tell you my very exciting story.** *(Both characters are seated but speak with animation.)*

Host: **We all know that you have been a great king for your country, Darius. You made good laws, and you put that famous man Daniel in charge of your whole kingdom.**

Darius: **That's right. Daniel was one of my favorite leaders. He did a great job. In fact, he did such a great job that my other leaders got jealous of him.**

Host: **Jealous? You mean they didn't want him to be in charge?**

Darius: **That's right. They all wanted his job. So they came up with an awful plan—behind my back—to get rid of Daniel. One day these leaders came to me with a suggestion for a new law. Now, you must remember that in a global kingdom such as mine there are many religions and people pray to many gods. My leaders thought it would honor me to have all the people pray to me.**

Host: **Pray to you?**

Darius: *(Looks a little embarrassed.)* **Only for 30 days! I must admit, even though it was silly, I went ahead and signed the law. But there was a trick in the law. No one in my entire kingdom would be allowed to pray to any other god during that time. I really was too busy to think about all the little details.**

Host: **But I thought that Daniel prayed only to the one true God. He was said to love God with all his heart.**

Darius: **Well, yes, that *was* the problem. Daniel apparently found out about the law and went straight home and prayed—not to me, but to his God—the one true God. You see, Daniel loved God very much and was in the habit of praying to God three times every day. He never missed it.**

Host: **Did Daniel get caught?**

Darius: **Yes. You see, my other leaders had set up this law as a trap. They watched Daniel pray, and then they came and turned him in to me. The leaders had set up the law to be one that even I couldn't break or change. Believe me, I looked for every loophole I could. By sundown that day, when the punishment was to take place, I hadn't found a way out for Daniel.** *(Gets up and paces across the stage.)*

Host: **What was the punishment?**

Darius: **To be thrown into a den full of hungry lions. It would be a terrible way to die. I really didn't want to lose Daniel. But at sundown, Daniel was taken to the lions' den. Just before they threw him in, I said to him, "Daniel, I really hope that your God will be able to save you." And then the guards threw him in.** *(Sits down in defeat.)*

Host: **That's awful!**

Darius: **Yes, it was terrible. I didn't sleep a wink all night. I didn't eat, didn't have my usual parties. I just paced the floor and hoped that Daniel's God was strong enough. At the crack of dawn the next morning I ran to the lions' den to find out what had happened. I hollered in through the opening, "Daniel! Was your God able to save you?"** *(Begins to choke up in tears.)*

Host: **Yes? What happened next?**

Darius: **I heard a voice. "Great king! My God sent His angel to shut the lions' mouths! I'm not hurt at all!" Daniel was alive and well! Right away I knew what to do. I had those evil leaders thrown right into the lions' den— they tried to have Daniel killed for nothing! And then I made another law that everyone in my entire kingdom must show respect for the God of Daniel.**

Host: **Wow, it sounds like Daniel loved God every day in every way—and God took care of him! Thanks for being on our show today, King Darius.**

Step away from the stage and discuss a few review questions with the children. **Why was Daniel in** trouble with his friend the king? (He broke the king's law and prayed to God.) **How did God help Daniel?** (God saved him from the lions.)

PRESCHOOL BIBLE STORY
Daniel Loves God (Daniel 6)

Supplies: Bible

Show the children Daniel 6 in the Bible. **Our story today comes from the part of the Bible called Daniel. Daniel loved God very much. Whenever you hear me say the name Daniel, draw a heart in the air with your fingers.** Show the children how to draw a heart shape in the air.

Daniel (draw a heart in the air) **worked for the king. The king liked his work. But some of the other men who worked for the king didn't like Daniel** (heart). **They wanted the king to like them just as much as he liked Daniel** (heart).

The jealous men tricked the king into making a special rule. The rule said that any man who prayed to anyone or any god except the king for the next 30 days would be thrown into the lions' den.

When Daniel (heart) **heard the king's rule, he went home just as he did on all the other days. Three times a day, Daniel** (heart) **knelt and prayed to God. Even though he could be caught, Daniel** (heart) **would show that he loved God.**

The jealous men spied on Daniel (heart). **They saw him praying to God. The men went to the king and asked, "What happens if we see someone praying to another god?"**

The king said, "If the law is broken, that person will be thrown into the lions' den."

The jealous men told the king that Daniel (heart) **had prayed to God. The king was sad. He like Daniel** (heart). **But even the king had to follow the rule. So the king's soldiers took Daniel** (heart) **and threw him into the lions' den. "I hope your God saves you!" the king told Daniel** (heart).

All night long the king worried in the palace.

What was happening to Daniel? (Heart.) **In the lions' den, Daniel** (heart) **was safe. God sent an angel to shut the lions' mouths.**

In the morning, Daniel (heart) **came out of the den. The king was so happy to see him! "Your God is the true God," the king told Daniel** (heart).

Bible review: **What did Daniel do?** (He loved God and prayed to Him.) **Who saved Daniel in the lions' den?** (God.)

NOAH'S PARK PUPPETS
Every way, Everywhere

Have a Noah's Park puppet lead the children to the puppet stage. Today's skit is found on page RP-83 of the Noah's Park *Puppet Skits Book.*

BIBLE MEMORY
Target Verse

Supplies: Poster board, marker, beanbags, (optional: masking tape)

Preparation: Choose a memory verse. Draw a target on poster board. The target should have three circles. Use the marker to write a number 3 in the small center circle, 2 in the next larger circle, and 1 in the largest outer circle. As an option, you could make the circles using masking tape on the floor.

Say the memory verse phrase by phrase with the children repeating it after you. Do this a few times.

Place the target on the floor. Divide the children into two groups. Have each group form a line a few steps back from the target. Let the first child say the memory verse and then toss the beanbag onto the target. Record the number of points the child received for his or her team. Then have a child from the other team say the verse and toss the beanbag. Alternate between the two teams until all members have had a turn. You might set the rule that whoever says the verse perfectly gets a second toss. Total up the points to see the highest score. Congratulate both teams on "winning" because they learned the verse.

Daniel loved God every day in every way. Let's show our love to God now by singing to Him.

SINGING PRAISES TO JESUS

Supplies: Noah's Park CD and CD player

Play the unit song, "It Pays to Obey," and let the children make up hand motions or movements that go with the words. Let the children practice singing and doing the motions at the same time. Let kids perform their song for their parents at pick-up time.

SHARE AND PRAYER
Popcorn Prayers

Supplies: None

We know we love God, but sometimes we don't stop and think about why. What are some reasons you love God? Let children suggest many reasons.

Today we are going to pray "popcorn" prayers, because you can each pop up whenever you want to finish the prayer sentence. It goes like this: I'll start a sentence, like "God, we love You because…" and then any of you can start popping up and finishing the sentence. You can pray in any order and you can pray over and over. Be sure the children understand. Then open the prayer time with a sentence-starter: **God, we love You because…** When the "popping" starts winding down, pray another sentence-starter: **And God, thank You for …** Let the children pop up some more.

Divide the children into age-appropriate groups for games, crafts, and a snack. Let the Park Patrol help the kids find where they need to go for each activity.

SNACK SHACK
Popcorn Prayer Snack

Today's snack suggestion is found on page RS-83 of the *Snacks and Games Book*. This snack is a reminder of the popcorn-like prayer time.

CAMPSITE CAPERS
The King's New Laws (Elementary)
Lion to Lion (Preschool)

The elementary-age kids will enjoy playing "The King's New Laws." The directions to this game are found on page RS-83 of the *Snacks and Games Book*. Preschoolers will play "Lion to Lion," found on page RS-84 of the *Snacks and Games Book*.

COZY CAVE CRAFTS
Heart Painting (Elementary)
Daniel Puzzle (Preschool)

The elementary craft, "Heart Paining," will need time to dry. You might consider moving this craft to an earlier spot in the lesson. Directions are on page RC-83 of the *Craft Book*. Preschoolers will work on a "Daniel Puzzle," on page RC-84 of the *Craft Book*.

CLOSING ACTIVITIES

Give a signal for all of the children to stop what they are doing and begin cleaning up. Let a Noah's Park puppet, worked by a Park Patrol member, circulate and say things like, "Helping the teacher is a way to show you love God." When finished, gather everyone together to wrap up the lesson.

Let volunteers say the Bible memory verse. You might let the children hold a puppet and make the puppet say the verse. If time permits, play the unit song and let the children practice the motions. If the kids are going to perform the song for their parents, arrange them in the area where they will perform.

Be sure the children pick up their crafts as they leave the room. Remind each child as he or she leaves to love God every day in every way.

OVERTIME ACTIVITIES

With any leftover time, let the children act out the Bible story (this time not as a talk show).

R40 Lesson: Believing in Jesus Changes Us

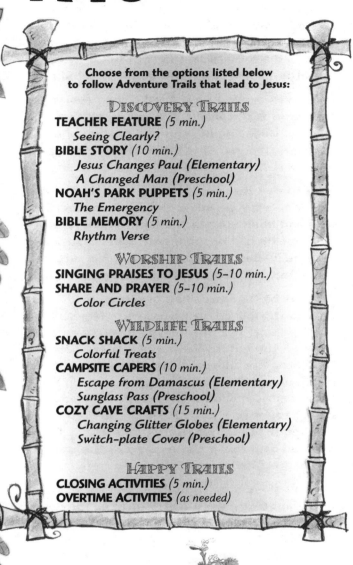

Choose from the options listed below to follow Adventure Trails that lead to Jesus:

DISCOVERY TRAILS
TEACHER FEATURE *(5 min.)*
   Seeing Clearly?
BIBLE STORY *(10 min.)*
   Jesus Changes Paul (Elementary)
   A Changed Man (Preschool)
NOAH'S PARK PUPPETS *(5 min.)*
   The Emergency
BIBLE MEMORY *(5 min.)*
   Rhythm Verse

WORSHIP TRAILS
SINGING PRAISES TO JESUS *(5–10 min.)*
SHARE AND PRAYER *(5–10 min.)*
   Color Circles

WILDLIFE TRAILS
SNACK SHACK *(5 min.)*
   Colorful Treats
CAMPSITE CAPERS *(10 min.)*
   Escape from Damascus (Elementary)
   Sunglass Pass (Preschool)
COZY CAVE CRAFTS *(15 min.)*
   Changing Glitter Globes (Elementary)
   Switch-plate Cover (Preschool)

HAPPY TRAILS
CLOSING ACTIVITIES *(5 min.)*
OVERTIME ACTIVITIES *(as needed)*

DISCOVERY TRAILS

TEACHER FEATURE
Seeing Clearly?

Supplies: Three visual aids (sunglasses, binoculars or telescope, a magnifying glass or a microscope)

Think about all the things you did this past week. You probably did some fun things, learned something, did chores, and went new places. Ask for a show of hands of who did these.

Now think carefully. Which parts of your body

did you use a lot to do those things? As the children discuss this, guide them to think about their senses—seeing, hearing, touching, tasting, and smelling. **God gave us five senses to help us get along in life. Not everyone has all five senses. When you did all these activities this week, you used most of your senses. Your probably used your ears and eyes quite a bit!**

Let's talk about our sense of sight. Not everyone can see well. In fact, many people use things to help them see better, like glasses or contacts. Other things might help you see better too.

Hold up a pair of sunglasses. **How many of you have ever worn sunglasses?** Allow for a show of hands. **How do sunglasses help us see better?** (They block the glare.) Hold up another eyesight aid, such as binoculars or a magnifying glass, and ask again. **How do binoculars (a telescope) help us see better?** (They make something that is far away seem a lot closer.) Hold up your third item, such as a magnifying glass or microscope. **How does a magnifying glass (microscope) help us see better?** (It makes something very tiny seem bigger.)

When we can see, we depend on our eyes. They give us lots of information. But did you ever notice that people often close their eyes when they're trying to think hard? Close your eyes and screw up your face as if you are thinking hard. **Sometimes, not being able to see helps us to think better. Our Bible story today tells us about someone who lost his ability to see because God knew he needed to think very hard about something very important.**

Separate, age-appropriate Bible stories are provided for the preschoolers and elementary-age children. Let your Park Patrol lead these two groups to their Bible story areas.

ELEMENTARY BIBLE STORY
Jesus Changes Paul (Acts 9:1-31)

Supplies: Bright or neon paper circles in these colors: green, red, yellow, blue, and purple; a rectangle of gray paper

Show the children where today's Bible story is found, Acts 9. **In the days after Jesus went up to heaven, the people who believed in Him tried their best to share the good news about Him with everyone. Believing in Jesus had changed them, and they were excited!** Hold up a green circle. Explain that the color green can mean new life or hope because it reminds us of new plants coming out in the spring.

There was a man named Saul who didn't believe in Jesus. In fact, Saul was really mad about these Christians who were telling everyone that believing in Jesus could change them. Hold up the red circle. Explain that red can remind us of anger. **Saul was an important man in the Jewish religion in Israel. He didn't think it was right to tell people that Jesus is the Savior. Saul was mad and tried to stop them.**

So Saul went to a city called Damascus to arrest the Christians. Hold up the red circle again. **He was traveling on the road with some men when suddenly a bright light from heaven flashed all around him.** Hold up the yellow circle and keep it up. **A voice said, "Saul, why are you hurting me?" They all heard the voice, but only Saul saw who was talking to him. "Who are you, Lord?" asked Saul. The voice said, "I am Jesus, the one you are hurting. Go to Damascus, and I'll tell you what to do."**

Then the bright light went away and Saul discovered that he was blind! Put down the yellow paper. **The men had to lead him. And for three days he wouldn't eat or drink anything.** Hold up the blue paper. Explain that blue is a color that sometimes means you're sad or thinking hard. **Saul was probably sad that he had been mean to Jesus' followers. He was thinking hard about who Jesus really was. Should he believe in Jesus? Did Jesus fit into God's promise to send a Savior?**

In another house in Damascus, Jesus appeared to a man named Ananias in a vision. Jesus told him to go find Saul and help him. But Ananias was afraid. Hold up the purple circle, which for now will represent fear. **Jesus explained, "I have chosen Saul to be My servant and to tell many people that I am the Savior."**

Hold up the purple circle again. **Even though he was afraid, Ananias went to the house where Saul was. Ananias spoke kindly to Saul, calling him a brother. And Ananias placed his hands on Saul's eyes and Saul was able to see again!** Hold up the green circle. **Saul was filled with hope! Jesus had forgiven him and healed him!**

He was so excited he started telling everyone that Jesus is the Savior. He no longer hurt anyone. Believing in Jesus had changed him! He even changed his name to Paul. Hold up the green circle.

Now some other people were mad. Hold up the red circle. **Everyone knew that Paul was the one who had been hurting the followers of Jesus— and now he had become one! Saul's old friends and the leaders were mad.** Hold up the red circle again. **They decided that Paul must die.**

The city of Damascus had big stone walls around it. Hold up the gray paper, to represent a block of stone. **The only way in or out was through the gates. The angry leaders watched the gates to catch Saul when he went out. But Saul heard about their plan.** Hold up the gray paper again. **One night his friends tied strong ropes to a large basket, and Paul climbed in. Then the friends quietly lowered Saul down the outside of the wall in the basket. He escaped!** Show the green circle.

Then Paul went to Jerusalem, but the Christians there were afraid of him. They didn't believe that Paul had really changed. But a Christian named Barnabas became Paul's friend. Hold up the green circle. **He helped Paul make friends with the other believers there. Everywhere Paul went he told people about Jesus, because Jesus had changed him.** Hold up the green circle.

Be sure children understood the main points of the Bible story: **What was Paul like before he met Jesus?** (He tried to arrest Christians.) **How was Paul different after he met Jesus?** (He told everyone the good news that Jesus is the Savior.) **What do we have to do to let Jesus change us?** (Believe in Jesus; give our lives to Him; etc.)

PRESCHOOL BIBLE STORY

A Changed Man (Acts 9:1-31)

Supplies: Bible, Bible-time outfit, sunglasses, flashlight

Preparation: Ahead of time, recruit a Park Patrol helper to pantomime the Bible story. Practice together, using the suggestions in parentheses in the story. The helper should dress in Bible-time clothes.

Our Bible story today is from the book of the Bible called Acts. Keep your Bible open to Acts 9 to reinforce that this story comes from the Bible.

The Bible tells us about a man named Saul. Have the dressed-up Park Patrol helper come in front of the class. **Saul was not a happy man.** *(Saul frowns and crosses arms.)* **He didn't like what Jesus' helpers were saying—that Jesus had died on the cross and came alive again so that people who believe in Him could go to heaven.** *(Saul shakes head "no.")*

Saul was so mad about what people were saying that he had a bad plan. *(Saul taps head as if thinking of a big idea.)* **He was going to travel to another city. There he would look for all the people who believed in Jesus and put them in jail.** *(Saul holds up muscle arms.)*

Saul started on his way. *(Saul walks around the room.)* **When he got close to the city, a bright light flashed around him.** Wave the beam of the flashlight around. *(Saul falls to the ground.)* **Then he heard a voice: "Saul, Saul, why do you hurt me?" Saul didn't know who was talking. Then he heard the voice again. "I am Jesus. Get up and go to the city. Listen to what you are told to do."**

Then Saul stood up. *(Saul stands up.)* **But he couldn't see!** Hand Saul the sunglasses to wear. **The men who were with Saul lead him to the city.** Have another helper lead Saul to a chair.

A man named Ananias visited Saul. He told Saul that Jesus had come to him in a dream. Ananias told Saul all about Jesus. *(Saul puts a hand by an ear as if listening.)* **Saul believed what Ananias said. Saul believed in Jesus.**

Then Saul could see again! *(Saul takes off the sunglasses.)* **Saul got up and was baptized.**

Instead of hurting the people who believed in Jesus, he helped them tell others. Saul was so changed that he got a new name—Paul. From then on, everyone called him Paul. Believing in Jesus changed Paul (or Saul).

Ask a few review questions to be sure the children understood the Bible story. **What did Saul want to do?** (Hurt the people who believed in Jesus.) **What happened on the way to the city?** (Jesus talked to Saul; Saul became blind.) **How did Saul change?** (He told others about Jesus.)

NOAH'S PARK PUPPETS

The Emergency

Let the Park Patrol lead the children to the puppet stage. Today's puppet skit is on page RP-85 of the Noah's Park *Puppet Skits Book.*

BIBLE MEMORY

Rhythm Verse

Supplies: Rhythm instruments

Preparation: Choose a Bible verse for the children to memorize to support today's lesson, or from Sunday school. Practice saying the verse in a rhythm that fits the words, figuring out where the beats fall.

Say the Bible memory verse for the children, using the rhythm you made up and clapping on the beats. Repeat, having the children clap on the beats as they listen. On the third time, have them say it with you.

Give out rhythm instruments, and let the group say the verse a few times while playing their instruments on the beats. When the verse is familiar, let volunteers "perform" the verse, using any instrument.

SINGING PRAISES TO JESUS

Supplies: Noah's Park CD and CD player

Introduce the Unit 10 song, "God Wants You," from the *Noah's Park Children's Church CD* by playing it while the children listen. If you have confident readers, you might project the words. See page 251 for reproducible lyrics. Sing the song a few times.

SHARE AND PRAYER
Color Circles

Supplies: Paper circles in red, green, yellow, blue, and purple; small envelopes

Preparation: Cut 2"-3" circles from red, green, blue, purple, and yellow paper, preferably bright or neon colors. (You can use the same paper from the Elementary Bible Story.)

Give each child a circle of each color and talk about what each represented in the Bible story. **These color circles remind us of all the things we can pray to Jesus about.** Hold up a red circle. **When we're mad, we can talk to Jesus and ask Him to help us do the right thing.** Hold up a green circle. **When we're happy, we can thank Jesus for whatever we're happy about.** Hold up a blue circle. **When we're sad, we can talk to Jesus about it, and He'll understand.** Hold up a purple circle. **When we're scared, Jesus helps us feel better.** Hold up a yellow circle. **And yellow reminds us to praise Jesus for being the Savior, who loves us and changes us.**

Divide the children into small groups. If possible, add a Park Patrol member to each group. **Let's pray with our color circles. When it's your turn to pray in your group, pick out a color and say a sentence prayer that the color reminds you of. For example, if you pick red, you might pray, "Dear Jesus, when I'm mad at my sister, please help me not be mean."** Let each small group pray at its own pace. Close the prayer time by thanking Jesus for changing us. Give each child an envelope to keep their circles in. and collect until the end of class.

Divide the preschoolers and elementary-age children, and send them to their craft and game areas with preassigned Park Patrol helpers.

SNACK SHACK
Colorful Treats

Today's snack suggestion is on page RS-85 in the *Snacks and Games Book.* Let a Park Patrol helper lead the children in thanking God for the food before eating.

CAMPSITE CAPERS
Escape from Damascus (Elementary)
Sunglass Pass (Preschool)

The elementary game, "Escape from Damascus," reinforces today's Bible story. Directions are on page RS-85 of the *Snacks and Games Book.* The preschoolers will be playing "Sunglass Pass," found on page RS-86.

COZY CAVE CRAFTS
Changing Glitter Globe (Elementary)
Switch-Plate Cover (Preschool)

The elementary craft directions for the "Changing Glitter Globe" can be found on page RC-85 of the *Craft Book.* The preschool craft, "Switch-Plate Cover," is on page RC-86.

CLOSING ACTIVITIES

Have the Noah's Park puppets, worked by the Park Patrol, encourage the children to help clean up the room. Then gather everyone together.

Let the children say the Bible memory verse, patting their legs on the beats. Close with a prayer, thanking Jesus for His ability to change us.

As children leave, be sure they get their crafts and an envelope of Color Circles from Share and Prayer time.

OVERTIME ACTIVITIES

While waiting for parents, let the children play with the Noah's Park puppets.

R41 Lesson A Willing Heart

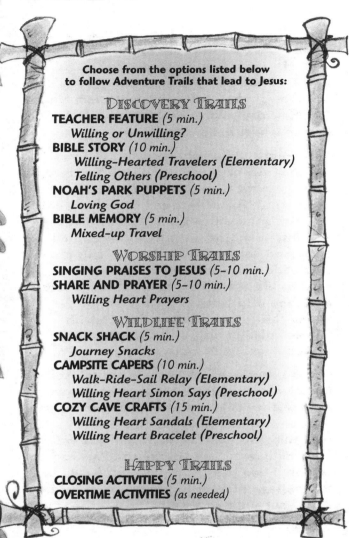

Choose from the options listed below
to follow Adventure Trails that lead to Jesus:

DISCOVERY TRAILS
TEACHER FEATURE *(5 min.)*
   Willing or Unwilling?
BIBLE STORY *(10 min.)*
   Willing-Hearted Travelers (Elementary)
   Telling Others (Preschool)
NOAH'S PARK PUPPETS *(5 min.)*
   Loving God
BIBLE MEMORY *(5 min.)*
   Mixed-up Travel

WORSHIP TRAILS
SINGING PRAISES TO JESUS *(5–10 min.)*
SHARE AND PRAYER *(5–10 min.)*
   Willing Heart Prayers

WILDLIFE TRAILS
SNACK SHACK *(5 min.)*
   Journey Snacks
CAMPSITE CAPERS *(10 min.)*
   Walk-Ride-Sail Relay (Elementary)
   Willing Heart Simon Says (Preschool)
COZY CAVE CRAFTS *(15 min.)*
   Willing Heart Sandals (Elementary)
   Willing Heart Bracelet (Preschool)

HAPPY TRAILS
CLOSING ACTIVITIES *(5 min.)*
OVERTIME ACTIVITIES *(as needed)*

DISCOVERY TRAILS

TEACHER FEATURE
Willing or Unwilling?

Supplies: Construction paper, masking tape, slips of paper, marker

Preparation: Make two signs on construction paper labeled "Willing" and Unwilling" with a heart underneath each word. Hang them up. On individual slips of paper, print willing and unwilling responses that kids might have, such as "I don't wanna," "Sure,

I'll do that," "Fine!" "Okay, I can come back to this later," "Can't I do it later?" "I'll stop what I'm doing and help," "That's not what I want to do," "I'll come right away," "Why do I have to?" "I'm happy to help you," "Why can't someone else do it?" and so on.

Have you ever been asked by your parents to help with something or go somewhere and you didn't want to do it? Think about what kinds of things you say when this happens. What you say and do shows whether your heart is willing or unwilling. Point to the signs and help the children read the words "willing" and "unwilling." **Let's figure out what this means.**

Today you'll all get to vote on kids with willing or unwilling hearts. Ask for volunteers to read aloud. Choose one for each statement you prepared, and have them line up in random order.

Tell the class that you will read some things that a parent might say to a kid. After each, one of your volunteers will read his or her statement. Then the class votes on whether that response shows a willing heart or an unwilling heart. That volunteer goes and stands by the matching sign. You may use these statements, adjusted to your class needs:

Can you help me with something?

We need to go run an errand.

It's time to come in for supper.

Can you keep an eye on your brother?

You need to turn off the TV now.

Don't forget to do your chores.

The dog needs some water. Can you get it?

Let's go pick up your sister.

Why don't you bring me another one?

I need you to do an extra chore today.

Once the class is finished voting, ask if anyone can describe the difference between having a willing or an unwilling heart. Let the children speculate. Thank the volunteers and let them be seated. **In our Bible story today, we'll see an example of when**

God asked someone to do some really hard things and if he had a willing heart or not.

Divide children into two groups, preschool and elementary, if you wish. Ask Park Patrol to lead them to their separate Bible story areas. Later, they'll come together again for the puppet presentation.

ELEMENTARY BIBLE STORY
Willing-Hearted Travelers (Acts 13)

Supplies: None

Today's Bible story comes from the Book of Acts in the New Testament. Show children Acts 13 in a Bible. Ask a volunteer to tell what happened in last week's lesson. (Paul was trying to arrest Christians; he met Jesus on the road to Damascus in a blinding light; he believed in Jesus and went to tell others about Him.)

Today we're going to follow Paul around on his adventures and see if he had a willing heart. Paul starts off in the church in a city called Antioch. Let's go there now. Have the group stand up and move to an open area of your room and be seated. **There were many teachers and prophets there. Paul learned a lot, and many of the Christians liked him now.**

One day they were all praying and worshiping the Lord. The Spirit of the Lord told the group, "I want Paul and Barnabas to do some special work for Me. Send them to travel and tell people about Me." Remind the children that Barnabas was the first Christian to believe Paul had really changed. **Paul could have had an unwilling heart and said, "Send someone else!" or "I'm happy here, I don't want to go!" But instead, Paul and Barnabas got ready right away, prayed with the church, and left.**

In Bible times, people had to travel by walking, riding a donkey or horse, or sailing on a ship. It took a long time and could be dangerous to travel far. Paul and Barnabas could have said, "That's too hard!" But they got on a ship and sailed. Have the class stand up and follow you one lap around the room, rocking back and forth like a boat. Have the children be seated again.

When Paul and Barnabas arrived on the island of Cyprus, they told everyone in the Jewish synagogue (house of worship) **about**

Jesus. **Then they traveled around the whole island, probably walking, visiting more synagogues.** Lead the children to a new spot to be seated.

In one town they found an important Roman leader who didn't believe in the one true God. He had a friend who did bad magic. Paul told him that was wrong and for punishment the Lord would make him blind for a few days. When that happened, the Roman leader believed in Jesus!

Then Paul and Barnabas had to sail again. Did they still have willing hearts? Yes. Lead the children to sail once around the room, landing in a new spot. **Again Paul and Barnabas went to a synagogue. There, Paul taught that the Old Testament promised that Jesus would come and be the Savior. He said Jesus is God's Son who died for our sins but came back to life again. Paul said, "Through Jesus, everyone who believes is forgiven for the wrong things they've done." The Jewish people couldn't wait to hear more. They invited Paul and Barnabas to come again.**

But the next week, the people weren't so friendly. Some of the synagogue leaders were jealous. They didn't believe in Jesus and didn't want anyone else to believe either. They said rude things to Paul and Barnabas. But did they still have willing hearts? Yes. Paul and Barnabas told them that now they would take the message of truth to non-Jewish people. Were Paul and Barnabas willing to change all their plans? Yes.

The synagogue leaders got the whole city mad at Paul and Barnabas. They got kicked out of the city! Did they still have willing hearts then? Yes. They walked or rode a very long way to another city and taught about Jesus there. Lead the children to "ride donkeys" to a new spot in the room and be seated. **Paul and Barnabas and all who followed Jesus were filled with joy. They did what God wanted with a willing heart. We also can do what God wants with a willing heart.**

Discuss a few review questions. **What did God want Paul and Barnabas to do?** (Travel and tell people about Jesus.) **What kind of attitude did they have?** (They had willing hearts.)

PRESCHOOL BIBLE STORY

Telling Others (Acts 13)

Supplies: Bible

Our story today is from the part of the Bible called Acts. Show the children Acts 13 in your Bible, and keep it open as you tell the story. As you do the actions in the story, encourage the children to repeat them.

Last week we learned about a man named Paul. The Bible tells us what Paul did after he believed in Jesus.

God sent Paul and his friend Barnabas on a trip. They were to tell others about Jesus. Paul and Barnabas walked to cities. Pat your knees as if walking. **They sailed on a ship.** Move your hands up and down in wave motions. **And they walked some more.** Pat your knees as if walking. **Everywhere they went, Paul and Barnabas told people about Jesus.**

One man they talked to was a leader in a city. He listened carefully to what Paul and Barnabas said. Cup your hand around an ear. **But one of the leader's helpers made fun of Paul and Barnabas and what they said. God made the helper blind. When the leader saw what happened, he believed in Jesus.**

There were other people to tell about Jesus. So Paul and Barnabas walked some more. Pat your knees as if walking. **They sailed on a ship.** Move your hands up and down in wave motions. **And Paul and Barnabas walked to cities.** Pat your knees as if walking. **Everywhere they went, Paul and Barnabas told people about Jesus.**

One day they went to the building where people worshiped God. The leaders of the church asked Paul and Barnabas if they had anything to tell the people. Paul stood up and talked. Cup your hands around your mouth. **Paul told them all about Jesus. The leaders asked them to come back in a week and tell more.** Hold up seven fingers for seven days. **Most of the people were happy to hear about Jesus.** Cup your hand around an ear.

The next week Paul and Barnabas went back. But some of the people weren't happy. Shake your head no. **They made Paul and Barnabas leave their city. Paul and Barnabas could** have been unhappy and quit. **But they had hearts that were willing to do whatever God wanted. So Paul and Barnabas walked to another city and told more people about Jesus.** Pat your knees as if walking.

Paul and Barnabas did what God wanted with willing hearts. We also can do what God wants with a willing heart.

Discuss some review questions with the children. **Who went where God told them?** (Paul and Barnabas.) **What did they do?** (They told people about Jesus with willing hearts.)

NOAH'S PARK PUPPETS

Loving God

Lead the children to the puppet stage. Today's show is on page RP-87 in the *Puppet Skits Book.*

BIBLE MEMORY

Mixed-up Travel

Supplies: Brown construction paper, scissors, marker

Preparation: Choose a Bible verse that reinforces today's lesson. Cut construction paper into fourths. On each fourth, draw a simple outline of a Bible-time ship, a donkey, or a sandal. Inside each picture print one word of the verse. Make a whole verse set of ships, donkeys, and sandals.

Divide children into three groups. Say the verse for the children a few times, and have them repeat each phrase after you. **In Bible times, people traveled by walking, riding, or sailing. These will help us learn our verse today.** Give each group a set of verse pictures. Have groups work together to lay out the pictures in word order on the floor or table. When all groups have the verse correct, let them trade pictures and repeat.

SINGING PRAISES TO JESUS

Supplies: Noah's Park CD and CD player

Sing together the Unit 10 song, "God Wants You,"

from the Noah's Park CD. Talk about any words or concepts that might be difficult for the children. Sing additional praise songs as time permits.

SHARE AND PRAYER
Willing Heart Prayers

Supplies: Construction paper hearts, markers

Preparation: From construction paper cut heart shapes three to four inches wide. On the board print "Do what God wants with a willing heart."

Give each child a paper heart and access to markers. Have the children copy the sentence from the board onto their hearts; they may use both front and back. They should add their names.

Have the children bring their hearts and gather in a circle for prayer. **What are some things that you need help doing with a willing heart?** Let the children brainstorm. (Doing chores, coming to church, obeying the teacher, being kind to a sibling, etc.) **Think about what you would like to ask God for help with. He will help you! And He loves it that you want to have a willing heart.**

I will start a prayer sentence. Any of you can finish the sentence in your own words as we pray around the circle. Begin a prayer time with, "Dear Lord, please help me have a willing heart with..." and let children pray aloud who wish to by simply finishing the sentence. If there is a lull, repeat the prayer starter. Close by thanking God for loving all the children very much.

The preschoolers and elementary-age children have separate, age-appropriate activities at this time. Let the Park Patrol help with each group.

SNACK SHACK
Journey Snacks

A lesson-related snack idea is provided on page RS-87 of the *Snacks and Games Book.* Ask Park Patrol members to wash tables off before and after snack time. A Noah's Park puppet could come and ask children questions about ways they have traveled.

CAMPSITE CAPERS
Walk-Ride-Sail Relay (Elementary)
Willing Heart Simon Says (Preschool)

Today's elementary game is a make-believe race called "Walk-Ride-Sail Relay." Directions are on page RS-87 of the *Snacks and Games Book.* The preschool game, "Willing Heart Simon Says," is on page RS-88 of the same book.

COZY CAVE CRAFTS
Willing Heart Sandals (Elementary)
Willing Heart Bracelet (Preschool)

The elementary children will be making "Willing Heart Sandals," described on page RC-87 of the *Craft Book.* The preschool craft, "Willing Heart Bracelet," is on page RC-88. Be sure children have their names on their crafts.

CLOSING ACTIVITIES

Play the unit song from the Noah's Park CD to signal that it is time to finish up activities and begin straightening the room.

Let the children bring their crafts to a large group wrap-up time. Let elementary volunteers tell the preschoolers about their crafts, and let preschool volunteers tell the elementary children about theirs. Have the whole group recite the Bible memory verse one more time. Before children leave, be sure they also have their Prayers from Share and Prayer time.

OVERTIME ACTIVITIES

As you wait for parents to arrive to pick up their children, let them work in groups to practice their memory verse using the picture cutouts.

R42 Lesson: We Give to Others

Choose from the options listed below to follow Adventure Trails that lead to Jesus:

DISCOVERY TRAILS
TEACHER FEATURE *(5 min.)*
  More or Less
BIBLE STORY *(10 min.)*
  Loving God by Loving Others (Elem.)
  Helping Others (Preschool)
NOAH'S PARK PUPPETS *(5 min.)*
  Giving It Away
BIBLE MEMORY *(5 min.)*
  Pass the Coin

WORSHIP TRAILS
SINGING PRAISES TO JESUS *(5–10 min.)*
SHARE AND PRAYER *(5–10 min.)*
  Prayer Holders

WILDLIFE TRAILS
SNACK SHACK *(5 min.)*
  Coin-shaped Treats
CAMPSITE CAPERS *(10 min.)*
  Roll It (Elementary)
  Gathering Gifts Relay (Preschool)
COZY CAVE CRAFTS *(15 min.)*
  Gift-giving Pouch (Elementary)
  Offering Basket (Preschool)

HAPPY TRAILS
CLOSING ACTIVITIES *(5 min.)*
OVERTIME ACTIVITIES *(as needed)*

DISCOVERY TRAILS

TEACHER FEATURE
More or Less

Supplies: Candies or small cookies, resealable plastic bags, paper lunch bags

Preparation: For most of the children in your class, place a handful of candies or small cookies in a resealable bag and then place each in a paper bag so no one can see what is in them. For the rest of the children, place only one candy or cookie in a plastic bag and also conceal each of these in a paper bag.

I have a treat for you today. Everyone come and get a paper bag. Your treats are in them. After you are seated again, you may open the bag and look inside, but don't eat yet.

Let the children follow these directions. Once all the treats are seen, the children will start commenting on the few children who got only one candy or cookie. Allow time for the class to interact about this. Some will say it's unfair; others will ask why the bags are like that. Simply explain: **When I was putting handfuls of treats in the bags, I started running out, so the last several baggies only got one each in them.** The children will probably keep talking among themselves. If no one suggests changing the situation, ask the children if anyone has any suggestions.

Most likely, some children with more will suggest sharing with those who have less. When that happens, allow those who wish to share some of their treats to do so. Then let everyone enjoy their snack.

How did it feel to have less than the others? Let volunteers respond. **How did it feel to share what you had with those who had less?** Let volunteers answer. **What made you want to share?** Allow children to try to put their motivation into words.

Our Bible story today is about some Christians who didn't have enough and what happened to them.

If elementary and preschool children usually separate for the Bible story, ask Park Patrol members to lead them to the right class area at this time. If you're keeping both groups together, use the Elementary Bible Story to teach the lesson.

ELEMENTARY BIBLE STORY
Loving God by Loving Others (Acts 19:21; Romans 15:25–27; 2 Corinthians 8:1-5)

Supplies: Bible, copies of the script for characters to hold, four chairs

Preparation: Invite three confident Park Patrol members to play Paul, a Jerusalem Christian, and a Macedonian Christian. Plan to play the host yourself. Rehearse the skit together. Set up four chairs in a semicircle at the front like a TV show stage.

Show children Acts, Romans, and 2 Corinthians in the Bible. Explain that Acts tells about the "actions" of the first Christians. Romans and 2 Corinthians are letters that Paul wrote to the Christians in Rome and Corinth. Tell the children that today they will get to be the audience of a TV talk show.

Host: (Enters.) **Welcome to the best talk show on TV! Today our famous guest is none other than Paul!** (Lead applause as Paul enters and both are seated.) **Welcome, Paul. I believe our studio audience has been learning about you—how you met Jesus in a blinding light and how you and Barnabas traveled all over the world to tell people about Jesus. Today we'd like to hear about your latest adventure.**

Paul: **Well, my latest adventure isn't really about me at all. But it is a story of international excitement and Christian churches on two continents. All I really did was travel.**

Host: **Paul, I think you're too humble. I have some more guests here to prove it. Please welcome a Christian from the church in Jerusalem!** (Lead applause as Jerusalem Christian enters and is seated.)

Jerusalem Christian: **I belong to the church in Jerusalem. That's in Israel. Things have been very hard there. There is not enough food. We all are very poor.**

Host: **And Paul helped you, didn't he?**

Paul: (Interrupts.) **Really, I didn't do anything but carry a message.**

Host: **Let's see about that. I have another guest you might know, here from the church in Macedonia!** (Lead applause as Macedonian Christian enters and is seated.) **Now, tell us about Macedonia and your church there.**

Macedonian Christian: **Macedonia is in Greece— a very long trip from Jerusalem. Paul came to teach us about Jesus. While he**

was there, he told us how much the church in Jerusalem was struggling. So we Christians in Macedonia decided to do something about it. We decided to collect money to send to Jerusalem.**

Paul: **Let me say that giving an offering was hard for the Macedonian Christians. I was struck by how poor they were themselves. They had next to nothing and they had been going through hard times too. Yet they wanted to give and give. They gave their money with joy, and they gave a lot—more than they could afford!**

Macedonian Christian: **We felt it was a privilege—a special treat—to be able to give to some other poor Christians.**

Jerusalem Christian: **Then Paul went out of his way to travel all the way back to Jerusalem to bring us the Macedonian offering. It helped so much! Not only did we have the money we needed, we were filled with joy that Christians far away were showing their love to us.**

Paul: **It was because they loved God that they gave their offerings. We all give because we love God.**

Host: **Thank you all for being on our show today.** (All exit.)

Discuss these questions to make sure the children understood the main points of the Bible story. **What problem did the Christians in Jerusalem have?** (They were very poor.) **What did the Christians in Macedonia do?** (They collected money even they though were poor too.) **What did Paul do?** (He took the offering to Jerusalem.) **Why did the people give money?** (Because they loved God.) **We also give to others because we love God.**

PRESCHOOL BIBLE STORY
Helping Others (Acts 19:21;
Romans 15:25-27; 2 Corinthians 8:1-5)

Supplies: Bible

Show the children the books of Acts, Romans, and 2 Corinthians. **Our Bible story today comes from three parts of the Bible called Acts, Romans, and 2 Corinthians.**

Tell the children that they will hear the question "What can we give?" during the story. Whenever they hear those words, they need to raise their hands out to their sides with palms up, as if asking a question. Practice a couple of times.

The people in the city of Jerusalem who believed in Jesus were very poor. They needed food. They need money to buy the food. What would they do?

Paul was in another country when he heard about the people in Jerusalem. The churches in that country were also very poor. But they asked, "What can we give?" Raise hands.

First, the people trusted in God. They knew that He would show them how to help the poor people in Jerusalem. So the people asked again, "What can we give?" Raise hands in question. **The people trusted in Paul to take the money to Jerusalem. Then the people gave as much money as they could—and even more!**

Paul wrote a letter to another city. The year before they had asked, "What can we give?" Raise hands in question. **They were happy to give money to help the poor people in Jerusalem. But they hadn't finished collecting the money. They had forgotten that they were giving because they loved God.**

So Paul asked the people to ask themselves, "What can we give?" Raise hands in question. **He wanted them to give what they could now. If they ever needed help, others would help them.**

Paul took the money that all the people in the different places had given. He brought it to the poor people of Jerusalem. They were thankful that people who loved Jesus had given money so that they could have food.

Review the main points of the Bible story with a few questions. **What did the people in Jerusalem need?** (Money to buy food.) **Who helped them?** (People who loved Jesus gave money.)

NOAH'S PARK PUPPETS
Giving It Away

Let a Noah's Park puppet begin to sing a praise song to get the children's attention over at the puppet stage. Then have the puppet invite the children to join him or her. When the children are seated, let the Park Patrol begin the puppet presentation. Today's skit is found on page RP-89 in the *Puppet Skits Book.*

BIBLE MEMORY
Pass the Coin

Supplies: A quarter or 50-cent piece, (optional: an offering basket)

Preparation: Choose a memory verse that supports the unit theme, "The Person Christ Needs." The verse learned in Sunday school may be a good choice to review and reinforce. Print the verse clearly on the board.

Have the children sit in a circle. Read the verse together as you point to each word. Be sure the children understand all the vocabulary. Read the verse together a few more times.

Give the coin to a child to begin. That child says the first word of the verse and passes the quarter to the next child in the circle. That child says the second word and passes the coin. Continue around the circle until the whole verse is said.

Repeat the game, encouraging the children to pass the coin faster as they get to know the verse. If they learn the verse quickly, begin passing an offering basket in the opposite direction at the same time that the coin is passing. The children must pay attention to both directions the verse is moving.

SINGING PRAISES TO JESUS

Supplies: Noah's Park CD and CD player

Let the children enjoy singing the Unit 10 song, "God Wants You," from the Noah's Park CD. If you have rhythm instruments, pass them out and let the children play along. Then let the children suggest additional songs to worship God with today.

SHARE AND PRAYER
Prayer Holders

Supplies: Paper or foam cups, brightly colored index cards, scissors, colored markers (if using plastic cups you will need permanent markers)

Preparation: Cut index cards into strips about an inch tall.

Give each child a cup and markers to decorate their cups with. They should include their name.

Because we love God, we show our love to others. One way to give to others is to "give" them our prayers. When we pray for others, we show that we love them. Give out the index card strips. **Think about people who could use your prayers. They could be family or friends. Or they could be other people you know who have a problem—a kid in your class, a neighbor, or teacher. Write each person's name on a slip of paper.** Have the Park Patrol circulate and help the children with spellings. After writing, have the children put their names into their cups.

You can use your Prayer Holders to remind you to pray for these people. At home this week, you can take one name out each day and say a prayer for the person. You can also add more names as you think of them.

Gather the children for prayer, with their Prayer Holders. Let each child pull out one name and say a sentence prayer for that person. You may want to begin and model how to say a brief but meaningful or specific prayer. When finished, have the children place the Prayer Holders in a safe spot until the end of class.

At this time, use the Park Patrol to help the children in the different age groups move to the appropriate areas for the snack, games, and crafts. If you prefer, you may keep all the children together for snack time. When they are finished, have the Park Patrol helpers take the children to their separate areas.

SNACK SHACK
Coin-shaped Treats

A lesson-related snack suggestion is offered on page RS-89 of the *Snacks and Games Book.* Ask Park Patrol members to wash and wipe tables before *and* after snack time. Have children wash or disinfect their hands before eating.

CAMPSITE CAPERS
Roll It (Elementary)
Gathering Gifts Relay (Preschool)

Today's games reinforce the content of the Bible story and get the children thinking about how to apply it. The elementary game, "Roll It," is described on page RS-89 of the *Snacks and Games Book.* The preschool game, "Gathering Gifts Relay," is on page RS-90.

COZY CAVE CRAFTS
Gift-giving Pouch (Elementary)
Offering Basket (Preschool)

The project for the elementary children, "Gift-Giving Pouch," is on page RS-89 of the *Craft Book.* The preschoolers will be making "Offering Basket." Directions for this craft are on page RS-90.

CLOSING ACTIVITIES

After children have finished their crafts, ask them to help clean up and straighten the room. Then gather everyone together for a brief review.

Ask for volunteers to say the Bible memory verse. Lead applause for all who try. Remind the children that they can give to others in many ways this week because they love God. Encourage the children to remember to pray for others using their Prayer Holders from Share and Prayer and to give of their money, using their crafts as a reminder. Close in prayer.

Be sure the children have their projects and belongings, and give all a hug as they leave.

OVERTIME ACTIVITIES

Review the songs from previous units. Let volunteers take turns making the Noah's Park puppets sing.

R43 Lesson: Jesus' Power Is for Real

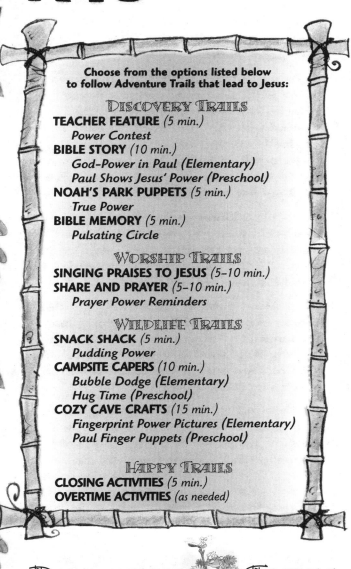

Choose from the options listed below
to follow Adventure Trails that lead to Jesus:

DISCOVERY TRAILS
TEACHER FEATURE (5 min.)
  Power Contest
BIBLE STORY (10 min.)
  God-Power in Paul (Elementary)
  Paul Shows Jesus' Power (Preschool)
NOAH'S PARK PUPPETS (5 min.)
  True Power
BIBLE MEMORY (5 min.)
  Pulsating Circle

WORSHIP TRAILS
SINGING PRAISES TO JESUS (5–10 min.)
SHARE AND PRAYER (5–10 min.)
  Prayer Power Reminders

WILDLIFE TRAILS
SNACK SHACK (5 min.)
  Pudding Power
CAMPSITE CAPERS (10 min.)
  Bubble Dodge (Elementary)
  Hug Time (Preschool)
COZY CAVE CRAFTS (15 min.)
  Fingerprint Power Pictures (Elementary)
  Paul Finger Puppets (Preschool)

HAPPY TRAILS
CLOSING ACTIVITIES (5 min.)
OVERTIME ACTIVITIES (as needed)

DISCOVERY TRAILS

TEACHER FEATURE
Power Contest

Supplies: Action figure of a strong superhero, toy truck, toy rocket, a star, or pictures of these things

Let's start today with a contest. Who would like to be in a contest of power? Choose five volunteers. **The rest of you will get to vote on the winner.** Line up the volunteers across the front. Put the tallest or strongest-looking one first in line.

All of our volunteers look strong. Do you feel strong today? Let the five answer. **What are some of the powerful things you can do?** Let any of the five name tasks they can do that require strength. **Well, I'm impressed. You are all very strong kids. Who's most powerful?**

Point to the first child. **You're the tallest here. Does that make you the strongest? It might. But what I didn't tell you is that some of our volunteers will get help to give them more power!** Give the action figure to the second child in line. **If** (name of second child) **was actually this action figure in real life, who'd be more powerful—our tallest friend or the superhero?** Let the class vote. **So there's some big power!**

Give the toy truck to the third child in line. **I'm giving you the power of a big truck. That's a lot of power! If this truck were life-size, which would be more powerful—the superhero or the truck?** Let the class vote. **That's tough. Some superheroes can stop trucks.**

Give the rocket to the fourth child. **Imagine a real rocket that has enough power to break the force of gravity and fly into space. Would this be the most powerful thing here?** Class votes.

Give the star to the last child. **If this were a real, fiery star out in space, who would have the most power in this line?** Let the class vote. **The star has power to destroy anything it touches. But there's something with even more power.**

Can you think of anything with more power than any of these people or things? Let the class give suggestions. **You all know Someone with ultimate power—it's Jesus. Let's see in today's Bible story just how powerful He is.**

If you divide your children for the Bible story, ask Park Patrol members to lead them to their areas.

ELEMENTARY BIBLE STORY
God-Power in Paul (Acts 19:11-20; 20:1-12)

Supplies: Bible, copies of the script, highlighter, something to use as a microphone

Preparation: Photocopy each person's part below, and highlight it. Prepare to be the reporter yourself.

Show the children where Acts 19—20 is in your Bible. Ask for volunteers to read parts in a skit. Spread out your volunteers around the room. Let the Park Patrol help them read through their parts. Have the rest of the children be seated in the center where they can turn around and see all the interviews as you "travel." Hold the "microphone" and begin the skit.

Reporter: **Thanks for tuning in to the Roman Empire News. I have a news story to report to you that will make your ears wiggle! And it all has to do with that famous follower of Jesus named Paul. Let's start in a city called Corinth.** (Moves to Corinthian 1.) **Good morning. What happened when Paul came to Corinth?**

Corinthian 1: **We had heard some things about Jesus. We wanted to believe in Him. Paul told us more. We believed and were baptized. Then the Holy Spirit came to us. We could speak in tongues and prophesy!**

Reporter: **Something only the Lord can make people do! What power! Thanks for sharing your experience.** (Moves to Corinthian 2.) **You also live in Corinth. What happened to you when Paul came?**

Corinthian 2: **I got to hear Paul teach about Jesus. He stayed here for two years. God did great miracles through Paul. God healed sick people when Paul prayed for them!**

Reporter: **Another miracle only the Lord can do! That really shows Jesus' power. Thanks for telling us what you saw. Let's sail now across the Aegean Sea to the city of Ephesus.** (Moves to another part of the room to the Ephesians.) **How did you meet Paul?**

Ephesian 1: **I had been doing evil things. I believed in fake gods and idols. I did bad magic. But I heard Paul teach about Jesus. I believed in Him. I wanted to change my life. So did lots of others.**

Ephesian 2: **Like me! We made a big bonfire and burned all the idols. We burned the evil scrolls we had used. It cost us a lot of money, but it was the right thing to do.**

Reporter: **Wow! Only God could change hearts like that. Jesus' power is for real!** (Moves to another part of the room to the Troas Disciples.) **Now we'll travel up the coast to the city of Troas. I heard that an amazing thing happened here.**

Troas Disciple 1: **That's right. I saw it happen. One night a lot of us met in a house where Paul was teaching. We were upstairs on the third floor. A young man named Eutychus was sitting in the window. Paul taught for a long time. And Eutychus got sleepy and fell asleep. He fell out the window!**

Troas Disciple 2: **When we ran down to get him, Eutychus was dead. But Paul wrapped his arms around Eutychus. Paul said, "Don't worry!" And then Eutychus came back to life! He even ate with us!**

Reporter: **What a relief! And what a miracle! It looks like the Lord has been doing many wonderful miracles through Paul. Jesus' power is for real! It was real for Paul and it's real for you and me too. Thanks for watching the Roman Empire News.**

Thank the actors and let them be seated. Discuss these questions to check comprehension. **How did Jesus show His power through Paul?** (By letting believers speak in tongues and prophesy, making evildoers change their ways, bringing a young man back to life.) **Can Jesus' power be real for us, too?** (Yes!) You may want to discuss ways the children might see Jesus' power in their own lives.

PRESCHOOL BIBLE STORY
Paul Shows Jesus' Power

(Acts 19:11-20; 20:1-12)

Supplies: Bible, Paul finger puppets (*Craft Book*, RC-92), scraps of cloth, a book or ledge

Preparation: Make a set of Paul finger puppets from page RC-92 of the *Craft Book*.

Open your Bible to Acts 19. **Our story today is from the book of the Bible called Acts.** Keep your Bible open to Acts as you tell the story.

The Bible tells us about Paul. Put the Paul finger puppet on one hand. **Paul traveled many**

places. He told people Jesus loved them.

When Paul wasn't telling people about Jesus, he sewed tents. When he sewed, he may have tied a handkerchief around his head to keep the sweat off. Put a scrap of fabric around the head of the Paul finger puppet. **Paul also may have put another piece of fabric around his waist like an apron.** Put a scrap of fabric around the waist of Paul.

In a city named Ephesus, God worked many miracles through Paul. When people who were sick touched the cloths that Paul had used when he worked, the people became well! Take the cloths off the Paul puppet. Put the sick man puppet on your other hand. Put one of the cloths on the sick man puppet. Act out the puppet being healed. **Paul showed that Jesus' power is for real.** Take off the sick man puppet and fabric.

One day, Paul was in another town named Troas. He wasn't going to be there very long. Have the Paul puppet on one hand. **So Paul spent many hours one night teaching a group of people about Jesus.**

One of the people listening to Paul teach about Jesus was a young man named Eutychus. Put the Eutychus puppet on the other hand. **It was very late at night and still Paul kept talking. Eutychus was sitting on a window ledge on the third floor, getting sleepier and sleepier.** Lay the Eutychus puppet down on the edge of a book or some type of ledge. **When Eutychus was sound asleep, he fell out the window! The people who ran downstairs and found him saw that he was dead.** Put Eutychus back on your hand, but lay your hand flat on the ground in front of you.

Paul went down to Eutychus and hugged him. Move Paul to Eutychus. Hold the two puppets close together. **"Don't be scared," Paul told the people. "He's alive!" Jesus' power had brought the young man back to life!** Make Eutychus stand up. **Then Paul went back upstairs and everyone ate supper and listened some more—even the young man.** Move Paul and Eutychus up "stairs." **Everyone was very happy.**

Paul showed by healing sick people and bringing Eutychus back to life that Jesus' power is for real. His power is for us, too.

Discuss a few review questions. **What happened when sick people touched the cloths that Paul wore?** (They were healed.) **What happened to Eutychus when he fell out the window and died?** (Paul hugged him and he became alive.) **What did Paul show?** (Jesus' power is for real.)

NOAH'S PARK PUPPETS
True Power

Let the children each pretend to be one of the Noah's Park animals and move in that animal's style to the puppet area. When all are seated, have the Park Patrol present the puppet skit from page RP-91 in the *Puppet Skits Book.*

BIBLE MEMORY
Pulsating Circle

Supplies: A Noah's Park puppet

Preparation: Choose a Bible memory verse that supports the lesson theme or Sunday school verse.

Have the children stand in a circle and hold hands. **We can't really *see* power happening. But sometimes we can feel it pulsing. Let's send a pulse of verse power around our circle!**

Begin by saying each word of the verse and have the class echo while lightly squeezing hands. Emphasize that the children should squeeze gently or their hands will quickly get sore. Then say the verse phrase by phrase and have the children repeat.

Pick a child to say the first word. He or she squeezes one hand to pass to the next person. That child says the second word of the verse and squeezes the hand of the third child. Continue around the circle in this fashion. In the beginning, a Noah's Park puppet, worked by the Park Patrol, might walk around behind the circle and whisper the next word of the verse when a child needs help.

As children learn the verse, increase the speed of the pulse around the circle.

SINGING PRAISES TO JESUS

Supplies: CD player and Noah's Park CD

Review the unit song from the Noah's Park CD. As time permits, sing other songs that praise Jesus' power.

SHARE AND PRAYER
Power Prayer Reminders

Supplies: Small stickers of superheroes, trucks, rockets, and stars; colorful index cards; markers

Preparation: Print "More Power Than..." on the board.

Give each child an index card, and let the children use markers to write "More Power Than..." along the top of *both* sides of their card. **Jesus' power is for real. What is Jesus' power bigger than?** Let the children offer answers. Pass out the stickers. **His power is bigger than superheroes, trucks, rockets, and stars, too, as we talked about in our opening Power Contest.** Let children add some stickers to *one* side of their card.

On the back of your card, we're going to explore how Jesus' power is real for *you.* **Think of some things in your life that you would like Jesus' help with.** Let volunteer name some, such as help with a mean kid at school, a relative who is sick, and so on. **Write down your things on the back of your card.** Let the Park Patrol help the children with spelling.

When finished, gather the children for prayer. Begin with a sentence-starter and let the children finish by naming something they wrote on their card. Begin with: **Jesus, we praise You for having power over...** You may have them take turns praying around a circle or simple let them call out their prayers random order. Whenever there is a lull, begin a new sentence, such as: **Jesus, please use Your power to help us with...** Collect children's cards and hold until the end of class.

This is the time to divide the class into two age levels: preschool and elementary. Play songs from the Noah's Park CD for the children to march to as they move to their next areas. You could leave the music playing during snack time.

SNACK SHACK
Pudding Power

You will need to plan a few extra minutes for today's "Pudding Power" snack. Details are on page RS-91 of the Noah's Park *Snacks and Games Book.* Let the children wash up before enjoying their refreshments.

CAMPSITE CAPERS
Bubble Dodge (Elementary)
Hug Time (Preschool)

Play "Bubble Dodge." Directions are on page RS-91 of the *Snacks and Games Book.* You may want to play this game outside. The preschool game is "Hug Time," on page RS-92.

COZY CAVE CRAFTS
Fingerprint Power Pictures (Elem.)
Paul Finger Puppets (Preschool)

Today's elementary craft, "Fingerprint Power Pictures," is on page RC-91 of the **Craft Book.** The preschoolers will make "Paul Finger Puppets," on RC-92. Have the children put names on their projects.

CLOSING ACTIVITIES

A few minutes before class is over, play the unit song from the Noah's Park CD to signal the children to begin cleaning up. When the room and supplies are clean, gather the kids for a brief wrap-up.

Let volunteers say today's Bible memory verse in pairs for the rest of the class. If they'd like, they may hold hands and "pulse" the words as they say the verse. Close the class in prayer, praising Jesus for His power.

As the children leave, be sure they have their crafts and "Power Prayer Reminders" from Prayer and Share.

OVERTIME ACTIVITIES

With an extra time while waiting for parents, let the children play some more "Bubble Dodge" (the elementary game) or just have fun blowing bubbles. Play the Noah's Park CD in the background.

R44 Lesson: God Is with Us in Hard Times

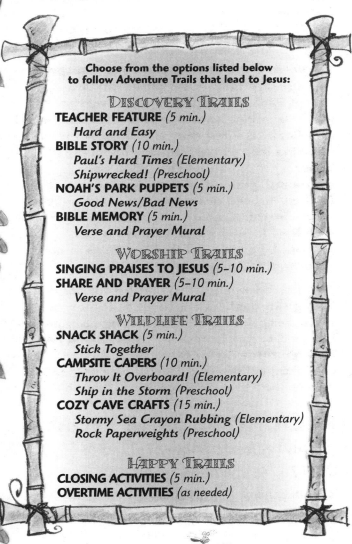

Choose from the options listed below to follow Adventure Trails that lead to Jesus:

DISCOVERY TRAILS
TEACHER FEATURE *(5 min.)*
  Hard and Easy
BIBLE STORY *(10 min.)*
  Paul's Hard Times (Elementary)
  Shipwrecked! (Preschool)
NOAH'S PARK PUPPETS *(5 min.)*
  Good News/Bad News
BIBLE MEMORY *(5 min.)*
  Verse and Prayer Mural

WORSHIP TRAILS
SINGING PRAISES TO JESUS *(5–10 min.)*
SHARE AND PRAYER *(5–10 min.)*
  Verse and Prayer Mural

WILDLIFE TRAILS
SNACK SHACK *(5 min.)*
  Stick Together
CAMPSITE CAPERS *(10 min.)*
  Throw It Overboard! (Elementary)
  Ship in the Storm (Preschool)
COZY CAVE CRAFTS *(15 min.)*
  Stormy Sea Crayon Rubbing (Elementary)
  Rock Paperweights (Preschool)

HAPPY TRAILS
CLOSING ACTIVITIES *(5 min.)*
OVERTIME ACTIVITIES *(as needed)*

DISCOVERY TRAILS

TEACHER FEATURE
Hard and Easy

Supplies: None

On the board, draw two columns and label them "Easy" and "Hard." Help the children read these words. **There are lots of things you have to do or deal with each week. Some of them are easy for you and some are hard. I'll name some things you might have done, and then** you'll vote by raising your hand. I'll count how many of you think it's easy and how many think it's hard and write down the numbers in these columns.

How many of you think it would be hard to change to a new school? Count the raised hands and record that number under "Hard." **How many think it would be pretty easy to make that change?** Count those hands and write that number under "Easy." Then move to more things children might do, and take a vote on each one. Choose some things that are very easy, some that are very hard, and some that children will disagree on. These are some ideas to vote on: climbing a tree, learning the ABCs, losing a pet, playing your favorite game, moving to a new house, going through a hurricane, feeding yourself, learning to add and subtract, having a very sick parent, having other kids mad at you, or giving hugs to a grandparent.

Some things are easy or hard for different people. Are there any things that are hard for all of us? Let the children offer ideas. Be encouraging and affirming to the children. **In our Bible lesson today, we'll see some really hard things that Paul went through, and we'll learn what helped him through hard times.**

If you separate elementary and preschool children before the Bible story, have Park Patrol members lead the preschool group and the elementary group to their respective class areas. Suggest to the children that they hop on the right foot five times, then on their left foot five times as they go to the Bible story areas. The groups will rejoin for the puppet skit.

ELEMENTARY BIBLE STORY
Paul's Hard Times
(Acts 21:27–36; 23:11–24; 27:1–44)

Supplies: Bible, poster board, markers

Preparation: Make some large cue signs from poster board, labeled: "Boo! Boo!" "Clap and Cheer!" and "Oh, no!"

Show the children the Book of Acts, where today's Bible story is found. Ask the class to tell you a little about Paul, who they've been learning about the past four weeks. As children share what they remember, emphasize that Paul always obeyed God.

In today's Bible story, Paul is still traveling all over the Roman Empire, telling everyone he can about Jesus. And he is still having exciting—and dangerous—adventures. Ask the children to help you tell today's story. Show the class the three signs. Explain that whenever you hold up the "Boo! Boo!" sign, the class should start booing. For the "Clap and Cheer!" sign, the children should clap and yell, "Yea!" For the "Oh, no!" sign, the children should say this once all together. Have the class practice these three signs a few times.

Paul was in the big city of Jerusalem. He loved to go to the temple to worship God and teach about Jesus. (Hold up the "Clap and Cheer" sign.) **But some of the people did not like Paul teaching about Jesus.**

One day, in the temple, they started shouting. "This man Paul teaches lies!" they shouted. "He is ruining what we believe about God!" The whole city got upset and came running. The people started booing Paul. (Hold up the "Boo!" sign.) **They grabbed Paul and started dragging him away, all the time shouting at him.** ("Boo!" sign.) **Then they started beating him.** (Hold up the "Oh, no!" sign.) **They were trying to kill Paul!** ("Again, hold up the "Oh, no!" sign.)

The Roman soldiers came running. They rescued Paul and carried him over their heads to take him to safety. ("Clap" sign.) **Paul asked to speak to the crowd, so the soldiers let him. Paul explained that he wasn't trying to make trouble. He told how he had met Jesus and that God had sent him to take this good news to the non-Jewish people. Paul knew that God was with him in hard times.**

The crowd interrupted and starting booing Paul! ("Boo" sign.) **The Roman guard took Paul to be whipped.** ("Oh, no!" sign.) **But Paul reminded him that this was against the Roman law.** ("Clap" sign.)

Later on, the leaders in Jerusalem got Paul arrested again. ("Oh, no!" sign.) **This time Paul was sent to the city of Rome to face an important judge. To get there, he had to sail on a ship with other prisoners. One day, a hurricane started blowing.** ("Oh, no!" sign.) **But God let Paul know that He was with him in this hard time.** ("Clap" sign.)

The winds blew for days and days. Everyone was just sure they would die—everyone except Paul. God had promised Paul that he would live. Paul encouraged the others. The ship finally crashed near an island. But it was breaking into pieces from the pounding waves. ("Oh, no!" sign.) **They all jumped overboard, grabbed a piece of broken wood to float on, and swam to shore. Paul and the others arrived safely.** ("Clap" sign.) **God was with Paul in hard times, just as He had promised.** ("Clap" sign.) **God is with us in hard times too.** ("Clap" sign.)

Ask a few review questions: **What hard times did Paul go through?** (Being booed and beaten by a crowd, being threatened with whipping, being in a hurricane, being shipwrecked.) **What helped Paul through these times?** (Knowing God was with him.) Point out that God does not promise to take away our hard times but to be with us through them.

PRESCHOOL BIBLE STORY
Shipwrecked! (Acts 21:27–36; 23:11–24; 27:1–44)

Supplies: Bible, masking tape

Preparation: Use masking tape to make the outline of a boat on the floor. The outline needs to be big enough to fit your entire class sitting down inside of it.

Lead the children to be seated outside the "boat." **Our Bible story today is from the book of the Bible called Acts.** Show the children Acts 21 in your Bible, and keep it open. Encourage the children to copy your actions as you tell the story.

Paul was in Jerusalem telling people about Jesus. Some of the people didn't like what Paul was saying. Shake head no. **While those people were trying to hurt Paul, some soldiers came and took Paul to jail.** Loudly clap hands one time to make the sound of a jail door shutting. **It was a hard time for Paul, but he knew that God was with him.**

Different leaders talked to Paul. Open and close your hands as if they were talking. **They didn't really know what Paul had done wrong, but they kept him in jail.** Loudly clap hands one time. It was a hard time for Paul, but he told the soldiers and leaders about Jesus.

Finally, the leaders decided to send Paul far across the sea to a city called Rome. The leaders there could find out what Paul had done wrong. The soldiers took Paul and his friends and put them on a ship. Lead the class to sit down inside the boat.

There was a huge storm where the ship was sailing. Rock back and forth. **The storm lasted for many days. The sailors were afraid. Paul told them not to be afraid.** Point up. **"God will keep us safe," he told them. "God is with us."**

The storm kept on blowing the ship. Rock back and forth. **Paul urged everyone on the ship to eat. They would need their strength.** Pretend to eat. **Even though it was a hard time, he knew God was with him.**

The next morning, the men on the ship saw a sandy beach through the stormy weather. Put your hands above your eyes as if peering into the distance. **They decided to try to sail the ship to the beach. On the way, the ship got stuck on some high land under the water and wouldn't go any farther. It started to break apart as the waves hit it. It was a very hard time for Paul and the rest of the people on the ship.**

But God helped them. Everyone either swam to shore or floated on wood till they got to the beach. Have the children get out of the boat and sit where you started to tell the story. **Everyone that was on the ship was safe!**

Paul had some hard times. God was with Paul in the hard times. God is with us in hard times too.

Use review questions to check the children's comprehension of the Bible story. **What happened to Paul?** (He was put in jail.) **What happened to the ship Paul was on?** (It was in a storm and started to break apart.) **Who was with Paul?** (God.)

NOAH'S PARK PUPPETS
Good News/Bad News

Move the children to the puppet presentation area while the Park Patrol involved in getting ready for the presentation. Today's puppet skit is on page RP-93 of the *Puppet Skits Book.*

BIBLE MEMORY
Verse and Prayer Mural

Supplies: Butcher paper, masking tape, marker

Preparation: Select a Bible verse that supports today's lesson theme, "God is with us in hard times." The verse the children started learning in Sunday school may work well. Tape a length of butcher paper along a wall. In bold letters print the memory verse. You might add a decorative border to the paper. This mural will be completed during Share and Prayer.

Have the children stand facing the verse mural on the wall. Read the verse together as you point to each word. Have the children pair up, with one person in each pair facing the mural and one facing away. **The Bible teaches that God is always with us. Right now you have a friend with you to help you learn the memory verse. The person with his or her back to the wall tries to say the verse. Whenever you need help with the next word, your partner can help you by reading the verse off the mural.**

Let the children begin. After each pair is finished, they switch places and the other partner has a chance to say the verse. Let the pairs switch places several times to help the children learn the verse. Then see if both partners in a pair can stand with their backs to the mural and say the verse in unison.

SINGING PRAISES TO JESUS
Supplies: CD player and Noah's Park CD.

Lead the children in singing the Unit 10 song, "God Wants You." You might help the children make up motions for key words in the song. If so, sing the song a couple more times to help the children remember the motions. Then sing additional praise songs as time permits.

SHARE AND PRAYER
Verse and Prayer Mural

Supplies: Verse and Prayer Mural from Bible Memory (still on the wall), colored markers

Have the children be seated at the mural with the memory verse. **This verse reminds us that God is always with us. Let's make this our prayer wall. Today you'll get to write and draw your prayers to God.**

What are some times when you would like to remember that God is with you? Let volunteers share some hard times they face.

We're going to spread out on this mural. You can write a prayer to God asking for His help with a hard time. Or you could draw a picture of the hard time. Or you could just draw a picture of Jesus and you. Whatever helps you talk with God about His being with you, that's what you can draw or write.

Give out colored markers and let the children write and draw all over the mural. Some children may prefer to simply decorate as they think about their personal prayers. Encourage the children not to worry about spelling, but do encourage the children to make this a quiet, prayerful time.

When everyone has had a chance to add a prayer to the mural, gather the children together and briefly wrap up prayer time by thanking God for being with us through everything we do, both hard and fun.

The following age-appropriate activities work best by separating the preschoolers from the elementary-age children. Let the Park Patrol lead the different groups to their activities.

SNACK SHACK
Stick Together

Today's lesson-related snack is described on page RS-93 of the *Snacks and Games Book.* The children will enjoy learning how God "sticks" with them through this edible object lesson. You may want to allow time for children to wash their hands after the snack.

CAMPSITE CAPERS
Throw It Overboard! (Elementary)
Ship in a Storm (Preschool)

Today's games reinforce the Bible teaching while letting the children use up some energy. Directions for the elementary game are on page RS-93 of the *Snacks and Games Book.* The preschool game, "Ship in a Storm," is on page RS-94 of the same book.

COZY CAVE CRAFTS
Stormy Sea Crayon Rubbing (Elem.)
Rock Paperweights (Preschool)

The crafts will give the children a tangible reminder that God is with them. The elementary craft, "Stormy Sea Crayon Rubbing," is on page RC-93 of the *Craft Book.* The preschoolers will make "Rock Paperweights," found on page RC-94. Be sure all the children have their names on their crafts.

CLOSING ACTIVITIES

A few minutes before class is over, encourage all the children to help with cleaning up. You might play music from the Noah's Park CD in the background.

Before leaving, let the class practice saying the Bible memory verse again. Point out the children's prayers on the Verse and Prayer Mural and remind the children that God will be with them all week. Close your class time in prayer. Give out the children's crafts as they leave.

OVERTIME ACTIVITIES
While waiting for parents, let the Park Patrol read the children a story so that you'll be free to greet and visit with parents as they arrive. Some children may enjoy playing a Campsite Capers game again.

R45 Lesson: The Promised Savior

Choose from the options listed below to follow Adventure Trails that lead to Jesus:

Discovery Trails

TEACHER FEATURE (5 min.)
  Promise-Keepers
BIBLE STORY (10 min.)
  God Promised a Savior (Elementary)
  God's Special Promise (Preschool)
NOAH'S PARK PUPPETS (5 min.)
  Saving from Death
BIBLE MEMORY (5 min.)
  Verse Scroll

Worship Trails

SINGING PRAISES TO JESUS (5–10 min.)
SHARE AND PRAYER (5–10 min.)
  Prayer Promises

Wildlife Trails

SNACK SHACK (5 min.)
  Sweet Scrolls
CAMPSITE CAPERS (10 min.)
  Scroll Search (Elementary)
  God's Promises (Preschool)
COZY CAVE CRAFTS (15 min.)
  Batik Promise Scroll (Elementary)
  Prophet Puppet (Preschool)

Happy Trails

CLOSING ACTIVITIES (5 min.)
OVERTIME ACTIVITIES (as needed)

Discovery Trails

TEACHER FEATURE
Promise-Keepers

Supplies: None

Preparation: Think through promise rhymes or "handshakes" you have known, or find out what kids do in your area to prove that their promise will "stick." Be prepared to share these with the class.

Ask the children to share about promise rhymes or handshakes that they know or that they've seen kids their age do to "prove" they'll keep a promise. For example, some children might know "Cross my heart and hope to die." Other children might know "pinky promise" with a pinky finger shake. Some children may raise their right hand or place their hand over their heart or perform a special handshake or fist-tapping. Let all volunteers demonstrate the "promise-keepers" to the class.

What does it mean when someone says or does one of these "promise-keepers"? (They will keep their promise.) **What if a friend just says, "I promise," but doesn't add anything special to it?** Let the children speculate on this. Some will believe there needs to be an extra-special promise, but others may realize that it's the person who's promising that makes the difference.

Who do you trust to keep their promises? Who would you not trust? Let children respond. **Why would you trust some of these people?** (Because they've always kept their promises, etc.)

Someone else makes promises to us, and that's God. In His Word, the Bible, God gave many promises. Some of them are for us now. Some were promises made thousands of years ago that came true hundreds of years ago. How do we know we can trust the Bible's promises? Because God made them. Let's learn about some of God's important promises.

At this time, divide the preschoolers from the elementary-age children and have a Park Patrol member lead them to their separate Bible story areas. If you choose to keep the groups together, use the Elementary Bible Story to teach the lesson.

ELEMENTARY BIBLE STORY
God Promised a Savior

(Isaiah 7:14; 9:1–7; Micah 5:2)

Supplies: Bible, Bible-time clothes

Preparation: Ask a Park Patrol member to read the part of Micah. Play the part of Isaiah yourself. Both of you should dress in Bible-time clothes.

Enter holding a Bible and looking as much like a prophet as you can muster. Greet the children warmly, and begin the monologue along these lines:

(Isaiah) **You may have heard my name before. I am Isaiah. Many of the things the Lord told me are written down in the Old Testament. I was one of His prophets.** Show the children the Book of Isaiah. **God gave me many messages for His people, Israel. Some of my favorites were about what God planned to do in the far future. These were great promises that His people could trust and look forward to.**

God knew that we really needed a Savior. Now, God had been planning this from the very beginning. He knew that people would do wrong things, called sin. He knew we had no way to work off our sins or be good enough to get to Him. So He planned to come down to us, through His Son, Jesus. It would be a long time, in human-years, before this could happen, so God told me promises I could give to the people so they would have hope during the long wait.

One of the first promises the Lord gave me was that a woman who had never been married would become pregnant, through God's power, and have a baby. That baby would be special, God's own Son.

Another promise God gave me was about how important the birth of His Son would be. The Lord knew that when we do wrong things, it's like walking in darkness. But God was sending a great light, to show us the way to Him. This Son of God would be called the Wonderful Counselor, the Mighty God, the Everlasting Father, and the Prince of Peace. He would be ruler of everything.

Hundreds and hundreds of years later, God made these promises come true. He kept His promises after all that time. Jesus' mother, Mary, had never been married. And Jesus grew up to be wise, peaceful, and wonderful. Because Jesus is God, He is in charge of everything and lives forever! I am so thankful that God gave me these promises to pass on to His people. Thank the children for listening and step aside for Micah.

Micah steps to the front and greets the children. He

or she takes the Bible from Isaiah and shows the children the Book of Micah. Then proceed like this:

(Micah) **This book here, Micah, is named after me—Micah! It's in the Bible because I was another one of the prophets that God gave messages to in the Old Testament. My messages don't take up a lot of room, but one of them was especially important to me. God told me to tell His people that He would send a Savior. And here's an important detail—the Savior would be born in the town of Bethlehem. I'm sure you've heard of Bethlehem. Who was born there? That's right, Jesus. And Jesus is the Savior God promised. He was born on earth hundreds of years after I gave this promise, but God kept His promise after all those years.**

Thank the children for listening, and remove your costume before asking a few review questions. **What did God promise?** (To send a Savior.) **Who did God give promises to about a Savior?** (Prophets who lived hundreds of years before Jesus was born—Isaiah and Micah.) **What did God promise?** (A young woman would have a baby by God, He would be a wonderful ruler who was really God, and He would be born in Bethlehem.)

PRESCHOOL BIBLE STORY
God's Special Promise

(Isaiah 7:14; 9:1-7; Micah 5:2)

Supplies: Bible, Prophet Puppet (Found in the *Craft Book*, p. RC-96)

Preparation: Make a Prophet Puppet using the pattern and directions on page RC-96 of the *Craft Book*. Bookmark Isaiah 7 and Micah 5 in your Bible.

Our story today is from the Bible. Set your Bible in front of you. **Today we have a visitor who would like to tell us our Bible story. His name is Mr. Prophet. Can you welcome Mr. Prophet to our class?** Put the Prophet Puppet on your hand and pretend to "walk" it up a staircase to bring in front of you. Then turn the puppet to face the children.

Move your hand to make the puppet talk as you speak for it. **"I am a prophet. I bring messages from God. I also tell people things that will happen in the future. In the Old Testament,**

God would speak to prophets. The prophets would then tell God's people His message. Sometimes prophets had bad news to tell from God. Sometimes it was good news.

"I'm going to tell you about two of my friends who were prophets. One was named Isaiah. He lived many, many years ago. Isaiah told a promise from God. God said He would send a Savior, someone to save us from the wrong things we do. Then God told my friend Isaiah more about that promise. He told the people that a young woman would have a son. He would have a special name called *Immanuel. Immanuel* means 'God is with us.'" Hold the puppet to the side.

Show the children where the Book of Isaiah is in the Bible. **What Isaiah wrote about God's promise in the Bible. It is in the book called Isaiah.**

Have the puppet talk as before. **"That isn't all Isaiah told about the Savior. He said the Savior would be from the family of David, our great king of Israel.**

"I'd also like to tell you about the prophet Micah. He lived at the same time as Isaiah. Micah also told about the promised Savior. He said that the Savior would be born in the town of Bethlehem." Hold puppet to the side.

Show the children where the Book of Micah is in the Bible. **What Micah wrote about God's promise is in the Bible. It is in the book called Micah.**

Have the puppet talk as before. **"Thank you for letting me come and visit today. I wanted to tell you that God promised us a Savior."** Have the puppet leave by turning him to the side and "walking" it down a staircase in front of you.

Ask a few questions to be sure the children understood the Bible story. **Which prophets told about God's promise?** (Isaiah and Micah.) **What did they say God promised?** (God promised a Savior.)

NOAH'S PARK PUPPETS
Saving from Death

Have Ponder lead the children to the puppet stage, asking what the Bible story was about. When the children are seated and listening present the puppet skit found on page RP-95 of the *Puppet Skits Book.*

BIBLE MEMORY
Verse Scroll

Supplies: Butcher paper, marker

Preparation: Select a memory verse about God keeping His promises, or choose the verse children started learning in Sunday school. Cut a long length of butcher paper into a strip about a foot tall. In wide letters, print the memory verse across it. Roll up the paper from both ends so it resembles a scroll.

Ask two Park Patrol helpers to stand in front of the class with the scroll between them and walk apart to unfurl the scroll. Point to each word of the verse as you lead the class in reading it together. Read it a few times so the children become familiar with it.

Have the helper holding the end of the verse roll up a few words, and have the class read the verse, including the words they can no longer see. Then unroll the end and have the helper at the beginning roll up the first few words. Repeat the verse in unison. Let the two helpers roll up different lengths at the beginning and end of the verse while the class says the verse after each change. Finally, roll up the whole scroll and see if the class can say the verse.

It's wonderful to be able to trust God to keep His promises. Let's praise Him now for keeping His promise to send the Savior, Jesus.

SINGING PRAISES TO JESUS
Supplies: Noah's Park CD and CD player

Introduce the new unit song, "Good News," by playing it on the CD and letting the children listen. You may choose to project the words on a screen. (Lyrics are provided on page 252.) Play the song a few times so the children can become comfortable with it.

SHARE AND PRAYER
Prayer Promises

Supplies: Quarter-sheets of paper with a Christian Christmas drawn symbol on them (star, crown, shepherd's crook, etc.), pencils

How good are you at keeping promises you make to others? Let volunteers describe. **Let's try keeping our promises today by promising to pray for a friend this week. Your prayers don't have to be long, but you can remember to thank God for that friend and ask Him to help that person.**

Divide the children into pairs. Be sure no one is left out or paired with someone that might feel awkward. If you have an odd number, let a Park Patrol member pair up with someone. Give every child a quarter-sheet of paper and pencil. **This symbol on your papers can remind you of Christmastime, when God promised to send a Savior. On your paper, write the name of your partner. Then ask that person if there's something you can pray about for him or her this week.**

Allow children time to talk. Encourage the children to name prayer requests, such as understanding a school subject, doing better at a sport they're trying, a sick family member feeling better, and so on, rather than general requests like "having a good week." Have the children jot down their partners' requests. The Park Patrol may help with spelling as needed. Children should write their names on their papers.

Open a prayer time for the class, and allow a minute for partners to say a sentence prayer for each other. You might model a short prayer by praying for a Park Patrol helper. Close by thanking God for keeping His promise to send a Savior.

You can promise your friend that you will pray for him or her this week. Then do your best to keep that promise. Collect the papers until the end of class.

The preschoolers and elementary-age children have separate activities for this part of the lesson. Let the Park Patrol use Noah's Park puppets to help the children transition and participate in their activities.

SNACK SHACK
Sweet Scrolls

Today's snack will remind the children of the scrolls used in Bible times. Directions are on page RS-95 in the *Snacks and Games Book*. Have the Park Patrol wipe off the tables before and after the snack. The children may need to wash their hands again after the snack to remove any stickiness.

CAMPSITE CAPERS
Scroll Search (Elementary)
God's Promises (Preschool)

Today's elementary game, "Scroll Search," is in the *Snacks and Games Book* on page RS-95. The preschoolers will be playing "God's Promises," described on page RS-96 in the same book.

COZY CAVE CRAFTS
Batik Promise Scroll (Elementary)
Prophet Puppet (Preschool)

The elementary craft will need time to dry during class. You might consider moving their craft time to an earlier spot in the lesson. Old Testament accounts were originally written on scrolls. The elementary children will be exploring this concept by making "Batik Promise Scrolls." Complete directions are on page RC-95 of the *Craft Book*. The preschool craft, "Prophet Puppet," is found on page RC-96.

CLOSING ACTIVITIES

A few minutes before class time is over, let the Park Patrol circulate with the puppets and ask the kids to finish up their activities and help straighten up the room. The puppets could give specific suggestions of chores to do. When finished, gather everyone together to wrap up the lesson.

Encourage the kids to sit with their prayer partner from Share and Prayer. Give out the Prayer Promises papers. Ask for volunteers of partners to stand and say the memory verse together. Then give out the crafts and be sure children have their belongings.

OVERTIME ACTIVITIES

While waiting for parents to pick up their children, play the unit song again and let the children make up motions for it or play rhythm instruments.

R46 Lesson: Jesus Is Both God and Human

Choose from the options listed below to follow Adventure Trails that lead to Jesus:

DISCOVERY TRAILS
TEACHER FEATURE *(5 min.)*
  More Than We Ask or Imagine
BIBLE STORY *(10 min.)*
  Human Baby, God's Son (Elementary)
  Jesus Is Coming! (Preschool)
NOAH'S PARK PUPPETS *(5 min.)*
  Two in One
BIBLE MEMORY *(5 min.)*
  Verse Groupings

WORSHIP TRAILS
SINGING PRAISES TO JESUS *(5–10 min.)*
SHARE AND PRAYER *(5–10 min.)*
  The Gift of Worship

WILDLIFE TRAILS
SNACK SHACK *(5 min.)*
  Bible-Time Foods
CAMPSITE CAPERS *(10 min.)*
  Gift Pyramid Relay (Elementary)
  Angel, Mary, Joseph (Preschool)
COZY CAVE CRAFTS *(15 min.)*
  God's Gift Pencil Topper (Elementary)
  Nativity Flannel Figures—Part 1 (Preschool)

HAPPY TRAILS
CLOSING ACTIVITIES *(5 min.)*
OVERTIME ACTIVITIES *(as needed)*

DISCOVERY TRAILS

TEACHER FEATURE
More Than We Ask or Imagine

Supplies: Toy car and a picture of a battery-powered, kid-driven car; fun-size candy bar and picture of a triple-scoop ice cream cone (or similar large dessert); cute stuffed animal and a picture of a live puppy; three gift boxes; Christmas wrapping paper

Preparation: Place the three pairs of objects and pictures into three boxes and wrap them in Christmas gift wrap. You may substitute pictures for any items you don't have.

Have you ever asked for something as a present and what you got ended up being much better than what you asked for? Let children share their experiences.

Hold up a wrapped gift. (You may open the gifts in any order. Adjust your words to match the gifts.) **Let's say you asked for a toy car.** Open the gift and take out the car and show it to the children. **You'd be pretty happy to get this shiny-new, cool-looking car. But what if you got this instead?** Take out the picture of the kid-size, battery-powered car. **But what if you got this real, super-duper, life-size car to play in? That would be really special. It's more than you asked or imagined your present could be!**

As you continue to lead the discussion, be sure to steer the conversation away from the getting of "better" stuff and toward the surprise of a gift being unexpectedly special.

Hold up another wrapped gift. **What if you wanted a treat or dessert?** Open the gift and hold up the simple, small candy bar. **This would be a tasty snack, wouldn't it? But what if the person giving you the gift decided you should have something extra-special?** Take out the picture of the large dessert. **Wow! Sometimes our presents are even better than what we thought we wanted or needed.**

Hold up the last gift. **Let's say you wanted a cute stuffed animal to hug at bedtime and play with during the day.** Open the gift. Hold up the stuffed animal or picture of it. **What if the person giving you the gift decided you needed something even more lifelike to keep you company?** Take out the picture of the real puppy. **You might get a real, live puppy to play with instead! Wouldn't that be a great surprise!**

Our Bible story today is about a very special present that God gave. This present was way more than anyone expected—way more

special that people could have asked for. Let's find out what it was and why it was special.

Have the Park Patrol lead the preschoolers and elementary-age children to their separate Bible story areas. The two groups will gather back together for the puppet show.

ELEMENTARY BIBLE STORY
Human Baby, God's Son
(Matthew 1:18–25; Luke 1:26–38; John 1:1)

Supplies: Bible, a picture of a baby, a picture of baby Jesus, box, Christmas gift wrap

Preparation: Place the two pictures in a gift-wrapped box.

Show the children the books of Matthew, Luke, and John in a Bible. **Today's Bible lesson comes from the beginning of the New Testament.** Show the wrapped gift you brought. **It's about a very special gift from God.**

There was a young woman named Mary. God sent an angel to her with a surprising message. "Greetings, Mary! God is very happy with you!" Mary didn't know what to think of this and was worried. But the angel said, "Don't be upset. God is so pleased with you that He has chosen you to have a baby boy. You should name Him Jesus. He will be the Savior of the world!"

Open the gift and hold up the picture of the baby. **Now having a baby can be very good news. What a wonderful gift! But Mary didn't understand how this could happen, since she wasn't married. The angel told her, "This baby will be special. God's own Spirit will come to you, and this baby will the Son of God!"** Take out the picture of baby Jesus. **The angel was telling Mary that her baby would be a human person and also God's Son. Jesus would be both God and human. That's even more wonderful than just having a baby!**

Place the pictures back in the gift box. **Now Mary had promised to marry a young man named Joseph. Mary and Joseph loved each other. When Joseph found out that Mary was going to have a baby, at first he was sad because he knew he wasn't the father of the baby. He decided he wouldn't get married to Mary after all.** Show the picture of the baby. **Joseph thought this gift of a baby wasn't so great.**

But then God sent an angel to Joseph in a dream. He had another surprising message. The angel said, "Joseph, don't be afraid to get married to Mary. It's true she's going to have a baby. But this baby is more special than any other ever born." Hold up the picture of baby Jesus. **"The Spirit of God came to Mary, and she will have a baby boy. This baby is the Son of God. You should name Him Jesus, and He will save the people from their sins."**

Then Joseph was happy. He understood that Jesus was both God and human. That's very hard for us to understand. How can someone be a person *and* be God? Only Jesus could be. And that makes Him the most special "Christmas present" ever.

Discuss a few review questions to be sure the children understand the main points of the Bible story. **What message did an angel bring Mary?** (That she would have a baby, Jesus, and that He would be the Son of God, etc.) **What message did an angel bring Joseph?** (That Mary's baby belonged to God and He would be the Savior, etc.) **What made baby Jesus more special than all the other babies every born?** (He is both God and human.)

PRESCHOOL BIBLE STORY
Jesus Is Coming!
(Matthew 1:18–25; Luke 1:26–38; John 1:1)

Supplies: Bible; figures of Mary, Joseph, and the angel (*Craft Book*, p. RC-98); flannel board

Preparation: Make a set of the Nativity Flannel Figures—Part 1 (Mary, Joseph, Angel) from page RC-98 in the *Craft Book*. Set up the flannel board at children's eye level so it is easy for them to see. You may want to hold it on your lap, or set it on an easel.

Show the children where Matthew and Luke are in your Bible. **Our story today comes from two books of the Bible—Matthew and Luke.**

Put the Mary figure on the flannel board. **The Bible tells us about Mary. She is happy. She is going to be married to Joseph.** Show the Joseph figure; then set it aside.

One day, something exciting happened to Mary. An angel named Gabriel appeared to her. Put the angel figure on the flannel board next to Mary. **The angel told Mary, "God is happy with you! God has sent me to give you a special message."**

Mary was a little scared. She had never seen an angel before. What special message could God have for her? But Mary listened carefully to what the angel said. He said, "Don't be scared. You are going to have a baby. You should name Him Jesus. He will be God's Son." Then the angel left.

Replace Mary with Joseph. Remove the angel. **This is Joseph. He was going to get married to Mary. Joseph was surprised to hear that Mary was going to have a baby. He and Mary weren't married yet. What should he do?**

Lay the Joseph figure down as if he were sleeping. **While Joseph was sleeping one night, an angel came to visit him.** Stand the angel next to Joseph on the flannel board.

The angel talked to Joseph in a special dream. "Don't be afraid to get married to Mary," the angel told Joseph. "The baby is God's Son. You should name Him Jesus." Remove the angel.

Stand Joseph up. **Joseph remembered the dream. He was happy. He could still get married to Mary.** Stand Mary next to Joseph. **She would have a special baby—God's own Son. Jesus, God's Son, was coming.**

Briefly discuss a few review questions to check the children's comprehension. **What did the angel tell Mary and Joseph?** (Mary would have a baby.) **Who was the baby?** (God's Son, Jesus.)

NOAH'S PARK PUPPETS
Two in One

Bring the preschool and elementary children back together for the Noah's Park puppet presentation. Today's lesson-related puppet skit is provided on page RP-97 of the *Puppet Skits Book*. Refer to the *Park Patrol Training Book* for suggestions on how best to present a puppet skit.

BIBLE MEMORY
Verse Groupings

Supplies: None

Preparation: Select a Bible verse that reinforces the unit theme, "Jesus the Savior." The memory verse taught in Sunday school may be a good choice.

Say the verse for the class, phrase by phrase, and have the children repeat it after you. Do this a few times until the verse becomes familiar. If you have good readers, you might also write the verse on the board.

Explain that you're going to name some groups and whoever fits in that group will stand and say the verse together. Call out something like, "Kids wearing blue." Have those children stand, say the verse together, and be seated. Continue calling out groups such as kids who are seven years old, all boys, kids who have pets, kids who like chocolate, kids who drank milk for breakfast, and so on.

Change the groups to fit your class, and try to choose groups that will have more than one child in them. Add groupings until all the children have had a few chances to say the verse.

Jesus deserves our worship because He is both God and human. Let's sing to Him now.

SINGING PRAISES TO JESUS

Supplies: Noah's Park CD and CD player

Play the unit song, "Good News," from the Noah's Park CD. If you have strong readers in your group, you may want to project the words of the song on the board or a wall for the children to read as they sing. Lyrics are provided in the back of this *Leader's Guide*. Let the children sing along with you as you play it again. Then let the children choose other praise or Christmas songs to sing to worship Jesus.

SHARE AND PRAYER
The Gift of Worship

Supplies: A small, gift-wrapped box for each group

It's just awesome that Jesus is both God and

human. It's great that He was willing to leave His home in heaven to come to earth and be our Savior. We can praise Him and worship Him every day for that!

Because Jesus was a real person living on earth, He understands everything we go through. And because He is God, He is powerful enough to help us. Divide the children into a few groups and have each group sit in a circle. Give a gift-wrapped box to each group. If possible, let a Park Patrol helper join each circle.

We'll pray twice around each circle. You pass the box to know whose turn it is to pray. If you don't want to pray aloud, just pass the box to the next person. The first time the box goes around your circle, you can say a sentence prayer asking Jesus to help you with something. Remember, because Jesus used to live on earth as a human, He understands what you're going through.

The second time the box passes around your circle, you can say a sentence of praise to Jesus. Because Jesus is God, we can worship and praise Him. Be sure the children understand what to pray. You may want to model a sentence prayer of each type. Then give the signal for the circles to begin praying, starting with the children holding the boxes.

When everyone has had a chance to pray twice, close the prayer time by praising Jesus for being Almighty God and for coming to show us His love.

Age-specific activities are provided here for snack, games, and crafts. Have the Park Patrol helpers lead the children to their areas and stay to help.

SNACK SHACK
Bible-Time Foods

A snack suggestion for today is provided on page RS-97 in the *Snacks and Games Book*. You might ask a child volunteer to thank God for the food before the class begins eating. Ask Park Patrol members to wipe off tables both before and after the snack.

CAMPSITE CAPERS
Gift Pyramid Relay (Elementary)
Angel, Mary, Joseph (Preschool)

Today's lesson-related games will get the children up and moving! The elementary game, "Gift Pyramid Relay," is explained on page RS-97 in the *Snacks and Games Book*. The preschoolers will play "Angel, Mary Joseph," found on page RS-98.

COZY CAVE CRAFTS
God's Gift Pencil Topper (Elementary)
Nativity Flannel Figures—Part 1 (Pre)

The elementary-age children will be making "God's Gift Pencil Topper" of the *Craft Book*. The directions are on page RC-97. The preschool craft, "Nativity Flannel Figures—Part 1," is described on page RC-98. Both crafts reinforce the Bible story. Be sure all the children put their names on their crafts.

CLOSING ACTIVITIES

After completing the activities, invite all the children to help straighten up the room. You might have the children pair up to find scraps of paper to pick up or supplies to put away. Then gather back together to finish the session.

Bring out one of the gift-wrapped boxes used earlier. Let volunteers hold the box and say the Bible verse from memory. If time permits, let volunteers from the elementary age-group show their craft to the preschoolers and explain it. Then let a few preschoolers explain their craft to the others. Close with a prayer, praising Jesus for being both God and human.

OVERTIME ACTIVITIES

With any extra time while waiting for parents to arrive, allow the puppets, worked by the Park Patrol, to come and visit with the children. The puppets might even read a storybook to children.

R47 Lesson: Good News! Jesus Is Born

**Choose from the options listed below
to follow Adventure Trails that lead to Jesus:**

DISCOVERY TRAILS
TEACHER FEATURE (5 min.)
Best News Ever
BIBLE STORY (10 min.)
Shepherds Hear the Good News (Elem.)
Jesus Is Born! (Preschool)
NOAH'S PARK PUPPETS (5 min.)
He's Born!
BIBLE MEMORY (5 min.)
Antiphonal Verse Calling

WORSHIP TRAILS
SINGING PRAISES TO JESUS (5–10 min.)
SHARE AND PRAYER (5–10 min.)
Shepherd's Staff Prayer Reminder

WILDLIFE TRAILS
SNACK SHACK (5 min.)
Animal Crackers
CAMPSITE CAPERS (10 min.)
Good News Relay (Elementary)
Shepherds Go to Bethlehem (Preschool)
COZY CAVE CRAFTS (15 min.)
3-D Shepherds Picture (Elementary)
Nativity Flannel Figures—Part 2 (Pre.)

HAPPY TRAILS
CLOSING ACTIVITIES (5 min.)
OVERTIME ACTIVITIES (as needed)

DISCOVERY TRAILS

TEACHER FEATURE
Best News Ever

Supplies: Several items or pictures of items that let people communicate news, such as a telephone or cell phone, TV, walkie-talkies, newspaper, computer (e-mail), pager, radio, magazine, etc.; box or bag

Preparation: Place the items or pictures you gathered in a box or bag so they are out of sight but available.

When you have really good news to tell someone, how do you get your news to them? Let the children discuss and give suggestions. Most children this age will start off with telling someone face to face. Affirm this as a great way to communicate.

To get the children thinking further, ask them how they might tell good news to an out-of-town grandparent (telephone or e-mail). Ask how the children might give an important message to a parent who's at the store (cell phone). Ask how a club or sport they're in might announce their good news of winning games or an accomplishment (newspaper, radio, or TV). As the children name each way of communication, pull that item out of the bag and show it to the children.

When the children have exhausted their ideas, bring out any extra items and let the children discuss how those thing could help spread news. Though not all children will have used all the items in your bag, they should all be familiar with them.

What's the best news you've ever heard? Let several children briefly share.

In Bible times, do you know which of these things was used to give good news? Have the children name or point to the things that were not available 2,000 years ago. Return each to the bag as it is named. You should end up with nothing.

In Bible times, people used the very first news spreader you named—the mouth. They told others the news. Sometimes there were big announcements to big groups, and other times people just told others one at a time. Today we'll learn about some good news that came as a big announcement.

Divide the children into two groups and have the Park Patrol lead them to their Bible story areas.

ELEMENTARY BIBLE STORY
Shepherds Hear the Good News
(Luke 2:1-20)

Supplies: Bible, Bible-time costumes to look like

shepherd clothing, (optional: staffs, long dowels, or walking sticks)

Preparation: Ask a few Park Patrol helpers to play shepherds with you. All they have to do is wear Bible-time costumes and nod in agreement when you explain important points that you "witnessed."

Begin by showing the children Luke 2 in a Bible. Explain that today's story comes from there. Step aside, pull on your costume, and return with the other "shepherds" to begin the story.

I am a shepherd. What does a shepherd do? We take care of sheep, of course! We have a hard job, don't we? (Look to other shepherds, who nod in agreement.) **I mean, the sheep are sweet and all that. They're very trusting and love to be near us. But sheep are pretty helpless, too. We have to lead them to good grass and clean water, and keep them safe from hungry animals.**

And we can't leave them alone—at all! That means we lead them around all day and then at night, we find them a safe place and we sleep with them—right out there in the fields. When we work together with our different flocks of sheep, we take turns sleeping and standing guard. We spend lots of time away from home.

Now, I'm here to tell you about one special night. We lived and worked in the fields outside of a little town called Bethlehem. We were all out watching our sheep one night, weren't we? (Look to other shepherds, who nod in agreement.) **Then suddenly, out of nowhere, came this huge light. It was the glory of the Lord shining all around us! An angel from God was there! I was pretty scared.** (Shepherds nod in agreement.) **He told us strange news.**

The angel said, "Shepherds, don't be afraid! I'm bringing you good news! Tonight in Bethlehem the Savior was born! He is Jesus Christ the Lord. If you go into town looking for Him, you'll find him in a manger." **That's a feeding trough for barn animals.**

And then, the whole sky lit up. It was filled with angels! And they were singing and praising God. It was just amazing. When the angels left, we turned to each other and said, "Let's go into Bethlehem and see this thing

that the Lord has told us about." (Other shepherds nod in agreement.) **So we did. We left our sheep right there—we figured this was pretty important news—and we went into town. We found baby Jesus right where the angels had said—in a manger.**

We knelt down and worshiped Jesus. His mother, Mary, was there. Joseph, who was married to Mary, was there too. I wondered why they were in a stable. It turns out that the town was so crowded with visitors that there was no room anywhere but there. We told Mary everything the angel had said, and she remembered those words all her life.

Well, we had to get back to our sheep. (Shepherds nod.) **But we just couldn't keep that good news to ourselves! As we walked through Bethlehem and through the countryside, we told everyone we met about baby Jesus being born! And we praised God for sending the Savior!** (All shepherds nod and exit.)

Be seated with the children and review the main points of the Bible story. **What was the good news the shepherds heard?** (That Jesus was born.) **How did the angels tell that good news?** (By telling the shepherds and singing.) **How did the shepherds spread the good news?** (By telling everyone they saw.) **We can spread the good news too!**

PRESCHOOL BIBLE STORY
Jesus Is Born! (Luke 2:1-20)

Supplies: Bible; completed flannel figures of Mary, Joseph, Angel, (used in Lesson 46); flannel figures of baby Jesus, shepherds, sheep (*Craft Book*, p. RC-100); flannel board

Preparation: Make a set of the Nativity Flannel Figures—Part 2 (baby Jesus, shepherds, sheep) from page RC-100 of the *Craft Book*. You will also need the figures of Mary, Joseph, and angel from Lesson 46.

Our story today comes from the book of the Bible called Luke. Show the children Luke 2 in your Bible and keep it open. Be sure the flannel board can be easily seen by all the children.

Mary and Joseph had traveled to a small town called Bethlehem. Put the figures of Mary and Joseph on the flannel board. **Bethlehem was very**

crowded with visitors. **So Mary and Joseph stayed in a barn, which is a place for animals.**

That night something special happened—a baby boy was born! It was Jesus! Place the figure of baby Jesus with the others. **Mary wrapped Him in cloth to stay warm. She didn't have a crib so she put Jesus in a manger, which is a box that holds the animals' food.** Take down the figures of Joseph, Mary, and baby Jesus.

Meanwhile, some men called shepherds were taking care of sheep near Bethlehem. Put the figures of the shepherds and sheep on the bottom middle of the flannel board. **Shepherds took care of sheep—even at night.**

Suddenly a bright light filled the sky. It was an angel! Put the figure of the angel above the shepherds and sheep. **God had sent the angel.**

The shepherds were afraid. But the angel said, "Don't be scared. I have good news. God has sent His Son, Jesus. He was born tonight in Bethlehem. You will find Him wrapped in cloths and sleeping in a manger."

Then other angels joined the first angel. They praised God because Jesus was born!

Remove the angel and sheep. **After the angels left, the shepherds hurried to Bethlehem. They found Mary, Joseph, and baby Jesus, just as the angel had said.** Move the shepherds to the left of the board. Put Mary, Joseph, and baby Jesus back in the middle of the board.

The shepherds were so happy! They had seen God's Son. They told everyone they met, "Jesus is born!"

Take the flannel figures off the board. Have the children put the correct figures on the board to answer the questions. **Who traveled to Bethlehem?** (Mary and Joseph.) **Who was born?** (Jesus.) **Who told the shepherds?** (The angel.) **Who went and told everyone, "Jesus is born"?** (The shepherds.)

NOAH'S PARK PUPPETS
He's Born!

As you lead the children to the puppet stage area, encourage them to whisper to one another, "Good news! Jesus is born!" Today's puppet presentation is found on page RP-99 of the *Puppet Skits Book.*

BIBLE MEMORY
Antiphonal Verse Calling

Supplies: None

Preparation: Choose a Bible verse for the class to memorize in support of today's lesson. The verse the children began learning in Sunday school may be a good choice.

Divide the class into two groups, and have the groups stand facing each other, about 10 steps apart. Add Park Patrol helpers to both groups. Say the verse, phrase by phrase, and have the whole class repeat it after you. Say it again, phrase by phrase, and have only one of the groups echo you. Repeat for the second group.

Then have one group call out the first phrase of the verse to the other group. The second group responds by calling the second phrase back. The first group says the third phrase, and the second group says the fourth phrase. Continue until the whole verse has been said.

Begin the verse again, this time with the second group beginning. Let the groups call the verse phrases back and forth to each other until the verse has been said again. If time permits, let volunteers say the verse individually.

There are many ways we can tell the good news. One way is to sing it! Let's sing now about Jesus' being born.

SINGING PRAISES TO JESUS

Supplies: Noah's Park CD and CD player

Invite the children to join in singing the unit song, "Good News." Let the children play rhythm instruments or clap as they sing. Encourage the children to sing from their hearts. As time permits, sing additional Christmas praise songs.

SHARE AND PRAYER
Shepherd's Staff Prayer Reminder

Supplies: Wide craft sticks, colored markers

Preparation: Make a sample shepherd's crook.

The shepherds told everyone they saw about Jesus' birth. It was good news! We also can tell our friends and family that Jesus was born and is still alive in heaven to help us. We can celebrate the story of Christmas all year long!

Let's make a shepherd's staff to remind us to tell people about Jesus. Give each child a wide craft stick and markers. Point out that the top curve of the stick looks like the curve of a shepherd's staff. Along one straight side could be the stick portion of the shepherd's staff. All the children need to do is draw a line to form the underside of the curve and a line down for the straight portion, forming the outline of a staff. On the back or the stick, the children may write: "Good news! Jesus is born!"

Have the children hold their craft stick staffs during prayer. Explain that you will open with a prayer-starter and the children may complete the sentence, praying in any order. Lead a prayer like this: **Dear Lord Jesus, we praise You for being born on earth to be our Savior. We want everyone to know this good news! Please help us to tell others about You. Please help these people to understand why knowing You is good news...** Encourage children here to tell names of friends or family. They may simply call out names from where they are seated. When the prayer time winds down, close by thanking Jesus for hearing the children's prayers.

The following age-appropriate activities work best by separating the older and younger children. Let the Park Patrol lead the different groups to their activities and help as you have assigned them.

SNACK SHACK
Animal Crackers

Today's lesson-related snack idea is in Noah's Park *Snacks and Games Book* on page RS-99. Give kids a chance to wash hands or use a liquid disinfectant before eating. While children eat, let Noah's Park puppets visit with children and ask them about any good news they know.

CAMPSITE CAPERS
Good News Relay (Elementary)
Shepherds Go to Bethlehem (Preschool)

Play up the theme of Christmas in summer by engaging the children in these funny and energetic games. The elementary, lesson-related game for today, "Good News Relay," is found on page RS-99 of the *Snacks and Games Book*. The preschool game that reinforces the lesson, "Shepherds Go to Bethlehem," is found on page RS-100.

COZY CAVE CRAFTS
3-D Shepherds Picture (Elementary)
Nativity Flannel Figures—Part 2 (Pre.)

The elementary craft, "3-D Shepherds Picture," is found on page RC-99 in the *Craft Book*. Let the Park Patrol help out as needed. Directions for the preschool craft, "Nativity Flannel Figures—Part 2," are found on page RC-100. Be sure children have their names on their crafts.

CLOSING ACTIVITIES

When only a few minutes remain, play the unit song as a signal for children to finish their activities and begin cleanup. When cleanup is finished, gather children into a large group to wrap up the lesson.

Ask for volunteers to say today's memory verse. Lead all in applauding those who try. Sing together the unit song if time permits. Remind the children to tell the good news about Jesus to some of their friends this week. Close the lesson with prayer.

Ask the Park Patrol to help the children collect their crafts, Shepherd's Staff Prayer Reminders (from Share and Prayer), and any belongings as they leave.

OVERTIME ACTIVITIES

While waiting for parents to arrive, you could set out construction paper and crayons and let the children make "Good News" cards. They may give these to the friends and family they prayed for today. As each child leaves, tell him or her: "Good news! Jesus is born!"

R48 Lesson: We Give the Gift of Worship

Choose from the options listed below to follow Adventure Trails that lead to Jesus:

DISCOVERY TRAILS
TEACHER FEATURE *(5 min.)*
  Like, Love, or Worship?
BIBLE STORY *(10 min.)*
  Wise Men Worship Jesus (Elementary)
  Visitors from Far Away (Preschool)
NOAH'S ARK PUPPETS *(5 min.)*
  Tell Him He's Great
BIBLE MEMORY *(5 min.)*
  Sock Toss

WORSHIP TRAILS
SINGING PRAISES TO JESUS *(5-10 min.)*
SHARE AND PRAYER *(5-10 min.)*
  Different Ways to Worship

WILDLIFE TRAILS
SNACK SHACK *(5 min.)*
  Christmas Cookies
CAMPSITE CAPERS *(10 min.)*
  Wise Man Caravan (Elementary)
  Follow the Star (Preschool)
COZY CAVE CRAFTS *(15 min.)*
  Pocket Present (Elementary)
  Nativity Flannel Figures—Part 3 (Pre.)

HAPPY TRAILS
CLOSING ACTIVITIES *(5 min.)*
OVERTIME ACTIVITIES *(as needed)*

DISCOVERY TRAILS

TEACHER FEATURE
Like, Love, or Worship?

Supplies: Three signs labeled "Like," "Love," and "Worship"; stuffed kitty; fake glasses with funny nose and mustache; candy bar; baseball and glove

Preparation: Place the three signs where all the children can see them and point to them during the discussion.

Ask for five volunteers to hold a prop and say something up front. You may ask for volunteers from the class to do these simple walk-on parts, or enlist the Park Patrol to say them. Take your volunteers off to the side, distribute the five props, and whisper their lines to them.

Return to the front of the class. **I have some people here today who have something to tell you.** Point to the three signs and read them together. **These volunteers will each tell you something. You must decide if what they mean is liking, loving, or worship.** If anyone asks what worship is, say that we'll decide that soon.

Call on the first volunteer, who walks across the stage hugging the kitty. He or she says with emphasis, "I looooooooove my kitty." Then have the children point to the sign they think really shows what this child feels—liking the kitty, loving it, or worshiping it. Then let that volunteer be seated at the front.

Call on the next child to come forward, eating the candy, and say, "I LOVE candy!" Again, let the children point to the sign they think is appropriate.

Call on the child wearing the fake glasses and mustache. He says dramatically, "I just love my wife." Let the class vote.

Have the fourth volunteer enter carrying baseball and glove (or other sport of your choice). This child should talk excitedly about how much he or she loves baseball.

Call on the last two volunteers to enter hugging each other and saying, "We're best friends. We love being together!"

What does it mean to love someone or something? Let the children offer ideas. **Do you think that this friend really "loves" candy?** Point to the volunteer with the candy. **Probably not. We do say "love," but we don't mean that we have strong, deep feelings like we do about our moms or dads or other people we're close to. Can someone really love their wife?** Point to the child with the moustache. **Yes, loving a wife is a good use of the word "love." What about a sport? What do we mean when we say we love a sport?** Let the children describe their excitement about the game. Also discuss loving pets and friends.

Let's look at the word "worship." Can you describe what it means? Let any volunteers define in their own words what worship might mean or involve. Worship is when we love someone so very much that we make them more important than anything or anyone. The Bible teaches that the only person we're ever supposed to worship is God. Let's learn more from our Bible story.

Have your Park Patrol members lead the children to the age-appropriate class area at this time.

ELEMENTARY BIBLE STORY
Wise Men Worship Jesus
(Matthew 2:1-12)

Supplies: Newsprint pad, easel, marker

Show the children where to find Matthew in a Bible, and explain that today's Bible story comes from these verses. Set up the newsprint and easel where all can see and the children drawing can reach.

Today you are going to help me tell the Bible story by drawing it. Your drawings will be clues to the rest of the class of what is going to happen next. Explain that not everyone will get a chance to draw.

Our Bible story begins with this. Ask for a volunteer to come up and draw. Whisper to that child to draw a star. Let the class guess what it is. Thank the volunteer and let him or her be seated again. When Jesus was born, God put a special star in the sky. Some very wise men lived in a country far to the east of Israel, where Jesus lived with his mother, Mary, and with Joseph. These men studied the Scriptures and watched the skies. When they saw the star, they did something.

Ask another volunteer to come up. Whisper to this child to draw a camel. You may use a fresh sheet of newsprint for each drawing. The wise men decided to make a long journey. They traveled, probably on camels, until they came to Israel. Once there, they went to the biggest city, Jerusalem, looking for someone.

Ask a third volunteer to come up, and whisper to draw two crowns. Once guessed, continue the story. The wise men were looking for two kings. One was King Herod. He was the king of the Jewish people. He loved being king but he was very mean about it. He didn't want anyone else to be a king. The wise men didn't know this. They thought it would be good to ask the king where to find the other king. The second king they were looking for was Jesus. King Herod learned that this new king would be born in Bethlehem. What did he do?

Ask a volunteer to come and draw an angry or sad face. Herod came up with a very bad plan. He didn't want any other kings around, so he planned to kill Jesus. Herod told the wise men to go and find Jesus and then come back and tell him where Jesus was. Herod lied and said that he wanted to worship Jesus too. So the wise men went on to Bethlehem.

Ask a volunteer to come and draw three gift boxes. The wise men followed the star and found Jesus. They gave Him expensive gifts, called gold, frankincense, and myrrh. They kneeled down and worshiped Jesus. They knew He was God's Son.

Ask another volunteer to come and draw another camel. This may fool the class to have a second picture of the same thing. God sent a dream to the wise men. He told them not to trust Herod. So the wise men sneaked out of Bethlehem and rode their camels home by a different road. They were long gone when Herod found out. But they were happy that they had found Jesus and given Him the gift of worship. We also can give Jesus the gift of worship.

PRESCHOOL BIBLE STORY
Visitors from Far Away (Matthew 2:1-12)

Supplies: Bible; completed flannel figures of Mary and Joseph (used in Lessons 46 and 47); Nativity Flannel Figures of toddler Jesus, wise men, the star, and the camels (Craft Book, p. RC-102); flannel board

Preparation: Make one set of the Nativity Flannel Figures of toddler Jesus, the wise men, the star, and the camels from page RC-102 of the Craft Book. You will also need the figures of Mary and Joseph used in Lessons 46 and 47.

Our story today comes from the part of the

Bible called Matthew. Show the children Matthew 2 in your Bible. Place the flannel board at children's eye level.

The Bible tells us about some very wise men. Put the figure of the wise men on the left side of the flannel board. They lived far away from Bethlehem, the town where Jesus was born. The wise men knew many things from stars.

One night, the wise men saw a special star in the sky. Put the star at the top, right-hand corner of the flannel board. They knew a king had been born! The wise men put everything they needed on their camels and started their journey. Add the camel figure near the wise men. The wise men traveled for a long time, following the special star. Move the wise men and camel figures across the board to the right side. Finally they came to a city called Jerusalem. They went to see the king, named Herod.

King Herod didn't know where the new king was born. But his helpers told him the wise men would find the baby in the town of Bethlehem. Move the star to the middle of the board with Mary, Joseph, and Jesus under it.

The wise men followed the bright star to Bethlehem. Move the wise men and camel figures to the center of the board. They found Mary, Joseph, and little Jesus. The wise men worshiped Jesus and gave Him special presents they had brought.

The wise men worshiped Jesus. They gave the gift of worship to Jesus. We also can give the gift of worship to Jesus.

Review the main points of the Bible story. What did the wise men follow to help them find Jesus? (A special star.) What did the wise men do whey they found Jesus? (They worshiped Him and gave Him special presents.)

NOAH'S PARK PUPPETS
Tell Him He's Great

Bring out the Noah's Park puppets needed for today's skit, found on page RP-101 of the *Puppet Skits Book*. You could have Ponder or one of the other puppets lead the children over to your puppet stage and direct them to be seated.

BIBLE MEMORY
Sock Toss

Supplies: Clean, old socks

Preparation: Choose a Bible verse for the children to memorize. It may be one learned in Sunday school or another verse that supports the unit theme. Tie a knot or two in each sock, preparing one sock for each small group.

Say the memory verse for the children, having them repeat each phrase after you. Explain any phrases they might not understand. Repeat a few more times

Divide the children into groups of four or five. Have each group stand in a wide circle, and give a knotted sock to each. The children in each group begin tossing their sock across the circle, saying one word of the verse on each toss. The children may toss to anyone in their circle in any order. Repeat until everyone has learned the verse well.

We worship Jesus when we sing to Him. We worship Him when we obey Him in our hearts and talk with Him. Let's spend some time worshiping Jesus now.

SINGING PRAISES TO JESUS

Supplies: Noah's Park CD and CD player

Review the Unit 11 song, "Good News," found on the Noah's Park CD. Since children have been learning this song for a few weeks, ask for volunteers to come up front with you and help lead the singing. Then encourage the children to suggest more songs that help them praise Jesus as Savior.

SHARE AND PRAYER
Different Ways to Worship

Supplies: None

We can give the gift of worship to Jesus. The Bible says there are different ways we can worship. We can worship with others, as in church. We can worship when we're alone, as when we say our bedtime prayers or quietly talk to Jesus during the day. We can worship standing up or sitting down or kneeling. As long as your heart is in it, you can worship!

Let's worship Jesus in two different ways today. In that spot you can pray with some friends. Point out one area of the room. Have the Park Patrol stay there to pray with the children as they come over. **In that spot you can pray by yourself.** Point out another area in the room. Explain that the children may pray silently or whisper their prayers there. And they may sit, stand, or kneel as they talk to Jesus.

What can you say to worship Jesus? You can tell Him why you love Him. You could praise Him for some of His wonderful qualities. You can thank Him for loving you and wanting you to be part of His family. Whatever you pray, it's your heart that counts. Explain that the children will be free to move at their own pace as they visit each of the two stations. Encourage the children to pray at least a few sentences to worship Jesus and to move quietly between the stations.

Be sure the children understand the directions; then set them free to move and pray. The Park Patrol may pray with the younger children. When a child has worshiped at both stations, encourage him or her to be seated. When everyone has had time to pray, move to the next activity.

Let the Park Patrol lead the preschoolers and the elementary children to their separate activities and be prepared to help as needed. If you prefer to keep the two groups together for snack time, you may want to have the preschoolers sit together at one table and have the elementary children sit together at another table.

SNACK SHACK
Christmas Cookies

For a fun snack idea, see page RS-101 in the *Snacks and Games Book.* Let the children wash up before eating, and ask for a volunteer to thank God for the food before beginning.

CAMPSITE CAPERS
Wise Man Caravan (Elementary)
Follow the Star (Preschool)

Today's elementary game requires teamwork and skill. You'll find the directions to "Wise Man Caravan" on page RS-101 of the *Snacks and Games Book.* For the preschool game, "Follow the Star," turn to page RS-102 in the same book.

COZY CAVE CRAFTS
Pocket Present (Elementary)
Nativity Flannel Figures—Part 3 (Pre.)

The elementary craft that supports today's lesson, "Pocket Present," is on page RC-101 of the *Craft Book.* The preschoolers will be making Part 3 of their "Nativity Flannel Figures." You will find the patterns on page RC-102. Remind children to put their names on their crafts. Set all projects in a safe spot until the children leave at the end of class.

CLOSING ACTIVITIES

A few minutes before class time is over, play the unit song from the Noah's Park CD as a signal for the children to begin cleaning up. Have the Noah's Park puppets, worked by the Park Patrol, visit each child and thank him or her for being helpful. Then gather everyone back together for closing activities.

Review today's Bible story by letting anyone who would like to do so to tell the class one thing about the story. Then have the class say the Bible memory verse in unison. Close the class with prayer.

As the children go out the door, hand out their crafts and remind the children that they can give the gift of worship to Jesus, as the wise men did.

OVERTIME ACTIVITIES

If you have time remaining while waiting for parents to pick up their children, you could let the children tell the Bible story to a Noah's Park puppet. Have Park Patrol members assist the children during this time to allow you to speak with the parents as they arrive.

R49 Lesson: Jesus Offers Eternal Life

Choose from the options listed below to follow Adventure Trails that lead to Jesus:

DISCOVERY TRAILS

TEACHER FEATURE (5 min.)
 Timeline
BIBLE STORY (10 min.)
 Nicodemus Meets Jesus (Elementary)
 Born Again? (Preschool)
NOAH'S PARK PUPPETS (5 min.)
 Eternal Life
BIBLE MEMORY (5 min.)
 Paper-turning Verse

WORSHIP TRAILS

SINGING PRAISES TO JESUS (5–10 min.)
SHARE AND PRAYER (5–10 min.)
 Antiphonal Prayer

WILDLIFE TRAILS

SNACK SHACK (5 min.)
 Never-ending Treats
CAMPSITE CAPERS (10 min.)
 "Hoop Race" (Elementary)
 "God Loves You" Train (Preschool)

COZY CAVE CRAFTS (15 min.)
 Eternally Turning Wind Spiral (Elem.)
 Jesus and Nicodemus Puppets (Preschool)

HAPPY TRAILS

CLOSING ACTIVITIES (5 min.)
OVERTIME ACTIVITIES (as needed)

DISCOVERY TRAILS

TEACHER FEATURE
Timeline

Supplies: Butcher paper, masking tape, marker

Preparation: Loosely tape butcher paper to a wall. Estimate ahead of time how much space you will need to allot for each timeline so you have room.

Let's make a timeline to show how long different things live. Some things live a very short time, like certain bugs. There's a kind of fly that lives for only one day. Print "Fly" on the far left of the paper and then draw a very short line out from the word to the right. Where the line ends write, "1 day."

How long does a dog or cat tend to live? Though some pets die early and some are long-lived, let the children briefly discuss the possibilities. **A dog or cat is considered old if it lives about 15 years. Let's mark that on our timeline.** Underneath "Fly," write "Dog" and draw a line to the right past the first mark. There write "15 years."

What about a person? How long do people live? Let the children offer opinions on this. **The average person lives to be about 75 or 80 years old, but it's not uncommon anymore to hear about people living to be 100. But there's no one who lives as long as 120.** Help the class come to a consensus on a fair age to use for the life span of people. Under "Dog," write "People" and draw a longer line out to the right. Write the years as well.

Not too many living creatures live longer than people. But some kinds of trees can live a couple hundred years. Add "Tree" to the chart and draw an even longer line to the right; include the number 200.

To help us understand how long or short these amounts of time are, let's mark when Jesus was born on earth. That was a little over 2,000 years ago. Write "Jesus born" under "Tree" and draw a line almost to the end of the butcher paper. **Jesus lived on earth for 33 years before He went up to heaven, but we're marking the 2,000 years to help us understand how long ago that was.**

Some scientists say that people have lived on earth for thousands of years, but our paper isn't long enough for that. Some scientists say that dinosaurs lived on earth millions of years ago. Our paper isn't long enough for that, either.

There's someone else we need to add to our timeline. How long does God live? (Forever.) Write "God" next on the list. **How do we mark that?** As the children give ideas, ask Park Patrol members to help you remove the timeline from the wall and hold the two ends together to form a circle with the butcher paper. Have the helpers stand inside the circle of paper to hold it up while you stay on the outside. You might tape the ends together. **Now our timeline has no beginning and no end.** Point with your marker next to God's name and begin walking around and around the paper as if you were drawing an endless timeline. **When should I stop? Never! It's hard for us to understand, but God never had a beginning and He will never have an end.**

In the Bible, never-ending is called "eternal" or "everlasting" because God lasts forever. Wouldn't it be great to live forever? Today we'll learn about eternal life—living forever—and how we can share it.

At this time, you can have Park Patrol helpers assist you by taking the preschool and elementary-age children to their separate Bible story areas. The groups will rejoin for the puppet show.

ELEMENTARY BIBLE STORY
Nicodemus Meets Jesus (John 3:1-21)

Supplies: Bible, Bible-time clothes, clipboard with copy of script, pencil

Preparation: Recruit a Park Patrol member to play the role of the reporter. Play Nicodemus yourself. Both of you should wear Bible-time clothing. The reporter should hold a clipboard with the script and pretend to take notes on the conversation. Both of you may glance at the script for help with lines.

Before beginning, show the children in a Bible that today's Bible story is from John 3. Then enter the room as Nicodemus next to the reporter.

Reporter: **Thank you, Nicodemus, for taking time to help with my magazine article.**

Nicodemus: (Looks around nervously.) **Shhh, I don't want anyone to see me. I might get in trouble. My friends and fellow leaders don't like me talking about Jesus.**

Reporter: **But, Nicodemus, isn't it true that you met with Jesus last night?**

Nicodemus: **Yes, though that was a secret too. You see, I had heard so much about Jesus. He taught about God and stood up for God's house of worship and did miracles. But He is very different from what the Jewish leaders like. They would look down on me if they knew I had been to see Him.**

Reporter: **Then why DID you go to see Jesus, Nicodemus?**

Nicodemus: **I really wanted to learn about God from Him. I could tell that Jesus taught the truth. Also, I could tell that He knew what believing in God was really all about—not just the rules that we keep.**

Reporter: **What did Jesus say?**

Nicodemus: **He welcomed me. And He got right to the point. He told me that I would not see God's kingdom—have eternal life—unless I was born again.**

Reporter: **Born again? What does that mean?**

Nicodemus: **That's what I asked! I told Him I could not go back inside my mother's body like a baby and be born a second time! But Jesus meant being born in a different way. To know God and have eternal life, we have to be born of God's Spirit, too.**

Reporter: **Hmmm, I guess I don't understand.**

Nicodemus: **I didn't understand either! And Jesus thought that I should. After all, my job is teaching people about God. But Jesus explained more. He said that to be "born again" as He called it, all we have to do is believe in Him. Then we will have eternal life. Jesus said it like this: "For God so loved the world that he gave his one and only Son, that whoever believes in Him shall not perish but have eternal life."**

Reporter: **Eternal life. Does that mean living forever?**

Nicodemus: **Yes, but it's our spirits that will live on forever after our bodies die. If we believe in Jesus—trusting Him and loving Him with all our hearts—we will live forever. Our spirit inside of us will live with God in heaven forever.**

Reporter: **Well, that's a lot of really good information for my magazine article. Thanks, Nicodemus! I think I'd like to get to know Jesus better.** (Both walk off.)

Return to the children and discuss a few review questions. **Why did Nicodemus go to Jesus?** (He thought Jesus was a good teacher and wanted to learn about God.) **What did Jesus tell Nicodemus about getting eternal life?** (That he should be born again by believing in Jesus.)

PRESCHOOL BIBLE STORY

Born Again? *(John 3:1-21)*

Supplies: Bible, Jesus and Nicodemus puppets (*Craft Book*, p. RC-104), flashlight, dark cloth, large book

Preparation: Make a complete set of Jesus and Nicodemus stick puppets from page RC-104 of the *Craft Book*.

Keep your Bible open to John 3 as you tell the story. **Our story today is from the part of the Bible called John.** Drape the dark cloth over a large book to use as a backdrop.

One night a man named Nicodemus came to talk to Jesus. With a puppet in each hand, stand the puppets in front of the backdrop. **Nicodemus was an important leader.**

Have Nicodemus stand a little bit forward of Jesus. **"Jesus," Nicodemus said. "You are an important teacher. You must be from God. No one could do the things You do unless God is with You." What do you think Jesus said?**

Move the Nicodemus puppet back. Move the Jesus puppet forward. **Jesus said, "I have something important to tell you. No one can go to heaven unless they are born again."**

Nicodemus didn't understand what Jesus was saying. What could "born again" mean?

Then Jesus explained what He meant. "You were first born a baby. But after that, you need to have the Holy Spirit in your heart. You will believe in God's Son. That will be the born again part."

Nicodemus still didn't understand what Jesus was saying. "How does that happen?"

Lean the puppets against the backdrop and pick up the flashlight. **"God loves the world very much,"** Jesus said. **"But the world is full of bad things that keep it away from God. It's**
like when it is dark. So God sent His Son. That is like the light from a flashlight.** Turn on the flashlight and shine it on part of the dark fabric so children can see the light. **If a person believes in God's Son, that person will go to heaven. That is the person who wants to be where it is light and not where it is dark.** Move the puppets so they are in the light of the flashlight. **People can see the person in the light. The person in the light shows other people God's love."**

Turn off the flashlight. **Jesus is God's Son. When we believe in Jesus, we will go to heaven.**

Ask a few questions to review the Bible story. **Who talked to Jesus?** (Nicodemus.) **What did Jesus tell him?** (He needed to believe in Jesus.)

NOAH'S PARK PUPPETS

Eternal Life

Today's puppet presentation, "Eternal Life," is found on RP-103 of *Puppet Skits Book*. Lead the children to the puppet stage by "sneaking" over there as if it were night and they were going in secret, as Nicodemus went to see Jesus in the cover of night.

BIBLE MEMORY

Paper-turning Verse

Supplies: Sheets of paper, marker, Noah's Park puppet

Preparation: Choose a Bible verse for the children to memorize that supports today's lesson, or use the verse from Sunday school. Print two words from the verse on each sheet of paper in order. (If the verse is short, write only one word per sheet.)

Ask volunteers to come up and hold the verse papers, standing across the front of the room in order. Wear the Noah's Park puppet and have it lead the children in saying the verse as the puppet points to each word. Repeat this a couple more times.

Then have the puppet tap a few verse-holders as a signal for them to turn their papers around so they can't be read. Lead the class in saying the verse. The puppet taps a few more verse-holders, and they also turn their papers around. If the puppet taps someone whose paper is already hidden, that child turns the paper back right-side-out again.

Once the verse becomes familiar, walk the puppet up and down the line, randomly and quickly tapping children as the class continues to repeat the verse, so that the verse papers are switching around even as the verse is being said.

SINGING PRAISES TO JESUS

Supplies: Noah's Park CD and CD player

Introduce the Unit 12 song, "Hallelujah! Jesus Is Risen," from the Noah's Park CD by playing it on the CD player as the kids listen. Play it a second time and let the children sing along. If your class has confident readers, you can project the lyrics on the wall for the children to follow. (Lyrics are in the back of this *Leader's Guide.*) Sing the song again, this time letting the Noah's Park puppets lead the singing. If time permits, sing another familiar song about Jesus' offering eternal life.

SHARE AND PRAYER
Antiphonal Prayer

Supplies: None

Ask the children to share about anything they might want prayer for. Jot down each request on the board. Explain that the children will take part in this prayer time by saying sentence prayers together. Divide the class down the middle. Teach one half to pray, "Help us, Lord," in unison. Teach the other half to pray, "Thank You, God."

Explain that you will say a sentence to pray for each request on the board. After each, you will point to the first group who will pray, "Help us, Lord," then to the second group who will pray, "Thank You, God." After each request, the groups will repeat their unison prayers. Be sure the children understand, and assign Park Patrol helpers to each group.

Separate suggestions are provided for preschoolers and elementary-age children. Divide the Park Patrol to help with both groups as needed.

SNACK SHACK
Never-ending Treats

Today's lesson-related snack suggestion is found on page RS-103 of the *Snacks and Games Book.* Let the children wash up before eating.

CAMPSITE CAPERS
Hoop Race (Elementary)
"God Loves You" Train (Preschool)

The elementary children will play "Hoop Race," found on page RS-103 of the *Snacks and Games Book.* For the preschool game, "'God Loves You' Train," see page RS-104 in the same book.

COZY CAVE CRAFTS
Eternally Turning Wind Spiral (Elem.)
Jesus and Nicodemus Puppets (Pre.)

The elementary-age children will make "Eternally Turning Wind Spirals," from page RC-103 of the *Craft Book.* Instructions for the preschool craft, "Jesus and Nicodemus Puppets," are on RC-104.

CLOSING ACTIVITIES

Allow a few minutes for the children to put away their activities and help straighten up the room. Then gather everyone together to review the Bible memory verse. Take a moment to discuss the eternal life that Jesus offers to be sure the children have an understanding of this concept and see if any children would like to pray with you (or with their parents at home) to accept Jesus. As children leave, be sure they have their crafts and belongings.

OVERTIME ACTIVITIES

While waiting for parents to arrive, let the children play with the Noah's Park puppets to become familiar with them. If the Park Patrol helps with these activities, you will be free to greet parents and see children off.

R50 Lesson: God Sent His Son to Die for Our Sins

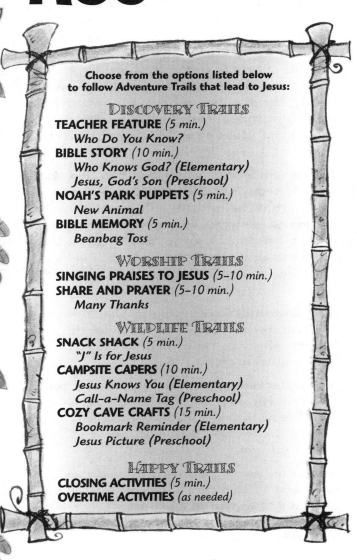

Choose from the options listed below
to follow Adventure Trails that lead to Jesus:

DISCOVERY TRAILS
TEACHER FEATURE *(5 min.)*
Who Do You Know?
BIBLE STORY *(10 min.)*
Who Knows God? (Elementary)
Jesus, God's Son (Preschool)
NOAH'S PARK PUPPETS *(5 min.)*
New Animal
BIBLE MEMORY *(5 min.)*
Beanbag Toss

WORSHIP TRAILS
SINGING PRAISES TO JESUS *(5–10 min.)*
SHARE AND PRAYER *(5–10 min.)*
Many Thanks

WILDLIFE TRAILS
SNACK SHACK *(5 min.)*
"J" Is for Jesus
CAMPSITE CAPERS *(10 min.)*
Jesus Knows You (Elementary)
Call-a-Name Tag (Preschool)
COZY CAVE CRAFTS *(15 min.)*
Bookmark Reminder (Elementary)
Jesus Picture (Preschool)

HAPPY TRAILS
CLOSING ACTIVITIES *(5 min.)*
OVERTIME ACTIVITIES *(as needed)*

DISCOVERY TRAILS

TEACHER FEATURE
Who Do You Know?

Supplies: Picture of the president of the United States or the White House (adjust if you live in another country); picture of your mother, preferably one of you and her together (or whoever you will use in the example); an example of an early elementary homework paper; newspaper

Hold up the picture of the president or White House. **If I told you, "I know the president of the United States and he's going to visit here in a few minutes," would you believe me?** Encourage the children to tell you why they would or wouldn't believe you. The children may find you a trustworthy person, but some may point out that you don't actually know the president. You may guide the children's thinking by asking: **How would I know what the president's schedule is?**

Hold up a picture of your mother. **If I told you that my mom (son, other close relative) was going to come help me with our class today, would you believe me?** Again, ask for opinions. Lead children to see that you actually know your mother (son, other relative), so they can believe that you have reliable information.

Why is it that you would believe something I tell you about someone close to me but not about a complete stranger? (Because you know the person, you have a chance to hear the truth about them and their schedule, you know what they're like, etc.)

And how about this example? Show the homework paper. **What if you got a phone call from a friend who said that she heard your teacher say that your class homework got cancelled, so you shouldn't do it? Would you believe it?** Let children speculate as to why or why not. **Now, what if it's your dad saying he got a phone call from your teacher saying that your class homework is cancelled. Would you believe it?** (Yes, because I trust my dad, he's more likely to get the message straight, he talked directly to the teacher, etc.)

Show the children the newspaper. **This happens with newspapers and TV news too. Reporters have learned that people want to be sure the news is true. Good reporters will talk with the actual person that the news is about.**

It's important to get our information from the right person. Otherwise, we might be trusting rumors and we might be hearing

things that aren't true. Our Bible story today is about knowing who knows who. Who really knows God? Let's find out.

If children usually separate into groups for the Bible story (preschool and elementary), ask the Park Patrol members to lead groups to their respective areas.

ELEMENTARY BIBLE STORY
Who Knows God?
(Mark 12:1–12; 15:24–39)

Supplies:

Preparation: Make two signs labeled: *They say they know God.* Make one sign labeled: *Hurt God's Son.* Make one sign labeled *They say they know the man* and one sign labeled *Hurt the son.*

Gather the children where you can hang the signs during the Bible story. Show the children Mark 11:27–33 in your Bible and explain that today's story comes from there.

Jesus went to the temple courtyard one day. Jesus had been teaching about God for three years and had many followers. The leaders and teachers at the temple did not like Jesus. They wanted to be the only ones to teach about God. They said they knew God the best. Hang up a sign: *They say they know God.* Read it with the children.

So the leaders said to Jesus, "What gives you the right to teach about God? Who put you in charge?" Jesus knew they were trying to trick Him. So He asked them a tricky question back. They couldn't answer it, so He didn't answer their question either. That just made them mad. They didn't believe Jesus was from God. They wanted to hurt Him. Hang up a sign beneath the first one: *Hurt God's Son.* Read it together.

Jesus knew what they were thinking. So He told them a story to explain who He was. He said, "A man planted a vineyard. That's a farm for grapes. He built the walls and planted the seeds and took good care of the vines. Then he had to go away for a while. He left servants to take care of it.

"These servants loved the vineyard so much that they wanted to keep it for themselves.

When harvest time came, the owner sent someone to collect the grapes. But the servants said, 'We know that man and we know how to keep all this for ourselves.' Hang the *Say they know the man* sign next to the first sign. **They beat him up and sent him away. The man sent other people to the servants; but the servants wouldn't send the man his grapes. Finally, the man sent his own son, whom he loved. But the servants beat him up and killed him."** Hang up a sign beneath the previous one: *Hurt the son.*

The temple leaders knew Jesus had told this story to show that they didn't really know God, just as the servants didn't really know the vineyard owner. So the leaders made a plan to get rid of Jesus so they could be the only ones to teach about God. Hang up the other *They say they know God* sign next to the first two.

Jesus knew this would happen. That's why He told the story. But Jesus chose to let this happen. He knew He needed to die to take the punishment for our sins.

Just as the vineyard owner sent his own son, God sent His own Son. The temple teachers didn't really know God, and Jesus really did, because He is God's Son. God sent His Son to die for our sins.

Discuss a few review questions. **Who said they knew God?** (The temple leaders and teachers.) **What did they plan to do to Jesus?** (Get rid of Jesus.) **Who really knew God?** (Jesus, because He was sent by God and is God's Son.)

PRESCHOOL BIBLE STORY
Jesus, God's Son *(Matthew 3;13–17; Mark 11:27–33; John 5:36–37)*

Supplies: Bible, picture of Jesus (*Craft Book,* p. RC-106), washable markers

Preparation: Enlarge the picture of Jesus, on page RC-106 of the *Craft Book,* so that it fits on a large piece of paper. Clip the picture to a sturdy backing.

Today's story comes from the books of the Bible called Matthew, Mark, and John. Show where Matthew, Mark, and John are in your Bible.

There was a man named John the Baptist. John lived near the Jordan River. People came down to the river to listen to him teach. He told them that they should be sorry for doing wrong things. These wrong things are called sins. John would baptize the people if they were sorry for doing wrong things. But John also told the people about God's Son. God's Son would save them.

One day Jesus came to see John by the river. Show the picture of Jesus. Color in the background of the picture. **Even though John knew that Jesus hadn't done any wrong things, John baptized Jesus. God's Spirit came down from heaven like a bird—a dove—and came to rest on Jesus. It was the Spirit of God. Then a voice spoke from heaven, "This is my Son. I love Him." Jesus is God's Son.**

Jesus did many special things to show that He was God's Son. One day Jesus helped a man so that he could walk. But the church leaders didn't like what Jesus was doing. Start to color in Jesus' hair and sandals and His skin. **"Who are you?" the leaders asked Jesus.**

Jesus told the leaders, "I am God's Son. God the Father has sent Me to do special work. John has told you about this." But the church leaders didn't believe Jesus. They didn't believe Jesus is God's Son. They didn't believe His special work was to save us from our sins.

Again, another day, the church leaders talked to Jesus. Jesus told people stories so they would know more about God. They didn't like what Jesus was doing or the stories Jesus was telling. Color in Jesus' sash. **"Who says you can do these things?" they asked Jesus. Jesus asked them many questions, but all they could say was "We don't know." But *we* know. God sent His Son to die for our sins.**

Briefly check the children's comprehension of the main facts of the Bible story. **Who did God send?** (God sent His Son, Jesus.) **What was Jesus' special work?** (To save us from our sins)

NOAH'S PARK PUPPETS
New Animal

Let the children stretch and swing their arms as they move to the puppet stage. When they are seated

and ready, have the Park Patrol present today's skit, found on page RP-105 of the *Puppet Skits Book.*

BIBLE MEMORY
Beanbag Toss

Supplies: Beanbag (one per group)

Preparation: Choose a memory verse that describes Jesus' coming as our Savior, either a new verse or one the children may be learning in Sunday school. Clearly print the verse on the board.

Begin to teach the verse to the class by reading it slowly while pointing to each word. Repeat the verse several times, encouraging the children to join you as they begin to remember it. The repetition and pointing will help non-readers.

When the verse is familiar to the children, divide the class into groups of about four or five children. The group sizes don't need to be identical. If possible, add a Park Patrol member to each group.

Have each group form a circle and toss a beanbag randomly around the circle. Whoever catches the beanbag says a word of the verse and then tosses it to another child, who says the next word, and so on. Let the children refer to the board or ask the Park Patrol helper if they can't remember the next word.

God sent His Son, Jesus, to die for our sins. We can be forgiven for the wrong things we do and live forever with Jesus! Let's worship Him now for His sacrifice for us.

SINGING PRAISES TO JESUS

Supplies: Noah's Park CD and CD player

Bring out some Noah's Park puppets to lead the children in singing the Unit 12 theme song, "Hallelujah! Jesus Is Risen." You could let the class make up motions to go along with each phrase or on key words of the song. Repeat the song so the children can learn the motions. If time permits, sing additional songs to thank Jesus for dying for our sins

.

SHARE AND PRAYER
Many Thanks

Supplies: Newsprint or butcher paper, marker, masking tape

Preparation: Choose a Bible verse that supports the Unit 12 theme, "Jesus the Sacrifice," or use a verse the children have been memorizing in Sunday school. On newsprint or butcher paper, draw a large bunch of grapes with each grape large enough to write a word or two in.

Gather the children where all can see the grapes. **God has given us so many wonderful things. We learned from our Bible story that He gives us salvation—that's when Jesus died on the cross for our sins.** Write "salvation" on a grape. **We learned last week that God gives us eternal life when we believe in Jesus.** Write "eternal life" on another grape.

What are some more good blessings that God gives us? Encourage all the children to contribute answers. They may include family, friends, pets, fun, sports, health, love, school, and so on. Accept all answers, and record each on a grape.

Lead the children in a time of prayer, thanking God for the many things listed on the grapes. Open the prayer time with: **Dear Father in heaven, thank You so much for the many great things You have given us. Thank You especially for . . .** Let any who wish speak up and name things listed on the grapes. If prayers wind down before most have prayed, add something like: **And Lord, thank You also for . . .** This may encourage more children to speak up in prayer.

Age-appropriate suggestions are provided for preschoolers and elementary-age children. Have the Park Patrol use Noah's Park puppets to lead the groups to their separate areas and help them get started. You may choose to have snack time with the groups combined.

SNACK SHACK
"J" Is for Jesus

Look on page RS-105 in the *Snacks and Games Book* for a lesson-related snack idea. Ask the Park Patrol to wipe off tables before and after the snack, and allow time for the children to wash their hands.

CAMPSITE CAPERS
Jesus Knows You (Elementary)
Call-a-Name Tag (Preschool)

The elementary-age children will play "Jesus Knows You," to reinforce the idea that Jesus knows who He died for. Instructions are on page RS-105 in the *Snacks and Games Book*. The preschool game, "Call-a-Name Tag," is on page RS-106.

COZY CAVE CRAFTS
Bookmark Reminder (Elementary)
Jesus Picture (Preschool)

Today's elementary craft, "Bookmark Reminder," will require some drying time if the shirt paint option is used. You may want to arrange to have this craft done earlier in the class time. Craft instructions are found on page RC-105 in the *Craft Book*. The preschoolers will be painting "Jesus Picture," described on page RC-106.

CLOSING ACTIVITIES

Encourage children to finish up their activities and help straighten up the room. You could use a puppet to offer encouragement and ideas of what to clean up. Play the unit song as children work.

When finished, have the children join in singing the unit song, using the motions they made up earlier. Ask for volunteers to say the Bible memory verse.

OVERTIME ACTIVITIES

While waiting for parents to pick their children up, let the Park Patrol interact with the children and play the preschool tag game for a few minutes.

R51 Lesson: Jesus Died for Us

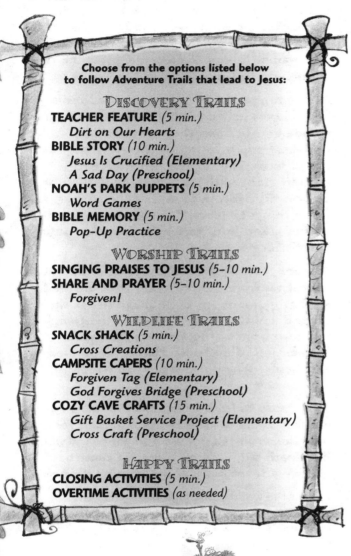

Choose from the options listed below
to follow Adventure Trails that lead to Jesus:

DISCOVERY TRAILS
TEACHER FEATURE (5 min.)
Dirt on Our Hearts
BIBLE STORY (10 min.)
Jesus Is Crucified (Elementary)
A Sad Day (Preschool)
NOAH'S PARK PUPPETS (5 min.)
Word Games
BIBLE MEMORY (5 min.)
Pop-Up Practice

WORSHIP TRAILS
SINGING PRAISES TO JESUS (5–10 min.)
SHARE AND PRAYER (5–10 min.)
Forgiven!

WILDLIFE TRAILS
SNACK SHACK (5 min.)
Cross Creations
CAMPSITE CAPERS (10 min.)
Forgiven Tag (Elementary)
God Forgives Bridge (Preschool)
COZY CAVE CRAFTS (15 min.)
Gift Basket Service Project (Elementary)
Cross Craft (Preschool)

HAPPY TRAILS
CLOSING ACTIVITIES (5 min.)
OVERTIME ACTIVITIES (as needed)

DISCOVERY TRAILS

TEACHER FEATURE
Dirt on Our Hearts

Supplies: One sheet of white paper (8 1/2" x 11"), white crayon, black or brown watercolor paint, paintbrush, and a cup of water

Preparation: Using the white crayon, draw and color in a large white cross in the middle of the white paper. Set the paper where all the children can see it. Have the black or brown watercolor paint, paintbrush, and cup of water nearby.

Have you ever gotten your clothes dirty playing outside? Let the kids briefly share some stories about getting their clothes dirty. **What color was the dirt you got on your clothes?** When the children answer "brown" or "black," show them the watercolor paint. **You're right. Dirt is usually brown or black, just like this paint.**

Well, the Bible tells us that we can get dirt on our hearts, too. In fact, it says that each one of us has gotten dirt on our hearts. This kind of dirt is called "sin." Every time we do, say, or even think of something that makes God sad, we sin.

There has only been one person who never sinned and whose heart never got dirty— Jesus, God's very own Son. What color do you think of when you imagine something that's perfectly clean and spotless without any dirt on it? When kids answer "white," show them the white sheet of paper. **Good. Now God could have decided to punish each of us for the wrong things that we think or do. But instead, because God loves you and me so much, He gave His very own Son, Jesus, to take the punishment for us.**

Get your paintbrush wet and dip it in the black or brown paint. As you continue talking, begin covering the entire sheet of white paper with paint. The paint will not stick to the white crayon cross in the middle of the paper. **Our hearts were dark and dirty, just like this paint. Then Jesus died on a cross so our hearts could be clean and spotless like His.** Finish covering the paper with paint.

What do you see on the paper? Wait for the children to answer "a cross." **What color is the cross?** Let the kids answer "white." **Wonderful! Because of the cross, all of the dirt on our hearts, the wrong things we say and do, can be washed clean. We can have pure hearts just like Jesus!**

If you are separating the elementary and preschool children for the Bible story, have your Park Patrol members lead them to the appropriate class area at this time. If you are keeping them together, be sure to use the Elementary Bible Story to teach the lesson.

ELEMENTARY BIBLE STORY

Jesus Is Crucified (Mark 11:27-33; 12:1-12; 15:24-39)

Supplies: Bible, blocks of wood, 2 for each child

Preparation: Gather or make hand-sized blocks of wood. You can use building blocks, cut up a 2" x 4" board yourself, or ask for scrap wood blocks from your local lumber yard.

Gather the children in a circle on the floor of your story area. Show them Mark 15 in your Bible and explain that today's story comes from there. Give each child two blocks of wood and explain that when you give the signal, children are to hammer their blocks of wood together three times.

Then tell the following story with drama.

Great crowds of people followed Jesus wherever He went. They couldn't wait to hear what He would teach them. Jesus said that God loves us and cares for us even when we have bad thoughts or do wrong things. He said when we are sorry for those things, God forgives us! It was the most wonderful news!

But not everyone was happy. The Jewish leaders and teachers were angry. They didn't believe the truth Jesus taught. And they were jealous of the great crowds of people that followed Him. So, they began to look for a way to kill Him. They asked the Roman rulers to put Jesus to death. *Signal the children to hammer three times by hammering with your closed fists.*

One day while Jesus was teaching, soldiers with weapons arrived and arrested Jesus. Jesus' closest friends were afraid and they ran away to hide. The soldiers took Jesus to the high priest and temple leaders. They asked Jesus questions. They tried to find things that Jesus had done wrong, so they could kill Him. But they could not find anything. Even though Jesus had done nothing wrong, they asked the Roman rulers to crucify Jesus. *Children hammer three times.*

Soldiers dressed Jesus in a purple robe and put a crown of thorns on his head. An angry crowd led Jesus outside the city to a small hill called Golgotha. The crowd mocked Jesus and made Him carry a heavy, wooden cross. When Jesus stumbled and fell, the soldiers forced a man named Simon to carry the cross the rest of the way to Golgotha. *Children hammer.*

At the top of the hill, they crucified Jesus. The soldiers nailed His hands and feet to the wooden cross. Then they set the cross upright. People passed by the cross and made fun of Jesus. The soldiers crucified two robbers along with Jesus, one on His left and one on His right. Even one of the robbers said mean things to Jesus. But after a while, one robber asked Jesus to forgive him. And Jesus did. *Children hammer.*

At noon, the sky grew dark. Jesus cried out to His Father from the cross and then He died. At that moment, an earthquake shook the ground and the heavy curtain in the temple was torn from top to bottom. The world seemed full of darkness. Had all hope died with Jesus? Why did this have to happen? *Children hammer.*

Jesus *chose* to let this happen. He knew He needed to die to take the punishment for our sins, the wrong things we do—yours and mine. But death did not stop Jesus. He came back to life. We'll learn more about that next week.

Collect the wood blocks from each child and then discuss a few review questions to check their understanding. **Who was angry with Jesus?** (The temple leaders and teachers.) **What did they do to Jesus?** (Had him arrested and killed on a cross.) **Why did Jesus die on the cross?** (Jesus chose to die; He took the punishment for our sin.)

PRESCHOOL BIBLE STORY

A Sad Day (Mark 11:27-33; 12:1-12; 15:1-39)

Supplies: Bible, sad-face signs

Preparation: Cut a three" circle from purple construction paper for each child, as well as one for yourself. Draw a sad face on each circle.

Our Bible story today comes from the book of the Bible called Mark. Show the children where Mark 11 is in your Bible.

Give each child a sad face sign. **We will use our sad face signs in our story today. When I hold up my sad face, you hold up your sad face.**

One day Jesus was at the temple. The temple was a type of church building. The leaders and teachers of the temple asked Jesus why He thought He could tell people about God. They didn't like what He was doing. The leaders and the teachers didn't know that Jesus was God's Son. Show the sad face.

But the leaders and the teachers didn't stop with questions. They began to not like Jesus more and more every day. How could they stop Jesus from telling people about God?

A couple of days later the leaders and teachers had a plan. They had Jesus put in jail—even though He had done nothing wrong. Show the sad face. **Some of the soldiers at the jail hurt Jesus, too.** Show the sad face.

It was a sad day—and it got sadder. The leaders and the teachers went to the ruler of the land. They told lies about Jesus. The ruler agreed to have Jesus put on a cross. Show sad face.

A couple of hours later, the ruler had some soldiers put Jesus on a cross. It hurt Jesus very much. Show sad face. **It hurt Jesus so much that He died.** Show sad face.

It was a very, very sad day when Jesus died on the cross. Show sad face. **But God had a plan that was bigger than the leaders and the teachers. Jesus could have chosen to not die on the cross. But by dying on the cross for our sins, Jesus saved us. Jesus died for us.**

Briefly check the children's comprehension of the main facts of the Bible story. **What happened to Jesus?** (He was hurt and put on a cross.) **Why did Jesus die on the cross?** (He died for our sins.)

NOAH'S PARK PUPPETS
Word Games

Lead the children to your Noah's Park puppet theater while the Park Patrol members get ready to per-

form the skit. You will find today's puppet script in the Puppet Skits Book on page RP-107.

BIBLE MEMORY
Pop-Up Practice

Supplies: None

Preparation: Choose a memory verse that describes Jesus' sacrifice that pays for our sin or that reviews a verse learned in Sunday school.

If most of your class can read, print the verse on the board, and let volunteers take turns leading the class in saying it. If you have non-readers, assign a Park Patrol helper to be their partner.

Then seat everyone in a circle. Choose a child to start by jumping up and saying the first word, then sitting down quickly. The next child pops up to say the next word, then sits down. Continue in this way around the circle. Go around the circle again, this time with each "popper" saying two or three words at a time. Challenge the kids to do it as quickly as possible with no mistakes.

God sent His son, Jesus, to take the punishment for our sins. We can be forgiven for the wrong things we do and live forever with Jesus! Let's worship Him now for His sacrifice for us.

SINGING PRAISES TO JESUS

Supplies: Noah's Park CD and CD player

Bring out some Noah's Park puppets to lead the children in singing the Unit 12 theme song, "Hallelujah! Jesus is Risen." You could let the class make up motions to go along with each phrase or on key words of the song. Repeat the song so the children can learn the motions. If time permits, sing additional songs to thank Jesus for His sacrifice for us.

SHARE AND PRAYER
Forgiven

Supplies: Construction paper in brown, gray, and

red, tape, scissors, pencils, glue

Preparation: Tape whole sheets of brown construction end to end on a blank wall or the floor to form the shape of a large cross. From the gray construction paper, cut 4" squares. Then cut the gray squares in half diagonally to make triangles. These will become "spikes" or nails; make one for each child. Cut one 5" heart shape from red construction paper for each child.

Jesus will forgive us when we sin—when we say, think, or do wrong things. In fact, Jesus died on the cross to take the punishment for our sin. He loves us that much! Whenever we sin, we can talk to Jesus about it. He knows when we are sorry for our sin. He promises to forgive us.

Give each child a "nail." Invite each child to think of something they've done wrong and want to be forgiven for (or something that they keep doing wrong and want help with). Have the children briefly write or draw on the "nail" what it is. Let the Park Patrol help the preschoolers or non-readers write. Then let children glue the "nails" to the cross.

Allow a few minutes for the children to talk to Jesus about needing His forgiveness and help. As you close prayer time, thank Jesus for His promise to always love us and forgive us.

When Jesus forgives you, He covers your sin with His love. He wipes away the sin and it's gone forever. Give each child a heart shape to glue on top of his or her nail, covering it completely. Make sure the hearts are glued down completely so the sins they wrote down are gone forever

The following age-appropriate activities work best by separating the older and younger children. Let the Park Patrol lead the different groups to their activities.

SNACK SHACK
Cross Creations

Look on page RS-107 in the *Snacks and Games*

Book for a lesson-related snack idea. Ask the Park Patrol to wipe off tables before and after the snack, and allow time for the children to wash their hands.

CAMPSITE CAPERS
Forgiven Tag (Elementary)
God Forgives Bridge (Preschool)

The elementary-age children will play "Jesus Knows You," to reinforce the idea that Jesus knows who He died for. Instructions are on page RS-107 in the *Snacks and Games Book.* The preschool game, "God Forgives Bridge," is on page RS-108.

COZY CAVE CRAFTS
Gift Basket Service Project ((Elem.)
Cross Craft (Preschool)

The elementary-age children will give a gift basket to a needy family in your church or community. Instructions for this project are found on page RC-107 in the *Craft Book.* The preschoolers will be making "Cross Crafts," described on page RC-108.

CLOSING ACTIVITIES

As class time draws near its end, encourage children to finish up their activities and help straighten up the room. You could use a Noah's Park puppet to offer encouragement and ideas of what to clean up. Play the unit song as children work.

When finished, have the children join in singing the unit song, using the motions they made up earlier. Ask for volunteers to say the Bible memory verse. Close the class time in prayer.

As the children go out the door, distribute crafts.

OVERTIME ACTIVITIES

If you have extra time while waiting for parents to pick up their children, you could play an extra round of "Run to the Tomb." Preschoolers will not be familiar with this game, but you might let the Park Patrol helpers teach them how to play. This will free you up to chat with parents as they arrive.

R52 Lesson: Jesus Is Alive!

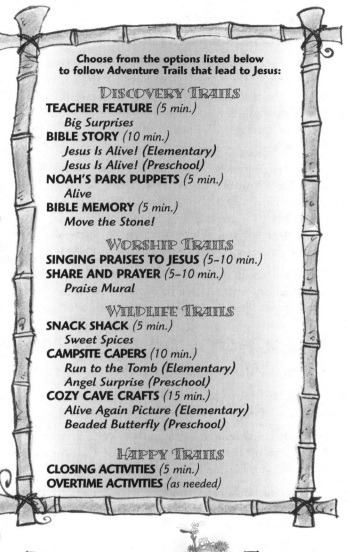

Choose from the options listed below
to follow Adventure Trails that lead to Jesus:

DISCOVERY TRAILS

TEACHER FEATURE *(5 min.)*
Big Surprises
BIBLE STORY *(10 min.)*
Jesus Is Alive! (Elementary)
Jesus Is Alive! (Preschool)
NOAH'S PARK PUPPETS *(5 min.)*
Alive
BIBLE MEMORY *(5 min.)*
Move the Stone!

WORSHIP TRAILS

SINGING PRAISES TO JESUS *(5–10 min.)*
SHARE AND PRAYER *(5–10 min.)*
Praise Mural

WILDLIFE TRAILS

SNACK SHACK *(5 min.)*
Sweet Spices
CAMPSITE CAPERS *(10 min.)*
Run to the Tomb (Elementary)
Angel Surprise (Preschool)
COZY CAVE CRAFTS *(15 min.)*
Alive Again Picture (Elementary)
Beaded Butterfly (Preschool)

HAPPY TRAILS

CLOSING ACTIVITIES *(5 min.)*
OVERTIME ACTIVITIES *(as needed)*

DISCOVERY TRAILS

TEACHER FEATURE
Big Surprises

Supplies: Paper, marker

Preparation: Make two signs, labeled "Big" and "Little."

Let's play a game to find out what kinds of things are surprising to you. Read the two signs with the children. Have two Park Patrol helpers hold them about 10 steps apart from each other.

I'm going to say some things that are surprising. If it would be a big surprise for that to happen to you, go stand by the "Big" sign.

If it would only be a little surprising to you, stand by the "Little" sign. I'll read these fairly quickly, so you'll have to think quickly and move between the signs to show your answer. It's okay if you don't all have the same answers.

Be sure the children understand the directions. Then read the following statements, adding your own if you'd like to spend more time on this activity:

Someone suddenly pops a balloon behind you.

You get a new puppy for Christmas.

Your grandparents come to visit.

You passed a hard test with a good grade.

Your parents tell you you're going to move.

Your teacher brings in ice cream for your whole class.

A good friend gets his or her hair cut off short.

Your parents throw you a surprise birthday party.

Your team wins the championship.

You just won a million dollars.

Ask the children to be seated. **What's the biggest surprise you've ever had?** Let several volunteers share. If any children share something sad or distressing, be comforting but don't dwell on it. **Some surprises are really big and really good. There's one in our Bible story today. Let's find out what was so special.**

Let the Park Patrol lead your two age groups to the preschool or elementary Bible story areas before continuing the lesson.

ELEMENTARY BIBLE STORY
Jesus Is Alive! *(Luke 24:1-12; John 10:17-18)*

Supplies: Bible, copy of the choral reading for each

child, butcher paper, markers, masking tape

Preparation: Hang butcher paper on a wall and draw on it a large tomb (life-size, if possible). Make it appear that the stone has been rolled to the side.

Show the children the passage from Luke 24 in a Bible. Invite them to be part of the Bible story. Explain how a choral reading works.

Divide the class into three groups: Angels, Women, and Disciples. You may want to have most of the girls read the Women part, most of the boys read the Disciples part, and the rest of the boys and girls read the Angels part. For non-readers, they may simply travel with their assigned group.

The sentences in parentheses are echoes. Have the Park Patrol read the echoes with the early readers to help them.

Have the Angel group stand near the tomb picture. The Disciples group stands across the room. The Women group begins in the middle of the classroom. Instruct the children to read slowly and clearly and try to keep together, as when they are reciting a memory verse as a class.

Begin by explaining: **This was the third day since Jesus had died on the cross. He was put in a tomb, cut in the rock. A big, heavy stone had been rolled across the entrance.**

Women: **Let's go to Jesus' tomb. (Let's go.)**

The Women group walks to the tomb.

Women: **Look! Look! The stone is rolled away! (Look! Look!)**

The Women pretend to look into the tomb.

Women: **Jesus is gone! (He is gone!)**

Angels: **Why are you looking for Jesus here? He is not here. (He is not here.)**

The Angels point at the tomb.

Angels: **Jesus told you He would be alive again. Remember! (Remember!)**

The Women move to the Disciples group.

Women: **Jesus is alive! (He's alive!)**

Disciples: **We don't believe you! (No! No!)**

The Disciples shake their heads no.

Disciples: **Let's go see! (Let's go!)**

The Disciples go to the tomb and look in. The Angels move away from it.

Disciples: **Jesus is not here! It's true! He's alive again! (He's alive!)**

All Groups: **Jesus is alive! Jesus is alive!**

Thank the children for taking part in the Bible story, and let them be seated. Be sure to tell the children that in the real Bible story a few women went to the tomb, two angels were there, and Peter and John were the disciples who ran to the tomb.

Use the following questions to check children's understanding of the main points of the story. **What did the women expect when they went to the tomb?** (To find Jesus' dead body.) **What did they find there?** (Angels telling them that Jesus had come back to life.) **What did the disciples do?** (Ran to the tomb to see that Jesus was really alive.)

Note: Although John is not specifically identified in either of today's passages, John 20:2 does record his presence at Jesus' tomb along with Peter.

PRESCHOOL BIBLE STORY
Jesus Is Alive! (Luke 24:1-12; John 10:17-18)

Supplies: Bible, completed Cross Craft from Lesson 50 (*Craft Book*, p. RC-106), bath towel, white cloth

Preparation: Spread out a bath towel under a table. Roll up the white cloth and put it at one end of the towel. Place a chair in front of the table.

Our story today is found in two books of the Bible—Luke and John. Show the children where Luke and John are in the Bible.

Hold the cross so the children can see it. **Last week we learned that some people didn't like Jesus. They didn't believe that Jesus was God's Son. The people had Jesus put on a cross. Later that day, Jesus died.**

Jesus' friends took His body off the cross, wrapped it carefully in cloth, and laid it in a cave. That's what people did in Bible times. A big rock was used as a door to the cave. Put a chair in front of the table.

That was a Friday. The next day was Saturday. The day after that was Sunday. Count the days on your fingers. **On Sunday morning, some women friends of Jesus went to put spices**

and perfume on Jesus' body. That's what people did in Bible times. When they got to the cave, the big rock door had been rolled away! Move the chair away from the table. The women looked in the cave, but Jesus' body was gone! Where was He? Have the children walk over to the table and look inside.

Suddenly, two angels stood by the women. They told the women, "Jesus isn't here. He isn't dead anymore. He came back to life, just as He told you He would."

The women ran to tell Jesus' helpers. Walk back to your starting place with the children. Jesus' helpers didn't believe the women. One of the helpers, Peter, ran to the tomb to see for himself. Ask a child to run to the table and look inside. He saw the cloth that Jesus' body had been wrapped in, but Jesus was no longer there. Have the child run back.

Later, Peter and the other helpers saw Jesus. He was alive! Jesus will always be alive!

Be sure the children understand the main facts of the Bible story. What happened when the women went back to the cave? (Jesus wasn't there.) What did the angels tell the women? (Jesus is alive!)

NOAH'S PARK PUPPETS
Alive

Let the children move to the puppet stage, and have the Park Patrol present today's puppet skit, "Alive." It is provided on page RP-109 of the Noah's Park Puppet Skits Book.

BIBLE MEMORY
Move the Stone!

Supplies: Balls, any size (one for every word or two of the verse), labels (or slips of paper and packing tape)

Preparation: Choose a Bible memory verse that reinforces the Unit 12 theme. The verse being taught in Sunday school may correspond. Print a word or two of the verse on individual labels and stick each to a ball. It's okay if the balls are different sizes.

Place the balls across the floor in the correct order. Point to each ball as the children read the word(s) on it. Do this a few times to help them become familiar with it.

Just as the angels moved the stone when Jesus came back to life, let's move these "stones" to help us learn the verse. I'm going to mix up these stones. When I say, "Move the stone!" everyone races to put them back in the right order. But be careful—they may keep rolling after you place them!

Lightly push the balls around to mix them up, not letting them get too far away. Then say, **Move the stone!** and let everyone put them back in order.

Encourage the children to work together and take turns. If you have a large group, you may want to assign different groups of children to have a turn each time you say the signal sentence.

SINGING PRAISES TO JESUS
Supplies: Noah's Park CD and CD player

Let the children enjoy singing along with the Noah's Park CD as they sing the unit song, "Hallelujah! Jesus Is Risen." Ask if anyone remembers the motions made up last week, and sing it again with the motions. If available, sing some Easter or resurrection songs with the group.

SHARE AND PRAYER
Praise Mural

Supplies: Tomb picture on butcher paper from Elementary Bible Story, markers

Preparation: Be sure the tomb picture is still hanging up where children can access it.

Today we are praising Jesus because He is alive! Because Jesus is God, He conquered death, proving He is Lord over the whole universe. He is just awesome!

Let's write and draw some prayers of praise. You can draw or write anything that expresses the love and joy you feel in your heart because Jesus is alive. You can write anywhere on this paper. (Show the butcher paper on the wall.)

As you draw or write, think about Jesus. After each thing you add to the picture, stop and silently say your prayer to Jesus. Then you can add more things and praise Jesus for each of those things too.

Set out colored markers and let the children all draw and write on the mural. Visit each child to offer ideas and to listen to what they are working on. Offer to pray a sentence prayer with each child. When your Share and Prayer time is up, close the large group with a brief prayer.

The following age-appropriate activities work best by separating the older and younger children. The kids could be in the same room at different tables and different areas. Or you could arrange to use separate rooms for the two groups. Let the Park Patrol lead the different groups to their activities.

SNACK SHACK
Sweet Spices

A lesson-related snack idea is offered on page RS-109 of the Noah's Park *Snacks and Games Book.* If you need to use the same tables for snacks as for crafts, you will need to have the tables wiped off in between activities.

CAMPSITE CAPERS
Run to the Tomb (Elementary)
Angel Surprise (Preschool)

The elementary game, "Run to the Tomb," is described on page RS-109 of the Noah's Park *Snacks and Games Book.* The preschoolers will play "Angel Surprise," found on page RS-110.

COZY CAVE CRAFTS
Alive Again Picture (Elementary)
Beaded Butterfly (Preschool)

The elementary-age children will work on an "Alive Again Picture." Instructions are on page RC-109 of the Noah's Park *Craft Book.* The preschool craft , "Beaded Butterfly," is found on page RC-110.

CLOSING ACTIVITIES

A few minutes before your class time is over, play the unit song from the Noah's Park CD as a signal that the children should stop their activities and begin cleaning up. When finished, gather the group together to wrap up the lesson.

Review the Bible memory verse. If there is time, get out the "stones" (balls) from Bible Memory time to give the class some fun in reviewing. Close the class with a prayer praising Jesus for always being alive to love us and be with us.

Let the Park Patrol help you give out crafts and get the children ready to leave. As children leave with their parents, remind each one, "Jesus is alive!"

OVERTIME ACTIVITIES

If you have extra time while waiting for parents to pick up their children, you could play an extra round of "Run to the Tomb."

Preschoolers will not be familiar with this game, but you might let the Park Patrol helpers teach them how to play. This will free you up to chat with parents as they arrive.

R53 Lesson: Jesus Opens the Scriptures to Us

Choose from the options listed below
to follow Adventure Trails that lead to Jesus:

DISCOVERY TRAILS
TEACHER FEATURE (5 min.)
All I Understand
BIBLE STORY (10 min.)
Jesus and His Friends in Emmaus (Elem.)
On the Road (Preschool)
NOAH'S PARK PUPPETS (5 min.)
The Opening
BIBLE MEMORY (5 min.)
Talk to the Beats

WORSHIP TRAILS
SINGING PRAISES TO JESUS (5-10 min.)
SHARE AND PRAYER (5-10 min.)
My Bible at Home

WILDLIFE TRAILS
SNACK SHACK (5 min.)
Cheesy Books
CAMPSITE CAPERS (10 min.)
Obstacles on the Road to Emmaus (Elem.)
The Emmaus Road (Preschool)
COZY CAVE CRAFTS (15 min.)
Mini Bibles (Elementary)
Bible Bookmark (Preschool)

HAPPY TRAILS
CLOSING ACTIVITIES (5 min.)
OVERTIME ACTIVITIES (as needed)

DISCOVERY TRAILS

TEACHER FEATURE
All I Understand

Supplies: Bible, a variety of objects that show different fields of knowledge, such as a toy rocket, a higher math book, a mechanic's box of tools, a portable sewing machine, a musical instrument, and so on.

There are probably loads and loads of things you understand how to do. Can you tell me some of them? Let volunteers name things, such as reading, tying shoes, putting together a transformer toy, mixing paint colors, and so on. Allow time for the children to name different skills and abilities.

But at your age—and even at my age—there are some things that we just don't understand. Bring out the rocket. If appropriate, you may pass around each object as you discuss it. **Some people have the job of building rockets—the real kind that go out into space. Do any of you understand how to make a rocket fly?** Some children may say they understand the basic principle of fire coming out the back to propel the rocket up, but focus on the knowledge needed to understand and build the rocket.

Bring out a higher math book. Let the children flip through it and look at the problems. **Math is important, and some need people to understand the hardest kinds of math to do their jobs. Can any of you do the problems in this book?** (No.) **What would you do if you wanted to learn how?** (Ask someone to teach me, go to school for many years, etc.)

Bring out each of the other items you brought and lead a similar discussion on each one. Lead the children to see that there are some things they just don't understand or can't yet do.

Because you can't do any of these things, does it mean you will never understand them? No, of course not. You could learn to understand any of these things if you have someone to teach you and you learn well. There's another area that's important for us to learn about. That's God's Word, the Bible. Hold up the Bible. **It's important for us to understand what's in here and what it means. So, how do we learn? We'll find out one way in our Bible story as we watch a couple of grown-ups who just don't get it.**

Ask the Park Patrol to lead the preschoolers and elementary-age children to their separate areas.

ELEMENTARY BIBLE STORY
Jesus and His Friends in Emmaus
(Luke 24:13-35)

Supplies: Bible, Bible-time clothes, copies of the script, three plates and cups (looking Bible-time, if possible), (optional: loaf of uncut bread)

Preparation: Ask three Park Patrol helpers to prepare the skit (or play one of the parts yourself). All three characters should wear Bible-time clothes. Set up a table with three chairs in the background of the Bible story area. You may choose to use real bread or just have the actors pretend.

Show the children Luke 24 in a Bible. Explain that these events happened on Easter Sunday, the day that Jesus rose from the dead. Then let the actors begin.

The two friends walk slowly back and forth across the Bible story area as if traveling a long way.

Friend 1: **I still can't believe it! Mary said Jesus was alive this morning!**

Friend 2: **But who can come back from the dead? That's too amazing!**

Friend 1: **I can't wait to tell our friends in Emmaus this news.**

Jesus: **Hello, may I walk with you to Emmaus?**

Friend 2: **Sure, we were just talking about the strange news about that man Jesus rising from the dead this morning.**

Jesus: **What do you mean?**

Friend 1: **Are you the only person in Jerusalem who hasn't heard about it? Jesus was sent by God. He was a great teacher. But the leaders killed Him, and His body was put in a stone tomb.**

Friend 2: **And what is more, it is the third day later, and our women friends told us that this morning they had seen the stone rolled away—and Jesus alive!**

Jesus: **Don't you know what God's Word teaches? It says that God's Son would have to die for the sins of all people. And it says that on the third day He would come back to life.**

Friend 1: **Really? Teach us more about what God's Word says.**

Jesus: **Everything that happened these past few days was told about in God's Word, all the way back to the beginning of the Scriptures. God is just making His Word**

come true and keeping His promises. God's Son had to rise from the dead on the third day to prove who He is.**

The three arrive at the table and are seated. They bow their heads briefly. Then Jesus pretends to tear open the bread loaf (or uses the real one).

Friend 2: **Look! It's Jesus!**

Friend 1: **Why didn't we recognize Him on the road? He really is alive!**

While the two friends are turned to talk to each other, Jesus quietly disappears.

Friend 2: **Where did Jesus go?**

Friend 1: **We have to go back to Jerusalem right away and tell the others.**

Friend 2: **Jesus really is alive! And because He taught us from God's Word, now we understand why.**

The two friends hurry off.

Thank the actors for their good job and have them return to the group. Discuss a few review questions to be sure the children understood the Bible story. **What were the two friends discussing on the road to Emmaus?** (What the women said that morning about Jesus' being alive.) **What did Jesus teach them as they walked?** (That God's Word foretold that He had to die and come back to life on the third day.) **When did the friends recognize that it was Jesus?** (When He gave them the bread.) You may need to explain that Jesus had His reasons for keeping the friends from recognizing Him sooner.

When we want to understand what the Bible teaches, we can pray to Jesus and He will help us. Jesus opens the Scriptures to us.

PRESCHOOL BIBLE STORY
On the Road (Luke 24:13-35)

Supplies: Bible

Open your Bible to Luke 24. **Our story today is from the part of the Bible called Luke.** Keep your Bible open to Luke 24 as you tell the story.

When you hear the words, "Tap, tap, tap," pat your knees. Show the children how to pat their knees. Encourage them to pat their knees whenever you pat your knees in the story.

Tap, tap, tap. Pat your knees. **Two of Jesus' helpers were walking on the road to a town called Emmaus. They were talking about how much they missed Jesus. They were sad that He had died on the cross. The two helpers thought they would never see Jesus again.**

Tap, tap, tap. Pat your knees. **Suddenly, another man started walking along with them. Tap, tap, tap went their feet on the road.** Pat your knees. **The man asked the helpers, "What are you talking about?" The two helpers didn't know the man was Jesus.**

They said, "Haven't you heard about Jesus? Some people didn't believe Jesus was God's Son. They put Him on a cross and He died. Some women say He is alive again. But we do not know what has happened to Him."

"Why didn't you believe what the Bible says?" asked Jesus. "It says that God's Son would die, but He would come back to life again." The three kept walking. Tap, tap, tap. Pat your knees. **As they walked along, Jesus told the two helpers everything that was written in the Bible about Him.**

Tap, tap, tap. Pat your knees. **By the time the three arrived in Emmaus, it was getting dark. The two helpers asked Jesus to stay and eat with them. So Jesus did. Jesus prayed and thanked God for the food. Then Jesus broke the bread into pieces and handed it to others.** Pretend to break a loaf of bread in two pieces. **Suddenly, the two helpers knew He was Jesus! As soon as they knew this, Jesus disappeared.**

The two were not sad anymore! They knew Jesus was alive! Pat, pat, pat. Pat your knees quickly. **They hurried back to where the rest of Jesus' helpers were. "Jesus is alive!" they told them. "We've talked with Him!"**

Jesus opened God's Word to the men. Jesus opens God's Word, the Bible, to us.

Discuss a few review questions. **Who did the two helpers meet on the road?** (Jesus.) **What did Jesus tell the two helpers?** (Everything in the Bible that was written about Him.)

NOAH'S PARK PUPPETS
The Opening

Let the children walk in pairs over to the puppet stage. You might have them link arms as they walk. When they are ready, have the Park Patrol present today's skit, "The Opening," found on page RP–111 in the *Puppet Skits Book*.

BIBLE MEMORY
Talk to the Beats

Supplies: Rhythm instruments, such as sticks, maracas, or finger cymbals

Preparation: Choose a Bible verse that supports the lesson focus or reviews a memory verse from Sunday school. Think of a way to naturally repeat the verse in a rhythm. Practice saying the verse in rhythm, emphasizing the beats.

Say the Bible verse for the class in rhythm. Play a rhythm instrument to help them pick up on the downbeats. Repeat and have the children pat their knees on the beats. Then give out rhythm instruments to the class and let them play along on the beats as they listen to you repeat the verse. They may begin to join in with the words as they become familiar.

Divide the class in half. One half plays their instruments while the other half says the verse. Then switch. Finally, have the whole class play and recite the verse at the same time.

When we don't understand something in the Bible, we can always pray and ask Jesus to help us. He wants us to understand His Word. Let's thank and praise Jesus for that now.

WORSHIP TRAILS

SINGING PRAISES TO JESUS

Supplies: Noah's Park CD and CD player

Play the unit song, "Hallelujah! Jesus Is Risen," on the Noah's Park CD and invite the children to sing along. Let them clap or march with the music. As time permits, sing additional familiar songs about Jesus' being alive and able to help us understand His Word.

SHARE AND PRAYER
My Bible at Home

Supplies: Half sheets of paper, pencils, small Bible stickers

Where do you like to read the Bible or listen to Bible stories at home? Let children share. Some may mention their bed at bedtime and others might mention the dinner table with the family. Some children may not read the Bible at home, so suggest they think of a spot that would be good.

Give out paper and pencils. Encourage the children to sketch the outline of their home. Then give each child a Bible sticker to stick on a spot where they read the Bible, or would like to read the Bible, in their home. Have children add their names to their papers.

Let's divide into small groups. You may pray one-sentence prayers. Ask Jesus to help you understand what you read or hear in the Bible. You could also ask Him to help you remember to read the Bible at home. Divide the children into groups of three or four. You may add a Park Patrol helper to each group. Allow time for all the children to pray. Then collect the pictures and set them in a safe spot until the end of class.

At this point, divide the preschoolers from the elementary-age children for age-appropriate games and crafts. Let the assigned Park Patrol members lead each group to the designated areas. The groups may have a snack together or separately.

SNACK SHACK
Cheesy Books

A snack idea for today's lesson is provided on page RS-111 of the *Snacks and Games Book*. Be sure a volunteer thanks God for the food before the snack is served to the children.

CAMPSITE CAPERS
Obstacles on the Road to Emmaus
(Elementary)
The Emmaus Road (Preschool)

The preschoolers today will enjoy a game of "The Emmaus Road," described on page RS-112 in the *Snacks and Games Book*. For the elementary-age children, see page RS-111 for instructions to play "Obstacles on the Road to Emmaus."

COZY CAVE CRAFTS
Mini Bibles (Elementary)
Bible Bookmark (Preschool)

The elementary-age children will make "Mini Bibles" with shrinkable plastic. You may want to do this craft a little earlier in the lesson to allow time for baking and cooling. Details are on page RC-111 in the *Craft Book*. The preschool craft, "Bible Bookmark," will help the children understand the lesson and is found on page RC-112.

CLOSING ACTIVITIES

Have the Noah's Park puppets invite all the children to work in pairs to clean up the room. The puppets may give suggestions as to what jobs the children may do and also offer affirmation for good work.

Gather the children together, and let volunteers practice saying the Bible memory verse to the puppets. You could also let the puppets ask the Bible story review questions for the children to answer.

Be sure all the children have their crafts and home pictures from Share and Prayer. Send each child off with a hug.

OVERTIME ACTIVITIES

While waiting for parents, let Park Patrol helpers play "Follow-the-Leader on the road to Emmaus" with the children. This will free you up to greet parents as they arrive.

SONGSHEETS

In the Beginning

Words & Music by
John H. Morton

When God Makes a Promise

Words & Music by
Phil Reynolds

God's Already There

Words & Music by
John J. DiModica

With assurance! (♩ = 116)

took some con - vinc - ing___ for Phar - aoh to see___ God

want - ed him to___ set___ Is - ra - el free.___ He

want - ed to take___ them to the Prom - ised___ Land,___ and

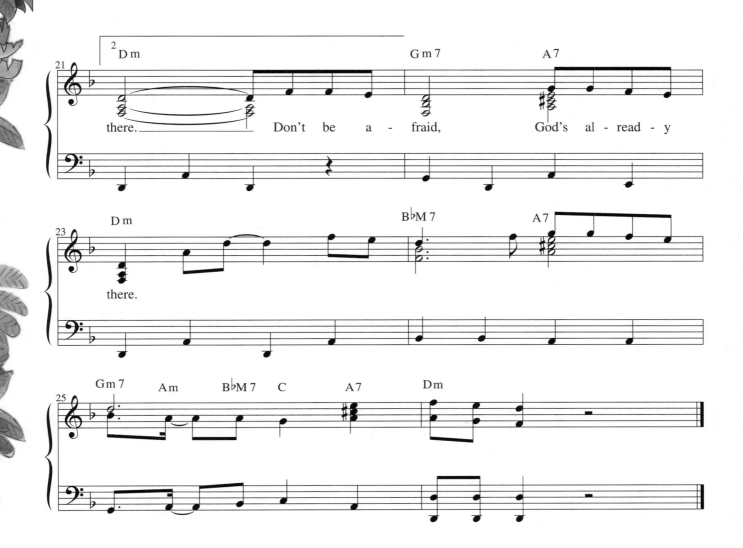

Glory to You

Words & Music by
Sarah Moore

Take a Stand

Words & Music by
Sarah Moore

Trust Him and Obey

Words & Music by
Darren Roos

I will lis-ten to the Word of God,

and I will choose to o - bey.

His pow'r is great-er than an - y - thing I face,

Living for You

Words & Music by
Shelly McFalls

I Wanna Live God's Way

Words & Music by
Phil Reynolds

It Pays to Obey

Words & Music by
John J. DiModica

God Wants You

Words & Music by
Phil Reynolds

Good News

Words & Music by
Sarah Moore

Hallelujah! Jesus Is Risen

Words & Music by
John H. Morton

SONG LYRICS

IN THE BEGINNING

Words and Music by John H. Morton

Chorus

In the beginning, God made the world.
He had a plan before He began.
He started with nothing,
But that didn't stop Him.
He spoke the Word and made all that we see.

Verse

He made the heavens and the earth.
He made the birds and fish in the sea.
He made the animals on the land.
The best He saved for last, you and me!
And then He rested.

Chorus

In the beginning, God made the world.
He had a plan before He began.
He started with nothing,
But that didn't stop Him.
He spoke the Word and made all that we see.

Verse

He made the heavens and the earth.
He made the birds and fish in the sea.
He made the animals on the land.
The best He saved for last, you and me!
And then He rested.

Chorus

In the beginning, God made the world.
He had a plan before He began.
He started with nothing,
But that didn't stop Him.
He spoke the Word and made all that we see.
He spoke the Word and made all that we see.

WHEN GOD MAKES A PROMISE

Words and Music by Phil Reynolds

When God makes a promise, He keeps it.
When He says He'll help you, believe it.
His Word never fails.
His Spirit will dwell in your heart;
Receive it.

When God makes a promise, He keeps it.
When He says He'll help you, believe it.
His Word never fails.
His Spirit will dwell in your heart;
Receive it.

When God makes a promise, He keeps it.
When He says He'll help you, believe it.
His Word never fails.
His Spirit will dwell in your heart;
Receive it.

GOD'S ALREADY THERE

Words and Music by John J. DiModica

Verse

It took some convincing for Pharaoh to see

God wanted him to set Israel free.

He wanted to take them to the Promised Land,

And He would lead them with His unseen hand.

Chorus

No matter where you are or wherever you go

There is something God wants you to know:

Whatever you face today or next year,

Don't be afraid, God's already there.

Verse

It took some convincing for Pharaoh to see

God wanted him to set Israel free.

He wanted to take them to the Promised Land,

And He would lead them with His unseen hand.

Chorus

No matter where you are or wherever you go

There is something God wants you to know:

Whatever you face today or next year,

Don't be afraid, God's already there.

Don't be afraid, God's already there.

GLORY TO YOU

Words and Music by Sarah Moore

Chorus

Glory to You.

Glory to You.

Glory to You, honor and praise.

All of my days I'll sing

Glory to You.

Verse 1

You created the world out of nothing,

And You filled it with purpose and life.

You know my heart, You know my needs,

You're my Provider,

And I thank You and give You the glory.

Chorus

Glory to You (to You).

Glory to You (to You).

Glory to You, honor and praise.

All of my days I'll sing

Glory to You.

Verse 2

You are perfect, righteous, and holy,

And You knew that I could not compare.

Yet in Your love, You made a way,

You're my salvation,

And I thank You and give You the glory.

Chorus

Glory to You (to You).

Glory to You (to You).

Glory to You, honor and praise.

All of my days I'll sing

Glory to You.

Glory to You (to You).

Glory to You (to You).

Glory to You, honor and praise.

All of my days I'll sing

Glory to You.

Glory to You.

Glory to You.

Glory to You.

TAKE A STAND
Words and Music by Sarah Moore

Verse 1

Let your choices show who you follow.

Take a stand for God.

He is greater than any problem.

Take a stand for God.

Chorus

Take a stand; don't run away.

Take a stand; don't be afraid.

Trust the Lord to see you through.

Take a stand; show you believe.

Take a stand; He'll meet your need.

Let the Lord take care of you.

Verse 2

Walk the way He leads

In your words and deeds.

Take a stand for God.

All who see will know

Who you follow.

Take a stand for God.

Chorus

Take a stand; don't run away.
Take a stand; don't be afraid.
Trust the Lord to see you through.
Take a stand; show you believe.
Take a stand; He'll meet your need.
Let the Lord take care of you.

Repeat Chorus

TRUST HIM AND OBEY
Words and Music by Darren Roos

I will listen to the Word of God,
And I will choose to obey.
His pow'r is greater than anything I face,
So I will trust Him ev'ry day.

Trust Him and obey.
There is no other way.

I will listen to the Word of God,
And I will choose to obey.
His pow'r is greater than anything I face,
So I will trust Him ev'ry day.

Trust Him and obey.
There is no other way.

I will listen to the Word of God,
And I will choose to obey.
His pow'r is greater than anything I face,
So I will trust Him ev'ry day.
So I will trust Him ev'ry day.
So I will trust Him ev'ry day.

LIVING FOR YOU
Words and Music by Shelly McFalls

Chorus

Give me the strength to keep on trying.

Give me the courage to do Your will.

Your love sends my heart to flying.

Living for You is such a thrill.

Repeat Chorus

Verse

I'm walking,

I'm running,

I'm climbing to You.

You are the reason we celebrate in ev'rything we do!

Chorus

Give me the strength to keep on trying.

Give me the courage to do Your will.

Your love sends my heart to flying.

Living for You is such a thrill.

Verse

I'm walking,

I'm running,

I'm climbing to You.

You are the reason we celebrate in ev'rything we do!

Chorus

Give me the strength to keep on trying.

Give me the courage to do Your will.

Your love sends my heart to flying.

Living for You is such a thrill.

Living for You is such a thrill.

Living for You is such a thrill.

I WANNA LIVE GOD'S WAY
Words and Music by Phil Reynolds

I wanna live God's way.

I'm learning to trust Him and obey.

I wanna live God's way.

I'm growing in faith each time I pray.

I wanna live God's way.

I'm going to follow Him each day.

I wanna live God's way.

I wanna live God's way.

I'm learning to trust Him and obey.

I wanna live God's way.

I'm growing in faith each time I pray.

I wanna live God's way.

I'm going to follow Him each day.

I wanna live God's way.

God is strong and powerful.

He has promised to take care of me.

I wanna live God's way.

I'm learning to trust Him and obey.

I wanna live God's way.

I'm growing in faith each time I pray.

I wanna live God's way.

I'm going to follow Him each day.

I wanna live God's way.

Live God's way!

IT PAYS TO OBEY

Words and Music by John J. DiModica

Verse

Let me tell you 'bout Daniel

And his three good friends

Who trusted God to what looked like

What would be the end.

And it ain't no joke

When they walked through the fire.

No, it ain't no joke;

They didn't smell like smoke!

Chorus

Obey, obey

Even when you feel like running away.

Obey, it pays to obey.

Obey, obey

Ev'ry single word that God has to say.

Obey, it pays to obey.

Verse

Let me tell you 'bout Daniel

And his three good friends

Who trusted God to what looked like

What would be the end.

And it ain't no joke

When they walked through the fire.

No, it ain't no joke;

They didn't smell like smoke!

Chorus

Obey, obey
Even when you feel like running away.
Obey, it pays to obey.
Obey, obey
Ev'ry single word that God has to say.
Obey, it pays to obey.

GOD WANTS YOU

Words and Music by Phil Reynolds

Chorus

God wants you to follow Him,

Believe, and change within,

Receive His Word and then

Share His love with the world.

God wants you to follow Him,

Believe, and change within,

Receive His Word and then

Share His love with the world.

Verse

Follow God with a willing heart.

Honor Him and do your part.

Jesus' power sees you through

All that God asks you to do.

Chorus

God wants you to follow Him,
Believe, and change within,
Receive His Word and then
Share His love with the world.

God wants you to follow Him,
Believe, and change within,
Receive His Word and then
Share His love with the world.
Share His love with the world.

GOOD NEWS

Words and Music by Sarah Moore

Good news, Jesus is born.
Good news, angels sang glory.
Good news, Jesus is born.
Tell the world the good news.

Precious Savior, Promised One.
Tell it, tell the good news.
Born of Mary, God's own Son,
Tell it, tell the good news.

Good news, Jesus is born.
Good news, angels sang glory.
Good news, Jesus is born.
Tell the world the good news.

Sing your praises, shout "hooray!"
Tell it, tell the good news.
Worship Christ the Lord today!
Tell it, tell the good news.

Good news, Jesus is born.
Good news, angels sang glory.
Good news, Jesus is born.
Tell the world the good news.
Tell the world the good news.
Tell the world the good news.

HALLELUJAH! JESUS IS RISEN

Words and Music by John H. Morton

Hallelujah! Jesus is risen.
Hallelujah! He's alive again.
Hallelujah! Jesus is risen.
Death could not keep Him.
He is risen; He is Lord!

Hallelujah! Jesus is risen.
Hallelujah! He's alive again.
Hallelujah! Jesus is risen.
Death could not keep Him.
He is risen; He is Lord!

Hallelujah! Jesus is risen.
Hallelujah! He's alive again.
Hallelujah! Jesus is risen.
Death could not keep Him.
He is risen; He is Lord!

Death could not keep Him.
Death could not keep Him.
Death could not keep Him.
He is risen; He is Lord!

NOTES

NOTES